UNDERSTANDING
RESEARCH FOR SOCIAL
POLICY AND PRACTICE

Other titles in the series

Understanding the finance of welfare
What welfare costs and how to pay for it
Howard Glennerster, Department of Social Administration,
London School of Economics and Political Science

"... a brilliant and lively textbook that students will enjoy."
Ian Shaw, School of Sociology and Social Policy, University of Nottingham
PB £17.99 (US$26.95) **ISBN** 1 86134 405 8
HB £50.00 (US$59.95) **ISBN** 1 86134 406 6
240 x 172mm 256 pages May 2003

Understanding social security
Issues for policy and practice
Jane Millar, Department of Social and Policy Sciences, University of Bath

*"This first-class text provides students with the most up-to-date review and analysis of social
security issues. It will fast become the definitive guide to the subject."* **Jonathan Bradshaw,
Department of Social Policy and Social Work, University of York**

PB £17.99 (US$26.95) **ISBN** 1 86134 419 8
HB £50.00 (US$59.95) **ISBN** 1 86134 420 1
240 x 172mm 360 pages May 2003

Understanding social citizenship
Themes and perspectives for policy and practice
Peter Dwyer, Department of Sociology and Social Policy,
University of Leeds

*"An excellent introduction to current debates about citizenship and the only general social policy
text on the subject. Highly recommended. Students will certainly benefit from reading this book."*
Nick Ellison, Department of Sociology and Social Policy, University of Durham
PB £17.99 (US$28.95) **ISBN** 1 86134 415 5
HB £50.00 (US$75.00) **ISBN** 1 86134 416 3
240 x 172mm 240 pages May 2004

Understanding the policy process
Analysing welfare policy and practice
John Hudson and **Stuart Lowe**, Department of Social Policy
and Social Work, University of York

*"Hudson and Lowe's book provides an excellent review of the issues about the policy process in a
changing society and a changing world."* **Michael Hill, Visiting Professor in the Health and
Social Policy Research Centre, University of Brighton**
PB £17.99 (US$28.95) **ISBN** 1 86134 540 2
HB £50.00 (US$75.00) **ISBN** 1 86134 539 9
240 x 172mm 288 pages tbc June 2004

Forthcoming
Understanding work–life balance
Policies for a family-friendly Britain
Margaret May and **Edward Brunsdon**
PB £18.99 (US$29.95) ISBN 1 86134 413 9
HB £50.00 (US$75.00) ISBN 1 86134 414 7
240 x 172mm 256 pages tbc July 2005

Understanding housing policy
Brian Lund
PB £18.99 (US$29.95) ISBN 1 86134 618 2
HB £50.00 (US$75.00) ISBN 1 86134 619 0
240 x 172mm 256 pages tbc October 2006

If you are interested in
submitting a proposal for
the series, please contact
The Policy Press
e-mail tpp-info@bristol.ac.uk
tel +44 (0)117 331 4054
fax +44 (0)117 331 4093

**INSPECTION COPIES AND
ORDERS AVAILABLE FRO**

Marston Book Services
PO Box 269 • Abingdon • Oxon
OX14 4YN UK
INSPECTION COPIES
Tel: +44 (0) 1235 465500
Fax: +44 (0) 1235 465556
Email: inspections@marston.co.u
ORDERS
Tel: +44 (0) 1235 465500
Fax: +44 (0) 1235 465556
Email: direct.orders@marston.cc

www.policypress.org.uk

UNDERSTANDING RESEARCH FOR SOCIAL POLICY AND PRACTICE

Themes, methods and approaches

Edited by Saul Becker and Alan Bryman

First published in Great Britain in June 2004 by

The Policy Press
University of Bristol
Fourth Floor, Beacon House
Queen's Road
Bristol BS8 1QU
UK

Tel +44 (0)117 331 4054
Fax +44 (0)117 331 4093
e-mail tpp-info@bristol.ac.uk
www.policypress.org.uk

British Library Cataloguing in Publication Data
A catalogue record for this book is available from the British Library

Library of Congress Cataloging-in-Publication Data
A catalog record for this book has been requested

ISBN 1 86134 403 1 paperback

Reprinted 2005

A hardcover version of this book is also available

Saul Becker is Professor-elect of Social Care and Health, University of Birmingham, UK. At the time of writing, he was Professor of Social Policy and Social Care at Loughborough University. **Alan Bryman** is Professor of Social Research at Loughborough University, UK.

Cover design by Qube Design Associates, Bristol.
Printed and bound in Great Britain by Hobbs the Printers Ltd, Southampton.

Contents

List of tables, figures and boxes

Tables

Figures

Boxes

Editors' note on authorship

There are 70 main sections and 47 illustrative boxes in this volume, not including the Introduction, Glossary and other additional material. Where chapter sections and boxes have been written by contributors other than the two editors, authorship has been clearly assigned to those contributors. A list of all contributors can be found on pages x–xii.

Saul Becker and Alan Bryman have been responsible for the concept for this volume, and for commissioning and editing all the contributions. They are also joint authors for 32 of the main sections and six illustrative boxes – one third of the total text – as well as writing or compiling all the additional material. Sections and boxes without an assigned author have been jointly written by Saul Becker and Alan Bryman.

List of contributors

[*Publishers note:* we have endeavoured to ensure that these details were correct at the time of going to print.]

David Abbott, Research Fellow, Norah Fry Research Centre, University of Bristol

Pete Alcock, Professor of Social Policy and Administration, University of Birmingham

Jo Aldridge, Research Fellow, Young Carers Research Group, Loughborough University

Charles Antaki, Reader in Language and Social Psychology, Loughborough University

Hilary Arksey, Research Fellow, Social Policy Research Unit, University of York

Karl Ashworth, Principal Methodologist at the Office for National Statistics

Marian Barnes, Professor of Social Research, University of Birmingham

Saul Becker, Professor-elect of Social Care and Health, University of Birmingham

Nigel Bilsbrough, Finance and Resources Manager, Centre for Research in Social Policy, Loughborough University

Jonathan Bradshaw, Professor of Social Policy, University of York

Julia Brannen, Professor of the Sociology of the Family, Institute of Education, University of London

John D. Brewer, Professor of Sociology, Queen's University, Belfast

Alan Bryman, Professor of Social Research, Loughborough University

Emma Carmel, Lecturer in Social Policy, University of Bath

Anne Corden, Research Fellow, Social Policy Research Unit, University of York

Louise Corti, Director of User Services and Qualidata, University of Essex

Gary Craig, Professor of Social Justice, University of Hull

Duncan Cramer, Reader in Psychological Health, Department of Social Sciences, Loughborough University

Alan Deacon, Professor of Social Policy, University of Leeds

David Deacon, Senior Lecturer in Communication and Media Studies, Loughborough University

David de Vaus, Professor of Sociology, La Trobe University, Australia

Barbara Dobson, formerly Research Fellow, Centre for Research in Social Policy, Loughborough University

Nigel Fielding, Professor of Sociology, University of Surrey

David Gordon, Professor of Social Justice, and Director of the Townsend Centre for International Poverty Research, University of Bristol

Arthur Gould, Reader in Swedish Social Policy, Loughborough University

Hilary Graham, Professor of Social Policy, Lancaster University

Martyn Hammersley, Professor of Educational and Social Research, The Open University

Stephen Harrison, Professor of Social Policy, University of Manchester

Alexa Hepburn, Lecturer in Social Psychology, Loughborough University

Michael Hirst, Research Fellow, Social Policy Research Unit, University of York

Lesley Hoggart, Senior Research Fellow, Policy Studies Institute

Lisa Holmes, Research Associate, Centre for Child and Family Research, Loughborough University

Roger Homan, Professor of Religious Studies, University of Brighton

Savita Katbamna, Research Fellow, Nuffield Community Care Studies Unit, University of Leicester

Perpetua Kirby, ex-Save the Children, now PK Research Consultancy Ltd, Hove

Jane Lewis, Barnett Professor of Social Policy, Oxford University

Janet Lewis, formerly Research Director, Joseph Rowntree Foundation

Ruth Lister, Professor of Social Policy, Loughborough University

Kate Louise McArdle, Lecturer in Organisational Behaviour, School of Management, University of Bath

Clare Madge, Lecturer in the Department of Geography, University of Leicester

Sue Middleton, Director, Centre for Research in Social Policy, Loughborough University

Jane Millar, Professor of Social Policy, University of Bath

Polly Neate, Editor, *Community Care* magazine

Henrietta O'Connor, Lecturer in the Centre for Labour Market Studies, University of Leicester

Robert Page, Reader in Democratic Socialism and Social Policy, University of Birmingham

Jan Pahl, Professor of Social Policy, University of Kent

Alison Park, Research Director, National Centre for Social Research

Elizabeth Peel, Lecturer in Psychology, Aston University

Sarah Pink, Senior Lecturer in Sociology, Loughborough University

Robert Pinker, Emeritus Professor of Social Administration, London School of Economics and Political Science

Jonathan Potter, Professor of Discourse Analysis, Loughborough University

Stephen Potter, Senior Research Fellow, The Open University

Peter Reason, Professor of Action Research Practice and Director of the Centre for Action Research in Professional Practice, School of Management, University of Bath

Brian Roberts, Principal Lecturer in Sociology, University of Huddersfield

Colin Robson, Emeritus Professor, School of Human and Health Sciences, University of Huddersfield

Karen Rowlingson, Senior Lecturer in Social Research, University of Bath

Roy Sainsbury, Senior Research Fellow, Social Policy Research Unit, University of York

Clive Seale, Research Professor, Department of Human Sciences, Brunel University

Joe Sempik, Research Fellow, Centre for Child and Family Research, Loughborough University

Noel Smith, Research Fellow, Centre for Research in Social Policy, Loughborough University

Bruce Stafford, Director, Centre for Research in Social Policy, Loughborough University

Elliot Stern, Head of Evaluation Studies, Tavistock Institute, London, and Independent Evaluation Consultant

Peter Townsend, Professor of International Social Policy, London School of Economics and Political Science, and Emeritus Professor of Social Policy, University of Bristol

Harriet Ward, Senior Research Fellow, and Director of the Centre for Child and Family Research, Loughborough University

Linda Ward, Professor of Disability and Social Policy, and Director, Norah Fry Research Centre, University of Bristol

Fiona Williams, Professor of Social Policy and Director, ESRC Research Group for the Study of Care, Values and the Future of Welfare, University of Leeds

Ken Young, Professor of Politics and Director, ESRC UK Centre for Evidence-based Policy and Practice, Queen Mary, University of London

Acknowledgements

We are grateful to our panel of 65 contributors who gave their time and expertise to make this volume possible. They all had to work to tight word limits and meet our requests for additional information (such as websites and questions for discussion). We hope that they are as pleased with the volume as we are.

We acknowledge with thanks the support of the Social Policy Association, and particularly the editorial support group that oversees the *Understanding welfare* series. We also acknowledge with thanks the helpful comments of three anonymous referees.

We are especially grateful to Jo Aldridge of Loughborough University, who provided valuable editorial assistance. Thanks also to Sophie Winfield who checked through all the cited websites.

Colleagues at The Policy Press have been wonderfully encouraging and helpful. Dawn Rushen has been our day-to-day contact and we are especially grateful to her for all her efforts and support, as well as to her colleagues, Helen Bolton, Laura Greaves, Julia Mortimer, Alison Shaw and Dave Worth.

Saul Becker and Alan Bryman
Loughborough University
March 2004

Introduction

Audiences

This book has been produced in order to meet the needs of several different audiences. One audience is made up of **undergraduate** and **postgraduate students** undertaking modules in research methods and conducting small-scale research projects as part of their degrees. The book will provide students with the knowledge and skills for critically appraising the research they read, a springboard for undertaking and writing up their own investigations.

A second audience includes **researchers** in the broad areas of social policy research. Researchers will benefit from the insights gleaned from an overview of the methodological issues and choices that relate to social policy research that have been written by leading authorities in social research methods generally and in the social policy field. Some of the sections, particularly the ones on managing budgets and staff and disseminating research, have been written with this audience in mind.

The third audience for the book includes **practitioners** (including social workers, health workers and the many others) with an interest or engagement in the broad areas of social policy implementation. Many of these practitioners are in a position where they need to evaluate existing research or to produce their own investigations. For this group, the insights from the book should be invaluable. Some of the sections will introduce practitioners to cutting-edge innovations in methodology and approaches that will be of particular significance to them and how they might go about conducting their own studies. For example, sections on user-participatory research, action research and evaluation research have been included with this group in mind. Additionally, discussions of the nature of evidence, what counts as evidence, and how research evidence can inform policy and practice, will be of especial interest to practitioners engaged in implementing social policies.

Aims

The overall aims of the book are to:

• help the reader to understand better the policy-making process (including how policy is made, delivered and implemented at the 'front line') (Chapter One);

- help the reader to understand the role that 'good' research plays within this process, and how it can be used to inform policy making and professional practice (Chapter One);
- equip the reader with a knowledge of approaches, issues, research methods and designs so that they are able to 'read' existing research on social policy in a more critical and informed manner, and are able to conduct and manage their own studies (Chapters Two, Three, Four, Five and Six);
- provide an understanding of how research can be disseminated effectively, to increase the likelihood of trustworthy and reliable evidence being used by policy makers and practitioners to inform their work (Chapter Seven);
- convey something of the breadth and excitement of social policy research. We have drawn research examples and illustrations from a wide range of policy fields, utilising a diversity of methodological and other approaches. In so doing, we want to show how broad and dynamic policy research can be, how challenging are the debates and issues that policy researchers must face, and how important are the research findings for the welfare and wellbeing of millions of citizens – be they on the 'receiving end' of social policies, or those charged with formulating or implementing them.

Structure

Chapter One provides much of the background to the book and should be read first as a foundation for the subsequent chapters. It deals with the questions of what we mean by social policy research and related terms and what kinds of factors are conventionally associated with 'good research' in this area. The chapter addresses the nature of the processes of policy making and implementation and the role that research can usefully play in relation to these activities. The chapter recognises that in a field like social policy, issues to do with values and politics frequently come into play and explores the significance of this fact. It also explores why we need research at all in relation to social policy and why there has been a drift in recent years to *evidence-based policy and practice*. The latter is very much at the heart of issues with which this book is concerned, namely, why we need *research-based* evidence in order to inform policy and practice. Finally in this chapter, a model of the policy research process is presented which seeks to show how many of the different elements of social policy research explored in this book are interconnected.

In this book, we emphasise how social policy research is and should be driven by research questions. These form the primary focus of **Chapter Two** where the issues of what research questions are and where they come from is examined. An important consideration here is the role that the existing published literature on a topic of inquiry has in helping the researcher to formulate research questions. The chapter emphasises the importance of conducting a literature review and the factors that need to be borne in mind when devising one. A related issue is what part *theory* plays in relation to social policy research. Theory can be used as a background and rationale to the research questions that are asked but equally research can inform theory. The nature of the interaction between theory and research figures prominently in the discussion.

The field of social policy research is beset with a diversity of methodological approaches and debates. **Chapter Three** provides a route through these issues. It begins by considering the well-known debate about the relative merits and significance of quantitative and qualitative research. It then goes on to explore a diversity of different approaches to social policy research that consider such issues as the role of feminism, the degree to which policy recipients can be involved in the social policy research process, the evaluation of policies and programmes and doing research cross-nationally. The discussion then moves on to explore issues to do with the examination of existing data and published research. As such, issues concerned with reviewing existing research and with the archiving and analysis of other researchers' data are emphasised. Finally, the chapter examines issues that are not unique to social policy research, but are ones which are especially relevant to it. This includes ethical considerations, matters to do with 'race' in relation to research, and how the researcher should take account of sensitive topics and vulnerable groups when conducting an investigation.

Chapter Four is concerned with the tools of *quantitative* research. It begins by examining the criteria quantitative researchers employ for assessing the quality of investigations with this research strategy. It then moves on to a consideration of the main types of research design that are employed by quantitative researchers. This entails an examination of four types of research design: the experiment; the cross-sectional design; the longitudinal design; and the case study. Research questions continue to loom large here too because a research design is presented as a framework that will allow a research question to be answered. There then follows a discussion of sampling in quantitative research, which includes a consideration of what it means to seek a representative sample from which generalisations can be forged and the factors that promote and detract from the ability to generate such a sample from different approaches to sampling. The chapter considers the main research methods associated with the collection of data and how data are coded to facilitate analysis. In this section, the following are examined: structured interviews and questionnaires in survey research, content analysis, structured observation, the use of official statistics and Internet surveys. Finally, the chapter contains a discussion of the main ingredients of quantitative data analysis.

Chapter Five forms a parallel chapter to Chapter Four. Thus, it begins with an examination of the criteria *qualitative* researchers employ for assessing the quality of investigations with this research strategy. There is then an examination of the main research designs in social policy research, which entails a primary focus on the case study, cross-sectional and longitudinal designs. The chapter then moves on to a consideration of issues to do with sampling. Here we find that the importance placed on generating a representative sample is less pronounced than in the context of quantitative research. There is then an examination of the main methods for collecting and sources of data. These include: semi-structured and unstructured interviewing; ethnography; focus groups; documents; and the use of the Internet for the collection of qualitative data. Finally, there is an examination of some different approaches to the analysis of qualitative data, such as grounded theory, conversation analysis, discourse analysis and narrative analysis. It also includes a discussion of computer-assisted qualitative data analysis, which has become increasingly prominent in recent years.

An important aspect of conducting good research that is easily overlooked is the quality and effectiveness with which it is *managed*. This issue lies at the heart of **Chapter Six**. Here the effectiveness of the management of social policy research is construed in terms of such issues as: the following of ethical principles; managing all stages of the research process; managing research staff; ensuring the safety of both researchers and research participants; managing confidentiality and protecting data collected from participants; managing budgets and time; and balancing the needs of those who fund research with the contingencies of the research process itself. In other words, the point of this chapter is to suggest that good research is not just to do with technical issues such as how well a sample is designed, the quality of a questionnaire or how well data are analysed. Management issues loom large in considerations of the quality of research and should not be marginalised.

Research is likely to be of little use to anyone unless it is *disseminated* and this is the main concern of **Chapter Seven**. In this chapter, the reader is introduced to what is meant by dissemination and the different forms it might take in the social policy research field. Practical advice is offered on how to write a report and how to plan a strategy for disseminating findings in this area. The role that the mass media can play is considered, since they are obviously the main springboard for bringing research to the attention of a much wider audience than can be envisaged by a report or article in an academic or practitioner journal. The degree to which research really can inform and influence policy and practice is also addressed.

Special features

In presenting discussions of these issues and topics, we make frequent use of a number of features to aid the reader's understanding:

- *Illustrative boxes:* many of the main expositions are embellished with boxed text that provides an example of the issue or method being discussed. In a small number of cases, a box is used to describe a particular facet of the main topic, for example, a box on visual ethnography in conjunction with the main exposition of ethnography.

- *Questions for discussion:* these can be used as the basis for individual revision, or in class-based discussions, to check out learning and as a catalyst for further work and discussions.
- *Further reading:* most sections and boxes are accompanied by further reading to guide the reader for examining an issue in greater depth.
- *Relevant organisations:* many sections and boxes are supplemented with information about organisations that are relevant to the topic. These include organisations concerned with methodological issues and ones with specific policy-related interests.
- *Website resources:* where appropriate, websites are given of relevant organisations or where further information relating to a research method or approach can be gleaned from a website.

one

Research for social policy and practice

Detailed contents

1.1 Introduction

This chapter provides the context for the rest of the book, and should therefore be read first. The overall aims of the book are to:

- help the reader to understand better the *policy-making process* (including how policy is made, delivered and implemented at the 'front line') (Chapter One);
- help the reader to understand the *role that 'good' research plays* within this process, and how it can be used to inform policy making and professional practice (Chapter One);
- equip the reader with a knowledge of *approaches, issues, research methods and designs* so that they are able to 'read' existing research on social policy in a more critical and informed manner, and are able to conduct and manage their own studies (Chapters Two, Three, Four, Five and Six);
- provide an understanding of *how research can be disseminated effectively*, to increase the likelihood of trustworthy and reliable evidence being used by policy makers and professionals to inform their work (Chapter Seven);
- convey something of the *breadth and excitement of social policy research*. We have drawn research examples and illustrations from a wide range of policy fields, utilising a diversity of methodological and other approaches. In so doing, we want to show how broad and dynamic policy research can be, how challenging the debates and issues are that policy researchers must face, and the importance of research findings for the welfare and wellbeing of millions of citizens – be they on the 'receiving end' of social policies, or those charged with formulating or implementing them

In this chapter we focus on the first two aims. We discuss:

- what is meant by terms such as *social policy*, *policy*, *policy research* and *good research*;
- how research can inform policy making and its implementation;
- the role that politics and ideology play in this process;
- how research evidence is an important *way of knowing* about the social world, and why it might be more reliable than, for example, personal beliefs or other sources of evidence;
- why there is a shift towards a greater emphasis on *evidence-based policy and practice*, and what the limits are to this development.

Finally, we provide a *model of the policy research process* that helps readers to understand the relationships between policy research, policy making and professional practice, and signposts how all the chapters in the volume 'fit' with the model and how they relate to each other.

1.2 Social policy and professional practice

Pete Alcock, *Professor of Social Policy and Administration, University of Birmingham*

What is social policy?

'Social policy' is an academic subject, studied by students in higher education as a discrete subject or as part of a broader social science programme. It is also incorporated into the professional training programmes for many public service professionals, such as social workers and nurses. Furthermore, it is the focus of research activity by academics who explore how and why policies have developed and how they operate within the social world.

Social policy is also the term used to refer to the practice of social intervention aimed at securing social change to promote the welfare and wellbeing of citizens. Social policies are pursued by government, and by non-governmental organisations, in order to improve individual life chances and social relations – for instance, through the provision of social security benefits, free school education, hospital treatment, public housing, and such like. Social policy refers both to the practice of, and academic study of, policy action. Most public service professionals therefore need to study social policy. It also means that social policy research is carried out not just by academics but also by policy makers and professionals – and by academics *for* policy makers and professionals/practitioners.

Policy, implementation and practice

This *relationship between analysis and practice* is thus right at the heart of social policy, and in particular it structures the way research on social policy is developed and carried out. Most (if not all) social policy research is linked directly or indirectly to the current or future development and implementation of social policies – for instance, social policy researchers work to monitor and evaluate the policy programmes implemented by government, and others. Social policy researchers, and social policy students, must therefore address this interface of theory and practice.

More pertinently perhaps, most social policy researchers and students *want* to do this. It is in order to understand, and then to influence, the policy process that most people are attracted to study and research in social policy. And the evidence is that this study and research have often had a significant impact upon the policy process – for instance, a famous study of the continuing problem of poverty in Britain despite the welfare reforms of the post-war era by Brian Abel-Smith and Peter Townsend (1965) forced government to admit that poverty was still a social problem and to develop new policy measures to respond to this (albeit not the measures that the authors might have been proposing at the time). Peter Townsend describes this research and its significance to social policy in **Box 1a**. Social policy is thus the study of policy practice in order to contribute to policy reform. It is not only a *descriptive* subject but also *prescriptive*. This is what makes it morally and politically attractive, and why it also makes research and practice in the field so complex, as the other contributions to this volume reveal.

Box 1a: National assistance and the rediscovery of poverty: *The poor and the poorest*

Peter Townsend, *Professor of International Social Policy, London School of Economics and Political Science, and Emeritus Professor of Social Policy, University of Bristol*

The idea for *The poor and the poorest* (Abel-Smith and Townsend, 1965) grew out of the long tradition of research in the UK on poverty. Booth, Rowntree, Bowley, Llewellyn-Smith and many more had pioneered surveys in various parts of Britain for the previous 100 years. But by the 1950s there was an air of complacency. It was widely believed, partly because of the Rowntree–Lavers report of 1951, that the post-war welfare state in the UK had virtually eliminated poverty (Rowntree and Lavers, 1951). Brian Abel-Smith and I had already set to work on the subject and believed that this conclusion was wrong and that a clear break from the traditional approaches to research had to be made to reach reliable conclusions. More convincing scientific investigation of low income and need, based on painstaking objective observations of social conditions and of personal and institutional behaviour, rather than on 'expert' or middle-class values, had to be organised. The values of social elites, and political entrepreneurs like Beveridge, continued to shape empirical enquiries – 'desert' was implicit in both the attitudes of investigators and the 'measures' believed to be appropriate. As a consequence poverty was minimised.

Two plans were devised. One was to undertake a new nationally representative survey of an unprecedently ambitious kind to develop objective, subjective and conventional institutional approaches to the investigation of poverty (see Chapter Four of this volume for a full discussion of survey methodology and sampling techniques). This was a programme of research approved and funded from 1964 by the Joseph Rowntree Memorial Trust. Inevitably it would take some years to complete. The programme resulted in a series of reports in the late 1960s and through the 1970s – on unemployment, disability, large families and lone-parent families, and later, the final comprehensive report that also included an analysis of the four poorest areas in the United Kingdom – *Poverty in the United Kingdom* (Townsend, 1979).

The second plan was to quickly draw together in a short book the best estimates that could be made from existing data of trends in the extent of poverty. In 1965, the book *The poor and the poorest* (preceded, as it happens, by papers to the British Sociological Association in 1962) was to form the centrepiece of the newly founded Child Poverty Action Group's campaign to mobilise effective anti-poverty action. The Prime Minister at the time, Harold Wilson, welcomed the authors to Downing Street in December. The book was based on a new idea; its authority, based on government data, was difficult to deny, and it quickly gained wide public and specialist support. The reaction to the publication "marked not only the campaign for what became child benefit, but also the arrival of the modern single-issue pressure group in British politics" (Timmins, 1995, p 257).

Because Sir William (later Lord) Beveridge had defined poverty as income insufficient to purchase the necessities of life, and intended to match national insurance benefits with that 'subsistence standard' of living, we hit on the idea of comparing the levels of benefits put in place after the war with information about the distribution of income – collected for other purposes by government. The method allowed some answer to be given to the questions: how many people's incomes fall below the government's standards of benefit? How adequate are the different benefits to lift people out of poverty?

We took advantage of a new Ministry of Labour survey of 13,000 households in 1953-54 (published in 1957) about the distribution of income and expenditure to rework the data they had collected to reveal how many in the population had lower income than the rates of National Assistance at the time. These rates can be regarded as 'institutionalised' measures of need rather than as measures that can be scientifically justified. The Ministry of Labour wanted to construct a more reliable cost-of-living index rather than review need and low income, and from 1957 conducted a smaller annual survey – the *Family Expenditure Survey*. With the Ministry's generous help, visits were paid to their offices in London and Watford – where completed questionnaires and schedules could be examined and checked individually to extract specific household income and expenditure and social information. To reduce costs a subsample of 25% of the 1953-54 households, numbering 3,225, formed the basis for comparison with the full sample of 3,540 in 1960. For reasons discussed in the book, expenditure was the criterion for a low level of living in 1953-54 and income in 1960. Supplementary research with subsamples on both income and expenditure helped to establish reliable conclusions about trends in low living standards.

A poverty 'line' was then constructed from the 'official' operational definition of the minimum level of living allowed in the National Assistance rates. In reaching conclusions about the numbers (including those in wage-earning households) who were in need, careful account had to be taken of types of income and capital ordinarily disregarded by the National Assistance Board in dealing with applications, as well as allowances added to the basic rates for special needs. The outcome was that in addition to the numbers found to have smaller incomes than the 'basic' national assistance rates there were others, generally in the range of income up to 40% above the basic rates, who would also be in practice within the government's standard of need. This explains the title of the book, *The poor and the poorest*. With certain expressed technical qualifications, we found that between 1953-54 and 1960 there was a distinct increase in the number and percentage of the population living below or just above the national assistance 'standard' of poverty.

Question for discussion
- In reopening the public debate about poverty, was *The poor and the poorest* innovative? Explain your answer.

References
Abel-Smith, B. and Townsend, P. (1965) *The poor and the poorest*, London: Bell.

Rowntree, S. and Lavers, G.R. (1951) *Poverty and the welfare state*, London: Longmans Green.

Timmins, N. (1995) *The five giants: A biography of the welfare state*, London: Harper Collins.

Townsend, P. (1979) *Poverty in the United Kingdom*, Harmondsworth: Penguin Books.

Further reading
Banting, K. (1979) *Poverty, politics and policy: Britain in the 1960s*, London: Macmillan.

Relevant organisations
Child Poverty Action Group
94 White Lion Street, London N1 9PF
Telephone 020 7837 7979; www.cpag.org.uk
Disability Alliance
Universal House, 88-94 Wentworth Street, London E1 7SA
Telephone 020 7247 8776; www.disabilityalliance.org

Low Pay Unit
10 Duke's Road, London WC1H 9AD
Telephone 020 7387 2522; www.lowpayunit.org.uk
National Pensioners Convention
9 Arkwright Road, London NW3 6AB
Telephone 020 7431 9820; www.natpencon.org.uk

Website resource
Office for National Statistics: www.statistics.gov.uk

The history of social policy is a history of the development of the interrelationship of the research and practice agenda. Most commentators on the subject in the UK trace its early roots back to the work of the **Fabian Society**, established at the end of the 19th century by Sidney and Beatrice Webb. The aims of Fabianism were to use social policy research to persuade government both to recognise the existence of *social problems* within Britain's capitalist society and to use the powers of the state to introduce public measures to ameliorate these. **Box 1b** uses the case of single motherhood to illustrate why a particular issue can come to be regarded as a social problem and why social policy responses to it may change over time. The Webbs were also committed to promoting the academic study of social policy and were instrumental in securing a base for this in the London School of Economics and Political Science (LSE), which they helped to establish.

Box 1b: Dilemmas in the study of social problems: the case of single motherhood

Robert Page, *Reader in Democratic Socialism and Social Policy, University of Birmingham*

We have seen how social policy (as an academic subject and as practice) has an underlying research interest with social problems, not least because they need to be understood and explained, but also because they raise major implications for policy making and implementation, for resources, and for the welfare and wellbeing of citizens.

The study of social problems is far from straightforward. Some writers remain sceptical about the use of this term on the grounds that it is used to deflect attention away from broader structural inequities (see Clarke, 2001). Those who accept the validity of the term may differ in their perceptions of social problems and the particular challenge each presents for society. There may also be disagreements over the extent of a particular problem (for example, opinion continues to be divided over the question of what constitutes the most appropriate measurement of poverty – see Garnham, 2001), the challenge it presents for a specific society, and the appropriateness of various policy responses. Moreover, there may be differences of opinion over why an issue is seen as problematic in one period of time but not in another. The case of single motherhood in the UK serves to illustrate some of these dilemmas.

Perception and values

The way in which single motherhood is perceived at any point in time tends to reflect the dominant social values of the age. In earlier periods, single motherhood was seen as problematic because of the threat it posed to Christian values concerning sexual relationships outside marriage and the sanctity of family life (Page, 1984). From the late 15th century onwards, the problem of single motherhood was seen predominantly as one of public dependency. Indeed, it was not until the early part of the 20th century that other dimensions of this problem, such as the welfare of illegitimate children, attracted public concern.

Up until the late 1960s, single motherhood continued to be perceived as problematic both for the women concerned and for the wider society. However, there was a growing tendency to see this group as 'victims' who could be rehabilitated rather than as 'deviants' in need of control (Kiernan et al, 1998).

In the more liberal climate of the late 1960s single motherhood became more socially acceptable. In consequence, it was the impoverished lifestyle of single mothers that came to be seen as problematic. However, the subsequent growth in the numbers of single mothers led some influential 'New Right' commentators to re-emphasise the negative aspects of this form of parenting. According to Charles Murray (1984, 1990, 1994) the overgenerosity of welfare provision was encouraging premature parenting among young, uneducated working-class women.

The policy response

The policy responses to the problem of single motherhood have also changed over time. In the 16th and 17th centuries public disapproval of this form of parenthood was expressed by means of physical punishments and detention in a House of Correction. Under the 1834 Poor Law Amendment Act single mothers applying for relief were required, like other members of the 'undeserving' poor, to enter the deterrent workhouse. In some of these institutions single mothers were required to wear a distinctive yellow uniform and undertake hard menial work (Longmate, 1974). They also faced the prospect of having their child forcibly adopted (Page, 1984).

Changing perceptions of the problem of single motherhood during the early part of the 20th century led to less punitive forms of policy. Mothers who had 'lapsed for the first time' were offered accommodation in a voluntary sector home rather than the workhouse (Middleton, 1971). More generous forms of state welfare support were also introduced during both the First and Second World Wars. Treating single mothers in a 'less eligible' way during wartime was regarded as inappropriate and impractical (Ferguson and Fitzgerald, 1954).

In the more liberal era of the late 1960s and 1970s, greater emphasis was given to the material deprivations experienced by single mothers. For example, the Finer Committee, which reported in 1974, made a number of policy recommendations to improve the economic and social position of all lone parents, including a Guaranteed Maintenance Allowance (*Report of the committee on one parent families*, 1974).

Since the late 1970s the policy response towards single mothers has changed in the light of their growing dependency on means-tested benefits. Attempts have been made by both Conservative and Labour administrations to increase the labour market participation of lone mothers by a combination of US style benefit reductions and work incentives (see Blank and Haskins, 2001).

Question for discussion
• What is a social problem? Why do social problems change over time?

References
Blank, R. and Haskins, R. (eds) (2001) *The new world of welfare*, Washington, DC: Brookings Institution Press.

Clarke, J. (2001) 'Social problems: sociological perspectives', in M. May, R. Page and E. Brunsdon (eds) *Understanding social problems*, Oxford: Blackwell, pp 3-15.

Ferguson, S.M. and Fitzgerald, H. (1954) *Studies in the social services*, London: HMSO.

Garnham, H. (2001) *Poverty: The facts* (4th edn), London: CPAG.

Kiernan, K., Land, H. and Lewis, J. (1998) *Lone motherhood in twentieth century Britain*, Oxford: Oxford University Press.

Longmate, N. (1974) *The workhouse*, London: Temple Smith.

Middleton, N. (1971) *When family failed*, London: Victor Gollancz.

Murray, C. (1984) *Losing ground*, New York, NY: Basic Books.

Murray, C. (1990) *The emerging British underclass*, London: Institute of Economic Affairs.

Murray, C. (1994) *Underclass: The crisis deepens*, London: Institute of Economic Affairs.

Page, R.M. (1984) *Stigma*, London: Routledge and Kegan Paul.

Report of the committee on one parent families (The Finer Report) (1974) vol 1, Cmnd 5629, London: HMSO.

Further reading
Manning, N. (ed) (1985) *Social problems and welfare ideology*, Aldershot: Gower.

May, M., Page, R. and Brunsdon, E. (eds) (2001) *Understanding social problems*, Oxford: Blackwell.

Rubington, E. and Weinberg, M. (eds) (2002) *The study of social problems* (6th edn), Oxford: Oxford University Press.

Website resource
Department for Work and Pensions: www.dwp.gov.uk

In the early development of social policy the links between academic study and policy practice were evident at the London School of Economics and Political Science (LSE). Clement Attlee, one of its first lecturers, became Prime Minister in the post-war Labour government which introduced much of the welfare state reform of the last century, and William Beveridge, one-time Director of the LSE, became the architect of the post-war social security reforms. In 1950 the LSE appointed the first Professor of Social Policy, Richard Titmuss, who went on to become not only the subject's leading scholar, but also an active member of advisory bodies and policy committees in the UK and abroad (see Alcock et al, 2001). Social policy is now studied across the university sector in the UK, and abroad, and its leading researchers are frequently actively involved in the development and evaluation of policy programmes.

Social policy has also moved beyond the relatively narrow concern with the development and implementation of UK public welfare services, which concerned the early Fabians. Theoretical debate has developed within the subject to embrace a more pluralistic concern, not only with what should be done through policy intervention, but also with why and where policy intervention might be justified (or not) and how its (sometimes contradictory) outcomes might be understood and explained. This broadening of approach was recognised symbolically by a change in the name of the subject from *social administration* to *social policy*, suggesting a move within study and research, from a concern with *how* things were done, to *why* they were done – or *whether* they should be done at all.

What is more, study and research in social policy have moved beyond a focus only on the policy programmes of the UK and its government. Within an increasingly global economic and social environment, and with the growing influence of supranational agencies (most notably the European Union), it is no longer possible to confine the understanding of social policy to one national context. Policies in the UK are affected by international influences, and social policy students and researchers must embrace the need for comparative analysis to engage with the ideas and forces at work internationally (see Section 3.9 and **Boxes 3f** and **3g** for a discussion of comparative and cross-national approaches in social policy research).

Social policy in the 21st century has therefore extended beyond its Fabian roots to become theoretically pluralist and internationally focused, and all current scholars and researchers now seek to embrace these broader influences in their work. Nevertheless the theory and practice interface remains at the core of modern social policy, just as it did in the days of Attlee and Beveridge. What drives scholarship and research is the commitment not just to understand policy, but also to change it – and this prescriptive dimension informs the work of all the contributors to this volume.

Question for discussion

• Why is social policy sometimes described as a 'prescriptive' discipline?

References

Abel-Smith, B. and Townsend, P. (1965) *The poor and the poorest*, London: Bell.
Alcock, P., Glennerster, H., Oakley, A. and Sinfield, A. (eds) (2001) *Welfare and wellbeing: Richard Titmuss's contribution to social policy*, Bristol: The Policy Press.

Further reading

Alcock, P. (2003) *Social policy in Britain* (2nd edn), Basingstoke: Palgrave.
Alcock, P., Erskine, A. and May, M. (eds) (2003) *The student's companion to social policy* (2nd edn), Oxford: Blackwell.
Hill, M. (2000) *Understanding social policy* (6th edn), Oxford: Blackwell.

Relevant organisations

The major organisation representing academics and researchers working in social policy is the **Social Policy Association** (SPA). It is a membership organisation and all staff and postgraduate students working in social policy can join. For more details see the SPA website: www.social-policy.com

Website resource

This website, 'An introduction to social policy', was developed and is maintained by Professor Paul Spicker at the Robert Gordon University in Aberdeen. It contains general material on the subject of social policy as well as some discussion of a range of policy issues: www2.rgu.ac.uk/publicpolicy/introduction/index.htm

---

1.3 Policy research

In understanding what we mean by 'policy research' we must first break down the term into its constituent parts: policy and research.

What is policy?

Levin (1997) suggests that when politicians and officials refer to **policy** they are referring to policy in a number of ways:'a stated intention to take a particular action', an 'organisational practice' or as some other form of activity/intervention. Figure 1a summarises what is meant by policy and identifies some of its key attributes and characteristics. It is these attributes, and particularly a commitment to some form of action, which help us to recognise when something is a policy. As we have seen in the previous section, **social policy** refers to the practice of social intervention aimed at securing social change to promote the welfare and wellbeing of citizens. Many organisations and agencies, and the people who work in or for them, are involved in formulating and implementing social policies.

Figure 1a: 'Policy' and the attributes of policy

What is policy?
- *'Policy' as a stated intention:* policy is a stated intention to take a particular action, or bring about a particular situation, in the future. This is found in, for example, the manifestos of political parties, in white papers, and so on.
- *'Policy' as a current or past action:* in other words, the government's policy is what the government is currently doing (or has done in the past).
- *'Policy' as an organisational practice:* policy is often used to denote the established practices of an organisation, the rules and regulations, the ways in which things are customarily done or attitudes that are customarily taken.
- *'Policy' as an indicator of the formal or claimed status of a past, present or proposed course of action:* a course of action is often described as a policy in a context where the term appears to denote a claim for status of some kind; for example, if a policy can successfully be labelled 'government policy' in the allocation of money or scarce

contd.../

resources, that policy will have a valid claim to priority over others not so labelled.

The attributes of policy

- *'Policy' denotes belongingness:* a policy belongs to someone, or some body (for example, the government's policy, departmental policy, and so on).
- *'Policy' denotes commitment:* a policy carries commitment on the part of those to whom it belongs. A stated intention, for example, is not just a proposal, it is a proposal to which the government/department or organisation is committed.
- *The description of a proposal or current course of action as 'policy' may also denote that it has, or is claimed to have, a certain status,* possibly conferred on it by a prior event of some kind (for example, a public announcement), or by being acted on even though no agreement to that effect has been reached.
- *A policy also possesses the attribute of 'specificity':* some stated intentions are quite specific, others less so. The less specific a policy, the more options it leaves open when it comes to translating the policy into action. The more specific it is, the closer it is to being a single blueprint for action. A policy must have at least some degree of specificity for it to be distinguishable from other policies.

Source: Adapted from Levin (1997, pp 15-19)

What is research?

Research in social policy, and research conducted by professionals employed in related spheres (for example, social workers, health workers, advice workers, and so on), is concerned with *understanding* social issues and social problems, social policies and actions, and the social world more generally. Policy research also aims to provide *answers* and *evidence* that can contribute to the *improvement* of 'policy' and policy making, can lead to better practice and interventions, the reduction of social problems and social distress, and the promotion of welfare and wellbeing. Finally, not only is policy research concerned to find answers to policy problems and improve policy action, but it is also concerned to identify the right *questions* to ask in the first place (Clarke, 2001, p 38).

Figure 1b shows that to 'count' as research the enquiry must be done in a systematic, disciplined and rigorous way, making use of the most appropriate research methods and designs to answer specific research questions.

Figure 1b: Three views of what constitutes 'research'

Research starts as an extension of common sense – finding out about things, looking for information about them, trying to make sense of them in the light of evidence and working out what evidence is needed.   (Abbott and Sapsford, 1998, p 3)

When we want to know something and there is no authority, or the authorities disagree, or we are just not ready to accept without question what the authority has told us, then we do research. When the existing literature on a subject does not answer the question we are asking, or we are dissatisfied with the answer, then we do research.... Research is a disciplined way to go about answering questions. This distinguishes research from other ways of answering questions. The fact that research is a disciplined process means that the answers are more reliable. (Bouma and Atkinson, 1995, pp 6-13)

Research is a systematic investigation to find answers to a problem. (Burns, 2000, p 3)

The term **policy-oriented research** has been used to refer to research designed to inform or understand one or more aspects of the public and social policy process, including decision making and policy formulation, implementation and evaluation (Becker, 2004). A distinction can be made between research *for* policy and research *of* policy:

- Research *for* policy is concerned to inform the various stages of the policy process (before the formation of policy through to its implementation).
- Research *of* policy is concerned with how problems are defined, agendas set, policy formulated, decisions made and how policy is implemented, evaluated and changed (Nutley and Webb, 2000, p 15).

Policy-oriented research (or 'policy research', as we refer to it in this volume) can simultaneously be research *for*, and research *of*, policy (Becker, 2004).

Methods and approaches in policy research

Policy research can serve several functions and can have a diverse range of audiences. It provides a *specialist* function of informing and influencing the policy process and the understanding of how policy works and 'what works', for target audiences of policy makers, policy networks and communities, research-aware professionals and service users, and academics; and a *democratic* or *enlightenment* function, where research findings contribute to the development of an informed and knowledge-based society as well as to the broader democratic process (Becker, 2004). Here the 'users' of research will include organised groups with vested interests, people whose lives are influenced by the policy and the public as a whole.

Policy research draws from the full range of research designs, methods and approaches outlined in this volume. Depending on the specific research question(s) to be addressed, in some cases just one method will be used. Chapter Four of this volume, for example, provides a discussion of quantitative research methods that can be employed in policy research, while Chapter Five focuses on qualitative ones. In other cases, there may be an integration of different methods either within a single piece of research or as part of a wider programme of research being conducted across multiple sites or cross-nationally (see Chapter Three). Each method and design has its own strengths and limitations, as will be seen in later sections of this volume. Ann Oakley, for example, has argued that policy research needs to make greater use of experiments and trial methodology, rather than rejecting these as inappropriate or part of an outdated positivist mentality. Experiments can contribute to the kinds of knowledge that academics, policy makers, professionals and the public are interested in. Indeed, "reliable information about the effectiveness of public policy and social interventions is hard to come by using any other means" (Oakley, 2000, p 323), because true experiments offer the most robust design for assessing cause and effect (see also Chapter Four, Section 4.3).

How an issue is perceived, and the policies in place (or not in place) to respond or to deal with it, will also influence how it is researched – the type of questions, the nature of the enquiries and the methodologies and approaches used. For example, where policies already exist to respond to the unique needs of lone mothers (for example, New Deals designed to 'encourage' them back into the paid labour market, or specific cash benefits or childcare strategies) then these can be *evaluated* using a number of approaches and research methods described in Chapter Three and throughout this volume. Where an issue has not yet been defined as a social issue or as a social problem (for example, young carers – see **Box 1c** later in this chapter), then other research approaches will need to be used, to highlight the issue for the first time and to bring knowledge of it to a wider audience, including policy makers. Qualitative studies (Chapter Five) are useful here, in that they can raise the profile of an issue such as young carers, drawing on a limited number of cases, because at an early stage it may be difficult or impossible to do large-scale surveys. In the example of *The poor and the poorest* (**Box 1a**), secondary analysis of large-scale government datasets enabled poverty to be reconceptualised and its extent to be measured.

Attributes of 'good' policy research

Abbott and Sapsford (1998, p 180) suggest that "Good research is the product of clear analysis of problems, clear specification of goals, careful design of fieldwork and thoughtful analysis and exposition afterwards". Cutting across these issues is the need for selecting the appropriate research method and design by reference to the precise research question(s), and the need to contribute to knowledge creation in a reliable, trustworthy and transparent way. Ann Oakley has suggested: "considerations of trustworthiness apply to all forms of research.... We need to examine all methods from the viewpoint of the same questions about trustworthiness, to consider how best to match methods to research questions, and to find ways of integrating a range of methods in carrying out socially useful inquiries" (Oakley, 1999, pp 165-6). Oakley also suggests that:

> ... the distinguishing mark of all 'good' research is the awareness and acknowledgement of error, and that what flows from this is the necessity of establishing procedures which will minimize the effect such errors may have on what counts as knowledge. (Oakley, 2000, p 72)

However, the notion of error is a contested concept for many qualitative researchers, as will be seen in Chapter Five.

In reviewing what researchers themselves understand to be 'good' social research, Denscombe (2002) has identified ten ground rules that help to define the attributes of good social research (Figure 1c).

Figure 1c: **Denscombe's ground rules for good research**

To qualify as social research, an investigation needs to:
- have clearly stated aims, that are
- related to existing knowledge and needs, and that are
- investigated within limitations imposed through time, money and opportunity.

Research needs to:
- contribute something new to knowledge, using
- precise and valid data,
- collected and used in a justifiable way, to
- produce findings from which generalisations can be made.

The researcher needs to adopt an attitude and approach that is:
- open-minded and self-reflective,

contd.../

- recognises the rights and interests of participants, and is
- cautious about claims based on the findings.

Source: Denscombe (2002, pp 2-3)

Question for discussion

- What are the characteristics of 'good' policy research?

References

Abbott, P. and Sapsford, R. (1998) *Research methods for nurses and the caring professions* (2nd edn), Buckingham: Open University Press.

Becker, S. (2004) 'Policy-oriented research', in M. Lewis-Beck, A. Bryman and T. Futing Liao (eds) *The SAGE encyclopaedia of social science research methods*, Thousand Oaks, CA: Sage Publications, pp 830-1.

Bouma, G. and Atkinson, G.B.J. (1995) *A handbook of social science research: A comprehensive and practical guide for students* (2nd edn), Oxford: Oxford University Press.

Burns, R.B. (2000) *Introduction to research methods*, London: Sage Publications.

Clarke, A. (2001) 'Research and the policy-making process', in N. Gilbert, *Researching social life* (2nd edn), London: Sage Publications, pp 28-42.

Denscombe, M. (2002) *Ground rules for good research: A 10 point guide for social researchers*, Buckingham: Open University Press.

Levin, P. (1997) *Making social policy: The mechanisms of government and politics, and how to investigate them*, Buckingham: Open University Press.

Nutley, S. and Webb, J. (2000) 'Evidence and the policy process', in H. Davies, S. Nutley and P. Smith, *What works? Evidence-based policy and practice in public services*, Bristol: The Policy Press, pp 13-41.

Oakley, A. (1999) 'People's way of knowing: gender and methodology', in S. Hood, B. Mayall and S. Oliver (eds) *Critical issues in social research: Power and prejudice*, Buckingham: Open University Press, pp 154-70.

Oakley, A. (2000) *Experiments in knowing: Gender and method in the social sciences*, Cambridge: Polity Press.

Further reading

Clarke, A. (2001) 'Research and the policy-making process', in N. Gilbert, *Researching social life* (2nd edn), London: Sage Publications, pp 28-42.

Levin, P. (1997) *Making social policy: The mechanisms of government and politics, and how to investigate them*, Buckingham: Open University Press.

1.4 Research, policy and practice

In most cases of policy formulation, development and policy change, it is difficult to be precise about the nature and degree of influence that research plays in informing the policy and legislative *process*, as well as the *practice* of social policy (in other words, the *implementation* of policy by professionals). Research can make a contribution to both policy and practice, even if it is not linear or direct. For example, **instrumental utilisation** of research can be said to have taken place when there is evidence of policy makers or practitioners *acting on* the findings of specific research studies. **Conceptual utilisation** occurs when research *influences* how policy makers and practitioners *interpret* and *think* about a social issue or problem – where, for example, it provides alternative ways of understanding and informs action strategies (Clarke, 2001, p 35).

In many discussions of the influence that research can have on policy and practice, there is an assumption that both policy and practice are influenced in the same way (and in the same direction). However, the connection between research and policy, and between research and practice, are markedly different (Bullock et al, 1998, p 11), and thus need to be considered separately. However, it must also be remembered that the distinction between policy (and policy makers), and practice (and professionals/practitioners) is not as clear-cut as might be inferred, as we shall see in the next section.

Models of policy making

In order to understand the relationship between research and policy we must first have some knowledge of the policy-making process. Figure 1d summarises two of the key models of the policy process: *rational* and *incremental* policy making.

Figure 1d: **Rational and incremental models of policy making**

Rational policy making
Rational, or top-down, theory is built on the assumption that "given the correct forms of implementation process – guidance, procedures, organisation, training and (especially in the past twenty years) management – policy implementation will proceed as intended by implementers at the top of organisations or Government" (Baldwin, 2000, p 15). The 'intended' policy itself will be determined through rational decision making, a process with a logical sequence, from problem awareness, to goal setting, to the formulation of clear

contd.../

objectives, to the selection from alternative strategies of the best means to accomplish the objectives, and finally, to the evaluation of outcomes (Smith and May, 1980, p 164).

Incremental policy making

In contrast is the incremental model of policy making, or what is often referred to as the 'bottom-up' approach. The writings of Charles Lindblom and Michael Lipsky are critical here. Lindblom (1959) argues that the pressures on policy decision makers are such that rationalism is unattainable in the policy process, that means and ends are often chosen simultaneously, and many decisions are incremental, involving 'successive limited comparisons' to what has been done before (Hill, 1993, p 159). Policy makers start not with ideal goals but with policies currently in force. "Decision making entails considering only incremental change, or changes at the margins. Only a rather restricted number of policy alternatives is reviewed and only a limited number of consequences is envisaged and evaluated for any given alternative" (Smith and May, 1980, p 166).

There are many criticisms of the rational model of policy making and the assumptions that underpin it (see Smith and May, 1980, for a thorough review). Given that the assumptions behind the model (that policy, following the consideration of all possibilities and options, can be defined rationally and unambiguously, with clear goals, aims and means, which are acceptable to, and accepted by, all parties and players) have been so challenged, it is perhaps surprising that the model still commands such respect among policy analysts. The reasons for its continuing importance lie not in its usefulness for understanding how policy *is* made, but in helping us understand how policy *ought* to be made. Gordon et al (1977, p 7) suggest that "The main explanation for its [the rational model's] continuing existence must lie in its status as a normative model and as a 'dignified' myth which is often shared by the policy-makers themselves". Baldwin confers: "This is a prescriptive and normative approach designed to assist those interested in implementation to understand the best way to proceed" (Baldwin, 2000, p 15). Thus, the rational approach offers a model for "ideal decision making procedures" (Smith and May, 1980, p 170).

Lindblom's (1959) 'science of muddling through' provides a critique of rationalist theory, noting that there is seldom such a thing as a 'new' policy. The incremental, bottom-up, model helps us understand why pro-inertia and anti-innovation are powerful characteristics of all human organisations and the policy-making process. In a later refinement of his thesis, Lindblom (1980) argues that disjointed incrementalism is a model that not only explains how policy is made in the real world, but, in his view, is also a model that illuminates how policy ought to be made.

Lindblom's importance is not just in his analysis of 'disjointed incrementalism'. He sees policy making as a process of political and social interaction involving negotiation and bargaining among groups promoting and protecting differing and competing interests and values – what Lindblom terms 'partisan mutual adjustment'. This political process is, in Lindblom's view, essential to policy making, and is in contrast with the centralised information-based decision making of rational approaches, which can ignore the voices of important stakeholders (see Gregory, 1989, for a full discussion of the Lindblomian paradigm). Indeed, Gregory suggests that Lindblom's enduring message is not about incrementalism in policy making, but rather that "public policy making has to be understood essentially as a political process, rather than an analytical, problem-solving, one" (Gregory, 1989, p 186).

Smith and May, however, suggest that the debate between rational and incremental models of policy making is an artificial one for two reasons:

> Firstly, the relationship between 'is' and 'ought' is confused and there are good grounds for suggesting that whereas incrementalist models may perform an explanatory function, rationalist models are largely confined to a prescriptive role. Secondly the debate does not consider seriously the issue of what it takes to act in accord with any set of decision making rules and thus neglects the way in which policy makers and administrators may use 'decision making' as a gloss for a range of practices. (Smith and May, 1980, p 172)

The influence of research on policy making

The relationship between research and any particular policy is perhaps most transparent when those responsible for formulating or implementing policy actually cite the research 'evidence' that informs their thinking and proposals. The 'rediscovery of poverty', as we have already seen, was informed directly by the work of Brian Abel-Smith and Peter Townsend (**Box 1a**). Their research utilised secondary analysis of government datasets to say new things about the meaning and extent of poverty, thus challenging accepted 'knowledge' and understanding of that time. There is a clear, and acknowledged, link between the Abel-Smith and Townsend research and a growing awareness and concern with poverty, the development of social policies and the growth of anti-poverty action – evidence of both *instrumental* and *conceptual utilisation* of the research. This example of research findings informing policy choices fits well with both the rational and incremental models of the policy process. In this case, research was used by the Labour government and by others (for example, the

Child Poverty Action Group) to inform their policy options and strategies, thus combining 'top-down' and 'bottom-up' elements.

While the rational model of policy making sees research findings feeding into the process of specifying goals and objectives and identifying consequences (Nutley and Webb, 2000, pp 25-6), the incremental model of policy making sees research evidence feeding into the policy process at many different points of time and being targeted on, and used by, different policy stakeholders in their negotiations and political interactions. Irrespective of which model is used to help us understand more clearly the workings of the policy process (and there are other models which can be referred to here – see Hill, 1993, for a review), what most of these models share is the value placed on *research knowledge informing policy decisions and choices.*

However, there are limits to the influence that research by itself can have on rational or incremental forms of policy making. In some cases, the impact of a *specific* piece of research is not particularly apparent, but policy has changed gradually as a consequence of growing social and political awareness, growing evidence of injustice or need, and as different policy networks have engaged with, and utilised, research findings. One such example is that of 'young carers' – children who provide unpaid care and support to other family members. As we can see from **Box 1c**, while research on young carers influenced significantly the development of policy and law for this group of children, it did not do this alone. The media, campaigning groups and children themselves played a significant part in bringing about awareness and developments in policy, and later, in professional practice. In this context, policy making combined both rational, top-down, and incremental, bottom-up elements, with research feeding into the process at various stages and being used by various stakeholders for different purposes, as part of a wider process of political negotiation, advocacy and policy development.

Box 1c: Research informing policy: the case of young carers

Jo Aldridge, *Research Fellow, Young Carers Research Group, Loughborough University*

Young carers are children and young people aged up to 18 who provide substantial, regular or significant care, often of an adult-like nature, to a family member – usually a parent – who has a need for care, support or supervision. In Britain during the 1990s policy, law and professional practice on young carers evolved and developed in a symbiotic relationship with the growing research literature which first described, and then explained, the experiences, circumstances and needs of this group of children and young people.

Prior to the 1990s, academics, policy makers and welfare professionals failed to recognise and account for children's caring responsibilities within the family. By the end of the decade a sea change had occurred: the number of dedicated young carers' projects grew from a handful to around 200; young carers were acknowledged in policy, guidance and law; they had legally defined rights to assessments, to services, 'direct payments' and other forms of provision both under community care and children's legislation; the government's national carers strategy made a series of policy commitments designed to support them; and young carers were also identified as a priority group in other health, social services and education spheres, including a new assessment framework for children in need and the Connexions service (Bibby and Becker, 2000).

In the early 1990s, small-scale qualitative studies helped cast some light on the experiences of this 'hidden' group of children (Bilsborrow, 1992; Aldridge and Becker, 1993). A small research team based at Loughborough University (the Young Carers Research Group: YCRG) were awarded a series of grants and contracts from various charities and health and social services authorities to undertake local, and then national, research in this field. Pursuing an active dissemination strategy (see also Chapter Seven in this volume), these and other researchers published extensively and made dozens of conference presentations. Their studies generated considerable media attention and interest from policy makers and politicians. A 1994 House of Commons Early Day Motion applauded the latest YCRG research and called on government to take more action for young carers. Over the next two years the Department of Health prepared guidance for social services departments, and young carers were included in the remit of the 1995 Carers (Recognition and Services) Act. Many organisations, particularly children's and carers' charities, the Social Services Inspectorate and social services and health authorities nationally, formed an ad hoc policy network that used research evidence to argue for further policy, procedural and legislative change (Becker et al, 1998; Aldridge and Becker, 2003).

The media also played a key role in using research to promote change (see **Box 7c** for a fuller discussion of the role of the media in reporting research findings). The weekly social care magazine, *Community Care*, ran a year-long campaign in 1995 – 'Young carers: back them up!' – to raise awareness among professionals. It commissioned the YCRG to undertake the first national survey of young carers (Dearden and Becker, 1995), which itself became the subject of a *World in Action* documentary seen by an estimated seven million people. Many young carers also became more vocal and 'politicised', with delegations of children attending meetings with MPs and policy makers, facilitated by children's and carers' charities.

A second national survey (Dearden and Becker, 1998) provided a profile of 2,303 young carers. This allowed, for the first time, a *statistical* analysis of the factors that influenced children's caring roles and their receipt of assessments and services. The then President of the Association of Directors of Social Services suggested that: "Information on over 2,000 young carers and those they care for must be heeded; central government and health, education and social services agencies must take notice and act in order to improve practice" (Taylor, 1998, p v). More qualitative and quantitative research followed. The media maintained its coverage of the 'human interest' stories as well as policy issues, and policy makers and politicians cited research evidence during Parliamentary debates (for example, *Hansard*, 2000) and in the growing body of policy guidance and government documents (HM Government, 1999). The then Department for Education and Employment developed its own responses to the growing evidence on young carers' educational and labour market difficulties (Dearden and Becker, 2000).

However, these developments did not receive universal appreciation. A critique against the 'young carers industry' was developed by some disability rights authors who proposed that, rather than focusing on and developing services for young carers, resources should instead be directed at disabled parents (Keith and Morris, 1995; Aldridge and Becker, 1996; Olsen and Parker, 1997). This critique, emerging from the young carers research, was to lead to the commissioning of new research on the needs of disabled parents, and to practice developments emphasising a holistic 'family approach' to meeting the needs of young carers *and* their families.

Question for discussion
- To what extent has qualitative and quantitative research on young carers informed the policy process? What are the other influential factors?

References
Aldridge, J. and Becker, S. (1993) *Children who care: Inside the world of young carers*, Loughborough: Young Carers Research Group, Loughborough University.

Aldridge, J. and Becker, S. (1996) 'Disability rights and the denial of young carers: the dangers of zero-sum arguments', *Critical Social Policy*, vol 16, pp 55-76.

Aldridge, J. and Becker, S. (2003) *Children caring for parents with mental illness: Perspectives of young carers, parents and professionals*, Bristol: The Policy Press.

Becker, S., Aldridge, J. and Dearden, C. (1998) *Young carers and their families*, Oxford: Blackwell Science.

Bibby, A. and Becker, S. (2000) *Young carers in their own words*, London: Calouste Gulbenkian Foundation.

Bilsborrow, S. (1992) *'You grow up fast as well...': Young carers on Merseyside*, Liverpool: Carers National Association, Personal Services Society and Barnardo's.

Dearden, C. and Becker, S. (1995) *Young carers: The facts*, Sutton: Reed Business Publishing.

Dearden, C. and Becker, S. (1998) *Young carers in the UK: A profile*, London: Carers National Association.

Dearden, C. and Becker, S. (2000) *Growing up caring: Vulnerability and transitions to adulthood – Young carers' experiences*, Leicester: Youth Work Press.

Hansard (2000) House of Lords official report, 23 June, vol 614, no 110, col 599.

HM Government (1999) *Caring about carers – A national strategy for carers*, London: DoH.

Keith, L. and Morris, J. (1995) 'Easy targets: a disability rights perspective on the "children as carers" debate', *Critical Social Policy*, no 44/45, pp 36-57.

Olsen, R. and Parker, G. (1997) 'A response to Aldridge and Becker – "Disability rights and the denial of young carers: the dangers of zero-sum arguments"', *Critical Social Policy*, no 50, pp 125-33.

Taylor, R. (1998) 'Foreword', in C. Dearden and S. Becker, *Young carers in the UK: A profile*, London: Carers National Association, p v.

Further reading

Aldridge, J. and Becker, S. (2003) *Children caring for parents with mental illness: Perspectives of young carers, parents and professionals*, Bristol: The Policy Press.

Becker, S., Aldridge, J. and Dearden, C. (1998) *Young carers and their families*, Oxford: Blackwell Science.

Relevant organisation
Young Carers Research Group
Centre for Child and Family Research, Department of Social Sciences, Loughborough University, Leicestershire LE11 3TU
Tel 01509 228355; www.ycrg.org.uk

Website resources
Carers UK: www.carersonline.org.uk
Children's Society: www.childrenssociety.org.uk
Children's Society website for young carers: www.youngcarers.hants.org.uk
Crossroads Caring for Carers: www.carers.org.uk

London Borough of Hammersmith and Fulham [award-winning site produced
   by young carers themselves]: www.bubblycrew.org.uk
Princess Royal Trust for Carers: www.carers.org

On other occasions, research fails to have any, or very little, impact on policy
making even though the 'quality' of the research is not in doubt. **Box 1d**
provides two examples drawn from social security and labour market research
where policy makers chose to ignore robust and trustworthy research evidence
because of, largely, political imperatives. Thus, not even 'good' policy research,
conducted to transparent 'ground rules' and high standards, will influence
policy if there is a strong political resistance, or apathy, to the findings.

Box 1d: Policy ignoring research: the case of Housing Benefit appeals and a New Deal

Roy Sainsbury, *Senior Research Fellow, Social Policy Research Unit, University
of York*

In an episode of *Yes, Minister* the hapless Minister for Administrative Affairs,
Jim Hacker, is faced with a piece of research which apparently shows conclusively
a failure of government policy. While this alarms the Minister, his Permanent
Secretary, Sir Humphrey, remains unruffled, advising Hacker that he can deploy
one or more of a range of responses to unwelcome research findings, such as
'it's out of date', 'the sample on which it was based was too small', 'the policy
has changed since the research was carried out' and 'the issues raised have
already been dealt with'. Whatever riposte is chosen, and whether or not it is
true, the effect is the same: the research can be ignored and no action is
required.

Not every researcher will have been the victim of cynical and manipulative policy
makers, but anyone who has carried out work intended to have an impact on
government policy will probably have a story or two about how their rigorous
and comprehensive piece of work ended up gathering dust. The general reason
for this is that research, when completed or even while still in progress, is part
of a wider, messier world of politics where rationality and logic are often trumped
by other considerations and where bigger forces can easily relegate the role of
research to a bit player (or no player at all). A couple of examples from the
world of social security and employment research will serve as illustrations. (I
have chosen these from work carried out from my research unit as I hesitate to
suggest anyone else's research has been sidelined.)

In the early 1990s, research funded by the then Department of Social Security (DSS) was carried out at the Social Policy Research Unit at the University of York into the arrangements for hearing appeals on Housing Benefit decisions made by local authorities (Sainsbury and Eardley, 1991). The main conclusion was reached that the system of using a board of local councillors to decide appeals failed at so many levels (it lacked independence, decisions were poor and claimants were effectively denied their appeal rights) that the case for transferring responsibility to the existing independent structure of Social Security Appeal Tribunals was 'compelling'. But nothing happened. Why? As it was explained to us some years later by a Departmental official, the argument was indeed seen as compelling but foundered on the twin rocks of local authority opposition and Treasury resistance. Local authorities did not want to relinquish any of their powers to central government, and the Treasury would not countenance increased expenditure, so plans for reform were dropped. Later in the 1990s, and without the aid for further research, government officials assessing the implications of the European Convention on Human Rights for domestic legislation concluded that Housing Benefit appeals contravened Article 6 of the Convention guaranteeing citizens an independent hearing in appeals against state agencies. The outcome is that, from April 2001, Housing Benefit appeals have been transferred from local authorities to the independent appeals system. Power of research: 0; Realpolitik: 1.

Being ignored is one unpleasant fate, but being rendered irrelevant is perhaps worse. In 1998, the DSS established a number of pilot schemes under the umbrella of the New Deal for Disabled People in which disabled people were assigned a 'personal adviser' to help them move from Incapacity Benefit towards and into paid work. The aim was to find out 'what worked' for the many and diverse sick and disabled people who were known from previous research to be disadvantaged in the labour market. An elaborate and expensive research project, involving a number of research organisations, was designed and started. Within six months of the two-year project, a new minister had changed the basis of the pilots. Finding out how to help people into work was no longer a priority; rather, getting as many people as possible into work was. The research methodology was therefore no longer the most appropriate. Furthermore, within a year policy makers had already decided the basic design of a national scheme to supersede the pilots, well before the research findings became available. Hence, when the research report appeared in 2001 (Loumidis et al, 2001) its utility to policy makers was hard to see. Power of research: 0; Realpolitik: 2.

This is not intended to be a Jeremiah vision of research; far from it, as this volume will demonstrate. However, the examples above do show that research did not play the part in the policy process that researchers expected. The message to remember is that, in our enthusiasm for social research, we should not overestimate or assume its role in the policy process. Research can be in the right place at the right time but it probably is not as much as we would like to think. And even if it is, the Hackers and Sir Humphreys might get you anyway.

Question for discussion
• Why does research not always play a prominent role in the policy process?

References

Loumidis, J., Stafford, B., Youngs, R., Green, A., Arthur, S., Legard, R., Lessof, C., Lewis, J., Walker, R., Corden, A., Thornton, P. and Sainsbury, R. (2001) *Evaluation of the New Deal for Disabled People personal adviser service pilot*, DSS Research Report, no 144, Leeds: Corporate Document Services.

Sainsbury, R. and Eardley, T. (1991) *Housing Benefit reviews*, DSS Research Report, no 3, London: HMSO.

Website resources

The government's official website on social security appeals can be found at: www.appeals-service.gov.uk

The Department for Work and Pensions' website containing information on the New Deal for Disabled People is at: www.newdeal.gov.uk/ newdeal.asp?DealID=NDDIS

There are a number of models that help us to understand the relationships between policy making and research (Figure 1e).

Figure 1e: **Models of the relationship between research and policy making**

• A 'knowledge-driven model' assumes that research (conducted by 'experts') *leads* policy.
• A 'problem-solving model' assumes that research *follows* policy, and that policy issues shape research priorities. Thus, research supplies the empirical evidence on which policy makers can base their decisions and choices.
• An 'interactive model' portrays research and policy as mutually influential.
• A 'political/tactical model' sees policy as the outcome of a political process, where the research agenda is politically driven. Here, research can become political ammunition or it can be ignored if it

contd.../

does not coincide with the answers that politicians want to see. Sometimes, the very fact that research is taking place is important for political and tactical purposes, rather than the findings themselves.

• An 'enlightenment model' sees research as serving policy in indirect ways, addressing the context within which decisions are made and providing a broader frame for understanding and explaining policy.

Source: Young et al (2002); see also Nutley and Webb (2000, pp 29-31); Clarke (2001, pp 35-27)

Abel-Smith and Townsend's research (**Box 1a**) falls largely within the knowledge-driven model, where anti-poverty policy and action developed out of robust research evidence. The young carers research (**Box 1c**) could be considered to be an illustration of both a knowledge-driven model and an interactive model, while the political/tactical model can help to explain the fate – or non-influence – of the social security research cited in **Box 1d**. However, as we shall see in the next section, the political climate of the time is also critical in determining the responsiveness of government and others to research evidence, and what they might do about, or with, research findings.

Politics and policy research

Politics is important on a number of levels. Some argue that the research process is itself a "political activity" (Mayall et al, 1999, p 5), where all aspects of research are constructed and reconstructed through the intersections of three sets of interests: those of the researchers, those of the researched (particularly disadvantaged individuals and groups); and those of socially dominant political structures, organisations, social groups and individuals (including policy makers, politicians, professionals, and so on). Researchers must manage these conflicting interests, and the demands and priorities of their organisations, funding bodies, and so on, as well as their own values, agendas, purposes and time constraints. In this context, research is political with a small 'p', and not some 'neutral' exercise in knowledge and evidence creation.

On another level, any intention by researchers to inform and influence the policy process is, by definition, a political activity. As we have already seen, policy research combines a number of aims and these include contributing to knowledge and understanding while also trying to *improve* the policy process, including policy making and implementation.

Additionally, the political climate of the time (not just which party is in power, but their ideologies and values, particularly their 'ideologies of welfare' – see George and Wilding, 1994) are important in determining in part the influence that research can have on policy ideas and policy making. Where research findings are consistent with government values and ideologies, there is some chance that the findings will be applauded and promoted, will 'count' as 'evidence', and may be used to justify a current policy approach or to usher in an 'evidence-based' change of direction. Where findings challenge the current approach of (government) policy making, they may be 'welcomed' (in the spirit of enlightenment and democratic governance), but there is also a very good chance that the research will be ignored, or seen as irrelevant, as **Box 1d** has illustrated.

Politics, and ideology, can also lead to the reframing of social issues and social problems, so that they are understood, and researched, in different ways. For example, Abel-Smith and Townsend's research on poverty, contained in *The poor and the poorest* (**Box 1a**), helped to define poverty *and* inequality as major *social problems* requiring widespread and concerted collective action. The Labour government of the time was responsive to the evidence and committed to some form of intervention. However, just nine years after its publication, Sir Keith Joseph – a Conservative politician whose influence on 'Thatcherism' is widely acknowledged – reframed the social problem of poverty into something quite different. He proposed that poverty was not the problem, but rather the issue was to do with a 'cycle of deprivation' – whereby deprivation was transmitted across generations through problem-creating parenting practices. This perspective, drawing on a different set of beliefs and ideologies of welfare, namely that post-war collectivism had failed to make a better society, and that poverty was more to do with the poor themselves rather than the social and economic structures around them, was a precursor to the Thatcher values that were to dominate government social and economic policy from the mid-1970s to the end of the century (Becker, 1997). These views helped to challenge the relatively new 'rediscovery' of poverty knowledge, by offering an alternative, more individualistic, way of understanding the issues. **Box 1e** shows how this reconceptualisation, from poverty to 'transmitted deprivation', led to a raft of research studies under the Conservatives, and how these issues have become popular again under the New Labour government, which has itself been responsive to 'new' research evidence on transgenerational inequalities. New Labour's responsiveness to this research evidence is consistent with its own political objectives of tackling poverty and social exclusion and promoting opportunities for all. However, there is some distance – conceptually and ideologically – between the current political concern with the transmission of poverty among some families (and groups, such as the so-called 'underclass'), and the spur to collective anti-poverty action generated by *The poor and the poorest* almost four decades earlier. Figure 1f summarises why issues of politics and ideology are important in the context of policy research.

Box 1e: Transmitted deprivation research

Alan Deacon, *Professor of Social Policy, University of Leeds*

Research on **transmitted deprivation** has two main objectives. First, it seeks to determine the extent to which problems of poverty and social exclusion recur in successive generations of the same families. Second, it tries to explain the continuities between generations that are found to exist. These explanations may emphasise the importance of social structures and inequalities. It may be argued, for example, that the children of poor families suffer more ill health, go to inferior schools and live in areas where there are few employment opportunities. As a result they achieve less in education and have to take insecure and low-paid jobs. Alternatively, explanations may emphasise the role of individual behaviours and attitudes. It may be argued that children who experience poor parenting go on to become inadequate parents themselves. They may even be trapped in a culture of poverty that limits their aspirations and leads them to spurn opportunities for self-advancement. These explanations are not, of course, mutually exclusive, and some studies of transmitted deprivation have put forward a sophisticated interpretation of the interaction of structure, behaviour and culture.

The influence of this kind of research and thinking on the policy process is a good example of what the historian Rodney Lowe calls the interplay between "circumstances and individual personality and ideas" (Seldon and Lowe, 1996, p 166).

The idea of a 'cycle of deprivation' was first popularised by the Conservative politician Sir Keith Joseph in a speech in June 1972. "Why is it", he asked, that deprivation has persisted in post-war Britain despite "long periods of full employment and relative prosperity". He suggested that "perhaps" there were processes by which parents "who were themselves deprived in one or more ways in childhood, become the parents of another generation of deprived children" (Joseph, 1972, p 32). At the time Sir Joseph was Secretary of State for Health and Social Services and at his instigation the government funded a seven-year programme of research into the 'transmission or recurrence of deprivation'. This encompassed nearly 40 separate projects, including literature reviews, small-scale qualitative studies of highly deprived families and communities, and highly technical analyses of the data from longitudinal surveys. A final report on the programme appeared in the early 1980s (Brown and Madge, 1982), although the findings of individual studies continued to be published until 1990.

Sir Joseph had expected that the research would focus on problem families, but in the event a majority of the studies emphasised the role of structural factors in what they came to call 'cycles of disadvantage'. Although Sir Joseph's original speech had aroused intense controversy, the findings of these projects attracted little attention. The Thatcher governments of the 1980s were not interested in discussions of poverty, while the great majority of academics took it as read that the research would discredit Sir Joseph's ideas. They believed that his concern with parenting was at best a red herring and at worst a distraction from the much more important issue of the generation and persistence of inequalities. As Richard Berthoud (1983, p 151) noted at the time, Sir Joseph's was a "kite that failed to fly".

Thirty years later the position seems very different. As Pete Alcock (2002, p 177) has put it, Sir Joseph's kite has been "taken out of the cupboard and dusted off for new trials". Tackling the 'cycle of disadvantage' is now at the heart of New Labour's approach to social exclusion, and there are striking parallels between some aspects of the government's thinking and Sir Joseph's ideas (Deacon, 2002).

This turnaround is due in part to the impact of new research evidence. In March 1999 the Treasury published what it described in a press release as "shocking conclusions" about the "passage of inequality from generation to generation" (HM Treasury, 1999). These conclusions were drawn largely from new analyses of panel data (Hills, 1999; see also Section 4.3 for a discussion of panel studies). This is not the whole story, however, since similar evidence had emerged in the 1980s (Such and Walker, 2002). What is new is New Labour's receptivity to this evidence. It could not be ignored by a government publicly committed to promoting equality of opportunity and reducing social exclusion. At the same time, New Labour is less resistant to Conservative ideas about welfare dependency than many on the left had been in the 1980s. It is willing to take tough measures to deal with what it deems to be inadequate or irresponsible parents, and it is this that has led it to incorporate some of Sir Joseph's ideas in its thinking about transmitted deprivation.

Question for discussion
- What are the major similarities and what are the major differences between New Labour thinking about the 'cycle of disadvantage' and Sir Keith Joseph's ideas about the 'cycle of deprivation'?

References
Alcock, P. (2002) 'Editorial', *Benefits*, vol 10, no 3, pp 177-8.
Berthoud, R. (1983) 'Transmitted deprivation: the kite that failed', *Policy Studies*, January, pp 151-69.
Brown, M. and Madge, N. (1982) *Despite the welfare state*, London: Heinemann.

Deacon, A. (2002) 'Echoes of Sir Keith? New Labour and the cycle of disadvantage', *Benefits*, vol 10, no 3, pp 179-84.

Hills, J. (ed) (1999) *Persistent poverty and lifetime inequality: The evidence*, HM

Treasury Occasional Paper 10, London: The Stationery Office.

HM Treasury (1999) *Tackling poverty and extending opportunity: The modernisation of Britain's tax and benefit system*, no 4, London: The Stationery Office.

Joseph, K. (1972) 'The cycle of deprivation', speech to conference of Pre-school Playgroups Association, 29 February, reprinted in *Caring for people*, London: Conservative Political Centre.

Seldon, A. and Lowe, R. (1996) 'The influence of ideas on social policy', *Contemporary British History*, vol 10, no 2, pp 160-77.

Such, E. and Walker, R. (2002) 'Falling behind? Research on transmitted deprivation', *Benefits*, vol 10, no 3, pp 185-92.

Further reading
Benefits (2002) 'The cycle of deprivation – thirty years on', vol 10, no 3.

Figure 1f: **Why politics matters**

- Politics and ideologies of welfare are important in determining the responsiveness of governments (or, for that matter, the responsiveness of organisations, key policy makers and professionals) to research evidence.
- Politics and ideological priorities can lead to some research questions (and answers) being ignored or suppressed, while others can be elevated and lead to extensions or new programmes of research and enquiry.
- Political ideologies help to determine what will be defined as a 'social issue' or as a 'social problem', and, over time, social problems can be reframed or redefined as something else (for example, 'personal or private troubles'). The reframing of social problems as 'non-problems', or private troubles as social problems, will have major implications for policy and practice.
- The nature of 'evidence' (and what 'counts' as evidence) is largely a political and social construct as well as a research and methodological issue. Research methods (the procedures for collecting research data and forming evidence) are themselves socially constructed, and represent particular views about the social world and about knowledge.
- And, of course, the values and political agendas of individual researchers and research units/think tanks influence how they define social issues and how they go about investigating them.

The influence of research on implementation and practice

What do we mean by the implementation of policy? Minogue (1983, p 17) suggests that it is "the crucial business of translating decisions into events: of 'getting things done'.... Implementation relates to 'specified objectives', the translation into practice of the policies that emerge from the complex process of decision making". Hill suggests that implementation should not be seen as somehow separate from the policy-making process: "Rather, implementation must be seen as part of policy-making" (Hill, 1993, p 213).

A model of implementation

The work of Michael Lipsky offers critical insights into how the implementation of policy actually works in practice. He focuses on the behaviour and actions of key implementers – what he refers to as 'street-level bureaucrats' – and their role in creating policy through their practice. As Hudson contends, "If we wish to understand policy implementation, we must understand the street-level bureaucrat" (Hudson, 1989, p 397).

Lipsky argues "that the decisions of street level-bureaucrats, the routines they establish and the devices they invent to cope with uncertainties and work pressures, effectively becomes the public policies they carry out" (Lipsky, 1980, p xii) – in other words, their day-to-day practice actually *constructs* policy. In response to organisational and workload pressures, street-level bureaucrats (including social workers, childcare workers and other social policy-related professionals) develop working practices which maximise their use of discretion. Discretion enables procedures to be adapted to the client or service user and the service user to be adapted to the procedures (Baldwin, 2000, p 83).

Lipsky's work is important in helping us to understand how policy is constructed through the practice of street-level implementers. Discretion is inevitable at the street level and thus policy making can never be truly 'rational', nor can implementation of policy ever be 'perfect' (Hogwood and Gunn, 1984). Nonetheless, the lessons for *improving* the implementation process, for making it less imperfect and perhaps more rational, do need to be learnt. The ten major 'blocks' to perfect implementation (Hogwood and Gunn, 1984) centre around organisational deficiencies in cooperation and communication, in defining objectives, and so on. An understanding of these organisational deficiencies helps explain the 'implementation deficits' that exist in all policy making, and particularly in complex and wide-ranging social policies that require implementation by many different organisations and professions from a range of sectors (statutory, private, voluntary, charitable and informal), with competing objectives and agendas, and working within predetermined budgets and, often, confusing political messages.

Practice and research evidence

"The term evidence-based practice assumes that it is practical and desirable to base practice on knowledge of what works" (Nutley and Davies, 2000, p 324). The extent to which research can inform professional practice is dependent on many factors. Research that does not come to the attention of professionals (or policy makers for that matter) cannot inform their decision making in any explicit or transparent way. How research is disseminated and communicated to target audiences, and what target audiences make or do with it – not just how research is 'done' and its 'trustworthiness' – are therefore critical to whether research can have an influence on practice.

Focusing on *how* research is communicated to professionals raises serious questions. Are professionals more likely to be informed and influenced by full, detailed research reports, or are short summaries of key findings a better vehicle for communicating research? Are *systematic* reviews of the literature more likely to be effective in influencing what professionals do in practice, than, say, a singe research-based article (which would most likely be read by academics)?

When research findings are able to reach and be read by practitioners, there is evidence to suggest that they are not sufficiently accessible to be understood and valued, or that practitioners do not have the time or skills to know what is relevant for their work (Needham, 2000, pp 135-6). How knowledge is diffused to, and adopted by, practitioners is one concern, but for practitioners to take any notice and *use* evidence as the base for practice also requires them to be committed to the ideology of evidence-based practice (Nutley and Davies, 2000, p 331).

Closing the gap between research and practice would also need practitioners to understand the relative strengths and weaknesses of different research methods and designs and how they answer, or provide evidence on, different questions. Practitioners (and also policy makers) need to recognise that there are differences between the types of data generated by research studies of different methodologies and designs. As Figure 1g shows, there are also other factors that need to be in place if the gap between research and practice is to be narrowed. These include the need for practitioners critically to appraise evidence and contribute to systematic reviews of research findings (Macdonald, 2000, p 130).

Figure 1g: Factors required for the development of evidence-based practice

- The generation of good quality data concerning effectiveness.
- A workforce critically able to appraise evidence and contribute to the process of systematic reviews of research findings.
- The dissemination of data and/or research syntheses in a readily accessible form to professionals, managers, policy makers and to service users – this is a methodological, as well as technical, challenge.
- A work and policy environment that facilitates, rather than impedes, the development of practices that reflect 'best evidence'.

Source: Drawn from Macdonald (2000, p 130)

Finally, it must be remembered that research evidence is only one among several influences on practice. Other influences include the legal structure determining practice and interventions, practitioners' knowledge gained through experience (tacit knowledge and craft routines), the views of service users, organisational structures and norms, and resources, to name but a few (Nutley and Davies, 2000). For research to inform practice, researchers (and the producers of research) must understand better and engage with the processes that lead to decision making and behaviour change, both at an individual and an organisational level.

Research for policy and practice

Figure 1h shows the circumstances that are favourable to research having an impact on *both* policy and practice. So, for example (and quite understandably), greater attention is paid to research findings when research is conducted by a trusted and authoritative source, or where research is timely and addresses an issue that is relevant with a methodology that is rigorously applied.

In a recent study on how local authorities use research, the authors found that having an effective structure for commissioning, undertaking and disseminating research within the authority was a necessary (but not sufficient) condition for research to have an impact on policy and practice. A centrally located, rather than devolved, research capacity results in more effective research, dissemination and adoption (Percy-Smith et al, 2002).

Figure 1h: The circumstances that are favourable to research having an impact on policy and practice

Greater attention is paid to research findings when:
- policy makers and practitioners understand and believe in the benefits of using evidence, and are clear of its relative merits vis-à-vis expert opinion;
- research is fully integrated into policy-making processes, practice training and delivery systems;
- users of research are partners in the process of evidence generation;
- research is produced by a trusted and authoritative source;
- research is timely and addresses an issue that is relevant with a methodology that is relatively uncontested;
- results support existing political ideologies, are convenient and relatively uncontentious, and do not represent a major challenge to existing policy;
- results are reported with low degrees of uncertainty, have clear implications for action and can be implemented without incurring high costs if the decision needs to be reversed;
- researchers, senior personnel and other key users seek implementation with skilful advocacy and great stamina;
- research outputs reach the right people in the right form at the right time, and these people have the requisite skills and motivation to interpret and apply the findings of research in their own context;
- research findings complement and confirm other 'ways of knowing', including theoretical and experiential knowing (See also Figure 1j)

Source: Drawn from Davies et al (2000, p 359) and Percy-Smith et al (2002, pp 43-5)

The discussion so far on policy and practice has assumed that there are strong advantages for policy making and professional interventions where and when research informs these activities. However, some writers, such as Bulmer, have urged a note of caution here, in that the close links between researchers and policy makers, while influencing policy, may divert attention from academic goals such as the improvement of the analytical procedures used to study social issues and processes: "To that extent, they contribute to the methodological weakness characteristic of much British social-policy research. Research carried out for explicitly political reasons is not necessarily the most objective or fruitful in its outcome" (Bulmer, 1991, p 162).

Questions for discussion

- What is the relationship between research, policy making, implementation and practice?
- How can you explain why research sometimes influences policy and practice, while at other times it may have little impact?

References

Baldwin, M. (2000) *Care management and community care: Social work discretion and the construction of policy*, Aldershot: Ashgate.

Becker, S. (1997) *Responding to poverty: The politics of cash and care*, Harlow: Longman.

Bullock, R., Gooch, D., Little, M. and Mount, K. (1998) *Research in practice: Experiments in development and information design*, Aldershot: Ashgate.

Bulmer, M. (1991) 'National contexts for the development of social-policy research: British and American research on poverty and social welfare compared', in P. Wagner, C.H. Weiss, B. Wittrock and H. Woolman (eds) *Social sciences and modern states: National experiences and theoretical crossroads*, Cambridge: Cambridge University Press.

Clarke, A. (2001) 'Research and the policy-making process', in N. Gilbert, *Researching social life* (2nd edn), London: Sage Publications, pp 28-42.

Davies, H., Nutley, S. and Smith, P. (2000) 'Learning from the past, prospects for the future', in H. Davies, S. Nutley and P. Smith (eds) *What works? Evidence-based policy and practice in public services*, Bristol: The Policy Press, pp 351-66.

George, V. and Wilding, P. (1994) *Welfare and ideology*, Hemel Hempstead: Harvester Wheatsheaf.

Gordon, I., Lewis, J. and Young, K. (1977) 'Perspectives on policy analysis', *Public Administration Bulletin*, 25, pp 26-30, reproduced in M. Hill (ed) (1993) *The policy process: A reader*, Hemel Hempstead: Harvester Wheatsheaf, pp 5-9.

Gregory, R. (1989) 'Political rationality or incrementalism?', *Policy & Politics*, no 17, pp 139-53, reproduced in M. Hill (ed) (1993) *The policy process: A reader*, Hemel Hempstead: Harvester Wheatsheaf, pp 175-91.

Hill, M. (ed) (1993) *The policy process: A reader*, Hemel Hempstead: Harvester Wheatsheaf.

Hogwood, B.W. and Gunn, L. (1984) *Policy analysis for the real world*, Oxford: Oxford University Press.

Hudson, B. (1989) 'Michael Lipsky and street level bureaucracy: a neglected perspective', in L. Barton (ed) *Disability and dependency*, Lewes: Falmer Press.

Lindblom, C. (1959) 'The science of muddling through', *Public Administration Review*, vol 19, no 2, pp 79-88.

Lindblom, C. (1980) *The policy making process* (2nd edn), Englewood Cliffs, NJ: Prentice Hall.

Lipsky, M. (1980) *Street-level bureaucracy: Dilemmas of the individual in public services*, New York, NY: Russell Sage Foundation.

Macdonald, G. (2000) 'Social care: rhetoric and reality', in H. Davies, S. Nutley and P. Smith (eds) *What works? Evidence-based policy and practice in public services*, Bristol: The Policy Press, pp 117-40.

Mayall, B., Hood, S. and Oliver, S. (1999) 'Introduction', in S. Hood, B. Mayall and S. Oliver (eds) *Critical issues in social research: Power and prejudice*, Buckingham: Open University Press, pp 1-9.

Minogue, M. (1983) 'Theory and practice in public policy and administration', *Policy & Politics*, no 11, pp 63-85, reproduced in M. Hill (ed) (1993) *The policy process: A reader*, Hemel Hempstead: Harvester Wheatsheaf, pp 10-29.

Needham, G. (2000) 'Research and practice: making a difference', in R. Gomm and C. Davies (eds) *Using evidence in health and social care*, London: Sage Publications, pp 131-51.

Nutley, S. and Davies, H. (2000) 'Making a reality of evidence-based practice', in H. Davies, S. Nutley and P. Smith (eds) *What works? Evidence-based policy and practice in public services*, Bristol: The Policy Press, pp 317-50.

Nutley, S. and Webb, J. (2000) 'Evidence and the policy process', in H. Davies, S. Nutley and P. Smith (eds) *What works? Evidence-based policy and practice in public services*, Bristol: The Policy Press. pp 13-41.

Percy-Smith, J. with Burden, T., Darlow, A , Dowson, L., Hawtin, M. and Ladi, S. (2002) *Promoting change through research: The impact of research in local government*, York: Joseph Rowntree Foundation/York Publishing Services.

Smith, G. and May, D. (1980) 'The artificial debate between rationalist and incrementalist models of decision making', *Policy & Politics*, no 8, pp 147-61, reproduced in M. Hill (ed) (1993) *The policy process: A reader*, Hemel Hempstead: Harvester Wheatsheaf, pp 163-74.

Young, K., Ashby, D., Boaz, A. and Grayson, L. (2002) 'Social science and the evidence-based policy movement', *Social Policy and Society*, vol 1, no 3, pp 215-24.

Further reading

Davies, H., Nutley, S. and Smith, P. (eds) (2000) *What works? Evidence-based policy and practice in public services*, Bristol: The Policy Press.

Hill, M. (1997) *The policy process in the modern state* (3rd edn), Hemel Hempstead: Prentice Hall/Harvester Wheatsheaf.

Nutley, S., Percy-Smith, J. and Solesbury, W. (2003) *Models of research impact: A cross-sector review of literature and practice*, London: Learning and Skills Research Centre.

1.5 Evidence and knowledge

Evidence

Research produces findings and 'evidence'. Whether findings count as evidence, and whether this evidence then informs or influences policy and practice, are quite separate issues and depend on many factors, not just the rigour and trustworthiness of the research itself, as we have seen in the preceding sections.

The dictionary defines **evidence** in various ways: 'means of proving an unknown or disputed fact', 'support for a belief', 'an indication', 'information in a law case', 'testimony' and 'witness or witnesses collectively' (Davies et al, 2000, p 2). Davies and colleagues observe:

> At one extreme, it might be argued that all evidence must conform to certain scientific rules of proof (the first definition). In other circumstances, any observation on an issue (whether informed or not) might be considered evidence (the last definition). However, perhaps the unifying theme in all the definitions is that the evidence (however construed) can be independently observed and verified, and that there is a broad consensus as to its contents (if not its interpretation). (Davies et al, 2000, p 2)

In addition to evidence from research there are other forms of evidence. For example, the legal structure and case law forms evidence that policy makers and practitioners must take account of in their decision making. Nutley and Webb (2000) also identify a number of other sources of what counts as evidence for policy making, including evidence generated through experience of 'doing the job', and evidence and knowledge from people who use services on a daily basis and who have become experts through experience:

> The raw ingredient of evidence is information. Good quality policy making depends on high quality information, derived from a variety of sources – expert knowledge; existing domestic and international research; existing statistics; stakeholder consultation; evaluation of previous policies; new research, if appropriate; or secondary sources, including the internet. Evidence can also include analysis of the outcome of consultation, costings of policy options and the results of economic or statistical modelling.
>
> There is a tendency to think of evidence as something that is only generated by major pieces of research. In any policy area there is a great deal of critical evidence held in the minds of both front-

line staff in departments, agencies and local authorities and those
to whom the policy is directed. (Nutley and Webb, 2000, p 23)

Additionally, there is evidence that contributes to knowledge drawn from
organisations themselves (such as the Social Services Inspectorate, the National
Audit Office and the Disability Rights Commission). These different sources
of evidence, including research evidence, contribute to knowledge – what we
know about things in general and on specific matters – and contribute to
policy and practice.

'Ways of knowing' and knowledge

In some areas of knowledge there is far less 'requirement' for any evidence at
all. For example, people's knowledge of religion, of art and beauty, are less
reliant on evidence and are far more matters of *faith* and *belief*. Where knowledge
is challenged or contested, we usually refer to it as 'beliefs'. This way of knowing
can be termed the *method of tenacity* (see Figure 1i). In policy terms, the
method of tenacity is closely related to political ideologies, or ideologies of
welfare. These ideologies often rest not on evidence to prove their claim to
truth or authority, but on beliefs about the world, about individuals and about
society, on rational logic and matters of judgement – not necessarily 'hard
facts or evidence' (Denscombe, 2002, p 198).

As Figure 1i also shows, a further way of knowing can be termed the
method of authority – where the claim to truth rests on the *authority* of the
person making the claim, not on the basis of the evidence itself. For example,
where a Prime Minister, or the head of a respected organisation, claims that
there is evidence for a particular policy or approach, they may be more likely
to be believed by the public than other people with less authority (even though
these other groups could have direct experience of the policy itself).

Figure 1i: Methods and ways of knowing

Method of tenacity: people hold on to the truth because they know it to
be true. This method of knowing rests on strong beliefs, which may not
be moved even in the light of contrary evidence.

Method of authority: a thing must be true, for example, if it is in the
Bible, Koran (and so on), or if we are told it by our leaders, teachers or
others in authority.

Theoretical knowing: where policy makers and practitioners recognise
different theoretical frameworks for thinking and responding to a
problem or issue. This is often used intuitively and informally.

contd.../

Experiential knowing: where craft and tacit knowledge build up over many years of experience. This can be very hard to make explicit.

Empirical knowing: where policy makers or practitioners may know how to respond on the basis of available research evidence. This is the most explicit form of knowing. It is the only way of knowing which allows self-correction through further research that can check and verify the knowledge base.

Source: Based on Brechin and Sidell (2000, p 4) and Burns (2000, p 5)

However, it is only *empirical knowing* that provides any systematic procedure for establishing the reliability and trustworthiness of the knowledge base and for assessing the superiority of one claim over another. It is for this reason that policy makers, professionals and researchers place such importance on evidence from policy research as the *base* for policy and practice.

The phrase 'research evidence' is used throughout this volume to refer *to the results or findings of systematic, robust and trustworthy empirical enquiry* – what has been referred to in Figure 1i as *empirical knowing*. Policy makers and professionals have expressed increasing commitment to draw on this research evidence to inform their policy or practice choices. Indeed, the term 'evidence-based policy and practice' is widely used across the whole range of social policy-related spheres. Those conducting policy research are involved in the process of knowledge creation to inform understanding, policy and practice. Research findings, and the conclusions reached, need to be based on the careful application of research designs, methods and analysis. The outcomes of this process (the data, findings and conclusions) can count as evidence for policy and practice if they are suitably substantial and have been collected in a rigorous, systematic and accountable way (Denscombe, 2002, p 196).

Towards evidence-based policy and practice*

Evidence-based social policy is not new – there has been a long-term move in advanced industrialised countries towards using research and evaluation to guide policy making. Arguably this is a cyclical process, and contemporary emphasis on evidence revisits tendencies that were prominent in the 1960s and 1970s. In the UK since the early 1960s government ministries have increasingly had their own research, statistics and evaluation departments which review research and even commission their own studies. However, the notion that policy and practice should be informed by research evidence has accelerated

* This section draws on additional material prepared by Elliot Stern and Ken Young.

in recent years. It is associated with the slogan 'what works' as a justification for public policy action. 'What works' suggests that unless we can be confident of success we should not waste public funds on new initiatives. Evidence-based policy as part of the performance ethic within the 'new public management' argues that effective and efficient public policy – and good returns to investment for taxpayers – requires that we understand what works before we spend.

This interest in evidence-based policy has been influenced heavily by a parallel set of concerns in the fields of medicine and healthcare. As we see in **Box 1f**, healthcare and medicine have developed systems for determining 'what counts as evidence' and what counts as the *most important* and trustworthy form of evidence. However, whether this hierarchy can be taken and applied to other areas of social policy is open to some debate.

Box 1f: Evidence-based healthcare as public policy

Stephen Harrison, *Professor of Social Policy, University of Manchester*

Recent interest in 'evidence-based' healthcare (EBHC) originates in the profession of medicine, although its logic has more recently been applied to the work of other clinical professions, especially nursing and midwifery, as well as to professions outside the health field. The definition of 'evidence-based medicine' (EBM) provided by its leading academic exponents is "the integration of best research evidence with clinical expertise and patient values" (Sackett et al, 2000, p 1). It seems difficult to object to such a formulation, and EBM (and its wider application as EBHC) has become an imperative of public policy in the UK National Health Service (NHS), and in many other countries (Woolf et al, 1999), rather than just an exhortation to professionals. Although few detailed studies have been conducted, it is likely that a range of factors have contributed to this policy centrality, including healthcare cost pressures (fuelled by technological development and ageing populations in the context of 'third party payment' systems of healthcare) and large variations in clinical practice between individual physicians (Harrison, 1998; Harrison and Moran, 2000; Harrison et al, 2002a, 2002b). EBM as defined above implies at least two questions. First, what is to count as 'best evidence'? Second, how is EBM to be implemented as a component of public policy?

Although not all exponents of EBM agree on every criterion, there is a strong orthodoxy of judging the quality of evidence as the avoidance of bias, so that the preferred primary research method is the randomised controlled trial (Cochrane, 1972), with non-randomised experimental methods in second place, and little weight given to uncontrolled studies. (A detailed account of this so-called 'hierarchy of evidence' is given in Sackett et al, 2000, pp 173-7; see also

Figure 1k, this chapter.) The main role of qualitative research is to contribute to the design and interpretation of quantitative studies. EBM seeks to cumulate research findings into a coherent 'body of knowledge', employing techniques such as statistical meta-analysis and other forms of 'systematic review' (Mulrow, 1994; see also Chapter Three, Section 3.12), techniques that rely heavily (but not exclusively) on the assumption that the relevant evidence can be found in electronic databases and specialist academic journals. Searches are underpinned by strict rules intended to ensure that review methods are in principle transparent and replicable (Centre for Reviews and Dissemination, 1996). EBM is largely atheoretical in the sense that 'theory' tends to be equated with 'hypothesis', implicitly discounting theoretical development as an objective of research or as a means of cumulating evidence.

The primary medium for implementation of EBM in the UK is the 'clinical guideline', that is, a statement (algorithmic in form, at least implicitly) specifying how a professional should treat a patient in stated circumstances. The choice of clinical guidelines as the main vehicle for implementing EBM is logical; it is obviously unrealistic to expect the average busy clinician to read and understand all research papers relevant to their own sub-specialty, to discriminate between acceptable and inadequate methods, to interpolate findings with existing knowledge, and to modify clinical practice accordingly. While it is rarely suggested that they should be followed in 100% of cases, the anodyne term 'guideline' should not conceal the intention of modifying clinical practice (Berg, 1997). This narrowing of professional autonomy is reinforced by the development of a raft of new NHS institutions such as the National Institute for Clinical Excellence and the Commission for Health Improvement as well as by more assertive management of health professionals through 'clinical governance' (Dowswell et al, 2002).

However, EBM/EBHC is not a technically neutral endeavour, and has opponents as well as supporters. Among the numerous critiques that have been offered are:

- The entry criteria for clinical trials are normally drawn narrowly, for instance, excluding older patients or those with multiple pathologies, and research is often conducted in specialist treatment centres. The consequence is uncertainty about how far the findings of such trials can be generalised to ordinary patients in ordinary settings.
- The focus of EBM on the outcomes of interventions rather than on the process by which they occur may run counter to the manner in which health professionals are trained to think and on which they base their practice (Tanenbaum, 1994). Physiology, pathology and aetiology are essentially the study of normal and disease *processes*, so that clinicians' reasoning may be

predominantly based on the 'logic of treatment' rather than the inputs and outputs of a 'black box' (Harrison, 1998).

- The 'hierarchy of evidence' may be inappropriate when employed to assess research into the outcomes of healthcare interventions or policies that are social (consisting largely of interactions between humans rather than the use of pharmaceuticals or technical equipment) and/or 'diffuse' (difficult to define precisely) and/or 'complex' (with numerous interconnecting elements: Campbell et al, 2000). Meta-analysis of randomised trials shows that 'stroke units' (hospital care for stroke patients involving multidisciplinary treatment and the involvement of patients' carers) reduce mortality (Langhorne et al, 1993). But it is hard to be confident that the meta-analysis aggregates like with like, since stroke units in different hospitals may differ in numerous respects (Stroke Unit Trialists' Collaboration, 1997).
- Important elements of knowledge and skill may remain 'tacit' (Polanyi, 1967), that is, incapable of being codified into explicit guidelines.
- Clinical guidelines are a species of bureaucratic rule and therefore subject to the classic 'dysfunctions' identified by sociologists. These might include 'goal displacement' in which following the rules becomes an end in itself (Blau, 1955), and the consequences of 'low trust' organisations in terms of reduced morale, lack of flexibility and lack of moral commitment (Fox, 1974; Fukuyama, 1995; Smith, 2001).
- EBM may be a politically untenable basis for public policy in the context of active pressure groups. Citizens may remain unconvinced by the evidence, as illustrated in contemporary controversies over the drug Interferon Beta in the treatment of multiple sclerosis, and the measles–mumps–rubella (MMR) triple vaccine for children. For Interferon Beta, economic analyses have suggested high costs for low levels of effectiveness, yet patient groups and many individual patients have argued that it produces worthwhile benefits. Many parents wish to avoid the MMR vaccine for fear that it might be associated with autism, even though the Department of Health asserts that there is no convincing evidence that it has different adverse effects from separate single vaccinations and the original medical research proposing a link was largely discredited in 2004.

Question for discussion
- What, according to proponents of 'evidence-based medicine', constitutes 'best evidence'?

References

Berg, M. (1997) 'Problems and promises of the protocol', *Social Science and Medicine*, vol 44, no 8, pp 1081-8.

Blau, P.M. (1955) *The dynamics of bureaucracy*, Chicago, IL: University of Chicago Press.

Campbell, M., Fitzpatrick, R., Haines, A., Kinmonth, A.L., Sandercock, P., Spiegelhalter, D. and Tyrer, P. (2000) 'Framework for design and evaluation of complex interventions to improve health', *British Medical Journal*, vol 321, pp 694-6.

Centre for Reviews and Dissemination (1996) *Undertaking systematic reviews on effectiveness*, Report no 4, York: University of York.

Cochrane, A.L. (1972) *Effectiveness and efficiency: Random reflections on health services*, London: Nuffield Provincial Hospitals Trust.

Dowswell, G., Harrison, S. and Wright, J. (2002) 'The early days of primary care groups: general practitioners' perceptions', *Health and Social Care in the Community*, vol 10, no 1, pp 46-54.

Fox, A. (1974) *Man mismanagement*, London: Hutchinson.

Fukuyama, F. (1995) *Trust: The social virtues and the creation of prosperity*, London: Hamish Hamilton.

Harrison, S. (1998) 'The politics of evidence-based medicine in the UK', *Policy & Politics*, vol 26, no 1, pp 15-31.

Harrison, S. and Moran, M. (2000) 'Resources and rationing: managing supply and demand in health care', in G. Albrecht, R. Fitzpatrick and S. Scrimshaw (eds) *The handbook of social studies in health and medicine*, New York, NY: Sage Publications, pp 493-508.

Harrison, S., Milewa, T. and Dowswell, G. (2002a) 'Public and user "involvement" in the National Health Service', *Health and Social Care in the Community*, vol 10, no 2, pp 63-6.

Harrison, S., Moran, M. and Wood, B. (2002b) 'Policy emergence and policy convergence: the case of "scientific-bureaucratic medicine" in the USA and UK', *British Journal of Politics and International Relations*, vol 4, no 1, pp 1-24.

Langhorne, P., Williams, B.O., Gilchrist, W. and Howie, K. (1993) 'Do stroke units save lives?', *Lancet*, vol 342, pp 395-8.

Mulrow, C. (1994) 'Rationale for systematic reviews', *British Medical Journal*, vol 309, pp 597-9.

Polanyi, M. (1967) *The tacit dimension*, London: Routledge and Kegan Paul.

Sackett, D.L., Straus, S., Richardson, W.S., Rosenberg, W. and Haynes, R.B. (2000) *Evidence-based medicine: How to practise and teach EBM* (2nd edn), Edinburgh: Churchill Livingstone.

Smith, C. (2001) 'Trust and confidence: possibilities for social work in "high modernity"', *British Journal of Social Work*, vol 31, pp 287-305.

Stroke Unit Trialists' Collaboration (1997) 'Collaborative systematic review of the randomised trials of organised inpatient (stroke unit) care after stroke', *British Medical Journal*, vol 314, pp 1151-9.

Tanenbaum, S.J. (1994) 'Knowing and acting in medical practice: the epistemological politics of outcomes research', *Journal of Health Politics, Policy and Law*, vol 19, no 1, pp 27-44.

Woolf, S.H., Grol, R., Hutchinson, A., Eccles, M. and Grimshaw, J. (1999) 'Potential benefits, limitations and harms of clinical guidelines', *British Medical Journal*, vol 318, pp 527-30.

Further reading

Harrison, S. (2002) 'New Labour, modernisation and the medical labour process', *Journal of Social Policy*, vol 31, no 2, pp 465-85.

Sackett, D.L., Straus, S., Richardson, W.S., Rosenberg, W. and Haynes, R.B. (2000) *Evidence-based medicine: How to practise and teach EBM* (2nd edn), Edinburgh: Churchill Livingstone.

Relevant organisations

Department of Health

Richmond House, 79 Whitehall, London SW1A 2NS

Telephone 020 7210 4850; www.doh.gov.uk/research/index.htm

National Institute for Clinical Excellence

11 The Strand, London WC2N 5HR

Telephone 020 7766 9191; www.nice.org.uk

National Co-ordinating Centre for Health Technology Assessment

Mailpoint 728, Boldrewood, University of Southampton, Bassett Crescent East, Southampton SO16 7PX

Telephone 023 8059 5586; www.hta.nhsweb.nhs.uk

UK Cochrane Centre

Summertown Pavilion, Middle Way, Oxford OX2 7LG

Telephone 01865 516300; www.cochrane.de/cochrane/general.htm

The evidence-based policy movement, like other tendencies in *evaluation* (see **Box 1g**), favours its own methods and methodologies – for example, pilot experiments using quasi-experimental methods or preferably random assignment; and meta-analyses and systematic reviews following traditions drawn from drug trials in medical research are much favoured (**Box 1f**). So also are prospective methods: model building, forecasting, impact assessments, feasibility studies and 'ex ante evaluations' would fall under this category. (At the same time, there are many who are part of the evidence-based policy and practice movement who draw on a far wider range of methods – qualitative and quantitative, longitudinal and naturalistic.)

Box 1g: Evaluation

Elliot Stern, *Head of Evaluation Studies, Tavistock Institute, London, and Independent Evaluation Consultant*

Evaluation is a set of research methods and associated methodologies with distinctive purposes. Evaluation research provides the means to judge actions and activities in the public sphere in terms of values, criteria and standards. This judgement or value-based orientation is one of the distinctive characteristics of evaluation. It has generated a considerable literature about how to accommodate the dimension of 'values' and from where these values should be derived. At the same time evaluation is also a practice that seeks to enhance effectiveness in the public sphere and make the success of public action more likely. This practice/improvement aspect of evaluation also has important implications. In order to improve as well as judge, there is a need to explain what happens and what would have to be done differently for different outcomes to be achieved. It is in this explanatory mode that evaluation overlaps most directly with mainstream social science.

Evaluation has become especially prominent in recent years because of the widespread consensus in advanced industrialised and in developing countries about the need to modernise and reform the public sector. Within this perspective, evaluation uses applied research methods to systematically strengthen public policy making, public management and the delivery of public services and public goods to citizens. There has therefore been a ready market for approaches and methods that can contribute to this process of modernisation and reform. Contemporary tendencies in evaluation such as 'performance management' and more particularly 'evidence-based' social policy are manifestations of this perspective.

Longer established traditions of evaluation are interwoven with the public sector reform agenda and performance and evidence-based tendencies – and are sometimes quite independent from this particular tradition. Examples of other traditions include democratic accountability, participative or 'bottom-up' policy making and continuous quality improvement. These traditions may concern efforts to increase the autonomy and self-management capacities of local communities or of decentralised service agencies, such as schools and hospitals; or support for grass-roots groups or front-line professionals in making their actions more effective or more (self-)understandable.

Perhaps the greatest divergence between some evaluation approaches and practice in other research domains concerns the stance of the evaluator in participative or developmental evaluations. Here the evaluator will often become an actor or participant – rather than an observer. In international development evaluation, for example, evaluation may seek to empower the recipients of international aid and the methods adopted will reflect this aspiration. In many regards 'empowerment' evaluation will then come to resemble in part social development methods and approaches. However, such participative methods are not confined to international development. Similar approaches can be found in urban regeneration or anti-poverty programmes in industrialised countries and in curriculum development approaches that seek to 'empower' the teacher, educational professionals, pupils and parents.

Evaluative enquiry draws on the full panoply of social and economic research methods and is consequently far broader in scope than a single set of tools or techniques. It is interdisciplinary and also draws (albeit selectively) on many social science disciplines – although from very particular perspectives. Despite the broad scope of evaluation, there is now an extensive literature with its own journals, handbooks and edited collections that operationally defines what has been called the 'trans-discipline' or even the 'emerging discipline' of evaluation. Yet it is important to recognise that evaluation is not simply an academic discipline. In many ways it bridges the worlds of academic research and the worlds of policy and practice. Key methods in evaluation seek to make this bridge and speak as much to the concerns of policy makers, politicians, administrators, public managers and citizens as to the interests of scholars. This emphasis is reflected in the positioning of evaluation within the academy. Until recently there have been few dedicated courses on evaluation in universities and even now it has a distinctive profile. For example, evaluation is likely to be embedded in particular courses: within health, education, social work, economic development, criminal justice, public administration, regional planning and international development. It is less likely to be located in evaluation departments – few of which exist. It is also more likely to be seen as a proper subject for teaching at a professional or continuing education level rather than at undergraduate or postgraduate research levels.

Evaluation research, despite serious attempts to build bridges, is scattered across many disciplines. Relevant material is to be found in within-discipline journals and books in social work, education, international development, technology assessment, health economics, criminology, urban and regional studies and many more. And context matters in evaluation. Each 'object' of evaluation (be it pupil performance, administrative effectiveness, the rate of technology transfer, healthcare programme success, and so on), demands particular configurations of evaluation methods. Sometimes this properly determines the way evaluators select their methods and data: in health, analyses of data about morbidity and mortality are relevant; while in education, concern for pupil performance demands quite different data and methods – alongside shared approaches to criteria/standard setting or causal inference. However, it is also true that some methods have become associated with evaluation in a particular domain for less sound reasons, probably associated with the isolated situation of evaluators in that domain.

The importance of practice in evaluation also has consequences. At a straightforward level there are methods and techniques with currency in the world of evaluation that have limited academic provenance. Thus evaluation practice leans heavily on various approaches to league tables, balanced scorecards, value added scores, benchmarking, profiling, project scoring and performance indicators. Not all of these would meet accepted research standards. At another level, methods in evaluation sometimes overlap with the methods of effective organisational practice – in other words, those organisational practices that are necessary for evaluation to be successfully implemented. For example, how to ensure that evaluation results are used and well-integrated into management practice within public agencies has been the subject of widespread research within the evaluation community. Methods developed to support the use of evaluation include how to consult and involve stakeholders (for validity as well as practical reasons) when designing evaluations; and the kinds of dissemination and dialogical techniques that are most likely to lead to evaluation uptake. Similarly, how to enhance transparency, democratic accountability and public participation (among the most important goals of the contemporary 'public sector reform' movement) as part of the evaluation process, are also important in some parts of the evaluation community. It is for this reason that various participative, consensus building, feedback, social development/empowerment and administrative control methods have evolved as an integral part of evaluation.

Further reading

Connel, J., Kubish, A., Schorr, L. and Weiss, C. (eds) (1995) *New approaches to evaluating community initiatives: Concepts, methods and contexts*, New York, NY: Aspen.

Pawson, R. and Tilley, N. (1997) *Realistic evaluation*, London: Sage Publications.

Shadish, W. Jr, Cook, T. and Leviton, L. (1991) *Foundations of program evaluation: Theories of practice*, London: Sage Publications.

Shaw, I.F. (1999) *Qualitative evaluation: Introducing qualitative methods*, London: Sage Publications.

In the late 20th century the emergence of the Campbell Collaboration (modelled on medicine's Cochrane Collaboration but concerned with social policies – see **Boxes 1f** and **1h**), and the UK's post-1997 New Labour government with its *Modernising government* agenda, both signify the growth of the evidence-based policy movement. Both the Campbell and Cochrane Collaborations "recommend making policy decisions on the basis of reliable evidence; both caution against the dangers of professional arrogance.... Campbell's conception of the social scientist's role in helping society towards his utopian vision was primarily that of the social scientist as methodological servant, giving policy-makers the tools with which to assess what *has* been done as a guide to decisions about what *might* be done in the future" (Oakley, 2000, p 321, emphasis in original).

The limits to evidence-based policy

Evidence-based policy has itself, however, become contested terrain. The term actually contains two terms, one referring to the way in which policy is made, the other to the evidential nature of social science itself. There are debates about method that mirror wider methodological and theory of knowledge debates: is there a hierarchy of evidence and is random assignment the 'gold standard'? There are disagreements about the generalisability of 'evidence' across different contexts: is there a single truth that can be designated as 'best practice' across all or many contexts? There are debates about values and interpretation: what criteria – or more pointedly *whose* criteria – are used to judge the 'truth' of evidence? And perhaps most importantly there are debates about the messy realities of politics: when evidence comes up against political mandates and expediency, which triumphs? (see also Section 1.4). There is now awareness that evidence itself is mustered selectively and the extent to which it shapes policy is contingent on factors that are not simply about the rigour with which data are collected or analysed, as we have already seen in earlier sections of this chapter.

There are, however, signs that the more simplistic approaches to what Ann Oakley (2000, p 318) termed "social science and evidence-based everything" are now losing ground to better-informed, more pluralistic and pragmatic approaches, concerned less with evidence-based policy than with developing the *evidence base for policy*. But realising even this more modest aim of strengthening the social science evidence base may require challenging some near-sacred assumptions about the value of established practices and methods, and, for example, the relative value of different publication modes (for example, publication in peer review journals versus professional magazines). It will require more of a partnership between research producers (those who 'do' the research) and the user community (those who need to make use of research to inform their policy or practice, and 'service' users themselves), so that the evidence base for policy is both robust, methodologically sound, undertaken and managed to high standards, and relevant to a wide range of stakeholders. It was to address these long-term strategic issues that the Economic and Social

Research Council (ESRC) launched its 'Evidence-based Policy' initiative in December 2000 (see **Box 1h**).

Box 1h: The UK Centre for Evidence-based Policy and Practice and the *EvidenceNetwork*

Ken Young, *Professor of Politics and Director, ESRC UK Centre for Evidence-based Policy and Practice, Queen Mary, University of London*

The ESRC UK Centre for Evidence-based Policy and Practice, established at Queen Mary, University of London, is charged with advancing debate on evidence-based policy while developing appropriate methods and capacities to meet the needs of the moment. To do so, the Centre works in partnership with eight associated research teams ('nodes', in ESRC parlance), covering a wide spectrum of social and economic policy issues from ethnicity and health to neighbourhood processes to research utilisation. Together, the nine ESRC-funded teams (several of them multi-centre) constitute the *EvidenceNetwork*, with specialist review work undertaken within the nodes, and collaborative work on methodological development taking place across the network. Apart from the Centre at Queen Mary, the other components of the *EvidenceNetwork* are:

- *What works for children?* – a development programme on the better use of evidence in policy and practice towards children and young people carried out by a team at Barnardo's, City and York Universities.
- *Centre for Evidence-based Public Health Policy* – a programme of systematic reviews of the impact of non-healthcare policies on public health undertaken by Glasgow, Lancaster and Liverpool Universities.
- *Centre for Neighbourhood Research* – providing a range of resources for researchers and practitioners pursuing the neighbourhood dimension to social and economic change jointly at Glasgow and Bristol Universities.
- *Centre for Economic Evaluation* – secondary analyses of data on labour markets, inequality, children and health are undertaken at the Institute for Fiscal Studies.
- *Research Unit for Research Utilisation* – examining and improving the contribution of research-based evidence in healthcare, education, criminal justice and social care at St Andrews University.
- *Centre for Evidence in Ethnicity, Health and Diversity* – providing reviews and syntheses of research evidence to inform policy and practice on ethnicity and health jointly at Warwick and de Montfort Universities.
- *Systematic Reviews in Social Policy and Social Care* – focusing particularly on health, social care, housing, employment, social security and the interactions between policy and practice in these fields undertaken by a team at York University.

- *Centre for Comparative European Policy Evaluation* – a team addressing European policy issues and UK policy issues with a European dimension selected from a number of areas including pensions, public service delivery, competition policy and regional policies, located at the Centre for Economic Policy Research.

For its part, the Centre undertakes bibliographic searching for the nodes and other customers, and runs an active training programme covering database awareness and use, and advanced information retrieval, aimed at building evidence-based policy capacity among both researchers and practitioners. The Centre additionally maintains a website on behalf of the Network, with an extensive and updated searchable bibliographic database and an information resources service. The Centre's website is also the base for the 'Associate' scheme, a loose association of more than 400 people with strong interests in evidence-based policy and practice. Associates are kept informed on a regular basis of developments in the evidence-based policy and practice arena, are provided with a facility based on their research or practice activities for making contact with each other, and can use the site's sophisticated multi-thread search engine to track down evidence-based policy and practice material. The Centre's Working Paper series is also mounted on the website, with individual papers downloadable, or available as hard copy from the Centre, as preferred. The papers cover a range of themes in the systematic review and synthesis of research evidence, as well as questions relating to the assessment of quality in social science publications.

These several services may be accessed by visiting the Centre's website where direct links to the nodes and other evidence-based policy-relevant centres may be found.

Question for discussion
- In what ways, and to what extent, are the methods of evidence-based medicine applicable in social policy research?

Further reading
Davies, H., Nutley, S. and Smith, P. (2000) *What works? Evidence-based policy and practice in public services*, Bristol: The Policy Press.

Oakley, A. (2002) 'Social science and evidence-based everything: the case of education', *Educational Review*, vol 54, no 3, pp 277-86.

Petticrew, M. (2001) 'Systematic reviews from astronomy to zoology: myths and misconceptions', *British Medical Journal*, vol 322, no 7278, pp 98-101.

Young, K., Ashby, D., Boaz, A.L. and Grayson, L. (2002) 'Social science and the evidence based policy movement', *Social Policy and Society*, vol 1, no 3, pp 215-24.

Website resources
The Campbell Collaboration [often referred to simply as 'C2', the relatively new Campbell Collaboration is analogous to the Cochrane Collaboration, but is concerned with the preparation, maintenance and dissemination of systematic reviews of studies of interventions in the social, behavioural and educational arenas]: www.campbellcollaboration.org

The Coalition for Evidence-based Policy [a US body, sponsored by the Council for Excellence in Government "to promote government policy making based on rigorous evidence of programme effectiveness, especially randomised controlled trials"]: www.excelgov.org/performance/evidence/execsumm.htm

The Cochrane Collaboration [a well-established international network of specialists developing the evidence base for medical practice on an open and responsive basis with regular updating of systematic reviews posted on the Collaboration's website]: www.cochrane.dk

The EPPI-Centre [the Evidence for Policy and Practice Information and Coordinating Centre established at London University's Institute of Education, to promote systematic reviews of research evidence, developing methodologies for systematic appraisal of different kinds of research studies, and facilitate user involvement throughout the review and dissemination process. The EPPI-Centre is concerned to develop systematic reviews beyond critical analyses of research reporting evaluations of policy and programme interventions to address, review and synthesise non-intervention research]: http://eppi.ioe.ac.uk

The ESRC Evidence Network [as described in the main text above]: www.evidencenetwork.org

What counts as the evidence base that should inform policy and practice will become a key issue for policy makers and professionals over the coming years. The advent of the Social Care Institute for Excellence (SCIE), to help identify the evidence base for social care policy and practice, mirrors the earlier advent of the National Institute for Clinical Excellence (NICE) in the medical/healthcare domain. This is important because, as Macdonald has observed, "Within social care, political ideology plays a major role in shaping policy and practice. The volatility inherent in the way that social problems are conceived, and therefore how they are responded to, also impacts on the shape and nature of social care provision" (Macdonald, 2000, p 118). Today, the evidence base for many fields of social policy, including social care, education, crime, social security, welfare reform and health, and for the associated professional practices in these spheres, could be considered to be less than robust, reliable and trustworthy.

Finally, it has been argued that evidence-based policy and practice is likely to be the exception rather than the rule because of the many 'enemies' of a more evidence-based approach. These enemies include: *bureaucratic logic* – the logic that says things are right because they have always been done that way; *politics* – the art of the possible rather than what is rational or what might work best; and *time* – there is scarcely room to think never mind time to think about evidence-based policy and practice (Nutley and Webb, 2000, p 36).

Research, particularly where it is trustworthy and robust, is a key source of evidence for policy and practice. But again it must be remembered that it is only one source, only one way of knowing, and that political imperatives, resources and other considerations also need to be taken into account by policy makers and especially by government: "Rather, research evidence is just one influence on the policy process and, while the research community is free to argue that it should receive greater attention, it would be anti-democratic to insist that research evidence should be the prime consideration" (Walker, 2000, p 163).

Evidence, 'proof' and the provisional nature of knowledge

Unlike political ideology or religious beliefs, proof is not a matter of faith; nor is it a matter of logic or the rationality of an argument alone. It requires corroboration by *empirical evidence* collected, analysed and reported to the highest standards: "What qualifies as evidence might vary between styles of research, but the need for research to verify its claims with reference to empirical evidence remains constant" (Denscombe, 2002, p 197). Thus, systematic reviews are a favoured form of evidence as they summarise, using a distinctive methodology, selected research evidence in a tightly defined area.

Proof, based on evidence, can either *verify* or *refute* existing knowledge and understanding. It can confirm what we already know about a social issue or social problem, or it can offer an alternative explanation – a competing form of knowledge or 'way of knowing'. In *The logic of scientific discovery*, Karl Popper (1959) argued that research evidence can support knowledge, but it can never prove it absolutely because new evidence may be found at a later date that will contradict or refute what we already know. He suggested that all knowledge, all theory, all evidence, must therefore remain *provisional* – the best available at the time – but always open to refutation by new evidence at a later date.

In this context, research should actively seek to test existing knowledge and theories in circumstances where they are most likely to be refuted. Rather than trying to prove existing knowledge and evidence as 'right', research should try to prove them 'wrong' (the notion of *falsification*). Where research (conducted to the highest standards of enquiry) cannot prove (through empirical evidence) that what we know already about something is wrong, then that knowledge base can be considered to be stronger and more robust than before. The amount of confidence and trust that can be placed in a theory or knowledge depends on its ability to withstand concerted efforts to refute it (Denscombe, 2002, pp 198-200; see also May, 2001, pp 30-4). While this approach to understanding knowledge creation is not universally accepted (see, for example, Kuhn's thesis [1970] on the nature of scientific revolutions), it does raise important challenges for evidence-based policy and practice, and these are outlined in Figure 1j. For research evidence to *refute* existing knowledge this would require more than one incidence of contra-evidence. It would also require contra-evidence to be genuine and based on high standards of social research practice; to occur repeatedly and be produced regularly and consistently by a variety of researchers; and not to be susceptible to accommodation within existing knowledge or theory. Refutation requires the *accumulation of a body of evidence* that the existing theory or way of knowing does not work (Denscombe, 2002, p 202).

Figure 1j: 'Falsification' and the challenges for evidence-based policy and practice

- Research to support evidence-based policy and practice should be directed at trying to prove existing evidence *wrong* as much as proving it *right*. This would lead to a more robust, reliable and trustworthy evidence base *for* policy and practice. So, for example, while it is important to generate evidence on 'what works' in the various fields of social policy, this evidence will be more trustworthy and reliable if it withstands concerted research attempts to disprove it. In reality, little, if any, research is primarily directed at proving existing evidence to be wrong.
- Policy research, and the evidence it produces either to support or to refute existing knowledge, needs to be considered as *provisional*, rather than as absolute, proof.
- Regarding the notion of 'what works', *whether* something works is the question of greatest interest to most practitioners and policy makers. *How* something works, and theories or models that might underpin the relationships between interventions and outcomes, are secondary questions.
- Given the provisional nature of evidence, proof and knowledge, then the need for research to be robust, rigorous and conducted to the highest standards – and open to verification or falsification – becomes even more necessary.

From a hierarchy to a continuum of evidence

Rather than adopting the influential medical and health approach which ranks different research methods and designs in a *hierarchy* of evidence (with several systematic reviews of randomised controlled trials at the top – see Figure 1k), it would be more useful for those involved in evidence-based policy and practice (including policy researchers, policy makers and professionals) to acknowledge the varying strengths and weaknesses of different research methods and designs and to consider them as a *continuum* rather than as a hierarchy.

Figure 1k: The traditional hierarchy of evidence in medical and health research

1. Several systematic reviews of randomised controlled trials or meta-analyses.
2. Systematic review of randomised controlled trials.
3. Randomised control trials.
4. Quasi-experimental trials.
5. Case control and cohort studies.
6. Expert consensus opinion.
7. Individual opinion.

Under the continuum approach, it would be acknowledged, for example, that systematic reviews, randomised controlled trials and other experimental designs provide the most appropriate form of evidence on 'cause and effect', while ethnography and other qualitative methods provide the most appropriate form of evidence on 'experiences and processes' – especially as understood by respondents themselves. This approach, which is also increasingly being recognised within the NHS Service Delivery and Organisation R&D Programme, allows the researcher to draw on the most appropriate method and design to answer specific research question(s). It also facilitates the integration of methods, breaking down the paradigm wars between quantitative and qualitative methods. Thus, the choice of method(s) to be used, and whether and how they may be combined, will depend largely on the research question(s):

> ... it is a question of carefully examining the research question, beginning with whether it has been asked and answered before, whether it makes sense to the people who might be asked to take part in the research, and identifying the other 'stakeholders' (including policy-makers); moving on to consider whether it is a question about evaluating the effect of something or about describing processes or events; whether it points to the generation

of theory and/or the production of widely applicable findings, and so on. All research takes place within the context of cost and funding and 'political' constraints; these will inevitably feed into decisions about what methods to use. (Oakley, 2000, p 305)

In this context, just as the debate between rational and incremental policy making can be seen to be artificial (Smith and May, 1980), so too can the paradigm wars between quantitative and qualitative methods. This is a theme we return to in Chapter Three.

Questions for discussion

- What should count as evidence in policy research? How can we know whether this evidence is trustworthy?
- Is it feasible, and desirable, to have evidence-based policy and practice? Give reasons for your answers.

References

Burns, R.B. (2000) *Introduction to research methods*, London: Sage Publications.

Brechin, A. and Sidell, M. (2000) 'Ways of knowing', in R. Gomm and C. Davies (eds) *Using evidence in health and social care*, London: Sage Publications, pp 3-25.

Davies, H., Nutley, S. and Smith, P. (2000) 'Introducing evidence-based policy and practice in public services', in H. Davies, S. Nutley and P. Smith (eds) *What works? Evidence-based policy and practice in public services*, Bristol: The Policy Press, pp 1-11.

Denscombe, M. (2002) *Ground rules for good research: A 10 point guide for social researchers*, Buckingham: Open University Press.

Kuhn, T.S. (1970) *The structure of scientific revolutions* (2nd edn), Chicago, IL: University of Chicago Press.

Macdonald, G. (2000) 'Social care: rhetoric and reality', in H. Davies, S. Nutley and P. Smith (eds) *What works? Evidence-based policy and practice in public services*, Bristol: The Policy Press, pp 117-40.

May, T. (2001) *Social research: Issues, methods and process* (3rd edn), Buckingham: Open University Press.

Nutley, S. and Webb, J. (2000) 'Evidence and the policy process', in H. Davies, S. Nutley and P. Smith (eds) *What works? Evidence-based policy and practice in public services*, Bristol: The Policy Press, pp 13-41.

Oakley, A. (2000) *Experiments in knowing: Gender and method in the social sciences*, Cambridge: Polity Press.

Popper, K. (1959) *The logic of scientific discovery*, London: Hutchinson.

Smith, G. and May, D. (1980) 'The artificial debate between rationalist and incrementalist models of decision making', *Policy & Politics*, no 8, pp 147-61, reproduced in M. Hill (ed) (1993) *The policy process: A reader*, Hemel Hempstead: Harvester Wheatsheaf, pp 163-74.

Walker, R. (2000) 'Welfare policy: tendering for evidence', in H. Davies, S. Nutley and P. Smith (eds) *What works? Evidence-based policy and practice in public services*, Bristol: The Policy Press, pp 141-66.

Further reading

Davies, H., Nutley, S. and Smith, P. (eds) (2000) *What works? Evidence-based policy and practice in public services*, Bristol: The Policy Press.

Denscombe, M. (2002) *Ground rules for good research: A 10 point guide for social researchers*, Buckingham: Open University Press.

Sheldon, B. (2001) 'The validity of evidence-based practice in social work: a reply to Stephen Webb', *British Journal of Social Work*, vol 31, pp 801-9.

Webb, S.A (2001) 'Some considerations on the validity of evidence-based practice in social work', *British Journal of Social Work*, vol 31, pp 57-79.

Website resources

NHS Service Delivery and Organisation R&D Programme: www.sdo.lshtm.ac.uk
Social Care Institute for Excellence: www.scie.org.uk
(See also **Boxes 1f** and **1h**.)

1.6 Modelling the policy research process

A dynamic research process

As we have seen from the preceding sections, policy research contributes to knowledge and can inform policy making and practice as part of a complex and dynamic process. It is possible to conceive of this process as a research cycle, moving from identifying and defining what we want or need to research, to undertaking that research, to actively promoting and disseminating the findings, to influencing policy and practice, to changes in the original situation, to ongoing monitoring and evaluation, and so on. While this model, as presented here, has a starting point (identifying an issue to research), this may not always be the starting point for every piece of policy research. Some people, for example, may be advocating or lobbying for a change of policy and then decide that research would be valuable to give them 'political ammunition', or to identify more precisely what needs changing, why and how. Others will be involved in evaluating policy and practice that is ongoing – with no obvious start or finishing point. Since 1997 it has been possible for government to 'pilot' social security reforms in local areas before they are 'rolled out' nationwide. In this case, research is concerned with (local) evaluation before full (national) implementation of the policy itself.

Irrespective of where the starting point for research occurs, it is possible to understand the research process (and its relationship with policy and practice) as a dynamic and ongoing cycle, which is made more complex and uncertain by a range of external factors – such as politics, ideologies, organisational structures, practitioners' training and skills, and so on – the very things that have been referred to throughout this chapter.

Here we present a model of this policy research cycle. The model is an attempt to simplify complex processes into some understandable and stylised form; to inform understanding of the relationship between policy research, policy making and professional practice; and to show how the remaining chapters of this volume (and, indeed, the preceding sections) 'fit' with the model.

A model of the policy research cycle

The research cycle is made up of four phases. These are:

- a cognitive phase;
- 'doing' research;
- dissemination and promotion;
- research adoption, utilisation and change.

While these phases are distinct from one another, they also merge into each other and it does not always follow that, for each piece of policy research, the cycle will start with a cognitive phase. Additionally, the cognitive – or thinking – phase extends throughout the others, while the dissemination and promotion phase extends some distance into the adoption, utilisation and change phase. The point of making a distinction between the four phases is that, at each phase, a particular activity ('thinking', 'doing', 'promoting' or 'changing') is more dominant than the others. For example (and rather obviously), we do not stop thinking when we are disseminating or promoting research findings – but our main purpose at these later phases is to disseminate and promote the research findings rather than defining what it is that needs to be researched in the first place. The phases of the research cycle are illustrated in Figure 1l.

Figure 1l: **The policy research cycle**

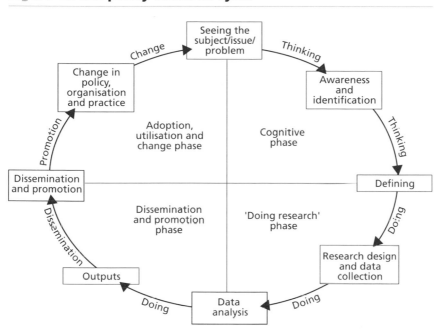

The stages of the research cycle

The cognitive phase

In this phase of the research cycle, researchers, research funders and others involved in the policy process (including professionals, service users, and so on), are involved in thinking about the issues or problems that confront them. They will need to move beyond seeing that there is an issue, to refining their thinking and becoming more precise and specific about what needs to be researched, why and how. Within this phase, therefore, there are at least three stages: seeing, awareness and identification and defining.

Seeing: policy researchers, policy makers and professionals observe things that concern them or that they may wish to change. These may be social problems (poverty, deprivation, poor housing) or social issues (the impact of community care changes on people with disabilities, the experiences of young carers, the practice of social workers in child protection cases). We need to 'see' these and other policy-related issues before we can start to work out how to investigate them. **Some of the themes and issues raised in Section 1.2, and Boxes 1a-1c, are pertinent here.**

Awareness and identification: here, researchers need a heightened awareness that an issue needs further exploration. Is this an example of an injustice? Why is it coming to light now? These are just a few of the things that need thinking about. **Some of the issues discussed in Sections 1.2 and 1.3 are relevant here.**

Defining: having identified the issue and a need for research, there is a need to define clearly and precisely what it is that requires investigation, why and how to go about it. What is already known about this issue? What literature and research already exist? Do we need new research on this topic? It is also very useful at this stage to have a view about how any new research will be reported – the type of 'output'. **The issues and themes discussed in Sections 1.3 and 1.4, and especially in Chapters Two and Three, will need to be considered here.**

'Doing' research

In this phase, the focus is on applying preparatory thinking to the actual mechanics of doing and managing policy research. Decisions will need to be taken about the most appropriate research methods and designs to be used or integrated, the fieldwork will be conducted, the data will be collected and analysed. This whole process needs to be conducted and managed to the highest standards if the research, and findings, are to be trustworthy. **All the issues and themes discussed in Section 1.3, and Chapters Three, Four, Five and Six, are central to this phase of the research cycle.**

Dissemination and promotion

Having conducted the research and analysis to the highest standards, the dissemination and promotion phase is initially concerned with 'outputs' (the type of report, article or presentation that reports the findings), and then moves into how the outputs can be disseminated and promoted to appropriate audiences. **The issues discussed in Chapter Seven are central here**. As we show in Chapter Seven, dissemination of research results can also take place throughout the research cycle, particularly in cases of action research and user participatory research. Here, interim findings can be shared and disseminated well before the formal end of the project.

Adoption, utilisation and change

Here, the focus is on the adoption of research evidence, and its use by individuals and organisations, to inform thinking and to change policy and practice. An intention here may be to use research to lead to better 'outcomes' (for service users, organisations, professionals, and so on) through the process of evidence-based policy and practice. **All the issues raised in Sections 1.4, 1.5 and 7.5 are central here.**

The chapters that follow provide details of the issues, themes and debates that need to be considered when thinking about, conducting and disseminating research to inform social policy and practice.

Questions for discussion

- Why can it be useful to have a model of the research cycle and its relationship with policy and practice?
- To what extent do you think the model reflects accurately the relationship between research, policy and practice? Can you identify any specific strengths and weaknesses?

two

Formulating research ideas and questions

Detailed contents

2.1 Introduction

The main goal of this chapter is to encourage readers to consider what research questions are, where they come from, and the role of existing knowledge – often referred to by the shorthand term 'the literature' – in formulating research questions. The ideas that derive from **the literature** are often referred to as existing **theory** and an important consideration is the relationship between theory and research in the overall research process: is it something that drives the formulation of research ideas and the collection and analysis of data, is it better thought of as an outcome of the collection of data, or is it better to think of the relationship between theory and research as having elements of both of these facets? At the very least, examining what is already known in connection with a research question should guard against the disconcerting possibility that when we complete a research project, we find or someone points out to us that the answers to the research question are already known.

In this chapter we discuss:

• how *research questions* are formulated and why they are important;
• the role of the existing *literature* in formulating research questions;
• the significance of a *literature review* and what kinds of considerations might be borne in mind when writing one;
• the role of *theory* in relation to research.

2.2 Formulating research ideas

Where do research topics and research questions come from? This is one of the most difficult areas for students and researchers to get to grips with, yet it is also fundamental. It connects with the issue of why we study the things that we do in fact study. There are, of course, several sources of research topics, issues and questions but before addressing the matter of sources it is worth spending a moment on our use of the terms used so far: *research topic*; *research issue*; and *research question*. Inevitably, these terms overlap but it is valuable to consider what lines we can draw between them.

Research topics, research issues and research questions

A research **topic** may be thought of as a fairly general focus. It might be something like informal family care. As a focus for research, it provides few (and arguably no) guidelines as to what should be studied and who should be included in any sample of people from which data might be collected. For example, is the research supposed to be on people with care needs, on the experiences of those who provide informal care, or should it be on the work of professionals charged with the responsibility to ensure that carers and their families receive the support they need, or on some other facet of the topic? Simply saying that the focus is on the topic of care tells us next to nothing.

A research **issue** begins to narrow the focus considerably. The issue may be something like how far informal carers receive support and recognition from the state and its agencies. Such a focus narrows things down to the experiences of carers and possibly to the perceptions of professionals responsible for assessing the needs of carers and the people they care for. At this point we are beginning to get a good understanding of what the research is about and why it is being done.

A research **question** takes things even further and will provide a guide to our research. It specifies in much more precise terms what the research is about by specifying a question. A research question is essentially a question that is put to the social world. Thus, for her research on informal care, Arksey (2002) essentially asked whether the 1995 Carers (Recognition and Services) Act provided informal carers with the recognition and support they need (see Figure 2a). The importance of a research question is that it acts as a routemap for research: it helps to guide the literature to be examined, who the focus of the inquiry should be, what kinds of questions might most usefully be asked in the research instruments (for example, an interview schedule or a questionnaire), and how the data should be analysed and interpreted.

A research question is not the same as a **hypothesis**. Hypotheses are better thought of as a kind of research question, namely, one that postulates a possible relationship between two variables. A hypothesis might be something like: the more affluent a household, the less likely they are to rely on informal carers. Such a hypothesis stipulates a relationship between two variables: household wealth and reliance on informal care. It is a form of research question, because it is asking whether there is a relationship between the two variables. However, not all research questions take this form, especially those emanating from qualitative research (see Chapter Five), where they tend to be less specific and less inclined to use the language of variables that is a particular feature of quantitative research. This issue of the distinction between quantitative and qualitative research is an important one that will be outlined in greater detail in Chapter Three.

Figure 2a: **Research topics, issues and questions**

Research topic – informal care

Research issue – state support and recognition for informal carers

Research question – does the 1995 Carers (Recognition and Services) Act provide informal carers with the recognition and support they need?

But to repeat the question posed at the outset: where do research topics and research questions come from? In social policy research, two sources stand out, although it is crucial not to drive a wedge between them in drawing this distinction for reasons that will hopefully become apparent. One source is that **events** in the social policy field may stimulate research ideas. New legislation, such as the 1995 Carers Act that was the focus of Arksey's (2002) research, is an example of the kind of event that may have this kind of impact. Equally, a growing awareness of a 'problem' group in society, as with the research on young carers described in **Box 1c** (Chapter One), may prompt researchers to conduct an investigation of the group concerned.

A second source of research questions is **existing theory** in the field. This issue is addressed more fully in Section 2.5 and **Box 2c**. The term 'theory' is a vague one and need not refer to the abstract ideas and concepts with which theories are often associated. Instead, 'theory' frequently refers to our existing knowledge and understanding surrounding an issue – what do we know about the issue?

However, in conducting research connected with the former kind of context – issues that present themselves in the social policy field – it is crucial to realise that it is still important to assess existing knowledge that is concerned with that issue. Research is never conducted in a vacuum. Even topics and issues that burst onto the scene as apparently unresearched areas still need to be assessed in terms of what we already know because it will almost certainly be the case that there will be cognate topics and issues that have been researched and whose findings will help to illuminate our understanding of our object of inquiry. This means that we need to conduct a *literature review* (see Section 2.3).

Question for discussion

- What are research questions and why are they important?

Reference

Arksey, H. (2002) 'Rationed care: assessing the support needs of informal carers in English social service authorities', *Journal of Social Policy*, vol 31, pp 81-101.

Further reading

Bryman, A. and Bell, E. (2003) *Business research methods*, Oxford: Oxford University Press, Chapter 2.

2.3 Writing a literature review

Why conduct a literature review?

A literature review is an assessment of existing knowledge – both empirical and theoretical – relating to our research topic, issue or question. There are several reasons for needing to conduct a literature review:

- Someone else might have carried out research relating to a research issue or research question. There is no point in going over the same ground unless you can add to what is already known. This may mean taking a different slant on what is already known by perhaps collecting data from groups who have been marginalised in previous research. Every experienced researcher at some time will have had the experience of thinking that he or she has suddenly uncovered a focus that has not been studied previously, only to find when looking at the literature that it has, in fact, already been covered. A literature review means that you will not be in a position of making incorrect claims about the 'unresearched' nature of your area of interest.
- Doing a literature review will help you to appreciate what gaps there are in existing knowledge about the phenomenon of interest. These gaps can be usefully mined to provide your own particular slant on the topic.
- A literature review will help to identify concepts and ideas that have been used to illuminate the area of interest. These may be helpful in giving you ideas about the kinds of data that need to be collected and also how to interpret the data that are collected.
- A literature review can give you ideas about who should be the focus of the enquiry, how they can be sampled, what kinds of lists are available for sampling them, and what is already known about them from surveys or from qualitative interview studies.
- A literature review is extremely useful for an appreciation of the research methods and research designs that have been used to examine this or related

areas of interest. This kind of information in itself might be useful in formulating a research question because it might suggest that a particular topic or research question would benefit from a different data collection strategy from the ones that have been used up to that point.

- At a later stage, a literature review will help you with the interpretation of your data and the formulation of conclusions. A literature review is helpful for providing 'pegs' on which to hang your data. There are invariably numerous ways that you can interpret and analyse your data. An understanding of the literature can provide you with some clues about which aspects of your data to emphasise because you will be able to, and should, relate your own data to aspects of the literature (see also **Box 7b**, Chapter Seven).

A useful aid to collecting materials for a literature review is to make use of computer software, such as a database. The potential of such software is described in **Box 2a**.

Box 2a: Managing references and a bibliography
Joe Sempik, *Research Fellow, Centre for Child and Family Research, Loughborough University*

Prior to the introduction of personal computers (PCs) one of the more tedious (and frequently neglected) tasks of managing a research project was the management of references and the bibliography. This required a boxful of index cards and an accurate transcription of author, title, journal and so on by hand. It is not surprising that this task was often neglected or often performed inaccurately.

However, with the advent of PCs the job of managing a bibliography is considerably easier. 'Reference managers' are computer applications specifically designed to hold and manipulate details of references and the bibliography. A reference manager also simplifies the task of writing papers and reports as it can be used directly with applications such as *Word* to insert references into the text while writing a paper.

There are at least two approaches to providing yourself with a reference manager. First, there are a number of excellent ready-to-use reference managers on the market, for example, *Endnote* and *Refman*. The distributors provide free demonstration copies (see Electronic sources) that perform all of the functions of the real thing but are time-limited. It is therefore possible to browse before you commit yourself to any particular one.

What reference managers can do:

- store bibliographical data;
- search for specific references by author or keyword;
- provide a bibliography in specific forms for particular journals;
- acquire reference information directly from some online databases during a literature search;
- import bibliographical information.

An alternative approach is to build a reference database yourself using an application such as *Microsoft Access*. The advantage of this method is that in the course of preparation you will learn a great deal about how databases are constructed and managed and how to use them. The construction and use of databases is an important element of many research projects. The disadvantage of this approach is that it takes time and effort, and even in this modern age of computers some researchers still struggle with them.

However, a custom-made reference database can be used to analyse and classify the content of published material for a literature review or systematic literature review. The analysis can also be displayed in exactly the form that you want, and this may be desirable when constructing a database that will be accessed by other users.

The screen shot below as figure included in box shows the main input form in an Access database designed to analyse the literature on *Social and therapeutic horticulture* (Sempik et al, 2003). In addition to fields containing the authors' names, article title, journal and so on, there are fields that help to physically manage the bibliography. These can hold information such as whether a copy is held or has been requested, whether the article has been reviewed and if it is to be used in a forthcoming report or publication.

Additional input forms (not shown here) are used to analyse the article. Tick boxes are used to show whether it is a review, descriptive, qualitative, quantitative and so on, and to describe the type of clients taking part in the reported study. Additional information can be added using text fields. Any of the fields can be searched using the *filter* function of *Microsoft Access* and more complex searches can be carried out by constructing *queries*.

Many colleges, universities and even commercial organisations have prepared tutorials on *Microsoft Access* and these are available on the Internet (see Electronic sources for examples). There are also a number of instruction manuals available – see, for example, Wempen (1999) or Catapult, inc (1999).

Screen shot showing the main input form in an *Access* database

If you do decide to construct your own reference database remember that the most important aspect is the design of the tables and their interrelationships. Elegant looking screens can be added later. Spend time on the design and get advice if necessary. If you don't think that you can cope with constructing your own database choose one of the commercially produced reference managers. But do it sooner rather than later!

Question for discussion
- What are the advantages and disadvantages of having an electronic system for managing your references and bibliography?

References
Catapult, inc (1999) *Microsoft Access 2000 step by step*, Redmond, Washington: Microsoft Press International.

Sempik, J., Aldridge, J. and Becker, S. (2003) *Social and therapeutic horticulture: Evidence and messages from research*, Reading: Thrive and Loughborough University.

Wempen, F. (1999) *Sams teach yourself Microsoft Access 2000 in 10 minutes*, Indianapolis, IN: Sams Publishing.

Website resources
Endnote home page: www.endonote.com
Refman home page: www.refman.com
FunctionX Microsoft Access Tutorial: www.functionx.com/access/index.htm

Writing the literature review

When writing your literature review there are a number of points that are worth bearing in mind:

- Be critical. This means that as you read the material that you have gathered start to think about what the contribution of each item is to the area you are investigating and about what its strengths and weaknesses are. Use these reflections in the literature review you write.
- Be sensitive to the need to make distinctions between different sources of literature and their quality. For example, peer-reviewed journal articles are a more reliable source of evidence than, say, an anonymous item off the Internet. These issues are discussed further in Section 2.3. When compiling material for a literature review you will need to make judgements about what to include and what to exclude.
- Adopt a narrative when writing the literature review. This means not simply summarising each item, but showing how each item contributes to a story that you are trying to construct about the literature in this area.
- Do not try to include in your literature review everything you read. This is very tempting, but is not a good strategy. You should use the literature in such a way that it helps to build the narrative you are devising. This will almost certainly mean omitting some items you have read.
- Read some articles in academic journals (or books) to see how the literature review is built up and how a narrative is constructed. **Box 2b** provides an example.
- Ensure that you keep full and accurate details of all the texts that you read. You may want to put these details on an electronic database (see **Box 2a**).

Question for discussion

- What are the main functions of a literature review?

Further reading

Hart, C. (1998) *Doing a literature review*, London: Sage Publications.
Potter, S. (2002) 'Undertaking a topic review', in S. Potter (ed) *Doing postgraduate research*, London: Sage Publications, pp 117-32.

Box 2b: Using the published literature to understand social policy issues

Rowlingson (2002) takes as her starting point government exhortations for over 20 years that individuals and families should take greater personal responsibility for their pension provision and should be weaned off a reliance on the state. Forty-one interviews were carried out with a cross-section of the population. The interviews are described as 'in depth', a term that usually denotes semi-structured interviewing, a topic covered in Section 5.8, Chapter Five. Her article takes a number of different sources for the literature review:

- Government sources. She cites various official documents such as Department of Social Security (DSS) (as it was then called) policy documents and statements by leading politicians, including Tony Blair, to give a sense of the 'official' position with regard to pension provision and any shifts in emphasis over time. Included here is a comment from the leader of HM Opposition at the time (2001) that is taken from an online BBC source at www.bbc.co.uk/. There is also a reference to the 1986 Social Security Act with a discussion of its implications for pension provision. This is used as a backcloth to a discussion of the 'reality of pensions policy' since the Act forms a yardstick against which the actual workings of pensions provision is considered.
- Academic commentary in academic books and journals concerning government policy as well as that in other countries where similar policies have been pursued. It also entails an examination of the principles underlying government thinking and policy in this area. Several of the journals referred to in Section 2.4 are among the academic sources employed. Rowlingson also cites the work of academic researchers who have published in refereed journals and academic books to expose the limits and limitations of government policy in this area, so that the gaps between official statements and the reality of pension provision can be exposed. The same kinds of source are also employed to present existing research on people's private pension planning and their understandings of pension issues.
- In addition, she cites a report from STICERD (The Suntory and Toyota International Centre for Economics and Related Disciplines) at the London School of Economics and Political Science concerning the risks of private pension planning and a report of the Institute/Faculty of Actuaries on the problems with government policy regarding means-testing for pensions. A DSS report based on research using group discussions with members of the public is cited to show the limitations of people's understanding of pensions-related issues.
- She also cites an article in a professional periodical, *Benefits*, which underlines some of the risks of private planning.

- A report from the Goode Committee of 1994, which examined the issue of pensions and fraud in the wake of the Maxwell debacle.
- The only online sources are news reports at sites like www.bbc.co.uk and an online lecture by Anthony Giddens in which he discusses the nature of risk (www.lse.ac.uk/giddens/reith.htm).

At the end of her literature review, Rowlingson concludes:

> It is clear, then, that there is a gap between, on the one hand, the aims and assumptions of policy and, on the other, the actual behaviour and attitudes of the general public. This is because policy-makers have assumed that people are future-oriented and actively consider the medium and long-term future. (Rowlingson, 2002, p 631)

She then outlines further "assumptions" about people and then writes: "The new research presented here aimed to explore these assumptions" (Rowlingson, 2002, p 631). In essence, Rowlingson's research question revolved around asking whether the assumptions of policy makers about people's pensions-related attitudes, understanding and behaviour are correct. The literature review is used to lead up to this research question by examining policy statements to demonstrate what the assumptions are, and existing research to suggest that perhaps these assumptions may not be realised in practice. This is a relatively simple but extremely effective narrative that uses a variety of sources to good effect to lead ineluctably to the research question.

In her conclusion, Rowlingson returns to the issues outlined by her literature review. She argues on the basis of the findings from her interviews that low levels of pension planning by individuals is not due to irresponsibility or irrationality, as implied by government policy regarding the need for individual responsibility, but because people "face constraints in thinking or planning ahead" (Rowlingson, 2002, p 639). She concludes in her final paragraph: "Current government policy does little to justify its emphasis on individual rather than collective planning and it currently misunderstands why people are not planning ahead as much as it would like" (Rowlingson, 2002, p 640). This is a strong conclusion that returns the reader to the issues spelled out in the literature review and relates these to the research findings. The issues of writing up research and relating findings to an established body of findings are further explored in Section 7.3 and **Box 7b**.

Reference

Rowlingson, K. (2002) 'Private pension planning: the rhetoric of responsibility, the reality of insecurity', *Journal of Social Policy*, vol 31, pp 623-42.

2.4 Evaluating sources for a literature review

When reviewing the literature it is important to realise that you will be dealing with a variety of materials that will have different purposes and statuses. **Articles in academic journals** such as the *Journal of Social Policy*, *Social Policy and Administration*, *Social Policy and Society*, *Critical Social Policy* and the *British Journal of Social Work* are often regarded as the highest status outlets for the kinds of material you are likely to read for a literature review. The articles that appear in these journals are only a proportion of those that are submitted. Many are rejected because they are not felt to be 'good' enough to be published in that journal or because the editors believe that the articles are outside the journal's brief. In addition to being read by an editor, all articles are also read by two, three and sometimes more referees who are authorities in the area covered by the articles. The refereeing process is 'blind', meaning that the referees do not know who the articles are written by, so that the possible halo effects of being a big name author are eliminated. Thus, articles appearing in such journals are the outcome of a set of rigorous quality control procedures, often requiring authors to go through one or more revisions of their articles before final acceptance.

Books by academic authors are also highly regarded, but not all publishers make substantial use of referees and, in any case, blind refereeing is usually not possible. Therefore, while some of the most important contributions to the field have been through books, it is also important to bear in mind that books have sometimes not gone through the same process that articles in refereed journals have.

Professional periodicals are valuable for a literature review because they give a good sense of how practitioners are approaching issues in fields such as community care or social work. They often provide useful reviews of policies and also give a sense of what is and is not working in a particular field. The articles in such outlets rarely have the same status as articles in academic journals and books, however, partly because the refereeing process is rarely as rigorous and partly because the periodicals are rarely addressing academic research concerns.

Another source you are likely to include in your review is reports from various **official and unofficial agencies**. For example, the Joseph Rowntree Foundation regularly provides reports of research it has commissioned and these can be very valuable in finding out about current findings in your area. You can also search out reports by local authorities and government departments that touch on social policy issues that are of interest to you.

The **Internet** is obviously an important source for students and researchers collecting material for a literature review. For one thing, many databases and journals are now available online, so searching the literature for articles and books in your field is likely to be carried out online. In addition, the Joseph Rowntree Foundation and other funding bodies, and local authorities and government departments, also have sites where reports can be found. In addition, of course, you can always do a general search using a search engine such as Google or Yahoo. However, be cautious about the material you accumulate through this kind of search procedure. Some of it is dubious in quality. So, by all means conduct such searches, but cultivate an attitude of scepticism towards them. Don't forget to keep good records of all the sites that you have searched, and the key words used to access them.

Question for discussion

- Are some kinds of literature more important and reliable than others from the point of view of writing a literature review?

Further reading

Hart, C. (1998) *Doing a literature review*, London: Sage Publications.

2.5 The role of theory in social policy research

Robert Pinker, *Emeritus Professor of Social Administration, London School of Economics and Political Science*

The **development and testing of theories** is an essential element in the conduct of social research. Theories set out explanatory and predictive propositions about the causal relationships between phenomena, such as, for example, the characteristics and incidence of poverty and the processes by which people become poor and escape from poverty.

The question as to whether theory construction develops out of social research or, conversely, research develops out of theory, is part of a wider philosophical debate between *deductivists* and *inductivists* concerning the origins and status of human knowledge, and the nature of scientific enquiry itself.

Deductivists and inductivists hold differing views about the sequence in which scientific research should be conducted. **Deductivists** start by formulating a theory and then proceed from this general proposition to a consideration of particular cases in order to test their theory. **Inductivists** start by drawing inferences from particular cases from which they proceed towards the formulation of general theoretical conclusions.

The central assumption of the inductivist approach is that "scientific knowledge grows out of simple unbiased statements reporting the evidence of the senses" (Medawar, 1984, p 98). "In real life", however, as Peter Medawar suggests, "discovery and justification are almost always different processes" and researchers seldom, if ever, start their enquiries with a clean sheet. They begin with a review of the relevant literature and some provisional ideas, or hypotheses, about the subject they wish to investigate.

Medawar argues that the weakness in the inductivist approach is its "failure to distinguish between the acts of the mind involved in discovery and proof". Induction, he points out, is "a logically mechanised process of thought which, starting from simple declarations of fact arising out of the evidence of the senses" purports to lead us on "with certainty to the truths of general laws". In Medawar's view, induction cannot fulfil these two functions of discovery and justification because "it is not the *origin* but only the *acceptance* of hypotheses that depends on the authority of logic" (Medawar, 1984, p 33).

For this reason, Medawar proposes that we "abandon the idea of induction and draw a clear distinction between *having an idea* and *testing it* or *trying it out*". We can then reconceptualise the relationship between the uses of imagination and sceptical criticism as the "*two* successive and complementary episodes of thought that occur in every advance of scientific understanding" (Medawar, 1984, p 33). The formulation of hypotheses requires an act of imagination. The testing of hypotheses requires the application of critical testing and experimentation.

Medawar's approach to the conduct of research shares much in common with that of Karl Popper. In Popper's **hypothetico-deductive method**, scientific enquiry starts with an imaginative conjecture, or 'hunch', which is set out in the form of a possible explanation of a causal relationship, a prediction, or a solution to a problem. A conjecture is the first stage in the development of a scientific hypothesis that will give focus to the research and direction in the collection of relevant evidence.

Scientific hypotheses, however, differ from conjectures insofar as they must be set out in forms that allow them to be tested and falsified by methods of observation and experiment. Scientific knowledge is distinguished from non-scientific knowledge insofar as it can be subjected to tests of falsifiability. Popper argues that we are never justified in deriving "universal statements from singular ones, no matter how numerous" because such statements may turn out to be false (Popper, 1972, p 27). In this crucially important respect, scientific knowledge is always provisional and never proven in status. Hypotheses and theories should not, therefore, be treated as propositions to be defended but as propositions to be tested, revised and, if necessary, abandoned in response to countervailing evidence (see also Chapter One, Section 1.5).

In Popper's approach to scientific research we must rely "upon the best tested of theories, which ... are the ones for which we have good rational reasons, not of course good reasons for believing them to be true, but for believing them to be the *best* available ... the best among competing theories, the best approximations to the truth" (Popper, 1978, p 95). On this basis, scientific knowledge will continue to advance through a "method of bold conjectures and ingenious and severe attempts to refute them" (Popper, 1978, p 81).

Popper's views have, in turn, been subjected to critical reappraisal by other philosophers. His claim that falsifiability is the hallmark of a scientific theory has been challenged on a number of grounds – as has his dismissal of inductivism. Not all scientific theories are predictive in character and it does not always follow that one negative finding invalidates a theory. It can also be argued that there are notably inductivist connotations to Popper's advice that we should rely on those theories that have, so far, stood up to rigorous testing.

In this respect, Putnam reminds us that, in the real world of policy making, people do make inductions and draw inferences from available evidence without reaching unwarranted conclusions about the truth or falsity of their theories. Putman suggests that Popper draws an unnecessarily sharp distinction between the worlds of theory and practice. In doing so, he overlooks the fact that ideas are "not just ends in themselves", but that they also "guide practice" and "structure whole forms of life" (Putnam, 1979, p 374).

There are, however, two good reasons why Popper's approach to scientific enquiry can improve the quality of social policy research. First, the ends and means of social policy are shaped by many *value judgements* that often conflict with each other. Policy researchers often hold strong political beliefs about the subjects they wish to investigate. Popper's injunction that theories are propositions to be tested is a useful corrective against value bias and partisanship in the conduct of research. Scholars test their propositions, ideologists defend them, if need be against all countervailing evidence. Second, a Popperian approach leaves open the alternative possibilities that theory can generate research and research can generate theory since hypotheses can emerge at any point in either of these two interactive processes. **Box 2c** provides an illustration of this process, in the context of the role that theory played in relation to a major research programme on health inequalities.

Question for discussion

- Start thinking about a possible research topic and see how far you get before you begin formulating hypotheses.

References

Medawar, P. (1984) *Pluto's Republic*, Oxford: Oxford University Press.
Popper, K. (1972) *The logic of scientific discovery*, London: Hutchinson.
Popper, K. (1978) *Objective knowledge: An evolutionary approach*, Oxford:
  Clarendon Press.
Putnam, H. (1979) 'The "corroboration" of theories', in T. Honderich and M.
  Burnyeat (eds) *Philosophy as it is*, London: Penguin Books.

Further reading

Leisuring, L. and Walker, R. (eds) (1998) *The dynamics of modern society:
  Poverty, policy and welfare*, Bristol: The Policy Press.
Lødemel, I. (1997) *The welfare paradox, income maintenance and personal
  social services in Norway and Britain, 1946-1966*, Oslo: Scandinavian University
  Press.
O'Brien, M. and Penna, S. (1998) *Theorising welfare: Enlightenment and
  modern society*, London: Sage Publications.

Website resource

Material on the philosophy of social science: www.geocities.com/orgscience/
  philos.htm

Box 2c: The role of theory in relation to the ESRC Health Inequalities Programme

Hilary Graham, *Professor of Social Policy, Lancaster University*

The UK is healthier and wealthier than it has ever been. But, as in other rich
societies, socio-economic inequalities in health remain (Whitehead, 1997).
Among working-age men, for example, death rates are three times higher
among unskilled manual workers than among professional men. Tackling these
inequalities is central to public health policies across the UK.

In 1996, a research programme was launched to shed light on the causes of
health inequalities (Graham, 2000). It was funded by the Economic and Social
Research Council (ESRC), the leading government-funded agency for UK social
science research. The *Health Variations Programme* drew on a rich seam of
research that had tested and disproved a set of theories about the socio-
economic gradient in health.   Previous studies had established, for example,
that health-related social mobility could not explain the gradient. While those
in better health are more likely to be upwardly mobile and those in poorer

health to slip down the social class ladder, the scale of mobility is insufficient to account for the scale of health inequalities in the UK.

Two broad perspectives have been proposed to explain how socio-economic position might exert its influence on health. The first perspective is that past socio-economic circumstances hold the key to understanding the socio-economic gradient in adult health. The second perspective argues that current circumstances are more important determinants. Developing and testing these perspectives requires longitudinal studies, where information is collected from the same people at different points in their lives. A set of projects in the Health Variations Programme drew on UK longitudinal studies to explore how past and present circumstances combine to shape health in adult life.

One project examined this question by analysing data from the 1958 birth cohort study, known as the National Child Development Study, which has followed children born in 1958 (Ferri, 1993; Power and Matthews, 1997). The researchers found that self reported health in adulthood (at age 33) was related to duration of exposure to socio-economic disadvantage: rates of poor health were highest among those who had been in disadvantaged circumstances at birth, through childhood and adolescence, and across adulthood to age 33 (Power et al, 1999; Power, 2000). Education was part of the pathway from childhood disadvantage to poor health, but did not explain the association between lifetime socio-economic circumstances and health. There was no evidence that one period of life had a greater impact than another, suggesting that, for this health indicator and in this age group, socio-economic circumstances across the life course contribute to the socio-economic gradient in health.

Other projects built on this finding, exploring how past and present disadvantage took its toll on health in older age groups. While confirming that disadvantage earlier in life contributed to the risk of poor health, these projects underlined the links between current circumstances and health. A project focused on the mental health of Whitehall civil servants in their mid-forties to mid-sixties found that factors related to current socio-economic position (such as working conditions and material disadvantage) were key predictors of depression (Stansfeld et al, 1998). A study of people aged 75-84 found that, while childhood disadvantage had an impact, poverty in old age was the most important predictor of poor self-reported health (Grundy and Holt, 2000).

What conclusions can be drawn from the Health Variations Programme about the two perspectives on health inequalities? Its findings suggest that theories emphasising early and later life influences offer complementary rather than competing explanations of health inequalities. There is evidence that disadvantage, both in childhood and in adulthood, makes an independent contribution to the socio-economic gradient in adult health, and that long-term exposure to disadvantage is especially detrimental to health. But it is never too late to intervene: current circumstances matter and, for some health outcomes, are likely to be more important than past circumstances.

Evidence on how health inequalities emerge across the life course lends support to policies to tackle health inequalities. Targeted interventions such as *Sure Start*, which aim to lift children heading towards long-term disadvantage onto more advantaged trajectories, have a role to play. But more important are the long-established welfare services that influence life chances and living standards across the population: education and social security, healthcare and personal social services, social housing and public transport. The reach of welfare policy goes further, too, to include employment and fiscal policies that moderate (or amplify) inequalities in income from 'the cradle to the grave' (Graham, 2002). As the government has stated, "tackling inequalities generally is the best way of tackling health inequalities in particular" (Secretary of State, 1998, p 12).

Acknowledgements

The illustration above draws on research funded under the ESRC Health Variations Programme, which ran from 1996-2001. Hilary Graham was Director of the Programme (grant number L128341002).

Question for discussion

• How has research on the life course helped to shed light on socio-economic inequalities in health?

References

Ferri, E. (ed) (1993) *Life at 33: The fifth follow-up of the National Child Development Study*, London: National Children's Bureau.

Graham, H. (2000) 'The challenge of health inequalities', in H. Graham (ed) *Understanding health inequalities*, Buckingham: Open University Press.

Graham, H. (2002) 'Building an inter-disciplinary science of health inequalities: the example of lifecourse research', *Social Science and Medicine*, vol 55, no 11, pp 2007-18 (www.elsevier.com/locate/socscimed).

Grundy, E. and Holt, J. (2000) 'Adult life experiences and health in early old age in Great Britain', *Social Science and Medicine*, vol 51, pp 1061-74 (www.elsevier.com/locate/socscimed).

Grundy, E. and Holt, J. (2001) 'Health inequalities in the older population', *Health Variations*, vol 7, pp 4-5 (downloadable from www.lancs.ac.uk/users/apsocsci/hvp/newsletters/grundy7.htm).

Power, C. and Matthews, S. (1997) 'Origins of health inequalities in a national population sample', *Lancet*, vol 350, pp 1584-9.

Power, C., Manor, O. and Matthews, S. (1999) 'The duration and timing of exposure: effects of socio-economic environment on adult health', *American Journal of Public Health*, vol 89, pp 1059-65.

Power, C. (2000) 'Duration and timing of exposure: effects of socio-economic environment on adult health', *Health Variations*, vol 5, pp 6-7 (downloadable from www.lancs.ac.uk/users/apsocsci/hvp/newsletters/power5.htm).

Secretary of State for Health (1998) *Our healthier nation: a contract for health*, Cm 3852, London: The Stationery Office.

Stansfeld, S.A., Head, J. and Marmot, M.G. (1998) 'Explaining social class differences in depression and well-being', *Social Psychiatry and Psychiatric Epidemiology*, vol 33, pp 1-9.

Whitehead, M. (1997) 'Life and death across the millennium', in F. Drever and M. Whitehead (eds) *Health inequalities*, Series DS No 15, London: Office for National Statistics.

Further reading

Independent Inquiry into Inequalities in Health (1998) *Report of the independent inquiry into inequalities in health* (Acheson Report), London: the Stationery Office (www.archive.official-documents.co.uk/document/doh/ih/ih.htm); reiussed by The Policy Press, 1999.

Kuh, D. and Davey Smith, G. (2000) 'The life course and adult chronic disease: an historical perspective with particular reference to coronary heart disease', in D. Kuh and Y. Ben-Shlomo (eds) *A life course approach to chronic disease epidemiology*, Oxford: Oxford University Press.

Relevant organisations

Health Development Agency

Holborn Gate, 330 High Holborn, London WC1V 7BA

www.hda-online.org.uk

Health Education Board for Scotland

Woodburn House, Canaan Lane, Edinburgh, EH10 4SG

www.hebs.scot.nhs.uk

Office for National Statistics [statistics and reports on health inequalities]

The Library, Office for National Statistics, Cardiff Road, Newport, NP10 8XG

www.statistics.gov.uk/cci/nscl.asp?id=5013

UK Public Health Association (UKPHA)

Room 111, Adamson House, Towers Business Park, Wilmslow Road, Didsbury, Manchester M20 1YY

www.ukpha.org.uk

World Health Organisation
Regional Office for Europe, 8 Scherfigsvej 2100, Copenhagen, Denmark
www.who.dk

Website resources

Department of Health (England) [policy documents and research on tackling
  health inequalities]: www.doh.gov.uk
Department of Health (Scotland) [policy documents and research on tackling
  health inequalities]: www.show.scot.nhs.uk/isd/index.htm
Department of Health, Social Services and Public Safety (Northern Ireland)
  [policy documents and research on tackling health inequalities]:
  www.dhsspsni.gov.uk
ESRC Health Variations Programme [summaries of research and publications
  from the Programme]: www.lancs.ac.uk/users/apsocsci/hvp
National Assembly Government (Wales) [policy documents and research on
  tackling health inequalities]: www.wales.gov.uk/keypubstatisticsforwales/
  about.htm
National Child Development Study:
  www.cls.ioe.ac.uk/Cohort/Ncds/mainncds.htm
  www.mimas.ac.uk/system/news/NCDS15.html

Methodological issues and approaches in social policy research

Detailed contents

3.1 Introduction

This chapter discusses key methodological issues, approaches and concerns that are related to, but which also transcend, quantitative and qualitative approaches to policy research. The chapter is divided into four parts.

Part One: Quantitative and qualitative research. In this introductory part of the chapter we examine the nature of, and debate about, *quantitative* and *qualitative* research, and how and why quantitative and qualitative methods may sometimes be combined (*integrated*).

Part Two: Approaches. In this part of the chapter we examine six *approaches* to social policy research, including:

- feminist research;
- user participatory research;
- action research;
- evaluation research;
- comparative research; and
- post–structuralist approaches.

While the approaches have something in common, they each, nonetheless, offer a different stance on investigating and understanding the social world, and raise important issues and challenges for policy research.

Part Three: Using existing research. Here we examine a number of issues that are to do with the use that can be made of published research and data that already exist and which have usually been produced by other researchers, including *secondary analysis*, *systematic reviews*, and the *archiving* of data.

Part Four: Themes. In the final part of the chapter we discuss four themes that are central to policy research: *ethical considerations*, *'race'*, *researching sensitive topics* and *researching vulnerable groups*. Ethical matters need to be taken into account in *all* policy research inquiries, as does the issue of *informed consent*. It would be hard to conceive of a piece of policy research that was *not* concerned with either a sensitive topic or a vulnerable group; how these inquiries are handled and managed, and how data are collected, analysed and interpreted, requires great care, sophistication and sensitivity. Here we are also reminded that the dimension of 'race' needs to be fully integrated into policy research studies.

   Throughout the chapter we illustrate these issues, approaches and themes by the use of a wide range of examples drawn from social policy research.

PART ONE: QUANTITATIVE AND QUALITATIVE RESEARCH

3.2 The nature of quantitative and qualitative research

The distinction between **quantitative** and **qualitative** research has had widespread currency in the social sciences for many years (particularly in sociology), but started to become a major area of debate and discussion in the late 1960s and early 1970s. Until then, *qualitative* research had occupied a position of near inferiority with respect to the far more pervasive and more revered *quantitative* methods. Qualitative methods were seen merely as different from quantitative ones and rarely warranted more than a brief discussion in research methods textbooks of the time, wherein they were typically described in rather unfavourable terms.

What is significant about the growing use of the **distinction** between quantitative and qualitative research and the very considerable increase in discussion about the latter is that qualitative research came to be seen as a coherent alternative to quantitative research. Each can be seen as having a distinctive cluster of concerns and preoccupations. Those associated with **quantitative** research can be viewed in the following terms (Bryman, 2004):

- *Measurement:* quantitative researchers seek to provide rigorous measures of the concepts that drive their research. Thus, there is often a great deal of concern in texts on quantitative research about how to *operationalise* concepts. The quantitative researcher searches for *indicators* to act as measures that can stand for or point towards the underlying concept. The very idea of a *variable* – an attribute on which people vary – which is so central to quantitative research, is indicative of this preoccupation with measurement. The emphasis on the measurement of prior concepts reflects a *deductive* approach to the relationship between theory and research (see also Chapter Two, Section 2.5).
- *Causality:* there is a concern to demonstrate causal relationships between variables, in other words, to show what factors influence people's behaviour, attitudes and beliefs. This preoccupation with causality can be seen in the widespread use of the terms *independent variable* and *dependent variable* to describe variables which, respectively, influence and are influenced by other variables.

- *Generalisation:* quantitative researchers invariably seek to establish that their findings apply more widely than the confines of their specific research context. Thus, there tends to be a concern to show that findings are representative of a wider population and this is responsible for the preoccupation in many research methods texts with *sampling* procedures that maximise the possibility of generating a representative sample (see also Chapter Four).
- *Replication:* one of the main ways in which the scientific orientation of quantitative research is most apparent is the frequent reference to the suggestion that the researcher should follow clearly explicated procedures so that a study is reproducible. As in the natural sciences, it is believed to be important for a study to be capable of being checked by someone else, in case it was poorly conducted or the biases of the researcher were allowed to intrude into the results of the investigation.

Box 3a provides an illustration of these concerns in quantitative research, by focusing on one published study of care management arrangements for older people with mental health problems (Challis et al, 2001).

Box 3a: Quantitative research: an example

Challis et al (2001) were interested in patterns of the management of care following on from community care legislation in the early 1990s (the 1990 National Health Service and Community Care Act). They note that the legislation was supposed to have led to a framework in which care would be assessed on the basis of individual needs and then to a plan for catering for those assessed needs and their subsequent monitoring. The authors note that the ambiguity inherent in the broad notion of care management and the lack of specificity in the guidance has allowed for considerable variation in the interpretation of the act and its implications. Unsurprisingly, Challis et al are able to draw attention to evidence that there has been considerable variety in the implementation of the post-1993 arrangements for the management of care. Indeed, they point to studies showing considerable confusion about even what the management of care means.

In response to this state of affairs, the Personal Social Services Research Unit at the University of Manchester was commissioned by the Department of Health "to undertake a programme of research to map and evaluate care management arrangements for older people and those with mental health problems" (Challis et al, 2001, pp 675-6). The researchers developed *key indicators* of possible variation and these were grouped into three headings:

- *Organisational arrangements:* an example is where the level of authority to purchase community-based care packages lies – whether at the first tier of management or below, or at the second tier of management or below.
- *Performance of core tasks:* examples are: whether health staff are involved in all core tasks; whether arrangements for the review of community and residential care for older people is fully fixed or not fully fixed; whether there is either usually or not usually continuity of assessment to other tasks of care management arrangements for older people.
- *Degree of differentiation:* examples are: whether there are care management staff based in specialist older people's teams; whether the average caseload size for older people is below 30 or 30+.

In 1997 and 1998, three postal questionnaires were mailed to English local authorities. A 75% response rate (98 out of 131 authorities) was achieved, which is very creditable for surveys based on postal questionnaires.

The authors found 63 different sets of care management arrangements by relating each of the different indicators to each other. They were then able to narrow down this diversity into six general patterns or types of care management arrangement which subsumed 78 (80%) of the authorities.

This study typified quantitative research in its preoccupation with measurement as a route to understanding. The main features of care management are outlined and operationalised through indicators, some of which are outlined above. The article itself does not deal with causality in that the authors are solely concerned with establishing the variety of arrangements. However, it could be imagined that at a later stage the authors might want to relate the six types of arrangement to a variety of variables, such as historical aspects of the local authorities, age and socio-economic profiles of the authorities, and so on. The issue of generalisation is interesting in the context of this research. Since questionnaires were sent to all local authorities, this is not a sample, since the whole population was included in the research. However, since not all replied (although a large percentage did), this could be taken to raise questions about the representativeness of those that did participate and hence the extent to which it is possible to generalise to all local authorities. On the other hand, since Challis et al did uncover a great deal of variety in the 75% that did participate, it is hard to believe that the other 25% would not also exhibit variety. Finally, replication of this study would be reasonably straightforward since the procedures for conducting the research and the measurement of the main concepts is clearly outlined. This would be an interesting replication since it would reveal how far arrangements have changed and in particular whether less variety was exhibited.

The article contributes a great deal to our understanding in this area and the authors show how their evidence links with the literature and policy context that guided their collection of data. As they observe, the high level of variation in arrangements "is interesting in the light of current policy regarding consistency in such areas as eligibility, assessment and review" (Challis et al, 2001, pp 682-3).

Reference

Challis, D., Weiner, K., Darton, R., Hughes, J. and Stewart, K. (2001) 'Emerging patterns of care management: arrangements for older people in England', *Social Policy and Administration*, vol 35, pp 672-87.

By contrast, **qualitative** research is seen as distinctive in the following respects:

• *Focus on actors' meanings:* qualitative researchers aim to understand the behaviour, values, beliefs, and so on of the people they study from the perspective of the subjects themselves. This tendency reflects a commitment that researchers should not impose their own understandings of what is going on.
• *Description and emphasis on context:* if you read an article or monograph based on qualitative research, it is difficult not to be struck by the attention to detail that is often revealed. There is frequently a rich account of the people and the environment. This is not to say that qualitative researchers are unconcerned with explanation, but that they provide detailed descriptions of the research setting. One of the chief reasons for the detailed description of research settings is so that behaviour and beliefs can be understood in the specific context of the research setting. The meaning of events is therefore to be sought in the prevailing value system and structures that are possibly unique to the setting being studied.
• *Process:* there is a tendency for social life to be viewed in terms of unfolding processes so that events are depicted as interconnected over time and not as disparate.
• *Flexibility:* much qualitative research is relatively unstructured so that the researcher is more likely to uncover actors' meanings and interpretations rather than impose his or her own understandings. The lack of structure has the additional advantage that the general strategy is flexible, so that if the researcher encounters unexpected events that offer a promising line of enquiry, a new direction can be absorbed and followed up.
• *Emergent theory and concepts:* typically, concepts and the development of theory emerge out of the process of data collection rather than appearing at the outset of an investigation, which is what occurs in quantitative research. This preference for an *inductive approach* reflects the predilection among qualitative researchers for interpretation to take place in subjects' own terms.

Box 3b provides an illustration of these concerns in qualitative research, by focusing on a published study of family ('lay') carers' involvement in healthcare, and their relationships with paid professionals (Pickard et al, 2003).

Question for discussion

- What are the main axes of difference between quantitative and qualitative research?

References

Bryman, A. (2004) *Social research methods* (2nd edn), Oxford: Oxford University Press.

Challis, D., Weiner, K., Darton, R., Hughes, J. and Stewart, K. (2001) 'Emerging patterns of care management: arrangements for older people in England', *Social Policy and Administration*, vol 35, pp 672-87.

Pickard, S., Jacobs, S. and Kirk, S. (2003) 'Challenging professional roles: lay carers' involvement in health care in the community', *Social Policy and Administration*, vol 37, pp 82-96.

Further reading

Bryman, A. (2004) *Social research methods* (2nd edn), Oxford: Oxford University Press, Chapters 1, 3 and 13.

Hammersley, M. (1996) 'The relationship between qualitative and quantitative research: paradigm loyalty versus methodological eclecticism', in J.T.E. Richardson (ed) *Handbook of research methods for psychology and the social sciences*, Leicester: BPS Books, pp 159-74.

Box 3b: Qualitative research: an example

Taking as their background the social policy environment within which lay carers' involvement in healthcare in the community takes place, Pickard et al (2003) examined the supposed implications of the various policy initiatives. These initiatives are predicated on a view of professionals as providing support for lay carers. The authors note that the boundaries of responsibility between the two parties – professionals and lay carers – is frequently unclear. As a result, the type and level of support tend to be worked out at the professional–carer interface where guidelines are uncertain and not always followed. They observe that changes in the boundaries of professional responsibilities have further made this an area in which the framework for professional–carer relationships and support is hazy and variable. After a review of the evidence and policy framework relating to this area, they take as the rationale for their research the "lack of clarity and detailed information that exists about who is doing what in the community" (Pickard et al, 2003, p 84).

To illuminate these issues, the authors draw on three research projects:

- a study of older carers of older people in two health authorities. Interviews were conducted with 24 frail elderly people aged 70 and over and with 24 professionals (district nurses and community psychiatric nurses);
- parent carers of children in the north of England who are dependent on technologies. Interviews were carried out with parents of 24 children and with 38 professionals involved in supporting the child at home. The parent carers were recruited via three specialist children's hospitals;
- home care workers involved in a Direct Payments scheme (whereby disabled people are given sums of money to employ personal assistants of their choice) in three local authority areas in England. Interviews were carried out with 42 users who received payments, with 15 personal assistants, and with 13 health professionals (district nurses, chiropodists, and so on).

Pickard et al state that all of the projects used *semi-structured interview* and *focus groups* (see Chapter Five, Sections 5.8 and 5.10, for an explanation of these terms). The data were collected on "the perspectives of both professionals and lay carers in order to ... enrich our understanding of the experience of different groups working together" (Pickard et al, 2003, p 84). The data from the three projects were analysed in terms of *core themes* relevant to all of them, such as: roles and activities being fulfilled by lay carers; how boundaries between lay and professional spheres are negotiated; professionals' and lay carers' perceptions of the appropriate lay–professional boundary; levels of support offered to lay carers; and the "different types of knowledge and expertise possessed by lay and professional carers" (Pickard et al, 2003, p 85).

In the article, the data are presented in terms of summaries of patterns in the findings, along with brief passages from transcripts of the interviews and focus groups. The authors find that lay carers have taken over many tasks and responsibilities formerly the domain of professionals. The latter tend to prevail when it comes to negotiations with lay carers about responsibilities and courses of action. Lay carers and personal assistants were found to possess a good deal of technical understanding of the nature of the care required by those for whom they are responsible, but often felt that their knowledge and expertise was ignored by professionals. The authors make a number of recommendations for current social policy to be fully realised.

This study exhibits the typical characteristics of a qualitative study. It emphasises the worldview and perspective of the people who were interviewed. This emphasis means that the points of view of several constituencies are covered – lay carers, professionals, disabled people and their personal assistants. Looking at issues from their points of view allows the contrasting positions to come across. There is quite a lot of descriptive information which is particularly apparent in the use of brief vignettes of cases. The stress on context is probably less apparent in this study than in ethnographic studies such as the one referred to in **Box 5d**, Chapter Five. Nonetheless, the descriptive information about the circumstances of some of the client groups helps to convey a sense of the environment within which care is negotiated and allocated. The study also brings out some of the processes that are involved in the negotiation over care. In this study, care does not appear as something that exists in a static state but as something that is in a state of flux as policies, decision-making processes, and professional–lay negotiations run their course. Finally, in adopting a semi-structured interview approach, a relatively flexible approach to data collection was taken.

The article provides a good illustration of qualitative research, provides some crucial insights into the world of informal care and its connections with the world of professionals, and ends up providing some important recommendations to be fed into the future discussions about the policy framework.

Reference

Pickard, S., Jacobs, S. and Kirk, S. (2003) 'Challenging professional roles: lay carers' involvement in health care in the community', *Social Policy and Administration*, vol 37, pp 82-96.

3.3 The debate about quantitative and qualitative research

At one level, any discussion about the nature of quantitative and qualitative research would seem to be about *technical* issues to do with the suitability or relevance of either stance in relation to a research question. However, discussions about the two research strategies have been bound up with debates about whether they reflect differing, even divergent, *epistemological* assumptions and commitments. This kind of discussion reflects a view that any research method is inextricably bound to a particular philosophy about how the social world ought to be studied. Such ruminations tie quantitative research and its associated research designs and research methods (such as experiments and questionnaire surveys) to **positivism**, which posits that social life can and should be studied according to the canons of the scientific method with its emphasis on directly observable entities. Similarly, qualitative research with its associated research designs and research methods (such as participant observation and intensive interviewing) is rooted in contrary views about how social life should be studied, such as **phenomenology**, which implies that the fact that people are capable of thought, self-reflection and language necessitates an alternative framework which ascribes priority to the actor's perspective. This perception of research methods can be seen very clearly in statements such as the following:

> ... the choice and adequacy of a method embodies a variety of assumptions regarding the nature of knowledge and the methods through which that knowledge can be obtained, as well as a root set of assumptions about the nature of the phenomena to be investigated. (Morgan and Smircich, 1980, p 491)

According to such a view the decision to engage in a research method such as participant observation represents not simply a choice of data gathering technique but a commitment to an epistemological position that is antithetical to positivism and that recognises the uniqueness of people and society as objects of study.

This kind of view of research methods has led some commentators to claim that *multi-strategy research*, which combines quantitative and qualitative research (the focus of the next section), is not genuinely possible. A participant observer may collect questionnaire data to gain information about a slice of social life that is not amenable to participant observation, but this does not represent an integration of quantitative and qualitative research because the epistemological positions in which participant observation and questionnaires are grounded are incompatible views of how social reality should be studied. This position conceives of quantitative and qualitative research as paradigms (following Kuhn's [1970] analysis of revolutions in science) in which epistemological assumptions, values and methods are inextricably interwoven and are incompatible between paradigms (for example, Guba, 1985). Therefore, when a researcher combines the use of participant observation with a questionnaire, he or she is not really integrating quantitative and qualitative research, since they are incompatible: the integration is only at a superficial level and within a single paradigm. Smith and Heshusius, for example, decry the integration of research strategies because it disregards the assumptions underlying techniques and transforms "qualitative inquiry into a procedural variation of quantitative inquiry" (1986, p 8).

One problem with this strapping together of epistemology and method is that it is not easy to sustain. Investigators who have attempted to explore connections between methods, on the one hand, and epistemological or theoretical positions, on the other, have often found that such supposed relationships are at best unclear and at worst simply wrong (see Bryman, 2004, pp 442-6, for a review of this evidence). A classic participant observation study such as Whyte's (1943) *Street corner society* contains many characteristics of a supposedly positivist approach, such as an exploration of the connection between bowling scores and group social position.

Linking epistemology and method also implies that researchers approach research problems with a host of epistemological commitments which determine their data collection strategy, rather than in terms of the fit between the problem and method, the resources available to them and methodological exemplars. Such technical and practical considerations are likely to loom very large in the way in which a researcher tackles a problem and authors of textbooks in social research methodology essentially advocate that this should be the case.

In other words, as several writers have argued (for example, Bryman, 2004; Hammersley, 1992), not only is it important not to exaggerate the differences between quantitative and qualitative research so that they appear to be warring positions, it is also important to recognise that research methods are not necessarily rooted to epistemological assumptions. Research methods can be far more free-floating than is generally appreciated. This recognition is crucial to the issue of combining quantitative and qualitative research, since it implies that the barriers to integrating the two research strategies are far less pronounced than is often suggested by writers who see methods as tied to particular epistemological positions.

Question for discussion

- To what extent are research methods inseparable from particular epistemological positions?

References

Bryman, A. (2004) *Social research methods* (2nd edn), Oxford: Oxford University Press.

Guba, E.G. (1985) 'The context of emergent paradigm research', in Y.S. Lincoln (ed) *Organization theory and inquiry: The paradigm revolution*, Beverly Hills, CA: Sage Publications, pp 79-104.

Hammersley, M. (1992) 'Deconstructing the qualitative-quantitative divide', in M. Hammersley, *What's wrong with ethnography?*, London: Routledge, pp 159-73.

Kuhn, T.S. (1970) *The structure of scientific revolutions* (2nd edn), Chicago, IL: University of Chicago Press.

Morgan, G. and Smircich, L. (1980) 'The case for qualitative research', *Academy of Management Review*, vol 5, pp 491-500.

Smith, J.K. and Heshusius, L. (1986) 'Closing down the conversation: the end of the quantitative-qualitative debate among educational enquirers', *Educational Researcher*, vol 15, pp 4-12.

Whyte, W.F. (1943) *Street corner society*, Chicago, IL: Chicago University Press.

Further reading

Bryman, A. (1984) 'The debate about quantitative and qualitative research: a question of method or epistemology?', *British Journal of Sociology*, vol 35, pp 75-92.

Bryman, A. (2004) *Social research methods* (2nd edn), Oxford: Oxford University Press, Chapter 21.

Hammersley, M. (1992) 'Deconstructing the qualitative-quantitative divide', in M. Hammersley, *What's wrong with ethnography?*, London: Routledge, pp 159-73.

3.4 Integrating quantitative and qualitative research

Writers and researchers who have been less wedded to the epistemological version of the debate about quantitative and qualitative research (see Section 3.3) have been very open to the possibility that the two research strategies can be fruitfully combined. Indeed, in the last 10–15 years, studies that integrate the two have become quite numerous, whereas before then it was relatively unusual to find such studies. In fact, the frequency with which **multi–strategy research** (research that combines quantitative and qualitative research) occurs has even begun to cast doubt in some researchers' eyes about the credibility of the distinction.

There are a number of different ways in which multi–strategy research might occur (Bryman, 2004, Chapter 22). The discussion below can only deal with the most prominent ways.

- *Triangulation:* the idea behind triangulation is that the credibility of findings are greater when more than one source of data is employed to tackle an issue. The term was originally devised in connection with quantitative research where it was argued that if a measure of a concept is devised and then cross–checked against another measure of the same concept, our faith in the findings will be greater. This notion has been extended into multi–

strategy research where it is often suggested that if quantitative and qualitative studies can mutually confirm each other, we will have more robust findings in which we will have greater faith.

- *Qualitative research facilitates quantitative research:* this second idea has been one of the most common justifications for combining the two research strategies, especially in the early years of multi-strategy research. The most common way of thinking about it is to suggest that qualitative research, because it is relatively unstructured, can provide quantitative researchers with a steady stream of hypotheses. Moreover, since qualitative researchers rarely employ random sampling procedures of the kind discussed in Section 4.1, Chapter Four, it is unlikely that we can generalise findings from it to populations. Also, it was sometimes suggested that since quantitative researchers generate 'hard' data (because the data are quantitative), we would get a better understanding of how much faith could be placed in the qualitative findings if they were treated as hypotheses which are subsequently confirmed by quantitative research. This kind of argument, which attaches a kind of epistemological priority to quantitative research, is less often encountered nowadays, since qualitative research is held in higher regard than was the case before the 1980s. Another way in which qualitative research is sometimes treated as being helpful in facilitating quantitative research is that it can provide quantitative researchers with ideas for structured interview or questionnaire questions and the correct language that should be employed (for example, Nassar-McMillan and Borders, 2002).

- *Quantitative research facilitates qualitative research:* the most common form of this context for multi-strategy research is mentioned in **Box 3c**, where Julia Brannen refers to a survey being employed (among other uses) as a means of purposively sampling individuals for qualitative interviews (semi-structured interviews). In this way, individuals can be selected in terms of characteristics that are relevant to the qualitative research.

- *Quantitative and qualitative research deal with different research questions or issues within a project:* this fourth approach to combining quantitative and qualitative research is probably the one that occurs most frequently nowadays. This orientation to multi-strategy research recognises that quantitative and qualitative research have different strengths and purposes and that a better overall picture will often emerge when the two are combined. It can be seen in **Box 3c** where the two research strategies had different roles in relation to the investigation. Another interesting example is a study by Taylor-Gooby (2001) in which he takes up the idea of a 'risk society' that was a significant influence on New Labour thinking and explores its implications for social welfare. As Taylor-Gooby observes, the implications of such thinking are substantial given their emphasis on a reduced role for government and greater individual responsibility. These issues were tackled in two ways. First, four focus groups made up of between eight and twelve participants were conducted. The discussions were concerned with "how people thought about risk, uncertainty and security in their daily lives" (Taylor-Gooby, 2001, p 200). Taylor-Gooby then went on to analyse the first seven waves of data collected from the British Household Panel Survey (BHPS) (see **Box 4a**, Chapter Four, for a brief description of the BHPS) "to examine the way in which some of the risks of modern social life affect particular groups" (Taylor-Gooby, 2001, p 200). He concludes:

> The focus groups produced suggestive evidence that individuals are aware of the new uncertainties associated with risk society, but that there are differences across social groups in people's confidence in their capacity to manage them and their potential need for state support.... The analysis of the BHPS shows that while most people regard the future with some optimism, many have difficulty in predicting their future circumstances accurately. (Taylor-Gooby, 2001, p 209)

In this way, through the use of multi-strategy research, different aspects of the phenomenon being researched could be explored.

Research that integrates quantitative and qualitative research has not only become more common and accepted but has also helped to bridge the gulf that has sometimes pitched quantitative and qualitative researchers against each other. However, as with all forms of research, it is still the responsibility of researchers to ensure that their research methods are tailored to their research questions. Multi-strategy research does not provide a short-cut around this necessity.

Question for discussion

- Do the supposed epistemological issues that relate to quantitative and qualitative research mean that they cannot be combined?

References

Bryman, A. (2004) *Social research methods* (2nd edn), Oxford: Oxford University Press.
Nassar-McMillan, S.C. and Borders, L.D. (2002) 'Use of focus groups in survey item development', *Qualitative Report*, vol 7, no 1, online journal (www.nova.edu/ssss/QR/QR7-1/nassar.html).
Taylor-Gooby, P. (2001) 'Risk, contingency and the third way: evidence from the BHPS and qualitative studies', *Social Policy and Administration*, vol 35, pp 195-211.

Further reading

Bryman, A. (2004) *Social research methods* (2nd edn), Oxford: Oxford University Press, Chapter 22.

Box 3c: Integrating qualitative and quantitative research: an illustration
Julia Brannen, *Professor of the Sociology of the Family, Institute of Education, University of London*

Studies may employ both qualitative and quantitative approaches. The way different types of approach come together varies according to the phase of the research process: the research design phase, the fieldwork phase, the analysis phase and the contextualisation phase. However, the issues of integration are rather differently addressed in the *context of the enquiry* from the *context of justification*.

In the context of the enquiry – the research design phase – decisions are made about its structure and content in relation to the study's research questions that cover substantive issues, policy concerns, theoretical approaches and practical matters. The issues here are: which questions will be addressed via which samples, and through which kinds of methods? In the following study example, two parts of the study were designed with two goals: (1) each part was designed to address differently framed research questions, and (2) the first quantitative part of the study was intended to assist access to the research participants (children in their families) and to provide a sampling frame for the second, qualitative part of the research. In terms of the second goal, qualitative samples were embedded within a larger representative sample.

Example 1: Children's concepts of care study (Brannen et al, 2000)
The study focused on children's concepts of care and their views and experiences of different kinds of family forms. In order to examine the ways in which children's views of care and their family practices were distributed across a wide range of children in the community, an extensive approach was employed: involving self-completion questionnaire surveys in a mix of mixed-sex state-funded secondary schools and feeder primary schools (in two London boroughs). These surveys were used to complement an intensive approach in which we sought to conduct qualitative interviews in order to elicit the perspectives of boys and girls. The 63 qualitative interviews were distributed equally across four types of family context: two parent, lone mother and stepfather families and foster care. We also used other methods during the interviews, for example network maps, vignettes and genealogical diagrams, which took account of

children's interests and competencies, while being attentive to the sensitivity of the topic of family life and family change. We included mothers' views of children's experiences since mothers were key figures in children's family lives and also because mothers could provide important contextual material about family change and children's relationships, especially with non-resident fathers about whom many children were reluctant to talk.

In the context of justification – when data are being analysed and written up and when the analyses are being contextualised in relation to other datasets – the issues are different. Each dataset – qualitative and quantitative – needs to be considered in relation to the ontological, epistemological and theoretical assumptions that underpinned each part of the enquiry, but also in relation to the contexts in which the data were generated (for example, face-to-face interview questions). Thus, the aim here is *not* to try to integrate the constituent parts of the study and the different types of data as if they constituted some rounded whole. Rather, the aim should be to show the particular contribution of each part of the study and how each type of data relate to the questions around which the enquiry was framed and was generated in the particular research context.

Example 2: Children's concepts of care study (Brannen et al, 2000)

Here is an example of *how the survey data (the quantitative part of the study) were used*. In order to assess children's normative views concerning the gendering of *particular parenting practices*, we employed extensive methods, in which children were asked to indicate whether they thought mothers, fathers or both parents ought to engage in particular parenting tasks. Similarly, we asked children which of their own parents performed a range of parenting practices. These structured survey data provided systematic responses to a list of parenting practices for a wide range and large number of children in the community.

Here is an example of *how the interview data with children and their mothers were used (the second part, the qualitative part of the study)*. In order to examine children's *relationships with their parents*, including non-resident parents, we asked children to locate household members, family members, and friends on their maps of significant others (the child was placed at the centre of the map which contained three concentric rings, each representing different degrees of closeness). In follow-up questioning, children were asked to explain why they had located them in that position and a number of other questions. However, children often said little at this juncture about their relationships with (non-resident) parents and, in some cases, were more forthcoming when responding to a vignette concerning a hypothetical individual child and their responses to parental divorce (the vignette was embedded in the interview). In terms of understanding the background to the study, children's family situations and their relationships – notably between children and their non-resident fathers – the mothers' interviews helped to fill the gaps in the story. In writing up the data concerning children's accounts of household change and relationships with non-resident parents, the story was often a 'between the lines' story in which it was important to make clear the contexts in which different responses were generated, including those in which children were reticent. We did not think it ethical to ask children to address relationships with parents and other highly personal matters in the public context of the school and the classroom in which the surveys took place. Moreover, we considered that children ought to be given a variety of 'contexts' within the interview to talk or not talk about family change and family relationships. The home setting provided a more secure environment for such disclosure. A responsible adult was present to provide children with support and who could refrain from posing questions to which children seemed unwilling to respond.

The mixed strategy approach greatly assisted the study's research design and sampling. It also provided a rich mix of different kinds of accounts from children and about children's family lives. The challenges were twofold: first, in exploiting the different data resources in order to show how accounts of sensitive topics such as family change are likely to be partial and understated; second, in knitting together the different types of data in the written products of the study. In this latter regard, it is notable that we did not draw directly on the focus groups that we conducted in the development of the interview phase (not referred to above) mainly because of the limitations of time, length of books and papers, and styles of presentation.

Question for discussion

- What are the benefits of a mixed strategy approach for research design? Discuss the main issues you may face in justifying the resulting different data analyses and their interpretation.

References and further reading

Brannen, J., Heptinstall, E. and Bhopal, K. (2000) *Connecting children: Care and family life in later childhood*, London: Routledge Falmer.

Brannen, J. (ed) (1992) *Mixing methods: Qualitative and quantitative research*, London: Gower (reprinted 1993 and 1994, paperback edn 1995).

Bryman, A. (2004) *Social research methods* (2nd edn), Oxford: Oxford University Press.

Hammersley, M. (1992) 'Deconstructing the qualitative-quantitative divide', in J. Brannen (ed) *Mixing methods: Qualitative and quantitative research*, Avebury: Gower, pp 39-55 (reprinted 1993 and 1994, paperback edn 1995).

Kaplan, A. (1964) *The conduct of enquiry*: *Methodology for behavioural science*, San Francisco, CA: Chandler Publishing Company.
Layder, D. (1998) *Sociological practice*: *Linking theory and social research*, London: Sage Publications.
Smith, J.K. and Heshusius, L. (1986) 'Closing down the conversation: the end of the quantitative-qualitative debate among educational inquirers', *Educational researcher*, vol 15, no 1, pp 4-12.

PART TWO: APPROACHES

3.5 Feminist Research

Lesley Hoggart, *Senior Research Fellow, Policy Studies Institute*

There is no simple model of feminist research, methodology, epistemology or research methods. Indeed, how and why feminists should undertake research has long been a matter of debate and disagreement amongst feminist researchers, although it would also be true to say that there are some generally recognised common concerns.

Feminists began by exposing what they understood to be a sexist bias in traditional social research, and by challenging positivism's claim to objectivity (Harding, 1987; Eichler, 1988). The 'myth' of value-free research was replaced by research in which the researchers' values and interpretations were acknowledged as central to the research process. "Feminism is in the first place an attempt to insist upon the experience and very existence of women. To this extent it is most importantly a feature of an ideological conflict, and does not of itself attempt an 'un-biased' or 'value-free' methodology" (Roberts, 1981, p 15). This was an important part of a broader trend within social research that criticised positivism, questioned the search for 'truth' and explored the role of the researcher in the production of knowledge. The feminist critique encompassed many areas of social science. In social policy, for example, an early feminist concern was to explain the gendered nature of existing welfare provision (Wilson, 1977; Dale and Foster, 1986; Pascall, 1986).

A broad definition of feminism offers a positive, non-prescriptive approach for feminist researchers. Feminism can be defined as *a position with the political aim of challenging discrimination against women and/or promoting greater equality between the sexes.* Feminist research, then, adds to our knowledge of these issues and is concerned with transforming gender relations. What has emerged over years of debate is not a blueprint, but a broad consensus about some guiding principles of feminist research (Figure 3a).

Figure 3a: **Some principles of feminist research**

1. Feminist research acknowledges the active presence of the researcher in the process of knowledge production.
2. Feminists value the experiences, concerns and opinions of women.
3. Feminists try to overcome the subject–object divide that places the researcher as the knowing subject and the researched as merely the object of research. This involves addressing power relationships and seeking to combine the knowledge and experience of researchers and researched.
4. Feminist research (while not excluding research on men) is politically for women and seeks to improve women's lives in some way. An important part of this may be sharing results with women whom the findings will benefit, and with the institutions responsible for policies.

The **Women, Risk and AIDS Project** (WRAP), a study into the sexual practices and beliefs of young women, is a good example of feminist research. In-depth interviews gave a voice to young women and the power relationship between the researcher and researched was acknowledged. The researchers located themselves as 'fallible' and subjective within the research process and made the process of data analysis transparent by exploring the relationship between the contributions of the young people and the interpretations of the researchers. The project also examined the exercise of power in existing gender relations and developed (and disseminated) policy recommendations aimed at empowering young women to take control of their sexual lives (Holland and Ramazanoglu, 1994; Holland et al, 1998).

Within the broad concerns outlined above (not all of which are necessarily applied to each piece of feminist research) there is room for a wide variety of approaches, as, indeed, different feminists have proposed. There is also room for a variety of research methods that can include both qualitative and quantitative approaches. Although many feminists favour qualitative research methods (such as unstructured interviews – see Chapter Five, Section 5.8) that facilitate open, in-depth expression of women's experiences and views, others challenge the divide between quantitative and qualitative research methods (Oakley, 1992). Indeed it has been argued that "[f]eminists should use any and every means available for investigating the condition of women in sexist society" (Stanley, 1990, p 12).

A key area of debate centres on the issue of subjectivity versus objectivity. Other debates include those around difference and diversity, representing others in research and what it means to be reflexive. A feminist methodology can involve an open acknowledgement of subjectivity. This is defended by pointing out that no research can be value free, and that to admit this at the outset is in fact a step towards more honest research (Roberts, 1981; Finch, 1991). Feminists also argue for reflexive research, which involves researchers being aware of, and making visible, their own experiences and presence in the research (Roberts, 1981; Stanley, 1990). How, and at what stage in the research process, this takes place has been variously interpreted. Mies (1981), for example, argued in favour of open partiality through identification with the research objects. This is an exclusionary model of feminist research that would preclude the study of some women, as well as women researching men and masculinity.

The further, distinct, claim that feminist research may be more objective than androcentric traditional research because it produces less distorted knowledge has been proposed by Harding (1987), who claims that knowledge grounded in women's experience of struggles against male domination can produce a more complete knowledge of gendered social lives than that based only on men's experiences. This is a central claim of the much disputed, and also varied, feminist standpoint which sought to develop new feminist knowledge of gendered social lives through 'women speaking their truth' (see Hartsock, 1997). Similarly, Eichler (1988) has suggested that once the sexist bias of traditional research is acknowledged, a woman-centred examination of the issues may lead to the establishment of a non-sexist paradigm.

In their criticism of Harding's approach which they claim uses 'sexism's weapons', Stanley and Wise (1983, 1993) argued that feminists should privilege subjectivity over objectivity, emotionality over rationality and experience over experiments. They argued that feminist claims to produce an alternative version of the truth have not made the necessary break with positivism and they proposed privileging subjective knowledge. One problem with this approach is that privileging subjective knowledge involves viewing reality as a matter of competing interpretations (an approach strongly associated with *postmodernism* – see Section 3.10 and **Box 7a**, Chapter Seven). This can become so removed from practical concerns that it undermines the value of social research. This is particularly problematic in social policy research. A more promising approach is to attack the binary thinking behind the subjective–objective, qualitative–quantitative dichotomy and acknowledge that no research can be wholly objective (Ramazanoglu, 2002). What feminists can do is to make their interpretations clear, and to see producing knowledge as problematic.

The growth of a number of different approaches to feminist research follows from a focus on women's experiences, on the need to acknowledge the role of the researcher, and, crucially, an understanding of the diversity of women's experiences. Lesbian research, postmodernist feminism, post-colonial feminist thought, research based on the experiences of disabled women, and many more, have all contributed to a view of feminist research as "a complex, diverse, and highly energized enterprise of which it can be said there is no single voice and no single voice can claim dominance" (Olesen, 2000, p 235). The distinctiveness of feminist methodology is the relationship between epistemology and feminist politics:"[f]eminist research is politically *for* women, feminist knowledge has some grounding in women's *experiences*, and in how it *feels* to live in unjust gendered relationships" (Ramazanoglu, 2002, p 16, emphasis in the original).

Question for discussion

• Can men undertake feminist research?

References

Dale, J. and Foster, P. (1986) *Feminists and state welfare*, London: Routledge.

Eichler, M. (1988) *Nonsexist research methods: A practical guide*, London: Routledge.

Finch, J. (1991) 'Feminist research and social policy', in M. Maclean and D. Groves (eds) *Women's issues in social policy*, London: Routledge, pp 194-212.

Harding, S. (ed) (1987) *Feminism and methodology*, Milton Keynes: Open University Press.

Hartsock, N. (1997) 'Comment on Hekman's "Truth and method: feminist standpoint theory revisited": truth or justice?', *Signs*, vol 22, no 21, pp 367-74.

Holland, J. and Ramazanoglu, C. (1994) 'Coming to conclusions: power and interpretation in researching young women's sexuality', in M. Maynard and J. Purvis (eds) *Researching women's lives from a feminist perspective*, London: Taylor and Francis, pp 125-48.

Holland, J., Ramazanoglu, C., Sharpe, S. and Thomson, R. (1998) *The male in the head: Young people, heterosexuality and power*, London: Tufnell Press.

Mies, M. (1981) 'Towards a methodology for feminist research', in G. Bowles and R. Duelli-Klein (eds) *Theories of women's studies II*, Berkeley, CA: University of California, pp 25-46.

Oakley, A. (1992) *Social support and motherhood: The natural history of a research project*, Oxford: Blackwell.

Olesen, V. (2000) 'Feminism and qualitative research at and into the millennium', in N. Denzin and Y. Lincoln (eds) *Handbook of qualitative research* (2nd edn), London: Sage Publications, pp 215-55.

Pascall, G. (1986) *Social policy: A feminist perspective*, London: Routledge.

Ramazanoglu, C. with Holland, J. (2002) *Feminist methodology: Challenges and choices*, London: Sage Publications.

Roberts, H. (ed) (1981) *Doing feminist research*, London: Routledge.

Stanley, L. (1990) 'Introduction', in L. Stanley (ed) *Feminist praxis: Research, theory and epistemology in feminist sociology*, London: Routledge, pp 3-19.

Stanley, L. and Wise, S. (1983) (revised edn 1993) *Breaking out: Feminist consciousness and feminist research*, London: Routledge.

Wilson, E. (1977) *Women and the welfare state*, London: Tavistock.

Further reading

Maynard, M. and Purvis, J. (eds) (1994) *Researching women's lives from a feminist perspective*, London: Taylor and Francis.

Ramazanoglu, C. with Holland, J. (2002) *Feminist methodology: Challenges and choices*, London: Sage Publications.

Ribbens, J. and Edwards, R. (1998) *Feminist dilemmas in qualitative research: Public knowledge and private lives*, London: Sage Publications.

3.6 User participatory research

Marian Barnes, *Professor of Social Research, University of Birmingham*

Other sections of this chapter discuss *how* research can be carried out. The focus of this section is on *who* undertakes it. First, a word about **terminology** and **scope**.

The term **user** is not accepted by all those who receive welfare services. For example, many recipients of mental health services prefer the term *survivor*. Many disabled people do not want to be defined by their relationship to welfare services. In other cases the term is simply inaccurate – people are not using services, but are directly affected by policy decisions – for example, residents in an area targeted by New Deal for Communities. The focus of this section is on the *involvement* of people who are or could be directly affected by welfare policy and practice in researching those policies or practices. This could include, for example, mental health service users carrying out research into the experiences of people subject to compulsion under the Mental Health Act (Barnes et al, 2000), or research into experiences of social exclusion carried out with local people in the areas concerned (Boeck and Ward, 2000). **Box 3d** provides an illustration of why and how young refugees can be involved in the research process.

Box 3d: Involving young people in policy research
Perpetua Kirby, *ex-Save the Children, now PK Research Consultancy Ltd, Hove*

Young people can take part in the many different stages of the research process and at each stage they can have varying levels of control about the decisions and action taken. In some instances young people play a large role in designing and implementing the research process (for example, writing questions, fieldwork and analysis), while in others they may be involved in just a few stages. The degree to which they are involved depends in part on the purpose of the research. Some projects may choose to involve young people to enable them to express their views and for their personal and political development. Whereas others emphasise traditional research approaches that are seen to be more objective. The decision about when and how much to involve young people requires consideration and balancing of the participation objectives and the rigorous requirements of traditional research (Dyson and Meagher, 2001).

Save the Children is committed to promoting young people's participation in decisions affecting their lives. As part of this work they recruited a group of young refugees (aged 16-21) to research the needs of young refugees and asylum seekers (HAYS, 1998). The group identified that they wanted to research educational support. They received research training and, supported by a researcher and a youth worker (himself a refugee), they designed and conducted interviews and focus groups with their peers. Researchers had to work hard to make the training and research process as enjoyable as possible. The young refugees were less interested and confident about undertaking some stages of the process, including the analysis and report writing, so workers took a lead in these tasks. It was considered more important for them to be informed and involved in making decisions than undertaking all the necessary research tasks (see Kirby et al, 2001).

In another study – an independent evaluation of a young refugee support project – the evaluators took a lead in designing and implementing all research stages (Kirby et al, 2004: forthcoming). Young people (and project workers) were involved in influencing decisions and taking action at some stages of the process. For example, the evaluators developed a short self-completion 'postcard' questionnaire for young people to complete (as objects of the research and sources of data). Around 10 young project users were asked to comment on the postcard and to help distribute them to other young refugees, including non-service users. The young fieldworkers received some initial training on how to ask and support others to complete the postcards. Towards the end of the two-year evaluation period, young people were invited to an analysis workshop with project staff and external agencies, to examine and help interpret the evaluation evidence. In this project, it was considered important to integrate young people's knowledge of their own needs, utilise their access to peers, test findings with them and ensure they had some ownership of the evaluation outcomes (for discussion on participatory evaluations with young people, see Kirby, 2002).

Question for discussion
- What criteria need to be considered when deciding how much to involve young people in research?

References
Dyson, A. and Meagher, N. (2001) 'Reflections on the case studies: towards a rationale for participation?', in J. Clark, A. Dyson, N. Meagher, E. Robson and M. Wootten (eds) *Young people as researchers: Possibilities, problems and politics*, Leicester: Youth Work Press.

HAYS (Horn of Africa Youth Scheme) (1998) *Let's spell it out: Peer research on the education support needs of young refugees and asylum seekers in Kensington and Chelsea*, London: Save the Children.

Kirby, P. (2002) *Measuring the magic? Evaluating and researching young people's participation in public decision making*, London: Carnegie Young People's Initiative.

Kirby, P., Pettit, B. and Simanowitz, A. (2004: forthcoming) *Young refugee project evaluation* (preliminary title), London: Lewisham NHS Primary Care Trust.

Kirby, P., HAYS young researchers, Wubner, K. and Lewis, M. (2001) 'The HAYS project', in J. Clark, A. Dyson, N. Meagher, E. Robson and M. Wootten (eds) *Young people as researchers: Possibilities, problems and politics*, Leicester: Youth Work Press, pp 11-21.

Further reading
Clark, J., Dyson, A., Meagher, N., Robson, E. and Wootten, M. (eds) (2001) *Young people as researchers: Possibilities, problems and politics*, Leicester: Youth Work Press.

France, A. (2000) *Youth researching youth: The triumph and success peer research project*, Leicester: Youth Work Press and Joseph Rowntree Foundation.

Kirby, P. (1999) *Involving young researchers: How to enable young people to design and conduct research*, York: York Publishing Services for the Joseph Rowntree Foundation.

Relevant organisations

Consumers in NHS Research Support Unit

Wessex House, Upper Market Street, Eastleigh, Hampshire, SO50 9FD

www.conres.co.uk

Institute for Development Studies, participation group

University of Sussex, Falmer, Brighton, East Sussex

www.ids.ac.uk/ids/particip/

Participatory research is one dimension of a shift in thinking – from notions of passive recipients of welfare to active subjects. Just as the practice of service delivery became opened up to challenge from service users during the 1980s and 1990s (for example, Barnes, 1997), so too did the practice of research. Users started to object to being the subject of research that they had no say in devising, in the same way that they objected to being the recipients of services that they had no say in designing. Gaining greater control over the research agenda became one aspect of the strategies developed by disabled people's and other user movements – not only to achieve change in services, but also a broader transformation in both lay and professional understanding of disablement, mental distress or living in poverty, and to achieve broadly based changes in people's lives (for example, Oliver, 1992; Faulkner, 1997; Beresford et al, 1999).

The challenge for researchers who were not also disabled, old, poor or in receipt of welfare services was to develop ways of researching with people, rather than on them (for example, Barnes, 1993; Priestley, 1999). An important aspect of that shift in focus is a preparedness to recognise and value knowledge and expertise deriving from direct experience, as well as to develop collaborative skills. Beyond a change in the relationship between researchers and service users in the context of any one research project, participatory research has involved changes in the way in which research is commissioned. Research funders, including government departments such as the Department of Health as well as independent funding agencies such as the Joseph Rowntree Foundation, now involve users in determining research priorities and research questions, and expect researchers to demonstrate how service users will take part in commissioned research (see also Chapter Six, Section 6.9).

User participatory research is based on a number of epistemological and political assumptions (Figure 3b).

Figure 3b: **Epistemological and political assumptions for user participatory research**

1. Knowledge is best generated *with* people (Reason, 1994).
2. 'Strong science' (Harding, 1991) necessitates looking at the world from different standpoints, particularly those of people normally excluded from powerful positions.
3. The aim of research is not solely to generate knowledge, but to achieve change – specifically change which will benefit users.
4. Claims to objectivity in research are both false and contribute to the oppression experienced by service users and disadvantaged citizens.
5. Taking part in the research process can be empowering in its own right (Fetterman et al, 1996).

Methodologically, participatory research does not presume any particular approach. Indeed, in the context of health services research there are examples of user involvement in the conduct of randomised controlled trials (RCTs). For example, women with breast cancer were involved in the design of an RCT of the use of hormone replacement therapy with women experiencing menopausal symptoms resulting from breast cancer treatment (quoted in Hanley et al, 2000). However, because of the commitment to understanding the subjective experience of those subject to welfare policy that underpins much research of this type, the majority of examples involve the use of qualitative methods. What *is* distinctive are the research relationships which are established. These involve collaboration at all stages: from defining research questions, designing and carrying out data collection, analysis and dissemination. The process is a dialogic one. At times researchers may be sharing their skills in questionnaire design with users, at other times researchers will be learning from users how best to negotiate access to people who are wary of researchers. In some cases access is only possible because service users are involved.

While participatory research does not prescribe research methods, there are a number of principles associated with this that have been expressed as guidance or good practice criteria. These emphasise the open and democratic relationships that typify such research. For example Hanley et al (2000) include the following:

• Avoid tokenism through involving more than one user on research committees.
• Be clear about the basis of people's involvement and agree how and what people want to offer.
• Spend time establishing and building relationships.

- Offer appropriate resources and support, including interpreters, signers and so on.
- Meet in users' venues.
- Think about different formats for working together.
- Set up a budget to meet expenses and payment to users.
- Consider the ethical implications for those taking part in the research.
- Ensure good communication and feedback to all those involved.

Question for discussion

- What would be the main differences between participatory and researcher-led approaches to a project that sought to investigate the needs of older people in danger of becoming isolated and socially excluded? How might you go about designing and conducting such a project?

References

Barnes, M. (1993) 'Introducing new stakeholders: user and researcher interests in evaluative research', *Policy & Politics*, vol 21, no 1, pp 47-58.

Barnes, M. (1997) *Care, communities and citizens*, Harlow: Addison Wesley Longman.

Barnes, M., Davis, A. and Tew, J. (2000) 'Valuing experience: users' experiences of compulsion under the Mental Health Act, 1983', *The Mental Health Review*, vol 5, no 3, pp 11-14.

Beresford, P., Green, D., Lister, R. and Woodard, R. (1999) *Poverty first hand: Poor people speak for themselves*, London: Child Poverty Action Group.

Boeck, T. and Ward, D. (2000) 'Social action research in practice: the Saffron Lane Project', in A.-L. Matthies, M. Jarvela and D. Ward (eds) *From social exclusion to participation: Explorations across three European cities*, Finland: Department of Social Sciences and Philosophy, University of Jyväskylä.

Faulkner, A. (1997) *Knowing our own minds: A survey of how people in emotional distress take control of their lives*, London: The Mental Health Foundation.

Fetterman, D.M., Kaftarian, S.J. and Wandersman, A. (eds) (1996) *Empowerment evaluation: Knowledge and tools for self-assessment and accountability*, Thousand Oaks, CA: Sage Publications.

Hanley, B., Bradburn, J., Gorin, S., Barnes, M., Evans, C., Goodare, H., Kelson, M., Kent, A., Oliver, S. and Wallcraft, J. (2000) *Involving consumers in research and development in the NHS: Briefing notes for researchers*, Winchester: Consumers in NHS Research Support Unit, Help for Health Trust.

Harding, S. (1991) *Whose sciences? Whose knowledge? Thinking from women's lives*, Milton Keynes: Open University Press.

Oliver, M. (1992) 'Changing the social relations of research production', *Disability, Handicap and Society*, vol 7, no 2, pp 101-15.

Priestley, M. (1999) *Disability politics and community care*, London: Jessica Kingsley Publishers.

Reason, P. (ed) (1994) *Participation in human inquiry*, London: Sage publications.

Further reading

Barnes, C. and Mercer, G. (eds) (1997) *Doing disability research*, Leeds: The Disability Press.

Kemshall, H. and Littlechild, R. (eds) (2000) *User involvement and participation in social care: Research informing practice*, London: Jessica Kingsley Publishers.

Website resources

Disability Research Unit: www.leeds.ac.uk/disability-studies/

Joseph Rowntree Foundation [strongly committed to funding participatory research]: www.jrf.org.uk

Mental Health Foundation 'Strategies for Living' project [search on 'Strategies for Living']: www.mentalhealth.org.uk

Norah Fry Research Centre [research involving people with learning difficulties]: www.bris.ac.uk/Depts/NorahFry/

SURESearch [mental health service user researchers linked with Birmingham University]: www.wmpmh.org.uk/wmpmembers/index.htm and search for 'SURESearch'

Folk.us [consumers and researchers who meet at Exeter University]: http:// latis.ex.ac.uk/folk.us/findex.htm

3.7 The theory and practice of action research

Peter Reason, *Professor of Action Research Practice and Director of the Centre for Action Research in Professional Practice, and* Kate Louise McArdle, *Lecturer in Organisational Behaviour, both at the School of Management, University of Bath*

Action research has a long history, going back to social scientists' attempts to help solve practical problems in wartime situations in both Europe and America. While many trace its origins to the work of Kurt Lewin in the 1940s to design social experiments in natural settings, and who is credited with the phrase "Nothing is as practical as a good theory", action research practice draws on a wide field of influence, including critical thinking (Kemmis, 2001), liberationist thought (Freire, 1970), pragmatism (Greenwood and Levin, 1998) and feminism (Stanley and Wise, 1983; Maguire, 2001). While many of the original forms of action research espoused participation, power was often held tightly by researchers. However, more recent developments place emphasis on a full integration of action and reflection and on increased collaboration between all those involved in the inquiry project, so that the knowledge developed in the inquiry process is directly relevant to the issues being studied. Thus, action research is conducted *by*, *with* and *for* people, rather than as research *on* people.

It is important to understand action research as an *orientation to inquiry* rather than as a methodology. Thus, a recent text describes action research as:

> ... a participatory, democratic process concerned with developing practical knowing in the pursuit of worthwhile human purposes, grounded in a participatory worldview.... It seeks to bring together action and reflection, theory and practice, in participation with others, in the pursuit of practical solutions to issues of pressing concern to people, and more generally the flourishing of individual persons and their communities. (Reason and Bradbury, 2001, p 1)

We can see how this 'bringing together' can occur by considering *three strategies of inquiry* which are highly interdependent. *Good action research will strive to stimulate inquiry at each of these levels and to create connections between levels*:

- *First-person research practices* address the ability of individual researchers to foster an inquiring approach to their own lives, to act awarely and choicefully, and to assess effects in the outside world while acting. First-person inquiry skills are essential for those who would provide leadership in any social enterprise.
- *Second-person action research/practices*, such as cooperative inquiry, address our ability to inquire face-to-face with others into issues of mutual concern, usually in small groups. In *cooperative inquiry* a small group of peers work together in cycles of action and reflection to develop both understanding and practice in a matter of mutual concern.
- *Third-person research/practice* includes a range of practices which draw together the views of large groups of people and create a wider community of inquiry involving people who cannot be known to each other face-to-face. Under this heading we include, for example, practices that 'network' small inquiry groups, the range of large-scale dialogue and 'whole system' conference designs, and the 'learning history' approach.

Action research typically involves creating spaces in which participants engage together in cycles of action and critical reflection. However, this basic process has been elaborated in different ways in different schools of practice.

Organisational change and work research. There is a long-standing tradition of action research in organisational settings that aims to contribute both to more effective work practices and better understanding of the processes of organisational change. This approach draws on a variety of forms of information gathering, feedback to organisation members, leading to problem-solving dialogue. This tradition is well represented in recent publications such as Toulmin and Gustavsen (1996), Greenwood and Levin (1998) and Coghlan and Brannick (2001).

Cooperative inquiry. A cooperative inquiry group consists of a group of people who share a common concern for developing understanding and practice in a specific personal, professional or social arena. All are both *co-researchers*, whose thinking and decision making contributes to generating ideas, designing and managing the project, and drawing conclusions from the experience; and also *co-subjects*, participating in the activity that is being researched. A typical inquiry group will consist of between six and twenty people. As co-researchers they participate in the thinking that goes into the research – framing the questions to be explored, agreeing on the methods to be employed, and together making sense of their experiences. As co-subjects they participate in the action being studied. The co-researchers engage in cycles of action and reflection: in the action phases they experiment with new forms of personal or professional practice; in the reflection phase they reflect on their experience critically, learn from their successes and failures, and develop theoretical perspectives which inform their work in the next action phase. Cooperative inquiry groups thus cycle between and integrate four forms of knowing: experiential, presentational, propositional and practical (Heron, 1996; Heron and Reason, 2001).

Action science and action inquiry. Much attention has been given by action researchers to the relationship between the theories we hold about our practices and what we actually do: to put it colloquially, do we 'walk our talk'? Action science and action inquiry are related disciplines that offer methods for inquiring into and developing congruence between our purposes, our theories and frames, our behaviour and our impact in the world. These practices can be applied at individual, small group and at organisational level. Their overall aim is to bring inquiry and action together in more and more moments of everyday life, to see inquiry as a 'way of life' (Friedman, 2001; Marshall, 2001; Torbert, 2001).

Learning history is a process of recording the lived experience of those in an action research or learning situation in which researchers work collaboratively with those involved to agree the scope and focus of the history, identify key questions, gather information through an iterative reflective interview process, distil this information into a form which the organisation or community can 'hear' and facilitate dialogue with organisation members to explore the accuracy, implications and practical outcomes that the work suggests (Roth and Kleiner, 1998).

Appreciative inquiry. Practitioners of appreciative inquiry argue that action research has been limited by its romance with critique at the expense of appreciation. To the extent that action research maintains a problem-oriented view of the world it diminishes the capacity of researchers and practitioners to produce innovative theory capable of inspiring the imagination, commitment and passionate dialogue required for the consensual reordering of social conduct. If we devote our attention to what is wrong with organisations and communities, we lose the ability to see and understand what gives life to organisations and to discover ways to sustain and enhance that life-giving potential. Appreciative inquiry therefore begins with the unconditional positive question that guides inquiry agendas and focuses attention towards the most life giving, life-sustaining aspects of organisational existence (Ludema et al, 2001).

Whole systems inquiry. Large group interventions or processes are events designed to engage representatives of an entire system, whether it be an organisation or a community, in thinking through and planning change (for descriptions see Bunker and Alban, 1997). What distinguishes them from other large meetings is that the process is managed to allow all participants an opportunity to engage actively in the planning (Martin, 2001). Rather than aim at a single outcome, in dialogue conference design (Gustavsen, 2001), and whole system designs (Pratt et al, 1999), the role of the researchers is to create the conditions for democratic dialogue among participants.

Participative action research. This term is usually used to refer to action research strategies which grew out of the liberationist ideas of Paulo Freire (1970) and others in countries of the South. Participatory action research (PAR) is explicitly political, aiming to restore to oppressed peoples the ability to create knowledge and practice in their own interests and as such has a double objective. One aim is to produce knowledge and action directly useful to a group of people – through research, through adult education and through socio-political action. The second aim is to empower people at a second and deeper level through the process of constructing and using their own knowledge: they 'see through' the ways in which the establishment monopolises the production and use of knowledge for the benefit of its members.

In keeping with the emphasis of PAR on inquiry as empowerment, specific research methodologies take second place to the emergent processes of collaboration and dialogue that empower, motivate and increase self-esteem, and develop community solidarity. Community meetings and events of various kinds are an important part of PAR, serving to identify issues; to reclaim a sense of community and emphasise the potential for liberation; and to make sense of information collected (Fals Borda and Rahman, 1991; Selener, 1997).

In **Box 3e** we provide an example of action research that integrates the three strategies and several of the methodological approaches discussed above.

By way of summary, we would emphasise that action research is not a methodology but an orientation that shapes methodological practices. There are no right answers, rather lots of choices, and quality of inquiry is shaped by the appropriateness of these choices and the way they are made.

Question for discussion

- What strategies are open to action researchers that will promote the participation in the research process of those whom action research is supposed to be for?

References

Bunker, B. and Alban, B. (1997) *Large group interventions: Engaging the whole system for rapid change*, San Francisco, CA: Jossey-Bass.

Coghlan, D. and Brannick, T. (2001) *Doing action research in your own organization*, London: Sage Publications.

Fals Borda, O. and Rahman, M.A. (eds) (1991) *Action and knowledge: Breaking the monopoly with participatory action research*, New York, NY: Intermediate Technology Publications/Apex Press.

Freire, P. (1970) *Pedagogy of the oppressed*, New York, NY: Herder and Herder.

Friedman, V.J. (2001) 'Action science: creating communities of inquiry in communities of practice', in P. Reason and H. Bradbury (eds) *Handbook of action research: Participative inquiry and practice*, London: Sage Publications, pp 159-70.

Greenwood, D.J. and Levin, M. (1998) *Introduction to action research: Social research for social change*, Thousand Oaks, CA: Sage Publications.

Gustavsen, B. (2001) 'Theory and practice: the mediating discourse', in P. Reason and H. Bradbury (eds) *Handbook of action research: Participative inquiry and practice*, London: Sage Publications, pp 17-26.

Heron, J. (1996) *Co-operative inquiry: Research into the human condition*, London: Sage Publications.

Heron, J. and Reason, P. (2001) 'The practice of co-operative inquiry: research with rather than on people', in P. Reason and H. Bradbury (eds) *Handbook of action research: Participative inquiry and practice*, London: Sage Publications, pp 179-88.

Kemmis, S. (2001) 'Exploring the relevance of critical theory for action research: emancipatory action research in the footsteps of Jürgen Habermas', in P. Reason and H. Bradbury (eds) *Handbook of action research: Participative inquiry and practice*, London: Sage Publications, pp 91-102.

Ludema, J.D., Cooperrider, D.L. and Barrett, F.J. (2001) 'Appreciative inquiry: The power of the unconditional positive question', in P. Reason and H. Bradbury (eds) *Handbook of action research: Participative inquiry and practice*, London: Sage Publications, pp 189-99.

Maguire, P. (2001) 'Uneven ground: feminisms and action research', in P. Reason and H. Bradbury (eds) *Handbook of action research: Participative inquiry and practice*, London: Sage Publications, pp 59-69.

Marshall, J. (2001) 'Self-reflective inquiry practices', in P. Reason and H. Bradbury (eds) *Handbook of action research: Participative inquiry and practice*, London: Sage Publications, pp 433-9.

Martin, A.W. (2001) 'Large-group processes as action research', in P. Reason and H. Bradbury (eds) *Handbook of action research: Participative inquiry and practice*, London: Sage Publications, pp 200-8.

Pratt, J., Gordon, P. and Plamping, D. (1999) *Working whole systems: Putting theory into practice in organizations*, London: King's Fund.

Reason, P. and Bradbury, H. (2001) 'Inquiry and participation in search of a world worthy of human aspiration', in P. Reason and H. Bradbury (eds) *Handbook of action research: Participative inquiry and practice*, London: Sage Publications, pp 1-14.

Roth, G.L. and Kleiner, A. (1998) 'Developing organizational memory through learning histories: organizational dynamics', *Organizational Dynamics*, vol 27, no 2, pp 43-61.

Selener, D. (1997) *Participatory action research and social change*, Cornell, NY: Cornell Participatory Action Research Network, Cornell University.

Stanley, L. and Wise, S. (1983) *Breaking out. Feminist consciousness and feminist research*, London: Routledge Kegan Paul.

Torbert, W.R. (2001) 'The practice of action inquiry', in P. Reason and H. Bradbury (eds) *The handbook of action research: Participative inquiry and practice*, London: Sage Publications, pp 250-60.

Toulmin, S. and Gustavsen, B. (1996) *Beyond theory: Changing organizations through participation*, Amsterdam: John Benjamins.

Further reading

Reason, P. and Bradbury, H. (eds) (2001) *The handbook of action research: Participative inquiry and practice*, London: Sage Publications.

Relevant organisations

Centre for Action Research in Professional Practice
School of Management, University of Bath, Bath BA2 7AY
www.bath.ac.uk/carpp

Box 3e: The practice of action research: an example

Peter Reason, *Professor of Action Research Practice and Director of the Centre for Action Research in Professional Practice,* and Kate Louise McArdle, *Lecturer in Organisational Behaviour, both at the School of Management, University of Bath*

An inquiry that integrates the three strategies and several of the methodological approaches discussed in Section 3.7 may be found in the research conducted by a group of Young Women in Management (YoWiM), initiated by Kate Louise McArdle as part of her PhD research (McArdle, in preparation). The YoWiM group was established as a cooperative inquiry, and was thus originally grounded in second-person inquiry practices (see Section 3.7), meeting together every four weeks for a half-day session to share their stories and ideas from a four-week action phase between meetings. For the YoWiM group one of the most valuable inquiry practices, which developed over the life of the group, was 'really listening' to each other (as something different from 'waiting to speak'), thus opening a space for new conversations about the experience of being young women in management. This helped them become aware of how their voices were largely absent in the organisation. Members brought their observations and concerns to the group, told stories of their experiences, and reported back the outcomes of action experiments that they undertook away from the group, and were encouraged and helped in developing new ways of responding to their experiences. Most important was the creation of a critical perspective, so that problems experienced by group members were no longer always 'their fault' but could be seen as part of the culture of a masculine-oriented organisation requiring a creative response.

Between meetings, the group continued to represent a supportive space that supported the members in their first-person inquiring practice. They paid increasing attention to their own behaviour and to that of their colleagues and managers, paid more attention to what was going on from the perspective of young women, and allowed themselves time to think through their role alone. They experimented with new behaviours, for example, finding ways of speaking out more effectively in the face of patronising and bullying behaviour on the part of male managers, and finding new value in more relational forms of behaviour.

As initiating facilitator of the group – and doing this for the first time (McArdle, 2001) – Kate McArdle paid particular attention to her own interventions in the group. In particular, she worked to model inquiring behaviour, to make her own action choices transparent to the group, and thus use her own inquiry practice to support and develop the inquiring practices of other group members. She kept careful records of her experience, in journals, e-mail correspondences, and the transcripts of the group sessions, and reviewed her behaviour 'off-line' (Rudolph et al, 2001) with colleagues and her PhD supervisor (Peter Reason).

We can see from this how first- and second-person inquiry practices become interdependent: as group members develop inquiring behaviour within the group context, they are more able to apply this working alone in their work situations; and as this first-person practice develops, the quality of the narrative brought back to the second-person forum of the inquiry group increases.

In the YoWiM group, the first- and second-person skills nurtured and developed in this way enable more engaged third person practice. The YoWiM group together held a half-day third-person inquiry with over 50 people, including other young women in the organisation and senior women in the company, to enable themselves and others to gain further understanding of issues of interest to women in the company. This may sound like nothing new – workshops happen all the time in organisations! However, because they had developed a second-person community of inquiry over a 10-month period, YoWiM group members were able to create and hold a wider *inquiring space*. They were careful not to recreate the hierarchy that existed 'in normal workshops' in the company, in which people were rewarded for 'knowing the right answers', but through quite simple means, such as arranging chairs in a circle without tables, sharing some of their own experience of inquiry, inviting other young women to tell their stories and really listen to each other, helping them to explore their experience; they countered the prevailing organisational culture and created a quite unusual experience for their peers.

In essence for the YoWiM group, third-person inquiry meant understanding when their moment had arrived, when they had gained sufficient confidence in themselves and in each other to be able to take a step away from each other, but with each other, to engage a bigger group of people in exploring issues that they had about a particular topic, in new ways. The depth of meaning created in first- and second-person inquiry over time cannot be recreated in a third-person inquiry of a one-off nature. However, the YoWiM experience shows how giving life to a different kind of fertile space in which others meet, often for the first time, to talk about things that *really matter to them*, sharpened the political edge of first- and second-person inquiry. In this sense, as Martin puts it, "the message sent by the event may have much more significance than the event itself" (Martin, 2001). Running a third-person inquiry of this nature took the YoWiM group into a cycle of inquiry about 'How were we/was I able to be in this wider space we created?'. This again highlights the dynamic and continually emergent relationship between first-, second- and third-person inquiry practices.

References

McArdle, K.L. (2001) 'Establishing a co-operative inquiry group: the perspective of a 'first-time' inquirer', *Systemic Practice and Action Research*, vol 15, no 3, pp 177-89.

McArdle, K.L. (in preparation) 'In-powering spaces: A co-operative inquiry with young women in management', unpublished PhD, Bath: University of Bath.

Martin, A.W. (2001) 'Large-group processes as action research', in P. Reason and H. Bradbury (eds) *Handbook of action research: Participative inquiry and practice*, London: Sage Publications, pp 200-8.

Rudolph, J.W., Taylor, S.S. and Foldy, E.G. (2001) 'Collaborative off-line reflection: a way to develop skill in action science and action inquiry', in P. Reason and H. Bradbury (eds) *Handbook of action research: Participative inquiry and practice*, London: Sage Publications, pp 405-12.

3.8 Evaluation research

Colin Robson, *Emeritus Professor, School of Human and Health Sciences, University of Huddersfield*

To state the obvious, evaluation research is both evaluation and research. The term is useful because, while evaluation is widespread in modern societies, much of what goes on is of dubious quality and unworthy of being labelled research. Evaluation is typically defined as *an attempt to assess the value or worth of something*. Both public services, and private businesses and other concerns, now work in a climate of accountability, efficiency, value for money, and so on, where managers and others press (or are pressed) towards some form of evaluation.

The argument for evaluation *research* is that, by following the canons of social science research, as discussed in this volume, you are likely to produce more trustworthy findings than you would get from simple informal evaluations.

Some academic researchers are very wary of evaluation research. They see a tension between the traditional tasks of research of describing, explaining and understanding, and evaluating, which focuses on assessing value. Also, evaluation research almost always has a clear political dimension. As Greene (1994, p 531) puts it, evaluation "is integrally intertwined with political decision-making about societal priorities, resource allocation, and power". However, there is increasing recognition that both values (including the values of the researcher) and political considerations permeate all social and policy research (see Chapter One, Section 1.4). Evaluation research is simply an area where they are more obviously inescapable, and where the conventions and procedures of formal research provide particularly valuable checks and balances (see also **Box 1g**, Chapter one). Murtagh (2001) provides a useful brief review of the 'politics and practice of urban policy evaluation'. He discusses the issues involved in carrying out evaluation research in this context, providing a case study of evaluation of urban policy in Derry/Londonderry.

Newcomers to evaluation commonly assume that its purpose is self-evident. Typically, is the policy (or programme, service, intervention innovation or whatever – the things which can form the focus of an evaluation are legion) effective in achieving its planned goals? A concern for *outcomes* is important, and not solely because this may well be top of the agenda for politicians and other paymasters. However, an evaluation can legitimately have other purposes, including finding out:

- if client needs are met (when a policy is in operation, or establishing currently unmet needs at an earlier stage);
- how a policy is operating (what actually happens; is it operating as planned or envisaged?);
- how it might be improved (for example, in meeting needs, or in effectiveness, or in efficiency);
- how the costs involved compare with the benefits that it provides (is it more or less efficient than possible alternatives?);
- why is it working (or not working)?

More than one purpose may be covered, with improvement almost always being of interest even if not stated as the main purpose. Murtagh's (2001) example, referred to above, includes two very different approaches to evaluation, stressing different purposes. He describes so-called *instrumental styles* which are primarily concerned with *performance measures* and *indicators of efficiency* in public spending in urban regeneration policy. *Interpretative styles* focus much more on the *processes* involved, exploring power relationships and the impact of policy on community competencies and self-learning.

Evaluation research is often commissioned research. Those commissioning the study may well not know what they need. A not uncommon request is to 'design a questionnaire to …'. This is an example of the 'method of data collection' cart being put before the 'research design' horse. It calls for sensitive exploration by the researcher. What is going to be most useful for the commissioner of research? Do they need to have hard outcome evidence by the end of the year? Or is there a suspicion that things might not be working out as envisaged and the concern should be mainly on what is happening in practice? However, unintended consequences of social interventions are found widely, and policy makers have been known to fight shy of funding an evaluation which might reveal some unpleasant truths. Evaluation research calls for well-developed personal, social and communicative skills in the researcher, to navigate these tricky waters (Robson, 2002, p 541).

Murtagh's (2001) study was part of an integrated system for establishing baselines, monitoring and evaluating, built into urban regeneration programmes funded by government and European Union initiatives. It was a large multi-level study carried out by external evaluators. Evaluations can, of course, also be small-scale when they are much more likely to be carried out by 'insiders' (Robson, 2000).

Broadly speaking, the fact that a study is an evaluation neither rules in nor rules out particular research designs or methods of collecting data. This is much more a question of the type of research question to which one is seeking answers (Robson, 2002, p 79), and of the purpose of the evaluation. Murtagh incorporates an impressive range of methods using both quantitative and qualitative methodologies. His two main approaches are 'community audit' and 'participatory action research'. The former was used primarily to record city-wide shifts in attitudes and behaviour using Likert scaling techniques (see Chapter Four, Section 4.2). The latter sought to examine the way in which groups benefiting from urban policy changed as a result of their participation. One finding was that the strict audit requirement arising from previous abuses of funding called for "a regime of business plans, feasibility studies, economic appraisals, and ultimately a skills base that deprived communities simply do not possess" (Murtagh, 2001, p 231). Hence, while groups felt that they had useful and meaningful inputs into the design of policy, they struggled when attempting to get funding for projects.

The study illustrates the point that any approach has its strengths and limitations. Murtagh concludes that "by focusing on local actors in [community audit] valid but silent interests can be missed and issues about ownership and control over action research can cause problems in the interpretation and use of data. However, combining a number of mutually supporting techniques within a single evaluation design might meet both the expectations of funders and funded" (2001, p 231).

An important outcome of the evaluation is a report. While sharing many characteristics with research reports in general, evaluation reports often differ in that they include *recommendations* for action arising from the findings. It is crucial that the report communicates with the intended audience(s). Different reports may be needed for different audiences (for example, funders or sponsors, professionals, clients, and so on) and may need to be very different in style and length. A one-page 'executive summary' is almost always useful (see also Chapter Seven, Section 7.4, for further discussion about tailoring outputs for different audiences).

Question for discussion

• How does evaluation research differ from other types of research?

References

Greene, J.C. (1994) 'Qualitative program evaluation: practice and promise', in N.K. Denzin and Y.S. Lincoln (eds) *Handbook of qualitative research*, Thousand Oaks, CA: Sage Publications, pp 530-44.

Murtagh, B. (2001) 'The politics and practice of urban policy evaluation', *Community Development Journal*, vol 36, pp 223-33.

Robson, C. (2000) *Small-scale evaluation: Principles and practice*, London: Sage Publications.

Robson, C. (2002) *Real world research: A resource for social scientists and practitioner-researchers* (2nd edn), Oxford: Blackwell.

Further reading

Robson, C. (2000) *Small-scale evaluation: Principles and practice*, London: Sage Publications.

Weiss, C.H. (1998) *Evaluation: Methods for studying programs and policies* (2nd edn), Upper Saddle River, NJ: Prentice-Hall.

Relevant organisations

American Evaluation Association
16 Sconticut Neck Road #290, Fairhaven, MA 02719, USA
http://trochim.human.cornell.edu/kb/evaluation.htm
European Evaluation Society
c/o Cour des Comptes, Rue de la Regence 2, 1000 Bruxelles, Belgium
www.europeanevaluation.org

3.9 Comparative research methods

Emma Carmel, *Lecturer in Social Policy, University of Bath*

Comparison is part of the way in which we think about our everyday lives as well as part of social policy research generally. **Comparison in social research** involves the identification of similarities and differences between two or more socio-economic or political phenomena. Usually the intention is also to explain and evaluate these similarities and differences as part of the comparison. **Comparative social research** (sometimes called cross-national research) refers to something more specific. Here the comparison is between socio-economic and political phenomena in two or more countries.

There are several reasons why we compare different countries, involving increasing levels of complexity from description, to classification, to explanation and theory generation and testing (Landman, 2002). The first aim is to describe the characteristics of phenomena in other countries, which we place side-by-side to implicitly compare them. To increase the value of this research, criteria can be adopted to identify similarities and differences, for example, by structuring descriptions in the same way for all countries being compared (Ginsburg, 1992).

This leads to the second aim, which is to classify welfare systems or policies. Classifications enable us to simplify the complexity and detail of cases to identify the most important similarities and differences. This information facilitates the 'benchmarking' of policies against those of other countries to analyse how they meet policy goals.

The third aim is to explain why these similarities and differences exist between the cases being investigated. Then it is possible to 'learn lessons' to evaluate why policies and institutions might work in some countries and not others. However, very different factors might be important in explaining apparently similar results in two countries. In order to make sense of this complexity, the final aim of comparative social research is to generate and/or test theories, providing generalised explanations of similarities and differences that apply to cases beyond those in a particular study.

The main methodological problem that arises in comparative social research is how to ensure comparability, or whether the research compares 'like with like'. The comparability problem emerges at several stages in research. First, when choosing which and how many cases to study. Second, when conceptualising the phenomena to be compared, and third, when collecting and analysing data. **Box 3f** illustrates the difficulties that can arise in comparative *poverty* research.

Box 3f: Comparative research on poverty
Jonathan Bradshaw, *Professor of Social Policy, University of York*

Since the 1990s, our capacity to analyse poverty comparatively has been greatly enhanced by the availability of new data. Thus, the Luxembourg Income Study (LIS) has included more countries, more sweeps and become the vehicle for very detailed comparative analysis of child poverty (UNICEF, 2000). The Organisation for Economic Co-operation and Development (OECD) (Oxley et al, 1999) have recently accumulated datasets for 16 countries and undertaken a detailed analysis of child poverty rates and trends over time. At last, the results of the European Community Household Panel Survey (ECHP) (European Commission, 2002) are emerging more quickly, with the promise that this could become a rich source of comparative analysis within the EU.

However, there are a number of problems:

* With the exception of the ECHP, poverty in these datasets is defined as an arbitrary point on the general distribution of income. Eurostat has recently adopted a threshold of 60% of equivalent median income (Atkinson et al, 2002).
* Most analysis has settled for using the modified OECD equivalence scale that is relatively more generous to small households and thus pensioner households as against families with children. The choice of equivalence scale influences the composition of the poor.
* Income is really only an indirect indicator of poverty and there is a dearth of comparative data using more direct measures (although the ECHP contains some relevant questions). Income does not take into account variations between countries in, for example, prices, domestic production or the value of free or subsidised services that might mitigate a low income. In short, income poverty is only a partial representation of deprivation, social exclusion, want or need.
* The results are sensitive to the general shape of the income distribution. Thus, UNICEF (2000) found that Slovakia and the Czech Republic had the lowest proportions (out of 25 countries) of children living in households with income below 50% of the median. But using the US official poverty line Slovakia had the second highest child poverty rate and the Czech Republic the fifth highest out of 25 countries.
* The results are sensitive to income 'lumping' at points of the distribution where large numbers of households are receiving the (same) minimum income.
* They fail to take account of the distribution of income within families – especially problematic for those (southern EU) countries with significant minorities of people living in multi-family households.

- Most analyses report poverty rates, not poverty gaps – how far below the poverty line people are.
- The cross-sectional datasets do not allow an analysis of how often or how long people are in poverty, although some comparative longitudinal results are beginning to emerge (Bradbury et al, 2001).

Perhaps the most important problem is that because poverty estimates are based on survey data these estimates take time to emerge – in 2002 researchers are working on the LIS data for circa 1995, the OECD data is 1993-95 and the latest published ECHP analysis of poverty is for the 1998 sweep (1997 income data).

Question for discussion
- What are the key problems in making comparisons of poverty between different countries?

References

Atkinson, T., Cantillon, B., Marlier, E. and Nolan, B. (2002) *Social indicators: The EU and social inclusion*, Oxford: Oxford University Press.

Bradbury, B., Jenkins, S.P. and Micklewright, J. (eds) (2001) *The dynamics of child poverty in industrialised countries*, Cambridge: Cambridge University Press.

European Commission (2002) *Joint report on social inclusion, employment and social affairs*, Luxembourg: European Community.

Oxley, H., Dang, T., Forster, M. and Pellizzari, M. (2001) 'Income inequalities and poverty among children and households with children in selected OECD countries', in K. Vleminckx and T. Smeeding (eds) *Child well-being, child poverty and child policy in modern nations*, Bristol: The Policy Press.

UNICEF (2000) *A league table of child poverty in rich nations*, Innocenti Report Card 1, Florence: UNICEF.

Further reading

Atkinson, T., Cantillon, B., Marlier, E. and Nolan, B. (2002) *Social indicators: The EU and social inclusion*, Oxford: Oxford University Press.

Vleminckx, K. and Smeeding, T. (eds) (2001) *Child well-being, child poverty and child policy in modern nations*, Bristol: The Policy Press.

Website resources

Child statistics:
   http://childstats.gov/intnllinks.asp?field=Subject1&value=Economic+Security
Eurostat: http://europa.eu.int/comm/eurostat/
Luxembourg Income Study (LIS): www.lisproject.org/keyfigures.htm

Office of Economic Co-operation and Development (OECD): www.oecd.org/
  home/
United Nations Children Fund (UNICEF): http://unicef-icdc.org

First, how do we decide what is a case, or the unit of analysis? Conventionally comparative social policy compares countries at the national level, but it might be more appropriate for the research to compare cities or regions in different countries (Schunk, 1996). The role of international organisations such as the European Union and the International Monetary Fund means that policies are not only made at national level. This requires the researcher to distinguish between local, regional, national and international policies and contexts (Kennett, 2001).

It is also necessary to decide whether to study a few ('small-N') or many ('large-N') cases (Peters, 1998, pp 58-78). If interested in detail and context, practical and resource issues usually dictate a *small-N* study, to focus on the nuances of the cases at hand. These studies often use *qualitative* research methods. Small-N studies are useful for generating theory that can be applied more generally later, and they can focus on subtle differences in experience and meaning that are otherwise difficult to capture. In small-N studies, however, the choice of cases is necessarily restricted. Comparing only cases that are similar might lead to the exaggeration of differences between them. If different cases are compared, it is possible that they will be too different to compare like with like. *Large-N* studies facilitate the study of a wide range and variety of countries. These studies are usually *quantitative* and are best-suited to searching for patterns in policies and outcomes, and for classifying a wide range of cases. Even in these studies, however, there may be problems of comparability between cases.

An important way to overcome comparability problems arising from the choice of cases is to select and apply concepts very carefully. When conceptualising the phenomenon to be analysed, it is necessary to ensure that the concepts capture its meaning in all the cases. The concepts must 'travel' from one country or language to another, without losing their meaning (Rose, 1991), so that they are focused enough to be precise, but general enough to be applied in different contexts (Sartori, 1974).

However, sometimes there is no way to translate a concept from one language to another, or the direct translation may be a 'false friend', and not mean the same thing in the second language as it does in the first (Mangen, 1999, pp 111-13). This is especially important for qualitative research, where the explication of meaning and experience expressed through language is one of its main benefits. It has been argued that this problem can be overcome by turning it to an advantage, so that a qualitative approach can explore the different meaning of concepts, such as 'care', or 'welfare', in different countries (Ferrari,

1990; Carmel, 1999). In this case, the concepts become the object of comparison, and a way to understand how countries' welfare systems have developed particular understandings of what constitutes social policy.

In quantitative comparative research, there is little scope for this exploratory approach, but variety in language and concepts remain important obstacles to clear research. One solution is to identify 'functional equivalence', where an institution or policy might be called different things in different countries, yet refer to broadly equivalent institutions or policies (that is, functions). This procedure creates comparability, although it can be used to make institutions appear the same when they are not (Dogan and Pelassey, 1990, p 37).

The final problem of comparability concerns data analysis. Regarding quantitative data, the main distinction is between harmonised and standardised data. **Harmonised data** are data which have been collected for particular purposes, and which are afterwards adjusted so that as far as possible the variables in different datasets measure the same thing – such as the number of hours that constitute part-time employment in all the countries. However, there are differences in measurement and calculation across countries and data cannot always be harmonised post hoc. This data must be analysed and read with caution to avoid drawing false conclusions about comparability. The alternative approach is to use **standardised data**, which are collected by using a common questionnaire in a range of countries. Standardised data can also be created by asking national experts to complete questionnaires on their respective countries using a common format, or formulae for the calculation of benefits and services for a 'model' person or family. Standardised data ensure a much greater degree of comparability, but problems of translation and meaning still arise in the questionnaire design, and these kinds of data are much less available than harmonised data.

For qualitative comparativists, language also remains an issue for data collection. As language and meaning is central to qualitative research, the process of translation must be part of the process of interpreting data. This is because translating interview or documentary data before starting the data analysis could result in the researcher losing important subtleties of meaning. As part of this process it is also especially important to be familiar with the socio-political and institutional contexts of the research (Chamberlayne and King, 1996). **Box 3g** illustrates some of the issues confronting the lone researcher wanting to study social policy in Sweden. Comparative research can also be conducted using national 'experts' from each country who collaborate as a cross-national team. Thus, each researcher brings to the investigation specific cultural knowledge that can enhance the overall findings.

Box 3g: Researching social policy in Sweden

Arthur Gould, *Reader in Swedish Social Policy, Loughborough University*

The comparativist is by definition interested in more than one country. Within the constraints of time and resources, equal attention should be given to each of the countries under consideration. Some of us prefer to examine one country in greater depth, exploring the social, economic and political context in which a specific set of policies has emerged. Such material contributes to our understanding of societies other than our own. The original researcher may have made no attempt to compare but others will do so explicitly or implicitly. To read about another welfare system automatically requires that we make some comparison with our own or others with which we are familiar. Although some of my work has been comparative, most of it has been about one country – Sweden. While of course there are many Swedes who have something useful to say about the country they live in, an outsider's view adds a different perspective.

In spite of a degree of retrenchment in recent years, Sweden remains the best example of a *Social Democratic* welfare state. There is much to learn from its policies, institutions and culture – now and historically. My approach to research in Sweden has been constrained by two important factors – I don't live there and I have preferred working alone to collaboration. In consequence, it has been necessary to seek funding which would enable me to visit Sweden for a few weeks at a time to carry out small-scale qualitative projects. These projects have normally included three elements: a search for published material, interviews with policy actors and interviews with welfare clients or beneficiaries. This triangulated approach has two principal advantages. Each element may reveal insights not revealed by the others; and each element acts as a check upon the others.

The search for published material is made easier by the fact that Sweden is a well-organised society in which bureaucratic records of all kinds are scrupulously kept and stored. Stockholm in particular has a number of local, national and academic libraries. Every agency that deals with a social issue – whether it be drugs, disability, unemployment or sexuality – will have a comprehensive library of its own, which visitors can ask to use. The *Riksdag* (parliament) has a complete record of government and parliamentary proceedings which make it possible to follow the progress of a specific social policy. A *Central Archive* also exists in which past policy documents can be obtained, including the responses to government proposals by interested parties. My searches would include not only public documents and academic journals but also newspaper and non-academic journal articles. The latter are frowned upon (especially by Swedish academics) but if used judicially provide the foreign researcher with a mass of useful information that could not be obtained in any other way. In recent years, Swedish websites (in English and Swedish) have multiplied enormously, giving the home-based researcher a wide range of up-to-date sources without leaving the office.

Websites can be particularly useful when it comes to organising interviews. Many of them include e-mail addresses that make arrangements much easier. More difficult to arrange are interviews with clients/beneficiaries. For these it is essential to have someone on the other side – working for local authorities, trades unions or employers – who can make the necessary contacts and draw up a timetable of visits.

While it is possible in a country like Sweden to do such research in English (many Swedes speak English and much material is published in English), without learning the language, its lack is a severe limitation. The task of learning a language may seem daunting at first but within a year or two, even a poor linguist (such as myself) can acquire sufficient skill to be able to read a great deal of useful material. Many non-English-speaking academics are likely to speak a second language as a matter of course. For British academics, this is much less so. Comparative research by British academics may depend much more on collaborative support from academics in other countries.

Question for discussion
• What are the advantages and disadvantages of doing comparative research (a) alone and (b) collaborating with foreign researchers?

Further reading
Gould, A. (1993) *Capitalist welfare systems: Japan, Sweden and Britain*, Harlow: Longman.

Clasen, J., Gould, A. and Vincent, J. (1998) *Voices within and without: Responses to long-term unemployment in Germany, Sweden and Britain*, Bristol: The Policy Press.

Gould, A. (2001) *Developments in Swedish social policy: Resisting Dionysus*, Basingstoke: Palgrave.

Gould, A. (2001) 'The criminalisation of buying sex: the politics of prostitution in Sweden', *Journal of Social Policy*, vol 30, no 3, pp 437-56.

Website resources
Institute for Social Research, Stockholm University [also makes available offprints in English of social policy journal articles]: www.sofi.su.se

Ministry of Health and Social Affairs: www.social.regeringen.se/inenglish/index.htm

Swedish Institute [publishes factsheets on every aspect of social policy – click on the British flag and information; also publishes 'Current Sweden', a series of occasional papers, some of which are about social policy issues]: www.si.se

Swedish Board for Health and Social Welfare: www.sos.se

Swedish parliament: www.riksdagen.se

Despite these problems of comparability in choosing cases, conceptualisation and data analysis, the value of comparative research remains. Whatever the caution and caveats we apply when doing and reading comparative research, it enables us to see other possibilities for organising social, economic and political life and new ways of understanding and theorising about societies.

Question for discussion

- What are the reasons why we undertake comparative research?

References

Carmel, E. (1999) 'Concepts, context and discourse in a comparative case study', *International Journal of Social Research Methodology*, vol 2, no 2, pp 141-50.

Chamberlayne, P. and King, A. (1996) 'Biographical approaches in comparative work', in L. Hantrais and S. Mangen (eds) *Cross-national research methods in the social sciences*, London: Pinter, pp 95-104.

Dogan, M. and Pelassey, D. (1990) *How to compare nations* (2nd edn), Chatham: Chatham House.

Ferrari, V. (1990) 'Socio-legal concepts and their comparison', in E. Øyen (ed) *Comparative methodology. Theory and practice in international social research*, London: Sage Publications, pp 63-80.

Ginsburg, N. (1992) *Divisions of welfare: A critical introduction to comparative social policy*, London: Sage Publications.

Kennett, P. (2001) *Comparative social policy: A critical introduction*, Buckingham: Open University Press.

Landman, T. (2002) *Issues and methods in comparative politics: An introduction*, London: Routledge.

Mangen, S. (1999) 'Qualitative research methods in cross-national research settings', *International Journal of Social Research Methodology*, vol 2, no 2, pp 109-24.

Peters, B.G. (1998) *Comparative politics: Theory and methods*, London: Macmillan.

Rose, R. (1991) 'Comparing forms of comparative analysis', *Political Studies*, vol 39, no 3, pp 446-62.

Sartori, G. (1973) 'Faulty concepts', in P.G. Lewis and D.C. Potter (eds) *The practice of comparative politics*, London: Longman/Open University Press, pp 356-91.

Schunk, M. (1996) 'Constructing models of the welfare mix: care options of frail elders', in L. Hantrais and S. Mangen (eds) *Cross-national research methods in the social sciences*, London: Pinter, pp 84-94.

Further reading

Hantrais, L. and Mangen, S. (eds) (1996) *Cross-national research methods in the social sciences*, London: Pinter [an edited volume with lots of examples, many from social policy research, discussing the use of quantitative and qualitative studies].

Landman, T. (2002) *Issues and methods in comparative politics: An introduction*, London: Routledge [although focused on politics, useful and very readable coverage of issues and approaches, full of examples, some of which are relevant to social policy].

Rose, R. (1991) 'Comparing forms of comparative analysis', *Political Studies*, vol 39, no 3, pp 446-62 [an excellent summary of the issues and debates, and a widely cited article].

Website resources

European Union [access documents from all EU institutions, including some cross-national data from Eurostat, the statistics section]: http://europa.eu.int

Organisation for Economic Co-operation and Development [an international organisation for the economically 'developed' world; includes cross-national data and some country and regional reports]: www.oecd.org

Social Policy Virtual Library [a useful gateway to many different national and international sources and sites]: www.social-policy.org

United Nations Development Programme [a gateway to international reports comparing 'human development index' for all countries]: www.undp.org

3.10 Post-structuralist perspectives

Fiona Williams, *Professor of Social Policy and Director, ESRC Research Group for the Study of Care, Values and the Future of Welfare, University of Leeds*

Much new thinking in social policy has been influenced by post-structuralist analysis, particularly the work of Foucault (1972, 1978). While post-structuralism refers to a school of *thought*, postmodernity refers to changing social and cultural *conditions* which contrast with modernity. This distinction is subject to dispute, but understanding the interplay of social change and social theory is important. It was modernity that saw the rise of the welfare state, and the practices of modernity were fed by the ideals of the 18th century Enlightenment. These centred on social and economic progress achieved through grand social and technological designs, on reason and rationality, and on a powerful and self-consciously political human subject (O'Brien and Penna, 1998). The development of the welfare state reflected these ideals in practice, with its belief in social progress, its collection of measurable facts about poverty, its categories of need and deserving and undeserving populations, its rational bureaucratic administration, and its scientifically trained experts.

If this characterised the 20th-century welfare state, then it was some of the political challenges to it that inspired a rethinking of welfare. For example, from the 1970s, social movements challenged the power of the profession to define the causes and solutions to people's problems, and revealed some of the cultural ways in which some groups were marginalised or excluded, such as minority ethnic groups, single parents or disabled people (Williams, 1989). Existing perspectives of welfare were found wanting: Marxism, with its focus on the logic of capital, class conflict and state power, or Fabian solutions of improving the technologies of government or the knowledge base of professionals, had little to say about disempowerment in the everyday experience of welfare users. Post-structuralist analyses, by contrast, offer an understanding of how scientific knowledges and state practices bring 'welfare subjects' into being in particular ways. Power resides in knowledge, in the discourses which inform our understanding about social groups and social problems. Thus, 'needs' are open to interpretation, and struggles over welfare benefits and services are about contestations over the interpretation of needs (Fraser, 1989).

This sort of analysis provides at least three new theoretical directions. First, policy texts, speeches and documents provide a window on to how social issues are 'spoken of' and how discourses constitute welfare subjects as, say, 'mentally ill', or 'scroungers' or 'carers' (Carabine, 2001). Second, this analysis unlocks welfare subjects from fixed, passive, universal and homogeneous categories, and resurrects them as creative, reflexive human agents who are embedded in social networks and who actively negotiate strategies to meet their welfare needs (Williams and Popay, 1999). For example, current policies for lone mothers in receipt of benefits have instituted a welfare-to-work programme. This reflects a structural analysis that paid work is a significant protection against poverty, but may fail to reckon with the fact that lone mothers are not a homogeneous group, who do not necessarily pursue rationally instrumental financial strategies. Duncan and Edwards (1999) found that different groups of lone mothers have different 'gendered moral rationalities' about combining paid work and motherhood which are informed by their identities as to what it means to be a 'good mother'. These are influenced by class and ethnicity, by their networks, as well as the cultural discourses, practices and resources of their localities.

Third, post-structuralist analysis has influenced a different approach to the state as it unpicks the many and varied sites of *governance* for the practices of power and resistance (Newman, 2001). Alternatively, an analysis of New Labour's *governmentality* focuses on the development of discourses of rights and responsibilities as a new form of ethico-politics where we are constituted as ethical and self-regulating subjects, negotiating the extent and limits of our responsibilities for self and others (Rose, 1999).

Such developments are not without criticism. The focus on subjectivity, identity and difference are seen to draw away from social policy's traditional concern with inequalities, or wider economic forces (Taylor-Gooby, 1994). In spite of an acknowledgement of contestation, the analysis of governmentality and the constitution of subjects seems to 'box off' possibilities for change. And, if post-structuralism involves a rejection of normative approaches, and knowledge is only ever provisional, how can one ever develop one's research in the direction of policy recommendations? These questions have generated attempts to bring to bear some of the new insights of post-structuralism on 'old' questions of justice and inequality (Thompson and Hoggett, 1996; Williams, 1996) and to develop a 'critical post-structuralism' that integrates post-structuralist thinking without losing sight of broader economic forces, the state, and the importance of normative and ethical judgements (Harris, 2001).

Question for discussion

- What does post-structuralist analysis offer and what difficulties does it pose for the study of social policy?

References

Carabine, J. (2001) 'Constituting sexuality through social policy: the case of lone motherhood, 1834 and today', *Social and Legal Studies*, vol 10, no 3, pp 291-314.

Duncan, S. and Edwards, R. (1999) *Lone mothers, paid work and gendered moral rationalities*, London: Macmillan.

Foucault, M. (1972) *The archaeology of knowledge*, London: Tavistock.

Foucault, M. (1978) *The history of sexuality*, New York, NY: Random House.

Fraser, N. (1989) *Unruly practices, power, discourse and gender in contemporary social theory*, Cambridge: Polity Press.

Harris, P. (2001) 'Towards a critical post-structuralism', *Social Work Education*, vol 20, no 3, pp 335-50.

Newman, J. (2001) *Modernising governance: New Labour, policy and society*, London: Sage Publications.

O'Brien, M. and Penna, S. (1998) *Theorising welfare: Enlightenment and modern society*, London: Sage Publications.

Rose, N. (1999) *Powers of freedom: Reframing political thought*, Cambridge: Cambridge University Press.

Taylor-Gooby, P. (1994) 'Post-modernism and social policy – a great leap backwards?', *Journal of Social Policy*, vol 23, no 3, pp 387-403.

Thompson, S. and Hoggett, P. (1996) 'Universalism, selectivism and particularism: towards a post-modern social policy', *Critical Social Policy*, vol 16, no 1, pp 21-43.

Williams, F. (1989) *Social policy: A critical introduction: Issues of race, gender and class*, Cambridge: Polity Press.

Williams, F. (1996) 'Postmodernism, feminism and the question of difference', in N. Parton (ed) *Social theory, social change and social work*, London: Routledge.

Williams, F. and Popay, J. (1999) 'Balancing polarities: developing a new framework for welfare research', in F. Williams, J. Popay and A. Oakley (eds) *Welfare research: A critical review*, London: UCL Press, pp 156-83.

Further reading

Fraser, N. (1989) *Unruly practices, power, discourse and gender in contemporary social theory*, Cambridge: Polity Press.

O'Brien, M. and Penna, S. (1998) *Theorising welfare: Enlightenment and modern society*, London: Sage Publications.

Rose, N. (1999) *Powers of freedom: Reframing political thought*, Cambridge: Cambridge University Press.

PART THREE: USING EXISTING RESEARCH

3.11 Secondary analysis

Karen Rowlingson, *Senior Lecturer in Social Research,
University of Bath*

What is secondary analysis?

Secondary analysis is when a researcher analyses data that they themselves did not collect (see Bryman, 2004). For example, a researcher (secondary analyst) can analyse statistics on a range of issues including the numbers of births, marriages, deaths, criminal convictions and immigration. These statistics, and many others, are collected routinely by government departments (see Chapter Four, Section 4.10, on official statistics). Government departments also carry out regular surveys to collect information on issues such as health, crime, income, employment, and so on. These data are then archived at the University of Essex Data Archive (www.data-archive.ac.uk) and can be analysed by other people outside government. This archive also has data from academically funded surveys, such as the British Household Panel Survey (see **Box 4a**, Chapter Four) and the British Social Attitudes Survey (see **Boxes 4b** and **4c**, Chapter Four). These too can be accessed and analysed.

On some occasions, secondary analysis is the analysis of data which the secondary analyst had collected in the past for a different purpose from the one that they now have. Perhaps they had been commissioned to collect some data on student debt and had carried out a survey of students and their finances. At a later date they decide to use these data to analyse student employment rates. This would also be secondary analysis.

Secondary analysis is usually thought of in terms of quantitative research but in recent years there have been attempts to encourage secondary analysis of qualitative data, for example, through the development of an archive for qualitative data at the University of Essex (Corti et al, 1995; see also Section 3.13). This section concentrates on *quantitative* secondary analysis.

Advantages and disadvantages of doing secondary analysis

As a research method, secondary analysis has a number of **advantages** and disadvantages. It is a relatively cheap method as data from the University of Essex Archive can be provided free through the Internet or sent through the post for a fee that may be nominal. The analyst does, of course, need a computer and appropriate software.

Secondary analysis is a relatively quick method of research as someone else has already been through the more time-consuming job of collecting the data. Having said this, it takes time for the analyst to get to know the data and to carry out the analysis, and sometimes it is easy to underestimate how time-consuming this method is.

Depending on the type of data used, analysts can gain access to surveys with massive sample sizes and there is therefore scope for considerable subgroup analysis (see Figure 3c).

Figure 3c: **Examples of major annual or continuous surveys**

Name (geographical area covered)	Effective sample size[a]	Response rate (%)[a]
British Crime Survey (England/Wales)	26,291	74
British Household Panel Survey (GB)	5,160	97
British Social Attitudes Survey (GB)	5,402	58
Family Expenditure Survey (UK)	11,424	63
Family Resources Survey (GB)	34,636	66
General Household Survey (GB)	11,831	72
International Passenger Survey (UK)	261,000	82
Labour Force Survey (UK)	59,000	76
National Readership Survey (GB)	54,074	60

Note: [a] This table draws on information in *Social Trends* (ONS, 2001). The effective sample sizes and response rates refer to the most recent survey included in *Social Trends*.

Another advantage of secondary analysis is that comparable data are increasingly available for other countries, enabling comparative analysis of secondary data (for example, through the European Community Household Panel). Data are also available over a number of years, enabling comparisons over time (for example, the General Household Survey started life in 1971, enabling three decades' worth of comparisons to be made).

In methodological terms, secondary analysis can be used for *triangulation* purposes. For example, some of the results of a smaller ad hoc survey can be compared with a much larger official survey to check the validity of the former. And secondary analysis of data can be replicated by another analyst to check on the reliability of the original research.

There are, however, **disadvantages** to the method. First of all, a certain degree of skill is needed in manipulating and analysing data which can often be large-scale and complex. For example, the Family Expenditure Survey comes in 175 different files and the documentation alone takes up to 13 megabytes of disk space. Secondary analysts therefore need a high level of skill in data handling and analysis and such skills are in relatively short supply in Britain. Other datasets, such as the British Social Attitudes Survey, are, however, much less complex.

Another problem with secondary analysis is that the available data do not always perfectly fit the secondary analyst's research question for a number of reasons. Perhaps the population is slightly different. Or perhaps the sample is not large enough to enable certain types of subgroup analysis. Or perhaps some key questions were not asked, or at least were not asked in exactly the way the secondary analyst would have liked.

Most official quantitative data are archived at the University of Essex and so are easily accessible. The data also come with comprehensive information about how they were collected. But some ad hoc surveys, particularly those carried out by commercial companies, may never be archived and so access may be very difficult to obtain. Once the data have been obtained there may be very little information about them. For example, the full questionnaire may not be available and so it would be impossible to see how the questions were asked.

Nevertheless, despite all the disadvantages to this approach, there is an enormous amount of quantitative information just waiting to be analysed and **Box 3h** gives one example of a secondary analysis project.

Question for discussion

- What types of research project are best carried out by means of secondary analysis? Summarise the pros and cons of carrying out secondary analysis.

References

Bryman, A. (2004) *Social research methods* (2nd edn), Oxford: Oxford University Press.
Corti, L., Foster, J. and Thompson, P. (1995) 'Archiving qualitative research data', *Social Research Update*, 10 (www.soc.surrey.ac.uk/sru/SRU10.html).
ONS (Office for National Statistics) (2001) *Social trends no 31*, London: The Stationery Office.

Further reading

Bryman, A. (2004) *Social research methods* (2nd edn), Oxford: Oxford University Press.

Miller, R., Acton, C., Fullerton, D. and Maltby, J. (2002) *SPSS for social scientists*, Basingstoke: Macmillan.

Website resource

University of Essex Data Archive: www.data-archive.ac.uk

Box 3h: Secondary analysis of wealth in Britain: an example

Karen Rowlingson, *Senior Lecturer in Social Research, University of Bath*

There has been relatively little research on wealth inequality. The main aim of our study (Rowlingson et al, 1999) was to analyse the role of the life cycle in explaining differences in the distribution of wealth, and the links between income and wealth. We used the 1995/96 Family Resources Survey (FRS) as this was a new dataset and was far superior to anything previously available on wealth. Information had been collected from 47,000 adults and 16,000 children. There was therefore ample opportunity to compare people in different subgroups. The FRS had been funded through central government and had been rigorously piloted. We were therefore confident in the reliability and validity of the data.

The research set out a clear definition of wealth (dividing it into three broad categories: housing wealth, pension wealth and financial savings) and was innovative in finding ways of operationalising wealth, given the limitations of data from a large-scale survey. It was particularly challenging to operationalise accumulated pension wealth (in other words, to capture what a person should be entitled to, were their pension provision to cease further operations tomorrow but with the pension providers honouring obligations already entered into without penalties for cashing in early). Given the range of different types of pension available, this was a very complex task. A similar challenge was to operationalise accumulated housing wealth given the extensive use of endowment mortgages.

The FRS was obtained from the University of Essex Data Archive and then, following on from our research objectives and our conceptualisations, we analysed the data using SPSS. The first task was to put the data in a manageable format. Then new variables were derived from the existing data. Then we investigated the relationships between different variables. This was very complex and required the advanced skills of a number of experienced analysts.

The research came up with the most reliable estimates to date on the extent and distribution of wealth in Britain. For example, it found that 50% of all wealth was owned by only 10% of the population. A third of the population had almost no wealth at all. It also produced new information about the links between income, wealth and the life cycle as these three variables are closely intertwined. For example, it identified a particular group of pensioners who were 'asset rich' but 'income poor'. The poorest families in terms of both income and wealth were young single people and lone parents. Older childless couples were best off in terms of both income and wealth.

Reference

Rowlingson, K., Whyley, C. and Warren, T. (1999) *Wealth in Britain: A lifecycle perspective*, London: Policy Studies Institute.

3.12 Systematic reviews for policy analysis

Jane Millar, *Professor of Social Policy, University of Bath*

Policy makers looking for answers to questions such as the impact of poverty on children, or the impact of class size on educational outcomes, or the impact of sex education on rates of teenage pregnancy will find that there are a very large number of research studies relating to these topics. These will include studies with different population groups, carried out at different times, perhaps in different countries, using different outcome measures and different techniques for the analysis of the data. The sheer amount of information can be very daunting and it can be extremely difficult to interpret and assess the volume of evidence. What if studies produce contradictory results? Or, even if results are not contradictory, what if they produce very different estimates of the size or strength of the effect? How can we decide which is the more accurate result?

Systematic reviews combine results from various different studies in order to provide the most robust assessments of the overall conclusions that can be drawn from many research studies. They are comprehensive reviews of the literature, with studies chosen in a systematic way and summarised according to explicit criteria. There are two main sorts of systematic review:

- *descriptive reviews* which compare studies looking for trends and patterns of results; and
- *meta-analytic reviews*, which apply statistical techniques to the results in order to produce summary measures (Fink, 1998).

The latter require quantitative data and are less common in policy research than the former, which can draw on many different types of data.

Carrying out a systematic review

Both descriptive and meta-analytical reviews proceed in a similar way:

- *Define the purpose of the review:* clear objectives are necessary in order to guide the selection of the studies to be included.
- *Set the criteria by which studies are to be selected for inclusion:* this might, for example, include time restrictions (such as only including studies carried out after a certain date), or geographical restrictions (for example, only include UK studies). Or it might include restrictions according to methodology (only include experimental studies), or according to some preset measures of quality (only include studies based on random sampling).
- *Search for and include all the studies that meet these criteria:* the aim is to be comprehensive. A key issue here concerns the inclusion (or not) of unpublished studies and 'grey' literature (conference papers, in-house reports, and so on). A review that includes only published literature risks missing studies that might provide a contradictory picture, or which are more speculative in approach. In the case of meta-analysis, which is based on quantitative studies, there is a risk that the published studies are biased towards studies that report positive or statistically significant results (studies that find no effects tend to be less likely to get published). This is known as the 'file drawer' problem.
- *Abstract the relevant features of the studies:* this should be done according to a standardised protocol. This might, for example, include the date of the study, the sample size, the age of respondents, the geographical coverage and key summary statistics.
- *Summarise/synthesise the results:* in the case of descriptive reviews this is often done in the form of summary tables, which provide an overview of the key characteristics and results of the studies reviewed. In the case of meta-analysis, this involves the application of statistical analysis to summary statistics (for example, means, standard deviations, the results from statistical tests) to produce a single summary statistic. This increases sample size, since the various samples are being 'pooled', and so provides greater statistical power. It should also cancel out differences between studies that are due to random errors. Fink (1998) and Kulik and Kulik (1989) discuss the origins of meta-analysis and outline the types of statistical analysis that can be applied.

Limitations

One of the main advantages of systematic reviews is that they can provide a concise synthesis of a large number of different studies. But there is also a danger that they will present a too simplistic picture and hide, rather than illuminate, important differences between the studies comprising the review. This is perhaps especially the case for meta-analysis, which can only be applied to quantitative studies that report their findings in statistical terms (and so limits the type of data that can be included). Kulik and Kulik (1989) point to four major criticisms of meta-analysis: that too much weight may be given to low quality studies; that they are too dependent on published results (and hence the publication bias discussed above); that they mix 'apples and pears'; and that sample sizes can be inflated if multiple results from the same study are included. More generally, systematic reviews have been criticised for being mechanistic and atheoretical, and for placing greater emphasis on quantitative, rather than qualitative, data, although as Gough and Elbourne (2002) point out, this need not necessarily be the case.

Descriptive reviews: some examples

As noted above, meta-analysis is relatively uncommon in policy-related research but much more use is made of systematic descriptive reviews (see Young et al, 2002, for a discussion of systematic reviews in the context of evidence-based policy making). For example, there have been a number of systematic reviews of the evaluation evidence on the impact of the 'New Deal' programmes (Hasluck, 1999, 2000; Millar, 2000; Evans et al, 2002). Kempson (1996) provides an interesting and unusual example of a systematic review of qualitative, rather than quantitative, data. This study examined 'life on a low income' by means of a review of 31 qualitative studies carried out in the early 1990s. Studies were selected for inclusion if they examined income, expenditure, household budgeting and the consequences of living on a low income. They were re-analysed to examine factors such as money management, the dynamics of making ends meet, the impact of poverty on family life, debt and so on. **Box 3i** discusses a systematic review of the outcomes for children of separation and divorce (Rodgers and Pryor, 1998).

Summary

Systematic reviews draw together the results from a number of different studies selected according to clear criteria, and summarise these using standard protocols. They have become increasingly popular in healthcare research because of their capacity to integrate the results of numerous findings. As with any other research methods, systematic reviews must be read critically and careful attention paid to the way in which studies have been selected and key terms defined.

Question for discussion

• What are the main stages involved in carrying out a systematic review?

References

Evans, M., McKnight, A. and Namazie, C. (2002) *New Deal for Lone Parents: First synthesis report of the national evaluation*, Report WAE 116, Sheffield: DWP.

Fink, A. (1998) *Conducting research literature reviews: From paper to the Internet*, London: Sage Publications.

Gough, D. and Elbourne, D. (2002) 'Systematic research synthesis to inform policy, practice and democratic debate', *Social Policy and Society*, vol 1, no 3, pp 225-36.

Hasluck, C. (1999) *The New Deal for Young People: Two years on*, Employment Service Report ESR41, Sheffield: Employment Service.

Hasluck, C. (2000) *The New Deal for Lone Parents: A review of the evaluation evidence*, Employment Service Report ESR51, Sheffield: Employment Service.

Kempson, E. (1996) *Life on a low income*, York: Joseph Rowntree Foundation.

Kulik, J.A. and Kulik, C.-L.C. (1989) 'Meta-analysis in education', *International Journal of Educational Research*, vol 13, pp 221-340.

Millar, J. (2000) *Keeping track of welfare reform*, York: York Publishing Services for the Joseph Rowntree Foundation.

Rodgers, B. and Pryor, J. (1998) *Divorce and separation: The outcomes for children*, York: Joseph Rowntree Foundation.

Young, K., Ashby, D., Boaz, A. and Grayson, L. (2002) 'Social science and the evidence-based policy movement', *Social Policy and Society*, vol 1, no 3, pp 215-24.

Further reading

Fink, A. (1998) *Conducting research literature reviews: From paper to the Internet*, London: Sage Publications.

Gough, D. and Elbourne, D. (2002) 'Systematic research synthesis to inform policy, practice and democratic debate', *Social Policy and Society*, vol 1, no 3, pp 225-36.

Kulik, J.A. and Kulik, C.-L.C. (1989) 'Meta-analysis in education', *International Journal of Educational Research*, vol 13, pp 221-340.

Macdonald, G. (2003) *Using systematic reviews to improve social care*, London: Social Care Institute for Excellence.

Young, K., Ashby, D., Boaz, A. and Grayson, L. (2002) 'Social science and the evidence-based policy movement', *Social Policy and Society*, vol 1, no 3, pp 215-24.

Website resources

Cochrane Collaboration: www.cochrane.org/cochrane/newcomer.htm

Meta-analysis in Educational Research, ERIC Digest: http://www.ed.gov/ databases/ERIC_Digests/ed339748.html

Box 3i: A systematic review of the evidence on the outcomes for children of divorce and separation

Jane Millar, *Professor of Social Policy, University of Bath*

The rise in marital breakdown and the growth of the number of lone-parent families has been a source of concern among some politicians and policy makers. There has therefore been much interest in research that examines the outcomes of these family changes on children, both in the short-term (for example, on school attendance) and long-term (for example, on their own patterns of family formation when they grow up). The topic is both very complex, with lots of potential factors to take into account, and highly political, with strong opinions and views about the consequences of these family trends. Finding a way through the various research findings is therefore very important. Different studies may have different results and it is easy for commentators to pick and choose among these, selecting only those that show particular types of results.

Rodgers and Pryor (1998) carried out a descriptive systematic review of the research evidence (see also **Box 7c**, Chapter Seven, for a brief discussion of this particular study from a *media* perspective). The *purpose* was to "provide an overview of where links between parental separation and outcomes for children have been well established and to pinpoint remaining areas of contention and ignorance", and "to understand factors that help explain the processes leading to particular outcomes" (p 8). The *criteria* for selecting studies were "intended to be as non-restrictive as possible" (p 14) but excluded studies which did not separately focus on marital separation (for example, those which also included children of unmarried parents). However, the authors give little further detail about their criteria and nor do they describe their *search* strategy in any detail. The *relevant features* of each study and the *summary of results* are presented in a set of tables which all use a standard format. Each table has information on the following relevant features:

- author reference;
- topic and location;
- date of birth of children in sample;
- age of children at time of outcome measure;
- outcome measure;
- effect size – none plus 3 categories (+, ++, +++) to indicate strength of effect.

The topics for which the results were examined included:
- socio-economic circumstances of families;
- socio-outcomes for offspring in adulthood;
- enuresis, childhood emotional problems, socialisation and mixed disorders;
- antisocial behaviour and delinquency in childhood and adulthood;
- educational attainment;
- physical health;
- age at leaving school;
- age at leaving home;
- sexual behaviour, partnership and parenthood;
- mental health and substance use in adolescence and adulthood.

Each of these included various different outcome measures.

They also include an appendix which discusses some of the limitations of the research. These include the fact that some of it is quite old, that longitudinal studies suffer from sample attrition, that sample sizes are sometimes too small for statistical analysis, that statistical tests are not always used appropriately, that studies do not distinguish between events and processes, that some outcomes have not been considered, and that there has been insufficient analyses of mediating and moderating factors.

However, Rodgers and Pryor do draw some substantive conclusions from their review. A key conclusion is that "there is no simple and direct relationship between parental separation and children's adjustment, and poor outcomes are far from inevitable" (pp 4-5). Adverse outcomes are more prevalent – roughly twice as likely – for children from divorced families as compared with children from intact families, but these disadvantages only apply to a minority of children. Rodgers and Prior also note that it cannot be assumed that the parental separation is the key cause and they point out that there are a "complexity of factors that impinge on families before, during and after separation" (p 5). Parental separation is a process, not a single event, but this has been difficult for research to untangle. **Box 7c**, Chapter Seven, illuminates how these findings were handled by the media.

Reference

Rodgers, B. and Pryor, J. (1998) *Divorce and separation: The outcomes for children*, York: Joseph Rowntree Foundation.

3.13 Data archiving

Louise Corti, *Director of User Services and Qualidata, University of Essex*

Data archiving is a *method of conserving expensive resources and ensuring that their research potential is fully exploited.* Unless preserved and documented for further research, data which have often been collected at significant expense, with substantial expertise and involving respondents' contributions may later exist only in a small number of reports which analyse just a fraction of the research potential of the data. Within a very short space of time the data files are likely to become lost or obsolete as technology evolves.

The key to data archiving is thus long-term preservation of data in a format that can be accessed by researchers, now and in the future. Ensuring long-term accessibility relies on strategies for data processing and creating informative documentation, and in the technical procedures for data storage, preservation, security and access.

Where are data archived?

Data are typically housed in data archives, which are resource centres that acquire, store and disseminate digital data for secondary analysis in research and teaching.

To provide a brief history, the data archiving movement began in the 1960s within a number of key social science departments in the US which stored original data from survey interviews. The movement spread across Europe and in 1967 UK Data Archive (UKDA) was established by the National Research Council for the Social Sciences. In the late 1970s many national archives joined a wider European professional organisation known as the Council of European Social Science Data Archives (CESSDA). These archives were established to promote cooperation on key archival strategies, procedures and technologies between disparate data services for the social sciences.

The first data archives collected data of specific interest to quantitative researchers in the social sciences. In the 1960s these were largely opinion poll or election data, but as the trend for large-scale surveys grew, by the late 1970s the UKDA began to acquire major government surveys and censuses. Because of their large sample sizes and the richness of the information collected, these national surveys represent major research resources for the social scientist. Examples of major British government series include the General Household Survey, the Labour Force Survey and the Health Survey for England. These series are used by government departments for planning, policy and monitoring purposes, and by other researchers to present a picture of households, families and people in Britain.

By the 1990s the UKDA collection had grown to thousands of datasets spanning a wide range of data sources, both historical and contemporary, relating to society. Microdata from surveys, censuses, registers and aggregate statistics derived from academic, commercial and public sector sources are available to the secondary analyst. Well-established UK-based academic large-scale surveys include the British Social Attitudes Survey, and the longitudinal and cohort studies, the British Household Panel Survey and the National Child Development Study, all referred to in other sections of this volume.

In the 1990s the research community recognised the needs of *qualitative* researchers by funding a Qualitative Data Archive (ESDS Qualidata) in 1994. A new culture of preserving and reusing qualitative data has thus grown, and research studies from Peter Townsend's career, such as *Poverty in the UK* (1979) (for which survey data are also available) and *The last refuge* (1962), are now preserved for researchers to consult. An increasing number of datasets acquired these days comprise data from both quantitative and qualitative methods.

Preparing data for archiving

Research data are created in a wide variety of types and formats depending on the research method used. Survey data are generally stored as numeric codes, while transcribed text from in-depth interviews and fieldnotes are typically stored as word-processed documents. Both types of data are usually managed and analysed by computer software, either using a statistical package or computer-assisted qualitative data analysis software (CAQDAS).

A key concern for a data archive is to ensure that the materials they acquire are in an appropriate format, are documented to a minimum standard that enables informed use, and cover topics that are anticipated to meet the demands of users. In order to smooth the transition from data collector to archive, it is important that potential depositors of data follow guidelines on documenting research projects, advocated by the data archiving community.

Data archives undertake data processing activities. First, the dataset is checked and validated, for example, by examining numeric data values and by ensuring data are anonymised to ensure that the risk of identifying individuals is minimal. Second, 'metadata' (data about data) are produced with the aim of producing high quality finding aids and providing good user documentation. Metadata cover information describing the study and the data and include enhancements added to a numeric data file (such as creating variable and value labels). A systematic catalogue record is always created for studies, detailing an overview of the study, the size and content of the dataset, its availability and terms and conditions of access. User guides contain further information on how the data were collected, the original questionnaires, and how to use the data.

Accessing and using data

Users typically request data from a data archive in a particular format, such as a statistical or word-processing package. These days, data can be accessed via instant download facilities available over the web or can be dispatched on portable media such as CD-ROM. The 21st century has seen a move towards sophisticated online analysis tools, where users can search, analyse, subset data via a web browser, such as NESSTAR (Ryssevik and Musgrave, 2001). Users are required to be registered with an archive and sign an agreement to the effect that they will not attempt to identify individuals when carrying out secondary analyses.

Data available from data archives can be used for a number of purposes. Secondary analysis (see Section 3.11) strengthens scientific inquiry, it avoids duplication of data collection and opens up methods of data collection and measurement. Archived data enable new users to: ask new questions of old data; undertake comparative research, replication or re-study; inform research design and promote methodological advancement. Finally, they provide significant resources for training in research and substantive learning, such as the measurement of poverty.

Question for discussion

- What kinds of sources of data would be available for an investigation into inequalities in health in Britain?

References

Ryssevik, J. and Musgrave, S. (2001) 'The social science dream machine: resource discovery, analysis, and delivery on the web', *Social Science Computing Review*, vol 19, no 2, pp 163-74.

Townsend, P. (1962) *The last refuge: A survey of residential institutions and homes for the aged in England and Wales*, London: Routledge.

Townsend, P. (1979) *Poverty in the UK: A survey of household resources and standards of living*, Harmondsworth: Penguin Books.

Relevant organisations

Economic and Social Research Council (ESRC)
The UK's leading research funding and training agency addressing economic and social concerns, aiming to provide high quality research on issues of importance to business, the public sector and government. The issues considered include economic competitiveness, the effectiveness of public services and policy, and quality of life.
ESRC, Polaris House, North Star Avenue, Swindon SN2 1UJ
Telephone 01793 413000; www.esrc.ac.uk

International Federation of Data Organisations (IFDO)
A network of social science data across the world, established in response to advanced research needs of the international social science community; the website provides information on the background and activities of the network of national data archives across the world.
IFDO, Zentral Archiv, Cologne, Zentralarchiv für Empirische Sozialforschung, Bachemer Strasse 40,D 50931, Köln
Telephone +49 221 476 940; www.ifdo.org

Joseph Rowntree Foundation (JRF)
One of the largest independent social policy research and development charities in the UK. It supports a wide programme of research and development projects in housing, social care and social policy and ensures that the findings are helpful in the development of better policies and practices across the UK.
JRF, The Homestead, 40 Water End, York, Y030 6WP
Telephone 01904 629241; www.jrf.org.uk

Office for National Statistics (ONS)
The UK government department that provides an up-to-date, comprehensive and meaningful description of the UK's economy and society compiled from government data sources. ONS carries out high quality survey research for government departments and other public bodies on a range of social issues to help develop government policies, inform public debate and monitor changes over time.
ONS Library, Cardiff Road, Newport, Wales NP10 8XG
Telephone 0845 601 3034; www.statistics.gov.uk

Qualitative Data Archive (ESDS Qualidata)
Based at the University of Essex, Economic and Social Data Service (ESDS) Qualidata provides information about availability and access to qualitative research materials in the social sciences. It also provides advice on the archiving and reuse of qualitative data; the website contains information on the availability of qualitative data resources in the UK, guidelines on preparing data for deposit, and reusing data.
ESDS Qualidata, UK Data Archive, University of Essex, Wivenhoe Park,
Colchester, Essex CO4 3SQ
Telephone 01206 873058; www.qualidata.essex.ac.uk

The UK Data Archive (UKDA)
Based at the University of Essex, UKDA hosts the largest collection of accessible

computer-readable data in the social sciences and humanities in the UK, standing at over 4,000 datasets. Data are acquired from many different sources including central government, academic researchers, opinion poll organisations and other data archives worldwide. Users can search the catalogue and indexes for datasets by subject or keyword, and order data in a variety of formats and media, subject to approval; the website contains relevant and up-to-date information on the provision and reuse of a broad range of social science data resources in the UK. UKDA, University of Essex, Wivenhoe Park, Colchester, Essex CO4 3SQ
Telephone 01206 872143; e-mail help@esds.ac.uk; www.data-archive.ac.uk

Website resources

Mruck, K., Corti, L., Kluge, S. and Opitz, D. (eds) (2000, December) Text. Archive. Re-Analysis, *Forum: Qualitative Social Research* [online Journal], vol 1, no 3, available at http://qualitative-research.net/fqs/fqs-eng.htm [this is a whole issue of the journal devoted to the sharing and reuse of qualitative data, and comprising some 40 papers on the topic].
UKDA catalogue record for Study Number 1671: Townsend, P. (1979) *Poverty in the UK: A survey of household resources and standards of living*, available at www.data-archive.ac.uk/findingData/snDescription.asp?sn=1671&key=poverty%20&catg=xmlTitle

PART FOUR: THEMES

3.14 Ethical considerations

Roger Homan, *Professor of Religious Studies, University of Brighton*

Research that engages human subjects in issues that may affect them involves the investigator in complex moral or ethical dilemmas. On the one hand, there is a quest for truth and a sense of the public right to know: the responsible researcher will want to publish those findings that might inform policy and enhance provision. On the other hand, human subjects are accorded rights to privacy and are entitled to withhold consent or to decline to participate; the duty to protect subjects and to honour their rights may mean that knowledge is not made available to the public or to specialist audiences for policy research. Further, those who are funding investigations may demand a degree of control upon the release of findings (see Chapter Six, Section 6.9). The honouring of the rights of participants and sponsors allows forms of censorship that are not easily reconciled with notions of intellectual freedom that have long been valued in the academic world.

Often, therefore, there are conflicts of value. Ethical standards are expressed as absolutes but must operate relatively. In this section we focus on some of the ethical considerations that need to be taken into account when conducting any piece of policy research – be it quantitative, qualitative or a multi-strategy approach. The aim here is to highlight some of the key issues that need to be thought through both *before* research is undertaken, as well as *during* the research process. We also return to some of these issues and related matters later in the volume, in Section 6.3, Chapter Six (where we consider *codes of ethics*), Section 6.6 (where we consider *safety* issues), and Section 6.7 (where we consider *confidentiality* and the protection of data).

Controls

The ethical standards of social researchers owe much to the world of medicine. The normative 1946 Nuremberg Code was a response to the practice of using the internees of prison camps as involuntary subjects in medical research; being oblivious of a right to decline, they had undergone such discomforts as freezing in investigations of the effects of frostbite. The Code made it clear that human subjects should be informed of what is involved in research participation and that they should not be compelled to take part. The principle of **informed consent** has come to be seminal in the codes and guidelines of all the professional bodies such as the British Sociological Association, the British Psychological Society and their American counterparts, and in the codes that operate for the ethical screening of research in health trusts and universities (see Section 6.3, Chapter Six, for further discussion of such codes). More recently, professional codes have addressed other considerations such as the conservation of the research environment for the purpose of further research, the need to maintain credibility for research findings and the reputation of the professional group or institution (see, for example, **Box 6a**, Chapter Six, on the research governance framework for health and social care).

Some, but not all, professional associations operate sanctions against those members who deviate from their codified standards. This is problematic when, as suggested above, ethical principles may be in conflict with each other. In recent years the more effective control has been the screening of research proposals by research ethics committees: these are now mandatory in health trusts and standard in universities. They are also becoming more common in social services departments.

Consent

Participation in almost all research is voluntary. The Registrar General may compel responses for the Census, so may the Inland Revenue and the local authority assessing the community charge. Government agents such as OFSTED also have rights of access. But these are the exceptions.

In reality, however, the voluntariness of participation is often compromised. Data collected for other purposes are filed and subsequently made available to researchers without retrospective consultation of those involved. The observation of transactions in committee and other groups is sometimes licensed not by the agreement of all participants but by the ruling of a chair or gatekeeper. The difficulty of allowing non-consenting individuals to withdraw from a committee or group is that the group will then be deprived of their contribution, and the absent person will be denied any benefits they might have enjoyed. Further, there is a sense in which some meetings such as local government committees are public and manage public money: as any one has the right to observe, the committee cannot close its doors to researchers. What is at issue is the public right to know: the entitlement to give or withhold consent, it is argued, should not be the basis of concealment. The legal or moral entitlement to observe, however, does not exempt the investigator from seeking consent. The consequence of not doing so may be a suspicion of, and refusal to cooperate with, future researchers and a hostile reception of any ensuing publication: there are thus tactics to consider as well as ethics.

The expectation is that participants in a research study – be they respondents to an interview or questionnaire or subjects of an observation – will know that research is taking place and will be appropriately informed of its purpose, implications and possible consequences. On the basis of this information they may decline to participate. However, it is in the nature of social research that enquiries are about the behaviour of more than one person. Interviews with claimants of benefits or studies of the allocation of housing are likely to invite participants to report on experiences that involve others, such as social workers. In a significant sense these other people become the subjects of such studies as well, and yet they have not given consent to be researched. Willing respondents are used as surrogate informants. Researchers investigating the experiences and perceptions of service users will need to cultivate a particular discipline in their written reports, recognising the sensitivity as well as the subjectivity of their data; they will want to resist the temptation to scavenge for sensational facts for the sake of catching public attention and thereby to expose those who have not willingly and wittingly participated. **Box 3j** provides an illustration of how one researcher went about getting the informed consent of her research participants.

Confidentiality and safety

Researchers are not in a position to assure human subjects of absolute confidentiality. If they discover evidence of the abuse of children, for example, they must report it to the police (see also Section 6.7 and **Box 6b**, Chapter Six). Nor is it always desirable to place the ethic of confidentiality above other considerations. Interviews with heavy users of drugs or alcohol, or with subjects who may have violent or volatile dispositions, may be more safely conducted in a public or accessible place such as the corner of a cafe than in private accommodation (see Section 6.6, Chapter Six).

In much social research the principle of confidentiality is reckoned to protect the privacy and identity of the relatively powerless. Receivers of social security benefits, for example, may give more candid responses if they can ensure that the information they convey will not work to their personal disadvantage. In social policy research, however, the ethic of confidentiality will often protect administrations, decision makers and managers. The responsibility to publish the findings of research is a complex one and it may be galvanised by a moral responsibility to expose and to eliminate perceived injustice. Do researchers have such an obligation to pursue truth that they should publish evidence that might weigh against the pretences or policy intentions of their sponsors? Should they leave such exposure to investigative journalists or the political opposition? If they breach confidentiality or trust, they and future researchers may well be denied further access. But if they only publish the findings that suit their subjects or their paymasters, they will damage the credibility of academic research in their field.

These are all complex issues that need to be thought about when conducting any piece of policy research. They are presented here to remind the reader that ethical considerations, including matters concerning confidentiality, consent, safety and the protection of data, are issues that must be considered during all stages of the research process. They are also concerns that we return to in Chapter Six (Sections 6.3, 6.6 and 6.7) when we consider how researchers must *manage* the *ethical context* of social policy research.

Question for discussion

- "Ethical standards are expressed as absolutes but must operate relatively." Give some examples of why and how these standards operate relatively.

Further reading

Oliver, P. (2003) *The student's guide to research ethics*, Maidenhead: Open University Press.

Box 3j: Gaining informed consent

Elizabeth Peel, *Lecturer in Psychology, Aston University*

Getting informed consent from research participants is ethically important. As a researcher, you have a responsibility to explain to the people taking part in your research what the study is about, the risks and benefits of taking part, and obtain their consent before involving them in your research. This is known as the *informed consent process*.

In a recent research project (Peel, 2002) my data collection was carried out in accordance with the British Psychological Society's *Ethical principles for conducting research with human participants* (BPS, 1997; see Brown, 1997 for a critique of standard ethical guidelines; and also Section 6.3, Chapter Six). I obtained informed consent from two groups of people. The first group were people who I interviewed about either their experiences of delivering lesbian and gay awareness training[1] or their views about attending lesbian and gay awareness training. The second group were trainees who were actually attending a training session. I asked for their consent for me to tape-record their training. Both these groups of people were over the age of 16 and were mentally able to understand what the research was about, and therefore were able to give their consent to taking part. Gaining *informed* consent is not always straightforward, however, and it can become a 'thorny issue' if participants physically deteriorate during the data collection period (Lawton, 2001), or are experiencing a mental impairment such as dementia (Sachs, 1998), or have learning disabilities (Stalker, 1998).

After I had clearly described my research – emphasising confidentiality and anonymity – I gave participants a *consent form*. The example consent form below outlines the information and steps needed to obtain informed consent.

Sample consent form (interviews)

My name is Liz Peel. I am a research student in the [name of Department] at [Name of University]. My supervisor is [name], who can be contacted at [address]. I am doing research on lesbian and gay awareness training. Thank you for agreeing to take part in my research. Before we begin the interview I would like to emphasise that:

---

[1] Lesbian and Gay Awareness Training (LGAT) is the term I chose to describe short experiential courses about sexuality provided by external trainers for (primarily public sector) organisations in the UK, as part of their employee training programmes. LGAT aims to provide a group of professionals – in a short space of time, often half a day – with a heightened awareness of lesbian, gay and bisexual sexualities.

- Your participation is entirely voluntary.
- You are free to refuse to answer any question.
- You are free to withdraw from the interview at any time.
- You may withdraw your data from this research within 2 weeks of this interview.

With your consent, the interview will be tape-recorded. Nobody except myself and my research supervisors will hear the tape of this training in its entirety. Small portions of the interview may be heard by other members of my research group. When the interview is transcribed, any information that may identify you will be removed. Under no circumstances will your name or identifying information be included in the reporting of this research. Parts of this interview may be used in my thesis and in publications arising from it. Please sign this form to show that you have read its contents, and consent to take part in this research.

Question for discussion
- What is informed consent, and how would you gain informed consent from research participants?

References
BPS (British Psychological Society) (1997) *Code of conduct, ethical principles and guidelines*, Leicester: BPS.

Brown, L. (1997) 'Ethics in psychology: Cui bono?', in D. Fox and I. Prilleltensky (eds) *Critical psychology: An introduction*, London: Sage Publications, pp 51-67

Lawton, J. (2001) 'Gaining and maintaining consent: ethical concerns raised in a study of dying patients', *Qualitative Health Research*, vol 11, no 5, pp 693-705.

Peel, E. (2002) 'Lesbian and gay awareness training: a critical analysis', unpublished PhD, Loughborough University, Loughborough.

Sachs, G. (1998) 'Informed consent for research on human subjects with dementia', *Journal of the American Geriatrics Society*, vol 46, pp 8602-14.

Stalker, K. (1998) 'Some ethical issues and methodological issues in research with people with learning difficulties', *Disability and Society*, vol 13, no 1, pp 5-19.

Further reading
Barrett, M. (2000) 'Practical and ethical issues in planning research', in G.M. Breakwell, S. Hammond and C. Fife-Schaw (eds) *Research methods in psychology* (2nd edn), London: Sage Publications, pp 22-41.

Doyal, L. and Tobias, J.S. (eds) (2001) *Informed consent: Respecting patients' rights in research and practice*, London: BMJ.

Ribbens, J. and Edwards, R. (eds) (1998) *Feminist dilemmas in qualitative research: Public knowledge and private lives*, London: Sage Publications.

Website resources

British Psychological Society [the website provides detailed professional guidelines about obtaining consent and confidentiality. They state that: "psychologists shall normally carry out investigations or interventions only with the valid consent of participants, having taken all reasonable steps to ensure that they have adequately understood the nature of the investigation or intervention and its anticipated consequences"]: www.bps.org.uk/about/rules5.cfm

British Sociological Association [the website provides a 'statement of ethical principles']: www.britsoc.org.uk

3.15 'Race' and social policy research

Gary Craig, *Professor of Social Justice, University of Hull, and* Savita Katbamna, *Research Fellow, Nuffield Community Care Studies Unit, University of Leicester*

Until quite recently, mainstream social policy texts have contained relatively little discussion of 'race' and ethnicity. This situation has begun to change since the mid-1990s, although the situation is still uneven (see for example Craig, 1999; Craig and Ahmad, 2002). In parallel with this, 'race' has also been the 'missing dimension' (Rai, 1995) in social research; again the situation has improved recently, and has been given given further impetus by recent debates on 'race', including the consequences of the murder of Stephen Lawrence, discussion of asylum-seeking and migration, and debates about the nature of multiculturalism. However, much social policy research still has an inadequate 'race' dimension. The reasons for this derive in part from institutional and individual racism, but also from methodological limitations of many studies, regardless of their auspices, limitations shaping each stage of the research process, the formulation of research questions, the employment of researchers, the commissioning of research, data collection and analysis.

One difficulty is that many research organisations, including university units, do not incorporate a specialist 'race' dimension in their work. It is thus often left to individual researchers to include 'race' issues. These researchers may be of minority origin themselves and can feel marginalised within their own workplace; there are disproportionately few senior black and minority ethnic researchers in a position to influence research agendas. Occasionally, funders or commissioners of research may specify consideration of 'race'–related issues in research studies. However, in a culture where research agendas are set by funding bodies in consultation with the research community, 'race' overall tends often to occupy an invisible space. An absence of organisational policy, strategy or practice ethos to address the 'race' dimension inevitably then results in ad hoc and inconsistent practice patterns. Issues of cost are certainly important and these need to be faced early on in discussion with funders; for example, as **Box 3k** shows, recruitment may take a much longer period of time, and translation and interpretation may also involve additional costs.

Box 3k: The experiences and needs of carers in the British South Asian communities

Gary Craig, *Professor of Social Justice, University of Hull, and* Savita Katbamna, *Research Fellow, Nuffield Community Care Studies Unit, University of Leicester*

While there is a large mainstream literature on carers, there is a particular dearth of literature on South Asian carers. Katbamna et al's (1998) study was based on the experiences of adult carers, aged between 20 and 65+, caring for people with a wide range of conditions including some with multiple and complex disabilities. Respondents were recruited using radio and television interviews asking for volunteers, and snowballing through word of mouth, a process which took about six months in all before an adequate sample was achieved. To enable male and female carers from a wide range of linguistic and social situations to participate in the study, group discussions and interviews were conducted by trained interviewers matched for carers' gender and language. The study found that many carers were providing care in very difficult circumstances due to a lack of information on care-giving, poor quality of consultation with health professionals, difficulties in accessing appropriate and relevant services, and implicit or explicit racism.

Carers not speaking English found that they were expected to take full responsibility for disabled relatives without adequate explanations about the disabilities involved. Carers claimed that they were rarely included in the decision-making process and their need for practical, financial and emotional support was often dismissed by professionals whose views were influenced by cultural stereotypes and myths about the availability of unlimited support within extended family networks. Practitioners were often unaware that female carers who were widowed, divorced and those, particularly in the Bangladeshi community, who had recently settled in Britain, were caring in isolated situations with little family support. Carers and their disabled relatives were often also subjected to racist comments from practitioners because their cultural and religious practices were at odds with their own.

Reference
Katbamna, S., Bhakta, P., Ahmad, W., Baker, R. and Parker, G. (1998) *Experiences and needs of carers from the South Asian communities*, Leicester: Nuffield Community Care Studies Unit, University of Leicester.

The small proportional representation of minority communities in the UK population (over 7% overall but considerably lower in most areas) is often used to justify their exclusion from general research intended to have wider applicability. In qualitative research, it is believed that low numbers of members from minority communities in small sample sizes lead to meaningless data and results. Research that addresses minority communities is believed always to incur high costs – allegedly because of the collection of data in minority languages – and require complex research designs. Both examples described in **Boxes 3k** and **3l** used researchers matched for language and culture and these did not involve significant additional costs although the slow recruitment process in the second example did cost more; but the quality of the research was certainly enhanced in each case as a result of taking these issues seriously.

In quantitative research, it is also argued that the low numbers of potential respondents from minority communities lead to results that are difficult to interpret statistically. The use of 'booster samples' is often viewed as an unsatisfactory solution, on the grounds that these require complex research designs with complicated and costly analysis – however, as **Box 3l** shows again, this need not be the case. Boosting a sample is often critical to ensuring an effective 'race' dimension to research but need not be more expensive. Many researchers have reservations about using common sampling techniques for minority communities. They argue here that samples drawn only from densely populated 'minority' areas are not representative and are biased against members of these communities who live elsewhere; given the concentration of these minorities in a relatively few areas, this seems a particularly inappropriate argument.

Box 3I: The needs of Black and Asian young people leaving school

Gary Craig, *Professor of Social Justice, University of Hull, and* Savita Katbamna, *Research Fellow, Nuffield Community Care Studies Unit, University of Leicester*

Britton et al (2002) interviewed 16- to 18-year-olds about their experiences of *not* being in education, employment or training. It was known that many young people of African-Caribbean and Pakistani and Bangladeshi origin had poor levels of educational attainment, so the study was disproportionately weighted towards these groups. Of the 64 young people interviewed, 41 were from these origins. The study found that a disproportionate number of vulnerable young people – including those of minority origins – had been in public care and that those of minority origin had experienced racism both within care and/or within the educational system, from social services departments or other organisations responsible for looking after young people. Many had been excluded from school or had dropped out early, in part because of racism. Six young South Asian women reported pressure to accept arranged marriages; in some cases threats had been accompanied by actual physical violence or by other forms of coercion, such as withdrawal of parental financial support from those wishing to pursue careers or go on to college.

Although the study found a disproportionate number of young people from minority origins not using the local careers service, the careers service itself had failed to identify this service issue because it had no effective 'race' dimension to its work: it therefore saw the problem as 'a white, male, working-class problem'. None of these findings would have emerged clearly from a study which had taken a proportional approach to sampling, which would have interviewed only seven young minority people or which had relied solely on recruiting respondents by traditional means. The young people were recruited using a standardised simple 'person specification' partly through formal agencies such as the Careers Service and Training and Enterprise Council but also through local community organisations working with disaffected young people in an area with a large minority ethnic population.

Reference

Britton, L., Chatrik, B., Coles, B., Craig, G., Hylton, C. and Mumtaz, S. (2002) *Missing connexions?*, Bristol/York: The Policy Press/Joseph Rowntree Foundation.

In Rai's (1995) study, many researchers were unsure how to address 'race' in research, citing uncertainty about which minority communities to include in particular research studies, and a lack of awareness of their specific cultural norms and social circumstances. A 'play safe' option has often therefore been adopted, resulting in ignoring minority communities in research, often with the implicit or explicit collusion of policy organisations which themselves have not incorporated an effective 'race' dimension in their own policies and practices (see Craig, 2001).

Arguments for having a clear 'race' perspective within social research are, however, important. First, without it, research is racist and incomplete. Second, the minority population in the UK, already substantial, is growing; in some areas, minority ethnic groups are actually the *majority* population or are a majority of children and younger people, and this will be increasingly the case, a result of demographic change. Third, the minority ethnic population, contrary to popular belief, is very diverse, a diversity reflected in significant differences which exist between but also *within* various subgroups – for example, as between Turks, Turkish Kurds and Turkish Cypriots. These differences are a product of migration histories, settlement patterns, languages, religious and cultural traditions, socio-economic circumstances and social support networks (Katbamna et al, 1997). The assumption of homogeneity, which influenced much previous research on minority ethnic groups, has had particularly unfortunate consequences for the development of appropriate and relevant policy to meet the needs of differing communities. Fourth, minority ethnic communities often face the severest social problems, with higher levels of unemployment and dependency on state benefits, poor housing and health, and having greater difficulty in accessing goods and services. These difficulties, again often the consequence of racism within institutions (Craig, 2000, 2001; Katbamna, 2000; Craig and Ahmad, 2002; Katbamna et al, 2002), lead to minority ethnic groups (including now many with refugee or asylum-seeker status) becoming 'invisibilised', particularly in areas with small minority populations (Craig and Manthorpe, 2000). In terms of issues of citizenship and social cohesion, the consequences for policy and politics of ignoring the difficult and diverse experiences and views of minority ethnic groups are clear – for example, the disturbances in northern cities during 2001.

However, although some minority ethnic groups – particularly those of Bangladeshi and Pakistani origin – experience higher levels of deprivation, this is not uniformly the case. Similarly, there are vast differences in the level of literacy in English, educational attainment and in the mother-tongue. These differences are often strongly associated with gender, where a higher proportion of older women in all subgroups do not speak English (Modood et al, 1997). This requires special efforts to engage non-English speakers (by, for example, interviews in the language of choice, as in both the examples below) as well as other marginalised groups. Thus, an increasingly strong theme in social policy research must be to trace the varied social and economic trajectories of different minority ethnic groups, incorporating different methodological approaches in qualitative and quantitative research to overcome language and communication problems, and sensitivity about gender-related cultural issues.

This would help a move away from problematising minorities (which, by ignoring structural causes of their disadvantage, itself feeds racism) and towards seeing minorities as citizens with needs, rights and contributions to society. Important steps in this direction would be for all research-related agencies effectively to monitor 'race' issues both for employees and users – as many public agencies are now required to do under the terms of the 2000 Race Relations Amendment Act – and for research funders to insist on an appropriate 'race' dimension in all research they support.

Question for discussion

- What factors should funding bodies take into consideration to ensure that the 'race' and ethnic dimensions of research are appropriately addressed in work they fund?

References

Craig, G. (1999) '"Race", poverty and social security', in J. Ditch (ed) *An introduction to social security*, London: Routledge, pp 206-26.

Craig, G. (2000) '"Race" and welfare', Inaugural lecture as Professor of Social Justice, Hull: University of Hull.

Craig, G. (2001) '"Race" and New Labour', in G. Fimister (ed) *An end in sight?*, London: Child Poverty Action Group, pp 92-100.

Craig, G. and Ahmad, W. (2002) '"Race" and social policy', in P. Alcock, A. Erskine and M. May (eds) *A student companion to social policy* (2nd edn), Oxford: Blackwells, pp 91-7.

Craig, G. and Manthorpe, J. (2000) *Fresh fields: Agendas for policy, practice and research in rural social care*, York: York Publishing Services.

Katbamna, S. (2000) *'Race' and childbirth*, Buckingham: Open University Press.

Katbamna, S., Bhakta, P., Parker, G. and Ahmad, W. (1997) *The needs of Asian carers: A selective literature review*, Leicester: Nuffield Community Care Studies Unit, University of Leicester.

Katbamna, S., Bhakta, P., Parker, G., Baker, R. and Ahmad, W. (2002) 'Supporting South Asian carers and those they care for: the role of the primary health care team', *British Journal of General Practice*, vol 52, pp 300-5.

Modood, T., Berthoud, R., Lakey, J., Nazroo, J., Smith, P., Virdee, S. and Belshon, S. (1997) *Ethnic minorities in Britain: Diversity and disadvantage*, London: Policy Studies Institute.

Rai, D.K. (1995) *In the margins: Social research amongst Asian communities*, Social Research Papers No 2, Hull: University of Humberside.

Further reading

Craig, G. (1999) '"Race", poverty and social security', in J. Ditch (ed) *An introduction to social security*, London: Routledge, pp 206-26.

Modood, T., Berthoud, R., Lakey, J., Nazroo, J., Smith, P., Virdee, S. and Belshon, S. (1997) *Ethnic minorities in Britain: Diversity and disadvantage*, London: Policy Studies Institute.

Rai, D.K. (1995) *In the margins: Social research amongst Asian communities*, Social Research Papers No 2, Hull: University of Humberside [part of the argument in Section 3.9 draws on this text].

Website resources

Membership network of researchers of South Asian origin that produces an occasional newsletter: Sasrf@yahoogroups.com

Social Science Information Gateway [a website which has useful information relevant to 'race' and ethnicity]: www.sosig.ac.uk/social_welfare/

3.16 Researching sensitive topics

John D. Brewer, *Professor of Sociology, Queen's University, Belfast*

A concern with ethics has always been a feature of social research because it involves human subjects. But discussions of ethical practice tended to be formulaic, focusing on the autonomy of the researcher and their obligations to protect subjects. Ethical debates thus became associated with issues like confidentiality and informed consent, on the one hand, and academic freedom, on the other (see also Sections 3.14, Chapter Six, Sections 6.3 and 6.7). However, reading the disclosures they made of their research (for example, Bell and Newby, 1977; Bell and Roberts, 1984), it was clear that social researchers were also struggling with other issues, only unsatisfactorily subsumed under ethics (for example, Rainwater and Pittman, 1966): issues such as handling the controversy surrounding their findings, the danger to themselves or their subjects during the research, and the difficulties in trying to get people to participate or talk about a certain topic, or of working with one group or set of people (see Punch, 1989, for difficulties in researching police corruption).

By the early 1990s these sorts of concerns became codified under the name **sensitive research**, first addressed in a special issue of *American Behavioral Scientist* in 1990 and published later as an extended edited collection (see Renzetti and Lee, 1993). Topics included research on the Royal Ulster

Constabulary, child abuse, cults, the informal economy and AIDS. Since then the literature has been extended by Lee's codification of both sensitive research (1994) and dangerous fieldwork (1995), and further collections of case studies on sensitive topics (Lee-Treweek and Linkogle, 2000). This growing focus on sensitivity fits two developments in modern social science: the recognition of risk as a feature of contemporary life, including risk behaviour in social research; and the injunction on modern researchers, particularly qualitative ones, to be reflexive and to identify the contingencies that bore on their practice and helped to shape the extant data.

Sensitive research can be described *as research that has potential implications for society or key social groups, and is potentially threatening to the researcher or subjects in bringing economic, social, political or physical costs.* Sometimes these implications derive from the topic because of its controversy, from the status or behaviour of the subjects which brings risks to them or the researcher from the study, the biographical features or conduct of the researcher and the problems arising from the general context within which the research is undertaken. Sensitivity is therefore often highly situational, depending on the topic, local circumstances and the people involved as subjects and researchers. What in one case may be unproblematic will be sensitive in another. It is for this reason that researchers often give considerable thought in the planning and design stage to what might be sensitive about their research, since it affects all stages, including identifying a topic and sample, negotiating access, data collection and publication of the results. The reflexive researcher, when writing up the results, will comment on how issues around sensitivity, among other things, affected their conduct and the data (for example, see Brewer, 1991, pp 16-30; 1993).

Research on sensitive topics is well suited to qualitative methods. While questionnaire design can address these topics, often using the technique of funnelling where respondents are led slowly through a series of increasingly more personal and revealing questions, 'closed questions', where respondents select from predetermined answers, are particularly inappropriate for the complexity and subtlety of people's responses or where evasion might be anticipated. Qualitative research often entails a more sustained contact with the respondent, developed gradually over time so that rapport is established. This helps with the management of sensitivity by putting respondents at ease, thus permitting risks and fears about the researcher or the topic to be assuaged, controversial topics to be raised in the context of trust, and provides an opportunity for maximising the potential for truthful answers. Some of the data collection techniques used in qualitative research are particularly suitable in this regard, such as in-depth interviewing, ethnography and unobtrusive methods such as personal documents and records (see Lee, 2000, and **Box 3m** for a description of the process involved in researching the sensitive topic of how a child's death affects a family's finances). The use of vignettes, for example, is particularly popular in work with sensitive groups such as children (Barter and Renold, 1999; Brewer, 2000, pp 74-6; MacAuley, 1996) and drug users (Hughes, 1998). Indeed, some of the areas where sensitivity can be most anticipated is research on socially disadvantaged and powerless groups, such as children, women, abused groups such as victims of domestic violence, older people, gays and lesbians, 'non-able-bodied' people and minority ethnic groups. These are respondents who are relevant to policy-related research by mostly being defined in policy terms as 'problem' or 'target' groups (see Hood et al, 1999).

Question for discussion

* Is research on some topics or with some groups or in some contexts best ruled out because of its sensitivity? If not, how can these problems be managed?

References

Barter, C. and Renold, E. (1999) 'The use of vignettes in qualitative research', *Social Research Update*, no 25 (www.soc.surrey.ac.uk/sru/SRU25.html).

Bell, C. and Newby, H. (1977) *Doing sociological research*, London: Allen and Unwin.

Bell, C. and Roberts, H. (1984) *Social researching*, London: Routledge.

Brewer, J.D. (1991) *Inside the RUC: Routine policing in a divided society*, Oxford: Clarendon Press.

Brewer, J.D. (1993) 'Sensitivity as a problem in field research: a study of routine policing in Northern Ireland', in C. Renzetti and R. Lee (eds) *Researching sensitive topics*, London: Sage Publications, pp 125-45.

Brewer, J.D. (2000) *Ethnography*, Buckingham: Open University Press.

Hood, S., Mayall, B. and Oliver, S. (1999) *Critical issues in social research*, Buckingham: Open University Press.

Hughes, J. (1998) 'Considering the vignette technique and its application to drug injecting and HIV risk and safer behaviour', *Sociology of Health and Illness*, vol 20, pp 381-400.

Lee, R.M. (1994) *Doing sensitive research*, London: Sage Publications.

Lee, R.M. (1995) *Dangerous fieldwork*, London: Sage Publications.

Lee, R.M. (2000) *Unobtrusive methods in social research*, Buckingham: Open University Press.

Lee-Treweek, G. and Linkogle, S. (2000) *Danger in the field*, London: Routledge.

MacAuley, C. (1996) *Children in long term foster care*, Aldershot: Avebury.

Punch, M. (1989) 'Researching police deviance', *British Journal of Sociology*, vol 40, pp 177-204.

Rainwater, L. and Pittman, D. (1966) 'Ethical problems in studying a politically sensitive and deviant community', *Social Problems*, vol 14, pp 357-66.

Renzetti, C. and Lee, R.M. (1993) *Researching sensitive topics*, London: Sage Publications.

Further reading

Lee, R. (1994) *Doing sensitive research*, London: Sage Publications.
Renzetti, C. and Lee, R. (eds) (1993) *Researching sensitive topics*, London: Sage Publications.
Lee-Treweek, G. and Linkogle, S. (eds) (2000) *Danger in the field*, London: Routledge.

Website resource

British Sociological Association [statement of research ethics]:
   www.britsoc.co.uk/index.php?link_id=14&area=item1
(See also the website resources for Sections 3.14 and Chapter Six, Section 6.3.)

Box 3m: Research with recently bereaved parents

Anne Corden, *Research Fellow, Social Policy Research Unit, University of York*

The Social Policy Research Unit (SPRU) was approached by a children's hospice in 1999 to undertake a small-scale study of the financial implications of the death of a child (Corden et al, 2001). There was little other literature or research which linked money matters and childhood death, areas of great sensitivity requiring care throughout. Three senior, experienced researchers shared responsibility for all stages of the work, working closely with senior staff at the children's hospice.

First, approval was sought from the relevant NHS Local Research Ethics Committee.

It was considered important to learn from other people's knowledge and experience, and this was approached in two ways. A project advisory group was recruited, including bereaved parents and staff from children's hospices and parents' support services, and this was particularly helpful in the early stages of the work. By joining the Bereavement Research Forum, a group of academics and practitioners meeting regularly to discuss issues around bereavement, the researchers learned from and shared experiences with others conducting bereavement research.

Sensitivities of both subjects and researchers had to be addressed. The research involved in-depth interviews with recently bereaved parents in touch with the children's hospice. The researchers followed normal good practice in research, paying particular attention to the way in which parents were approached (taking advice from the advisory group), language used in letters and interviews, and the timing of interviews. Taking advice from hospice staff, researchers did not approach families around the anniversary of their child's birthday or death, and there was a break in recruitment and fieldwork in the run-up to Christmas.

The researchers took cues from parents as to how much they wanted to talk about the child who had died, and whether and how brothers and sisters of the child who had died were drawn in. As the work proceeded some parents initially not selected for the research asked to take part, and the researchers responded positively.

What was talked about was very sad, but it proved possible to discuss money matters with recently bereaved parents (Corden et al, 2002). Hospice staff were ready to discuss these interviews with any parents who wanted this. The researchers' letters thanking parents provided opportunities for sending other contact addresses which might be helpful, for example employment advisers.

When a summary of research findings was available, the researchers checked before mailing whether parents still wanted these. Some parents decided not to receive a summary, after all, a further indication of the particular care needed when researching such sensitive topics.

Interviews about sensitive subjects make particular demands on researchers as well as subjects and the research funder (Joseph Rowntree Foundation) agreed to fund access to some professional support. Meeting a group psychotherapist before starting fieldwork to consider what personal impact and effect there might be helped the team prepare positively. At the end of the project, a further group meeting enabled discussion of the experience. This way of supporting researchers working in areas which might be risky to emotional health was considered useful (Corden et al, forthcoming).

Question for discussion
- At what stage in a research project should you pay attention to possible sensitivities in the area of study?

References
Corden, A., Sainsbury, R. and Sloper, P. (2001) *Financial implications of the death of a child*, London: Family Policy Studies Centre.
Corden, A., Sainsbury, R. and Sloper, P. (2002) 'When a child dies: money matters', *Illness, Crisis and Loss*, vol 7, no 4, pp 125-37.

Corden, A., Sainsbury, R., Sloper, P. and Ward, B. (forthcoming) 'Using a model of group psychotherapy to support social research on sensitive topics', *International Journal of Social Research Methodology.*

Further reading

Gilbert, K. (ed) (2001) *The emotional nature of qualitative research*, Washington, DC: CRC Press.

Hindmarch, C. (2000) *On the death of a child*, Abingdon: Radcliffe Medical Press.

Lee, R.M. (1993) *Doing research on sensitive topics*, London: Sage Publications.

Relevant organisations

Association of Children's Hospices Palliative Care Forum
151 Whiteladies Road, Bristol, BS8 2RA
Social Research Association
4 Tintagel Crescent, London, SE22 8HT
www.the-sra.org.uk

3.17 Researching vulnerable groups

Linda Ward, *Professor of Disability and Social Policy, and Director, Norah Fry Research Centre, University of Bristol*

Since 1988 we have seen a new emphasis in legislation and official guidance on consulting children and adults about the services they use and involving them in their planning and development (for example, the 1989 Children Act; 1990 NHS and Community Care Act; Valuing People – DoH, 2001). This emphasis has been paralleled within social research, where increasing attention has been given by researchers and research funders (for example, Ward, 1997a, 1997b; Ward and Watson, 2001) to ways of appropriately involving people who use services in research studies about them (*Disability, Handicap and Society*, 1992). Equal opportunities legislation in the 1980s and 1990s and the government's social inclusion agenda have been reflected in a new attention to inclusiveness in the research process, to ensure that the perspectives and experiences of disadvantaged and vulnerable groups are reflected in research findings – and the evidence-based practice which may ensue.

It is arguable that there will always be a power imbalance between researcher and researched, given that the researcher is in control of the agenda. But some groups are particularly 'vulnerable' within the research process as they are in the wider society – for example, people with learning difficulties (intellectual impairments), children, disabled people, people with mental health problems, older people and others living in residential care provision. This section focuses particularly on ethical and methodological issues arising in research involving adults with learning disabilities and disabled children and youngsters, but the key points are just as applicable to other 'vulnerable' groups.

Involving vulnerable people as research respondents

- *Vulnerable people are key informants about their lives:* this may seem self-evident, but, until recently, it was parents (or professionals) who were asked about issues to do with adults with learning disabilities and disabled children and youngsters, *not* those individuals themselves.
- *The ethical issues posed by research with vulnerable people require careful consideration:* Alderson (1995) points out that ethics are based on centuries of patriarchal law and philosophy, some of which discriminate against women and children (and other vulnerable groups). Traditional ethics have carried a strong theme of avoiding (potential) harm. But alternative harms have tended to be ignored: protecting children and other vulnerable groups so much that they, and their voices, are excluded from research (see also Sections 3.14 and Chapter Six, Section 6.3).
- *Making information accessible:* if potential research participants are to make an informed choice to be involved in a research study, they need information on which to make up their mind. Alderson (1995) provides a sample leaflet for young people explaining the implications of joining a research project. Different vulnerable groups will require different kinds of information to ensure its accessibility to them: for people with learning disabilities this may be an illustrated leaflet or tape (Townsley, 1999).
- *Consent:* ethical research with vulnerable groups needs their informed consent to participation (**Box 3j**). Where children are concerned, the law over consent remains uncertain. A key issue is competence – whether or not a child or adult can be appropriately involved in making decisions about whether to take part (Ward, 1997b). There is a growing literature on the practicalities of gaining proper consent from children, young people and other vulnerable groups to participate in research projects (Alderson, 1995; Ward, 1997b).
- *Preparation and practicalities:* research with vulnerable groups demands careful preparation. (Where and when can interviews be undertaken appropriately? It may be desirable to interview respondents on their own; but youngsters living away from home, or older people or adults with learning disabilities living in residential provision, may only have access to their bedrooms as a private space, which may pose other ethical dilemmas for the interviewer.)

Where a respondent has communication impairments then a facilitator (chosen by them) may be necessary (Morris, 1998).

- *Communication:* where respondents do not read English, or have difficulty understanding complex information, alternative methodologies must be devised (Beresford, 1997; Stalker, 1998).
- *Closure and 'aftercare':* where it is possible that respondents may become distressed during or after an interview or request information, appropriate sources of help, referral or advice should be collated beforehand, with the researcher careful not to take on inappropriate roles (for example, counsellor) themselves (Morris, 1998).
- *Payment to the research respondents:* (often by gift voucher) is increasingly recognised as an appropriate way of acknowledging their contribution to the research process (Ward, 1997b).
- *Accessible outputs:* research participants should have access if they want it (see Chapter Seven, Section 7.4) to a summary of research findings in a format accessible to them, for example, an illustrated leaflet and tape such as *Plain facts* (Townsley, 1998). This takes time and money which needs to be costed into the research budget (see Chapter Six, Section 6.8).
- *Research is an iterative process:* a project advisory group, comprising key stakeholders, with a mandate to scrutinise all aspects of the research process including their ethical implications, will increase the chances of ethical and methodologically sound practice throughout (Ward and Watson, 2001; see also Chapter Six, Section 6.9).

Box 3n illustrates how disabled children were involved in a research study examining their experiences and feelings of attending boarding school.

Box 3n: Involving disabled children in research
David Abbott, *Research Fellow, Norah Fry Research Centre, University of Bristol*

Finding out about the experiences of disabled children at boarding schools
The research question in this study (Abbott et al, 2001) was how well the law safeguards the interests of disabled children who go away to boarding schools. A key component was finding out how children feel about being at boarding school. To do this we needed to think about how to find out information from disabled children of different ages, with different levels of learning difficulty and with different ways of communicating (including non-verbal).

Getting advice from other young disabled people
The research team got advice from a 'reference group' of young disabled people who had been to residential school. We asked them about the kinds of questions

to ask and how to ask them. The group thought that the first draft of our interview schedule was 'very serious' and had missed out some important topics relating to leisure and friendship. The group told us what information we should give to help people decide whether or not to take part. The group gave us their views on getting consent and on the question of confidentiality that we took account of.

Getting access to training

Many disabled children who go to residential school have quite high levels of support needs and may well not use any words to communicate. These children have often been excluded from research as it has been assumed that they will not be able to take part. The research team attended training provided by Triangle (see below) to learn more about how to find out information by 'being with' children and young people. We also looked at resources and research done by other people in this area (Children's Society, 1997, 2001; Marchant et al, 1999; Triangle/NSPCC, 2001; Morris, 2002). The training helped us feel more confident about spending time with disabled children who don't use speech to communicate.

Doing it

We carried out interviews with a number of children some of whom used words and some of whom could communicate 'yes' or 'no' by using body language. We spent time together practising getting this right. With other children we spent at least a whole day at school with them joining in activities and finding out about their feelings by being with them.

Checklist: some important points when finding out about the experiences of disabled children and young people

- Assume that everyone can communicate.
- Recognise the barriers that will be put in your way, for example, adults telling you that a child won't be able to take part.
- Be flexible about when you can go – don't just offer weekdays.
- Allow lots of time for setting up the visit.
- Take things with you like paper, pens, toys, pictures – but be prepared to use none of them.
- Don't feel bad about making mistakes. Don't feel bad about not understanding when someone is trying to tell you something: persevere.
- Send a 'thank you' card after the visit and maybe a gift voucher.
- Make sure your project budget has enough resources for the time it takes to do this work properly.

Source: Adapted from Morris (1998)

Finally, think about how you are going to let disabled children and young people know what your research has found out in ways that are interesting and accessible to them.

Question for discussion
- What steps would you need to take so that disabled children and young people could take part in the different stages of a research project?

References
Abbott, D., Morris, J. and Ward, L. (2001) *The best place to be? Policy, practice and the experiences of residential school placements for disabled children*, York: Joseph Rowntree Foundation/York Publishing Services.

Children's Society (1997) *I'll go first: The planning and review toolkit for use with children with disabilities*, London: The Children's Society.

Children's Society (2001) *Ask us*, CD-ROM summarising key messages from a multimedia project to involve disabled children in policy development on Quality Protects, London: The Children's Society.

Marchant, R., Jones, M., Julyan, A. and Giles, A. (1999) *Listening on all channels: Consulting with disabled children and young people*, Brighton: Triangle.

Morris, J. (1998) *Don't leave us out: Involving disabled children and young people with communication impairments*, York: Joseph Rowntree Foundation/ York Publishing Services.

Morris, J. (2002) *A lot to say: A guide for social workers, personal advisors, and others working with young people with communication impairments*, London: Scope [this publication is available free from Scope, 6 Market Road, London N7 9PW. Telephone 020 7619 7100].

Triangle/NSPCC (2001) *Two way street* [training video and handbook on communicating with children who do not use speech or language], Leicester: NSPCC.

Further reading
Morris, J. (1998) *Don't leave us out: Involving disabled children and young people with communication impairments*, York: Joseph Rowntree Foundation/ York Publishing Services.

Morris, J. (2003) 'Including all children: finding out about the experiences of children with communication and/or cognitive impairments', *Children and Society*, vol 17, no 5.

Ward, L. (1997) *Seen and heard: Involving disabled children and young people in research and development projects*, York: Joseph Rowntree Foundation/ York Publishing Services.

Relevant organisations
Council for Disabled Children
8 Wakley Street, London ECI 7QE
Telephone 0207 843 6059
Norah Fry Research Centre
University of Bristol, 3 Priory Road, Bristol BS8 1TX
Telephone 0117 923 8137; fax 0117 946 6553; minicom 0117 928 8856
The Children's Society
Edward Rudolf House, Margery Street, London WC1X 0LJ
Telephone 0845 300 1128; www.the-childrens-society.org.uk
Triangle
Unit 310, 91 Western Road, Brighton BN1 2NM
Telephone 01273 241015; www.triangle-services.co.uk

Involving vulnerable groups in the research process

Increasingly, those who have traditionally been the 'subjects' of research – for example, disabled people – are arguing for more involvement in shaping and undertaking it themselves. There is now a growing body of literature describing how different groups can be involved in this way (Tozer and Thornton, 1995; Ward, 1997a, 1997b; Morris, 1998; Kirby, 1999; Patel, 1999; Williams, 1999; Worrall, 2000) and examples of their involvement throughout the research process:

- formulating the initial ideas for research;
- helping to plan it;
- providing consultancy to the research project on a paid basis;
- sitting as members of project advisory or reference groups;
- undertaking interviewing and other research work;
- being involved in analysis and production of material;
- taking part in the dissemination of project findings (Ward, 1997b; see also Section 3.6 on user participatory research, and 3.7 on action research).

In some cases, so called 'vulnerable' groups, such as people with learning difficulties, have undertaken funded research projects themselves (Swindon People First, 2002).

Most people from vulnerable groups, like any other members of society, will need support and training to undertake research successfully. There are a growing number of resources now available to facilitate this, including outputs from the Mental Health Foundation's 'Strategies for living' project on research by mental health service users (Faulkner and Nicholls, 1999).

Question for discussion

- If you were considering research involving 'vulnerable' people, what would you need to think about to ensure that the study was appropriate methodologically and ethically?

References

Alderson, P. (1995) *Listening to children: Children, ethics and social research*, London: Barnardo's.

Beresford, B. (1997) *Personal accounts: Involving disabled children in research*, London: The Stationery Office.

Disability, Handicap and Society (1992) vol 7, no 2; special issue on 'researching disability'.

DoH (Department of Health) (2001) *Valuing people: A new strategy for learning disability for the 21st Century*, London: The Stationery Office.

Faulkner, A. and Nicholls, V. (1999) *DIY guide to survivor research*, London: The Mental Health Foundation.

Kirby, P. (1999) *Involving young researchers: How to enable young people to design and conduct research*, York: York Publishing Services for the Joseph Rowntree Foundation/Save the Children.

Morris, J. (1998) *Don't leave us out: Involving disabled children and young people with communication impairments*, York: York Publishing Services for the Joseph Rowntree Foundation.

Patel, N. (1999) *Getting the evidence: Guidelines for ethical mental health research involving issues of 'race', ethnicity and culture*, London: MIND/Transcultural Psychiatry Society.

Stalker, K. (1998) 'Some ethical and methodological issues in research with people with learning difficulties', *Disability and Society*, vol 13, no 1, pp 5-19.

Swindon People First (2002) *Journey to independence*, Kidderminster: British Institute of Learning Disabilities.

Townsley, R. (1998) 'Information is power: the impact of accessible information on people with learning difficulties', in L. Ward (ed) *Innovations in advocacy and empowerment for people with intellectual disabilities*, Chorley: Liseux Hall Publications, pp 77-90.

Townsley, R. (1999) 'Putting it plainly: producing easy to understand information for people with learning difficulties', *Frontline*, no 40, pp 12-13.

Tozer, R. and Thornton, P. (1995) *A meeting of minds: Older people as research advisers*, York: Social Policy Research Unit, University of York.

Ward, L. (1997a) 'Funding for change: translating emancipatory disability research from theory to practice', in C. Barnes and G. Mercer (eds) *Doing disability research*, Leeds, The Disability Press, pp 32-48.

Ward, L. (1997b) *Seen and heard: Involving disabled children and young people in research and development projects*, York: York Publishing Services for the Joseph Rowntree Foundation.

Ward, L. and Watson, D. (2001) *Doing research – and doing it right*, London: Community Fund.

Williams, V. (1999) 'Researching together', *British Journal of Learning Disabilities*, vol 27, no 2, pp 48-51.

Worrall, S. (2000) *Young people as researchers: A learning resource pack*, London: Save the Children.

Further reading

Alderson, P. (1995) *Listening to children: Children, ethics and social research*, London: Barnardo's.

British Journal of Learning Disabilities (1998) vol 26, no 4; special issue on 'research and ethics'.

Ward, L. and Watson, D. (2001) *Doing research – and doing it right*, London: Community Fund.

Relevant organisations

Consumers for Ethics in Research
PO Box 1365, London N16 0BW
Consumers in NHS Research Support Unit
Wessex House, Upper Market Street, Eastleigh, Hampshire SO50 9FD
Telephone 023 8065 1088; www.conres.co.uk
Mental Health Foundation (Strategies for living project)
7th Floor, 83 Victoria Street, London SW1H 0HW
Telephone 020 7802 0300; www.mentalhealth.org.uk
Norah Fry Research Centre (including Plain Facts team)
University of Bristol, 3 Priory Road, Bristol BS8 1TX
Telephone 0117 923 8137; www.bris.ac.uk/Depts/NorahFry

Website resources

Community Fund: www.c-f.org.uk
Joseph Rowntree Foundation:www.jrf.org.uk
Plain Facts: www.bris.ac.uk/Depts/NorahFry/PlainFacts

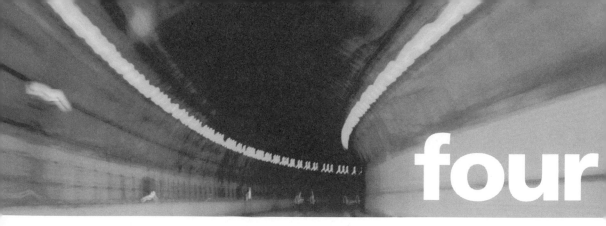

Quantitative research

Detailed contents

4.1 Introduction

In this chapter we address the main aspects of conducting quantitative research. The chapter is divided into three parts:

Part One: Fundamentals of quantitative research. This section begins by addressing the nature of quantitative research and the significance of the criteria that are conventionally employed by practitioners to establish the quality of their investigations. It then moves on to discuss two aspects of quantitative research that are fundamental aspects of social policy research associated with this strategy: the different kinds of research design employed by quantitative researchers (including experimental, cross-sectional, longitudinal and case study designs) and the approaches to sampling that they use.

Part Two: Methods for collecting and coding quantitative data. This part begins by noting the importance of coding to the processing of data. The significance of coding lies in the importance of generating data that can be quantified. The methods for the collection of quantitative data that are discussed are:

- structured interviews and questionnaires in survey research;
- content analysis;
- structured observation;
- official statistics; and
- Internet surveys.

Strictly speaking, two of these methods – content analysis and official statistics – are not methods for collecting data. The former is a method of handling unstructured data and information such as media reports, and official statistics are a source of data. However, they are important sources of quantitative data and as such are treated as similar to methods for the collection of data.

Part Three: The analysis of quantitative data. This final section deals with the basic elements of conducting an analysis of quantitative data.

PART ONE: FUNDAMENTALS OF QUANTITATIVE RESEARCH

4.2 Quantitative research

We have already encountered quantitative research in Chapter Three as an approach to social policy research that draws on principles associated with the natural sciences for its fundamental principles. The main concerns and preoccupations of quantitative researchers can be viewed as stemming from this commitment. The four main concerns and preoccupations were described as being: measurement; causality; generalisation; and replication. Therefore, although the term *quantitative* research seems to imply that quantification is the sole distinguishing characteristic of this research strategy, it is clear that there is more to quantitative research than the mere presence of numbers.

As Bryman (2004) points out, in addition to its epistemological roots in a natural science view of the research process, quantitative research tends to have two important features that further distinguish it from qualitative research. First, the approach taken by quantitative researchers typically involves a *deductive* approach to the relationship between theory and research. This term was encountered in Robert Pinker's discussion of the role of theory in social policy research in Chapter Two, Section 2.5. A deductive approach involves the drawing of research questions from an established body of knowledge which are then tested for their soundness. As Pinker points out, according to Popper, we are unlikely to be able to demonstrate a definitive truth through such a process, since all we can have is a temporarily confirmed knowledge.

Second, quantitative research adopts an **objectivist** position with respect to the nature of social reality. This means that social phenomena and social reality are generally construed as 'out there' for social actors, as entities that confront them as out of their scope of influence. Thus, something like a social network can be viewed as a thing that is independent of the people who participate in it and as such a sphere in which they can have limited impact. It is viewed as a collection of connections between individuals and groups and little more. A **constructionist** position, which tends to be associated with qualitative research, tends to challenge this standpoint by paying greater attention to the role that individuals play in constructing that network and having an influence over it. In thinking of social reality in an objectivist manner, quantitative researchers display their commitment to a natural science model of the research process since the natural order is frequently conceptualised as a pre-existing phenomenon awaiting the analytic tools of the natural scientist.

Quality criteria in quantitative research

One of the ways in which the natural science leanings of quantitative research are particularly evident is in the criteria that are employed for assessing the quality of research. Quantitative researchers have developed a well-understood and clear set of criteria that influence the way research is done and written about. To a certain extent, these criteria will be unsurprising because they exhibit clear connections with the four concerns and preoccupations among quantitative researchers that were outlined in Chapter Three.

Reliability

Reliability has to do with the consistency or stability of findings. This issue is most clearly apparent in connection with measurement issues. To have a reliable measure means having one that is consistent. There are two main aspects of this notion. First, a measure needs to be *externally reliable*, meaning that it should not fluctuate over time. To take a simple example: if we develop a measure of client satisfaction with a social service provider, we would not expect people's levels of client satisfaction to fluctuate other than due to changes in such things as their personal circumstances or the manner in which the service is provided. In order to assess external reliability, the researcher might administer a series of questions (let us say ten) about the levels of client satisfaction in a sample. This series of questions might be designed to establish a scale so that respondents' replies can be aggregated to form a level of client satisfaction for each respondent and indeed for the sample as a whole. The questions might take the form of what is known as **Likert scale** items like:

Staff are always responsive to my needs

| Strongly agree | Agree | Neither agree nor disagree | Disagree | Strongly disagree |

I find the rules for getting the particular service I need difficult to understand

| Strongly agree | Agree | Neither agree nor disagree | Disagree | Strongly disagree |

With a Likert scale, the respondent is provided with a series of statements that are designed to establish his or her feelings about an issue by getting the respondent to indicate the degree of agreement with the statement as in the two 'items' above. Each answer is 'coded' (see Section 4.5 for a discussion of coding) so that answers can be aggregated.

Let us say that we administer the scale to a sample of home care recipients to measure their degree of satisfaction with the service. We would find out each individual's level of client satisfaction. If we then administered the same measure again a month or two later, we would hope that unless something very significant has happened in the meantime (such as an influx of new staff or a new set of administrative procedures), there will be a good correspondence between people's answers over the two time periods. If there is not a good correspondence, the measure is externally *un*reliable.

Internal reliability is an issue that is predominantly to do with what are known as multiple-item scales such as a Likert scale. It asks the question: are all the items that make up the scale coherent? In other words, are they all connected to each other? If they are not, perhaps because one of the items is poorly related to the other items, it is not going to be an internally reliable measure. After all, it is unlikely that you would want a scale, one of whose constituent items is unrelated to the others. Internal reliability is often established using a check known as *split-half reliability*. In the case of our imaginary measure of client satisfaction, this would mean taking the ten items and randomly dividing them into two groups of five and then examining whether respondents' scores on one half correlate well with their scores on the other five items.

Validity

Validity is concerned with the issue of whether a measure that has been devised, such as our imaginary measure of client satisfaction, really gauges the underlying concept that it is presumed to be tapping. In other words, if we devise a scale of client satisfaction, how do we know that it is measuring client satisfaction and not something else? For a start, the measure must be reliable. If a measure is either internally or externally unreliable it cannot be a valid measure. If a measure fluctuated without explanation over time or if one or two of its constituent items was inconsistent with the others, it could hardly be valid. However, establishing reliability is only a first step in ensuring that a measure is valid. Several other approaches to estimating the validity of a measure are often used, of which two are discussed below. Other validity tests are discussed in Bryman (2004, pp 72-5).

At the very least, a measure should have *face validity*. This means that the researcher should determine that, as far as we can tell, the measure has a very good chance of tapping the underlying idea (client satisfaction). A close reading of the literature on client satisfaction will help to increase confidence since this should help to map out the main issues. In addition, face validity can be boosted by asking others to check the items that make up the measure. These people might include researchers in the field, a supervisor, practitioners and clients themselves. As regards the latter, it might be useful to use a group discussion to help devise questions and to hold another discussion to get feedback on the items that have been designed.

A further way of looking at validity is *concurrent validity*. Here, the researcher employs a criterion for establishing how far people differ on the measure in terms of the criterion. It may be that there is an external criterion that might be used, such as whether people have complained in the previous six months about the service. If it were possible to relate respondents' replies to whether they have launched a complaint, this would enable us to gauge concurrent validity. If clients who were dissatisfied with the service were more likely to have complained than those who were satisfied, our confidence in the validity of the measure would be enhanced.

In addition to the question of the validity of measurement, there is the issue of the validity of the findings from an investigation. In this connection, it is common to distinguish between *internal validity* and *external validity*, although other notions of validity exist (Bryman, 2004). Internal validity is to do with the issue of the robustness of the findings from a quantitative research investigation in terms of how sure we can be about the causal connections that we might infer from the research. In other words, if we find that income affects health, how sure can we be that it is income that affects health differentials and not something else? This issue will be dealt with in greater detail in the section on research design below, since the issue of how confident we can be in our causal findings is a major consideration and one in which the classical experimental design or randomised controlled trial is frequently regarded as a 'gold standard'. External validity is concerned with the issue of generalisation – to what populations and groups can we generalise our findings? If a study is externally valid, then it is generalisable to a specific population. The issue of generalisation is the focus of the next section.

Generalisation

Quantitative researchers typically want to be able to generalise their findings beyond the scope of the specific group (for example, a sample of respondents) on which they have conducted their investigation. This emphasis is connected with the adoption of natural science principles, since the focus on generalisation can be seen as sharing a predilection for findings that have a similar importance and features of scientific laws.

This emphasis on generalisation reveals itself particularly in the attention given to ways of maximising the chances of securing a representative sample (see Section 4.4). In this context, sampling procedures that adopt probability and random sampling principles are seen as crucial because they are most likely to produce a sample that is representative of the population from which the sample was selected. Convenience and purposive samples are often held in low esteem because they are not based on these principles and hence likely to be of unknown representativeness.

Replication

Scientists are frequently concerned that their findings should be capable of being replicated so that another scientist could, if they wanted to, attempt to reproduce their investigations. The idea behind the faith in replication is that findings should be (and be seen to be) independent of the person producing them. There is always the possibility that a scientist has distorted his or her findings or has not taken care to eliminate all possible contaminating factors that might have had an impact on the findings. Replication offers the opportunity to check those findings. This means that the scientist needs to spell out the procedures followed and instruments used so that someone else can follow the same route that was taken.

This principle of being able to spell out the ways in which research was conducted, the instruments used, and the procedures for analysing data has been absorbed into quantitative research, where the ability to conduct a replication is a valued feature of a research design. In the social sciences, the potentially contaminating effects of the values of the researcher are more likely to intrude than in the natural sciences, so that replication has potentially greater significance.

Honouring in the breach

To take a cue from *Hamlet* (I. iv.16), many of these principles, when it comes to research practice are customs that are honoured more in the breach than in the observance. In other words, while they are widely regarded as important principles, they are not universally observed. External reliability testing is potentially time consuming and the findings deriving from it can be ambiguous (how do we know that intervening events have not had an impact in the period between the two periods of data collection?). Validity testing can be similarly extremely time consuming once we go beyond establishing face validity. Generalisation from representative samples is often difficult because in social policy research certain populations may not lend themselves to the probability sampling principles outlined in Section 4.4 because it is hard to know what the population is like (for example, homeless people, informal carers). Finally, replications are rarely carried out in either the natural or the social sciences because replication is a relatively low status activity; instead, it is probably more accurate to say that it is the ability to replicate – *replicability* – that is regarded as an important quality criterion rather than replication as such.

Question for discussion

- What is the difference between reliability and validity and what is the importance of these two ideas?

Reference

Bryman, A. (2004) *Social research methods* (2nd edn), Oxford: Oxford University Press.

Further reading

Bryman, A. (2004) *Social research methods* (2nd edn), Oxford: Oxford University Press, Chapter 2.

Litwin, M.S. (1995) *How to measure survey reliability and validity*, Thousand Oaks, CA: Sage Publications.

4.3 Research design

The terms *research design* and *research method* have a superficial similarity and are often used interchangeably if not synonymously. In this book, we draw a distinction between the two. *A research method is a technique for gathering data, like a questionnaire, interview or observation. A research design is a structure or framework within which data are collected.* As de Vaus (2001, p 9) points out: "The function of a research design is to ensure that the evidence obtained enables us to answer the initial questions as unambiguously as possible". Understanding the nature of research design and the differences between the various types of design that will be outlined below is important because a research design provides the structure that will enable the research questions we start out with to be answered. A research design is selected for its capacity to answer the research questions that drive an investigation.

Research methods can serve different designs. In other words, a method of data collection such as a questionnaire can be employed in connection with all of the research designs that will be delineated in this chapter. Decisions about appropriate research methods are in a sense subsidiary to decisions about an appropriate research design, since it is the research design that provides the framework for answering research questions. An important principle to appreciate is that there is no universally superior research design (or indeed research method) – they are only as good as their suitability to the research questions being asked. It is important, therefore, to wean yourself off a personal preference for a research design or method because it may be blinding you to alternative and possibly more suitable ways of answering research questions.

In this section, we will cover the four major types of research design:

• experimental (including quasi-experimental);
• cross-sectional (including social survey);
• longitudinal;
• case study.

Experimental design

The term *experiment* is often used vaguely, particularly in everyday speech. In social research methodology, however, it has a specific meaning as a type of research design whose strength lies in its ability to demonstrate relatively clear findings which demonstrate internal validity, that is, that one variable (the independent variable) really does have a causal impact on another (the dependent variable).

Imagine that we hypothesise that client satisfaction with Housing Benefit departments is affected by the type of training that staff have received, in particular, whether they have received training in anger management. We are expecting the independent variable (training) to affect the dependent variable (satisfaction). A true experiment could have the following elements:

• Manipulation – the experimental treatment (training).
• Two groups – an *experimental group* that receives the anger management training and a *control group* that does not.
• Equivalence – of the experimental and control groups. This means that staff in the experimental and control groups must be equivalent in terms of their personal characteristics. This is ideally achieved through random assignment. In this case, staff in a Housing Benefit department would need to be randomly assigned to the two conditions, so that one group would have the training and the other (the control group) would not.
• Time order – client satisfaction will be measured before (pre-test) *and* after (post-test) the experimental treatment.

Thus, the structure of the experiment takes the form of a specific design sometimes called a *classical experimental design* or *randomised controlled trial*.

Figure 4a: Experimental design for examining the impact of training in anger management on client satisfaction with service provision

	Pre-test	**Experimental treatment**	**Post-test**	*Experimental group*
	Client satisfaction	Training	Client satisfaction	

Random assignment

	Pre-test	**No treatment**	**Post-test**	*Control group*
	Client satisfaction	No training	Client satisfaction	

In this experiment, the experimental treatment involves some staff attending training in anger management and others not attending the training (see Figure 4a). The two groups must be randomly assigned, otherwise any differences observed between the experimental and control groups could be attributed to differences in the memberships of the two groups. If we find that anger management training does make a difference, so that client satisfaction increases in the experimental group whereas in the control group it does not, we have strong, internally valid evidence to suggest that training in anger management does indeed have an impact on client satisfaction because it eliminates such alternative possible explanations as:

• Client satisfaction might have increased anyway. This can be discounted because if that were the case it would have shown up in the control group.
• The attitudes of research participants may have changed. Again, because of the control group this can be discounted.
• Differences between the two groups. Random assignment allows this possible factor to be discounted.

Moreover, there is no ambiguity about which variable influences which, a problem that does occur in connection with a cross-sectional design. However, whether it fares as well in connection with the issue of external validity may be a different matter. The benefit office where the research was conducted is unlikely to be typical in part because it is difficult to imagine what a typical office is.

It is often the case that when researchers seek to conduct experiments, for various reasons they are not able to randomly assign participants to the experimental and control groups. Managers may be unwilling to allow researchers that much control since it may have an impact on the efficient running of the department. Therefore, researchers have to make do with what is known as a *quasi-experiment*, in which all of the features in Figure 4a are met other than random assignment.

Cross-sectional design

A cross-sectional design is typified by a social survey. Unlike an experimental design, there is no manipulation of a setting, almost always because the variables in which the researcher is interested are not capable of being manipulated for practical or ethical reasons. Examples of variables that are often regarded as independent variables but are not capable of being manipulated are gender, education, age, ethnicity, income and occupation. In the case of all of these variables, we cannot make research participants male or female, well or poorly educated, old or young, wealthy or poor, and so on. The cross-sectional design contains the following features:

- It is based on existing differences between people rather than differences that are created by the experimenter.
- Data are usually collected on a large number of variables so that the connections among a wide range of variables can be studied.
- The design is usually based on the collection of data from a large number of cases, which may be people, organisations, newspapers, regions, etc.

The social survey in which the researcher collects a large amount of data from many people using a questionnaire or structured interview is one of the main ways in which the cross-sectional design appears in social policy research.

There are two chief problems for the user of a cross-sectional design relative to an experimental design. First, the groups are not equivalent. For example, if we are interested in the relationship between age and client satisfaction, the people in different age bands are not equivalent to each other. Thus, 30- to 39 year-olds will differ from each other in terms of such factors as ethnicity, education, gender, income and occupation, all of which might have a connection with client satisfaction. Second, there is ambiguity about the direction of causality. If we are interested in whether client satisfaction and the reported demeanour of staff are related, if we do find a relationship it is difficult to know which way around the causal connection works. Does demeanour influence client satisfaction or does client satisfaction influence demeanour? As a result, it is sometimes suggested that cross-sectional designs are weak in terms of internal validity, although it is important not to exaggerate this point. Sometimes there is little ambiguity about the causal direction, for example, if we found that age and client satisfaction were related, it is impossible to imagine that client satisfaction affects age. Variables such as age, ethnicity and gender can be regarded as givens that are always independent variables. Further, statistical analysis can be used to remove some of the alternative explanatory variables that might contaminate relationships between variables when compared to the experimental design (see Bryman and Cramer, 2001, Chapter 10).

Longitudinal design

With a longitudinal design, there is no manipulation of variables (as in the cross-sectional design), but, unlike the cross-sectional design, data are collected on at least two occasions. Users of longitudinal designs are typically concerned to capture change over time and also in many cases to deal with the time order problem that was outlined in the previous section as representing a problem for the cross-sectional design.

While there are several different types of longitudinal design, there is a crucial and basic distinction between the *panel design* and the *cohort design*. The **panel design** entails collection of data on the same group of people on at least two occasions. A major example of a panel design that has been used for addressing social policy research issues is the British Household Panel Survey (BHPS). This survey started in 1991: 10,000+ individuals in 5,000+ households based on probability sampling. Respondents are interviewed annually. See **Box 4a** for the use of this survey for social policy research.

Box 4a: The British Household Panel Survey: a longitudinal perspective on informal care

Michael Hirst, *Research Fellow, Social Policy Research Unit, University of York*

Longitudinal studies are rich sources of data and analysis on key policy issues such as poverty and unemployment, social exclusion, family formation and dissolution, educational outcomes and health inequalities. By gathering information about the same individuals on two or more occasions, longitudinal research highlights their changing needs and circumstances, enabling us to understand the dynamics of people's experiences – their duration, sequence and timing – and the processes at work. Longitudinal designs also serve to establish the temporal order of events, identify the factors associated with particular outcomes, and increase confidence in the size and direction of causal associations (Menard, 1991).

The British Household Panel Survey (BHPS) began in 1991 with an initial sample of some 10,000 adults recruited in a design not unlike that of any cross-sectional household survey (Buck et al, 1994). Since then, it aims to interview those same individuals, and their natural descendants on turning age 16, every year; other adults currently living with them are also interviewed. By including all household members, each wave is broadly representative of the population living in private households in England, Scotland and Wales.

Many of the questions asked in 1991 are repeated in later interview waves and by comparing individuals' circumstances year-on-year, it is possible to build up a movie-like picture of their lives. What happens between waves may not be precisely known, however, and repeated interviewing or changing perceptions of concepts and constructs over time can undermine monitoring trends and outcomes. Loss of panel members who have died, moved overseas or cannot be traced further complicates longitudinal research, especially if those lost to follow-up differ in systematic ways from those who remain in the sample. Adjusting for panel attrition and non-response, by weighting the sample at the analysis stage, is an important consideration when measuring change across sequences of waves.

The BHPS has been used to investigate poverty and its consequences (Benzeval and Judge, 2001), and the dynamics of disability (Burchardt, 2000). It also provides useful data for exploring transitions into and out of informal or unpaid care (Hirst, 2002). Identifying key turning points in carers' lives is important for ensuring positive outcomes, and preventing or alleviating adverse consequences (Aneshensel et al, 1995; Heaton et al, 1999; Hirst and Arksey, 2000; Howard, 2001). Taking on a caring role, especially one that involves a heavy or extended commitment over time, is associated with poor psychological health, limited social participation, reduced employment prospects and financial hardship (Schulz et al, 1990; Holzhausen and Pearlman, 2000; Hirst and Hutton, 2001; Arksey, 2002).

The persistence of adverse effects indicates a need for continuing support during the care episode and beyond (Hancock and Jarvis, 1994; McLaughlin and Ritchie, 1994). The end of a protracted spell of care can be particularly difficult for carers when the cared-for person enters institutional care (Nolan and Dellasega, 2000), or dies (Schulz et al, 1997; Corden et al, 2001; see also **Box 3m**, Chapter Three). Thus, transitions into and out of a caring role point to areas where the assessment of carers' needs, and audit of service performance and professional practice, could be usefully focused.

The population of carers is constantly changing as people stop providing care and others take on a caring role. As a result, more individuals are involved in caregiving across service planning, commissioning and budgeting cycles than are found in cross-sectional surveys. One implication is that the adequacy of resources for supporting carers depends on the frequency and duration of care episodes over time.

Longitudinal estimates of carer transitions also show that most people are involved in caregiving at some point in their lives, especially in late middle and early older age. However, the demand for care varies considerably over the life course, driven by changing health needs within and between the generations. Caring relationships are therefore extremely diverse, as are carers' characteristics, family structures and household circumstances.

Policy measures that are responsive to this diversity, and geared around key transitions, are likely to be most effective in supporting carers. Such measures would benefit a large section of the population over time.

Question for discussion
- What are the strengths and weaknesses of an annual prospective panel design, such as the BHPS, for investigating change and transition between social roles?

References

Aneshensel, C., Pearlin, L., Mullan, J., Zarit, S. and Whitlatch, C. (1995) *Profiles of caring: The unexpected career*, London: Academic Press.

Arksey, H. (2002) 'Combining informal care and work: supporting carers in the workplace', *Health and Social Care in the Community*, vol 10, pp 151-61.

Benzeval, M. and Judge, K. (2001) 'Income and health: the time dimension', *Social Science and Medicine*, vol 52, pp 1371-90.

Buck, N., Gershuny, J., Rose, D. and Scott, J. (1994) *Changing households: The British Household Panel Survey 1990-1992*, Colchester: ESRC Research Centre on Micro-Social Change, University of Essex.

Burchardt, T. (2000) 'The dynamics of being disabled', *Journal of Social Policy*, vol 29, pp 645-68.

Corden, A., Sainsbury, R. and Sloper, P. (2001) *Financial implications of the death of a child*, London: Family Policy Studies Centre.

Hancock, R. and Jarvis, C. (1994) *The long term effects of being a carer*, London: HMSO.

Heaton, J., Arksey, H. and Sloper, P. (1999) 'Carers' experiences of hospital discharge and continuing care in the community', *Health and Social Care in the Community*, vol 7, pp 91-9.

Hirst, M. (2002) 'Transitions to informal care in Great Britain during the 1990s', *Journal of Epidemiology and Community Health*, vol 56, pp 579-87.

Hirst, M. and Arksey, H. (2000) 'Informal carers count', *Nursing Standard*, vol 14, no 42, pp 33-4.

Hirst, M. and Hutton, S. (2001) *Informal care over time*, York: Social Policy Research Unit, University of York.

Holzhausen, E. and Pearlman, V. (2000) 'Carers' policies in the UK', *Benefits: Journal of Social Security Research, Policy and Practice*, no 28, pp 5-8.

Howard, M. (2001) *Paying the price: Carers, poverty and social exclusion*, London: Child Poverty Action Group.

McLaughlin, E. and Ritchie, J. (1994) 'Legacies of caring: the experiences and circumstances of ex-carers', *Health and Social Care in the Community*, vol 2, pp 241-53.

Menard, S. (1991) *Longitudinal research*, London: Sage Publications.

Nolan, M. and Dellasega, C. (2000) 'Supporting family carers during long-term care placement for elders', *Journal of Advanced Nursing*, vol 31, pp 759-67.

Schulz, R., Newsom, J., Fleissner, K. et al (1997) 'The effects of bereavement after family caregiving', *Aging and Mental Health*, vol 1, pp 269-82.

Schulz, R., Visintainer, P. and Williamson, G. (1990) 'Psychiatric and physical morbidity effects of caregiving', *Journal of Gerontology*, vol 45, pp 181-91.

Further reading

Berthoud, R. and Gershuny, J. (eds) (2000) *Seven years in the lives of British families: Evidence on the dynamics of social change from the British Household Panel Survey*, Bristol: The Policy Press.

Nocon, A. and Qureshi, H. (1996) *Outcomes of community care for users and carers*, Buckingham: Open University Press.

Nolan, M., Grant, G. and Keady, J. (1996) *Understanding family care: A multidimensional model of caring and coping*, Buckingham: Open University Press.

Relevant organisations

Carers UK

20-25 Glasshouse Yard, London EC1A 4JT

www.carersonline.org.uk

Help The Aged

207-221 Pentonville Road, London N1 9UZ

www.helptheaged.org.uk/

The Princess Royal Trust for Carers

142 Minories, London EC3N 1LB

www.carers.org/home/

Website resources

British Household Panel Survey: www.iser.essex.ac.uk/bhps/index.php

Data Archive: www.data-archive.ac.uk/

ESRC Research Centre on Micro-social Change: www.iser.essex.ac.uk/misoc/index.php

ESRC UK Longitudinal Studies Centre: www.iser.essex.ac.uk/ulsc/index.php

Government policy, services and other help for carers: www.carers.gov.uk/

By contrast, a **cohort design** takes everyone born in a particular period and follows them through at regular intervals. A major example of a cohort design that has been used for addressing social policy research issues is the National Child Development Study (NCDS), which is based on 17,000 children born in Britain between 3-9 March 1958. The cohort has been followed up at ages 7, 11, 16, 23 and 33 (see also **Box 2c**).

All longitudinal designs suffer from the problem of attrition (dropouts), whereby some people refuse or are unable to continue their participation. This can be a problem if the dropouts differ systematically from those who remain. There is the related issue of knowing how to deal with the issue of people who move away from an area or country, die or leave a household, although this issue affects the panel rather than the cohort design. There is also a related issue of addition, namely, how to deal with people who might become candidates for later inclusion on grounds of maintaining representativeness of the sample. Examples of groups that might raise this issue are new household members or an influx of new migrants.

Given a suitable length of time, the panel design allows the researcher to distinguish between the effects of age on respondents and cohort effects (effects due to similarities among those born at a similar time, for example, 'baby boomers'), since members of the sample will have been born at different times. Because members of a cohort design will be of the same age, cohort effects cannot be targeted.

Case study

The case study is typically the detailed and intensive examination of one or a very small number of cases. But what is a case? A case might be an organisation, a person, a community, a household, or even an event (for example, a decision and its effects or the implementation of a policy). While the case study is typically associated with a single case, some case study research entails more than one case and is probably better described and thought of as a *multiple case study design*.

As the discussion of the case study in Chapter Five, Section 5.4 suggests, the case study is primarily associated with qualitative research and with ethnography in particular (see also Section 5.9 on this point). However, this association between the case study and qualitative research should not be exaggerated. Case studies can involve the collection of quantitative data either exclusively or as part of a multi-strategy research design of the kind discussed in Chapter Three, Section 3.4.

With a case study, the researcher is not treating the case as a sample of one. The case study researcher does not claim that the chosen case is somehow representative and can therefore be generalised to a wider universe of cases. Instead, the arguments for case studies are largely to do with the ability to generate findings that are theoretically interesting and are capable of being taken up by other researchers for further elaboration. In this connection, Yin's (1984) use of the term *replication logic* is interesting. The term is used mainly in connection with multiple case study research. Yin argues that case studies using similar procedures on a research question will enhance our understanding. Also, any interesting differences in findings might be attributable in interesting ways to contrasts between the cases. The idea behind a replication logic, then, is that the researcher should aim to replicate findings using similar procedures across cases. This idea can be extended to suggest that when a researcher conducts a single case study, the findings may be taken up by another researcher to extend the findings (perhaps exploring some further implications) or to examine a somewhat contrasting case to see if the findings hold there.

Question for discussion

- To what extent is it legitimate to argue that only true experiments allow the researcher to establish cause and effect?

References

Bryman, A. and Cramer, D. (2001) *Quantitative data analysis with SPSS 10 for Windows: A guide for social scientists*, London: Routledge.

de Vaus, D. (2001) *Research design in social research*, London: Sage Publications.

Yin, R.K. (1984) *Case study research: Design and methods*, Beverley Hills, CA: Sage Publications.

Further reading

Bryman, A. (2004) *Social research methods* (2nd edn), Oxford: Oxford University Press, Chapter 2.

de Vaus, D. (2001) *Research design in social research*, London: Sage Publications.

4.4 Sampling

Karl Ashworth, *Principal Methodologist at the Office for National Statistics*

Why sample?

We select a sample either to say something about a particular class of units, or to compare two classes of units to see if they differ in certain ways. A sample is a selection of units from the entirety of all such similar units, known as a population. The sample is a means to understanding the population.

It is seldom practical to collect information from all population members, and unnecessary when sampling offers a practical, cheaper and quicker option. Typically, the number of units sampled is substantially smaller than the total number of units in the population. So we need to be confident that our sample is representative of the population. It is through an understanding of how the sample is drawn that we can address this question.

It is convenient to distinguish two broad sampling methods (probability and non-probability), each of which has various advantages and disadvantages that need to be weighed within the context of the research question and resources.

Probability sampling

The essence of probability sampling is that each member of the population has a (known, non-zero) chance of being included in the sample: it is an objective procedure, the selection process is unbiased and the precision of population estimates can be calculated.

Usually, a sample is used to estimate an average[1] value of some population characteristic, for example, the average height of adults in Britain or the average number (proportion) of working-age people in work. The more similar population members are to each other in this characteristic the more likely it is that the sample mean will be close to the population mean. The variance typically is the statistic used to measure variability, and is also an important component of the equation to estimate the precision of the sample estimate of the population mean.

The formulae used to calculate the mean and variance are presented here (***Table 4.1***). These pertain to the case of simple random sampling, described below, but generalise to other more complex sampling schemes.

---

[1] Corresponding formulae for totals or ratio estimates are available, for example, Cochrane (1977).

The formulae are given using two different notations to emphasise that we are using sample statistics to estimate population parameters. The population parameters typically are denoted in upper case to distinguish them from sample statistics (for example, Kish, 1965; Kalton, 1983). However, as is apparent from *Table 4.1*, the mechanics of the calculation are the same:

- n is the number of units in the sample.
- N is the total number of units in the population.
- y_i and Y_i are the observations on unit i, in the sample and population, respectively.

Table 4.1: *Formulae for calculating the sample and population mean and variance*

	Sample statistic	Population parameter
Mean	$\bar{y} = \sum_{i=1}^{n} y_i / n$	$\bar{Y} = \sum_{i=1}^{N} Y_i / N$
Variance	$s^2 = \sum_{i=1}^{n} (y_i - \bar{y})^2 / (n-1)$	$S^2 = \sum_{i=1}^{N} (Y_i - \bar{Y})^2 / (N-1)$
Standard error	$s_{\bar{y}} = (s / \sqrt{n}) * \sqrt{1 - (n/N)}$	

It is important to realise that the idea behind the standard error of the mean arises from the notion of a *sampling distribution of means*. In other words, if we were to repeatedly sample, an infinite number of times, from the same population (replacing each sample before drawing the next) we could array each sample mean as a frequency distribution. The resulting distribution is approximately normally distributed with a mean value equalling the population mean. As the mean of the sampling means equals the population mean, the sample mean is an unbiased estimator of the population mean[2]. This does not guarantee that the mean arising from any one sample will be the same as the population mean; chance selections, arising from sampling variability, may result in different groups of units producing different sample means. However, using the standard error, we can estimate, with a given degree of confidence, the range within which the population mean will fall.

---

[2] The same is true of the sample variance (using the denominator n-1), which is an unbiased estimator of the population variance.

The confidence intervals are given by:

$$\bar{y} - (ts/\sqrt{n})\sqrt{1-n/N} \leq \bar{Y} \leq \bar{y} + (ts/\sqrt{n})\sqrt{1-n/N}$$

Where t is the value returned from the t-distribution corresponding to the desired confidence probability level[3]. For example, a hypothetical sample size of 196 students selected from a campus population of 2000 had an average daily consumption of 5 units of alcohol, with a variance of 4 units. So, we can be 95% sure that in this hypothetical campus student population the average daily intake of alcoholic units was in the range of:

5 ±-((1.96*2)/14)*0.95 = 5 ± 0.266

The value of 1–n/N, more commonly symbolised as 1–f, is known as the *finite population correction* (fpc), and f is the *sampling fraction*. With a small sampling fraction, the fpc is close to unity and has little effect on the estimate of the standard error. The effect of ignoring the fpc is negligible with a large sample and small sampling fraction, when the sampling fraction is 5% or less the fpc can be ignored (Cochrane, 1977).

It is apparent that the standard error of the mean is influenced by three factors. The fpc is one factor, typically with a small effect. A second is the population variance; a smaller variance enables more precise estimates. Finally, the critical factor is the sample size – larger samples give more precise results. It is worth reflecting on the fact that what is important is the actual size of the sample and not the size of the sampling fraction, as long as the sampling fraction remains small. In other words, provided the two populations have the same variance, we can get virtually as precise an estimate from a sample of 400 from a population of 500,000 as we can from a sample of 400 from a population of 50,000.

Sample designs

Simple random sampling

Simple random sampling (srs) is a scheme that requires each unit in the population to have an equal probability of selection (epsem). Typically, it requires a list (sampling frame) of the members of the population and the assignation of a unique number to each member. We then require a selection method that meets the epsem condition. One type of method is the urn–

---

3   The values of t can be derived from tables of the normal distribution. However, with a small sample size, say 50 or less, the value can be taken from Student's t-distribution, using the appropriate degrees of freedom.

based approach, where a list of numbers is written, each on a separate piece of paper; these are then placed in an urn, thoroughly mixed and as many draws as required are made. The British National Lottery follows a machine equivalent procedure of randomly sampling six balls from 49. Other methods use random digit tables (for example, described in Kalton, 1983). Today, the easiest approach is to use a computer to generate the numbers. However, often srs is impractical and other approaches are used in practice.

Stratified sampling

Stratification is the process of splitting the sampling frame into separate subgroups (strata) that are defined using supplementary information on the sampling frame. The selection procedure is still random, because within each subgroup (stratum), elements are selected at random. A principal reason for stratification is that it can produce more precise variance estimates than srs, when the stratification factors are associated with the outcome(s) under investigation. However, stratification by factors that do not influence the research question does not result in any gain in precision. In addition, stratification can be used to ensure that certain groups are represented in the sample. For example, stratification by geographic region ensures that people from each region in the country are covered (see **Box 4b**).

Another reason for stratification might be to over-sample some comparatively rare subgroups of the population to ensure that sufficient numbers of them were available for robust analysis. Here the sampling fractions vary between the strata, and weighting adjustments to correct for this must be made in the analysis.

Box 4b: The British Social Attitudes Survey: sampling

Karl Ashworth, *Principal Methodologist at the Office for National Statistics*
[The author acknowledges the helpful comments made by Alison Park of the National Centre for Social Research]

The British Social Attitudes Survey (BSA) is an ongoing annual survey, started in 1983, and conducted by the National Centre for Social Research (formerly Social and Community Planning Research or SCPR). **Box 4c** provides further details of the BSA and how it is conducted and reported. The BSA provides a useful example of sampling individuals in an applied context. The details of the sampling procedure are given as an appendix in the annual BSA reports, on which this illustration is based, and although the detail varies from year to year, the technique essentially remains the same.

The target population for the survey is British adults (aged 18 or over) living in private households. This is achieved by drawing a sample of addresses from the Postcode Address File (PAF), a list of Post Office 'delivery units' (or addresses) organised geographically by postcode (prior to 1993, the Electoral Register was used). To minimise fieldwork costs, clusters of addresses within the same location are selected.

A multi-stage sampling procedure is used, with three stages of selection. In the first stage 200 postcode sectors are selected from all British postcode sectors south of the Great Glen and Caledonian Canal in Scotland (because of the disproportionate costs of interviewing there), with probability proportionate to the number of addresses in each sector. Prior to selection, the sectors are stratified by region, population density and home ownership. The stratification is designed so that there are about equal numbers of sectors in each stratum and ensures a nationwide geographical spread covering inner city, urban and rural areas and different types of tenure.

Once the postcode sectors have been selected, a fixed number of addresses are selected within each postcode, typically around 30. These are selected using a systematic sampling procedure, where the sampling interval varies between sectors to reflect the number of addresses in that sector. Because some addresses in Scotland contain more than one accommodation space (for example, a tenement), addresses there are listed as many times as they contain accommodation spaces (2.3% of addresses in Scotland).

If, on reaching an address, an interviewer finds more than one household resident, the correct number is determined and one randomly chosen. In addition, if more than one adult is resident at the selected household, one is selected using a computer-generated random number.

This procedure does not ensure that individuals have equal selection probabilities. There are three potential sources of bias. First, in Scotland, addresses known to contain more than one accommodation space will have a greater chance of selection than addresses containing only one accommodation space. Second, where more than one household lives at an address, individuals in these households have a lower selection probability than individuals living at addresses containing only one household. Finally, the probability of selection is lower for an adult who shares a household with other adults than for one who does not; the probability decreases with the number of adults in the household.

For these reasons, the data are weighted during analysis to adjust for these different selection probabilities. As the sample is clustered, design effect calculations are also supplied in the Appendix.

Systematic sampling

Systematic sampling involves randomly choosing a starting position on the list and selecting every kth element from the starting point. The sampling fraction determines k, so that if we were to select 150 employers from a list of 1,200, k=150/1,200 = 1/8, so that a random number between 1 and 8 would be selected. If the number were 3, the 3rd, 11th, 19th and so on would be selected. This is similar to splitting the sampling frame into k strata and selecting one element from each stratum.

Any naturally occurring ordering in the list could potentially have a detrimental effect on the sample. For example, a list of employees might be ordered by department and level of pay, so that the kth element corresponded primarily to higher (or lower) earners because of the ordering in the list. In general, while the properties of the sample mean as an estimate remain unbiased, unless the ordering is random, variance estimates could be detrimentally affected.

Cluster and multi-stage sampling

Cluster sampling embodies the notion that the population units can be aggregated into meaningful higher order units and assigned exclusively to a higher order unit. For example, in Britain residential addresses can be aggregated to postcode sectors and districts.

Out of the approximately 9,600 postcode sectors, a fixed number is chosen, and these are usually selected with probability proportionate to size (pps), that is, the number of addresses within the sector (see **Box 4b**). The pps requirement ensures that an equal probability of selection is given to each address, sectors with more addresses are more likely to be chosen.

A principal disadvantage of cluster sampling is that units within the cluster are likely to be correlated with each other, for example, people who live in the same neighbourhood tend to have more in common with their neighbours than with other randomly selected members of the general population. This has a number of consequences, particularly on the precision of the estimate. However, a design effect can be calculated which shows the loss of precision incurred relative to srs.

Multi-stage sampling is the repeated act of sampling lower units from higher order units and **Box 4b** demonstrates a three-stage process of drawing samples of sectors, addresses and individuals.

Non-probability sampling

There are times when probability samples either cannot be used, for example in the absence of a sampling frame, or when the cost is prohibitive. In these circumstances, other non-probability sampling procedures are available.

The essence of non-probability sampling is that a judgement is made about the specific units that are included in the sample. The process is not objective, all units do not have a known chance of inclusion and, strictly speaking, estimates of precision usually should not be calculated. The value of these methods very much depends on the objectives of the research.

Quota sampling

Quota sampling is particularly common in market research and in electoral polls. It is similar to stratified sampling in that the population is subdivided into groups in advance of selection, for example, controlling for sex and social class. A quota – the number of required interviews – is set within each control (stratum), for example 30 men and 30 women within each of social groups 1, 2 and 3. The underlying assumption is that the control variables account for systematic differences in the research variables of interest. In other words, once these control variables have been accounted for, the only difference between people within a control group is caused by random variation.

It is the method of selection that makes the procedure non-random because interviewers are allowed to select any people who meet these characteristics. This could lead to a whole range of potential biases. For example, if interviewing only took place on weekdays during the day, workers are likely to be under-represented. However, proponents argue that it is better able to guarantee a representative sample than are probability samples.

Haphazard/availability/convenience sampling

These approaches use units that happen to be available. This is relatively common in experimental social science. In circumstances where a high degree of similarity between units is likely, it can be useful. For example, among young healthy people, the impact of a stimulus on neuronal conductivity might not vary greatly. It would therefore be justifiable to allocate randomly students to an experimental or control group to test the impact of a stimulus. However, generalising the findings to the wider population of human beings assumes that only very minor random variation exists between individuals in the sample and population. Where a population estimate is required, generally it is not a recommended approach.

Question for discussion

- What are the key elements of a 'good' sample, and how might these vary if considering between a probability and quota sample?

References

Cochrane, W.G. (1977) *Sampling techniques* (3rd edn), New York, NY: John Wiley & Sons.

Kalton, G. (1983) *Introduction to survey sampling*, Sage Publications University Paper Series: Quantitative Applications in the Social Sciences, no 35, Beverly Hills, CA: Sage Publications.

Kish, L. (1965) *Survey sampling*, New York, NY: John Wiley and Sons.

Further reading

Sampling techniques are described in many introductory books on methodology, too numerous here to mention. However, the two Chapters by Lynn (Chapters 16 and 17) are recommended in:

Greenfield, T. (ed) (1996) *Research methods: Guidance for postgraduates*, London: Arnold.

The text by Kalton 1983, referenced above, provides an excellent general purpose introduction to the area. The other two referenced works are much more advanced.

The British Social Attitudes Survey series has, at the time of writing, produced 18 reports and the sampling procedure is described in the Appendix of each. The most recent publication, at the time of writing, is:

Park, A., Curtice, J., Thomson, K., Jarvis, L. and Bromley, C. (eds) (2002) *British social attitudes: Public policy, social ties, The 19th Report*, London: Sage Publications.

Website resources

The following website connects to many other useful sites and is highly recommended: http://gsociology.icaap.org/methods/surveys.htm

ICAAP, the International Consortium for the Advancement of Academic Publication, sponsors the site.

On conducting surveys: http://www.amstat.org/sections/srms/whatsurvey.html

PART TWO: METHODS FOR COLLECTING AND CODING QUANTITATIVE DATA

4.5 Overview of methods for collecting and coding quantitative data

In the next part of the chapter, the main methods for collecting and coding quantitative data are examined. Five main approaches are examined:

- structured interviews and questionnaires;
- using the Internet for the collection of quantitative data;
- content analysis;
- structured observation;
- official statistics.

Each of these approaches to the collection and coding of data is underpinned by the preoccupations outlined in relation to quantitative research in Sections 4.2 and 4.3. Content analysis is not a research method in the sense of a way of collecting data; it is an approach to the analysis of unstructured data so that the data can be quantified. The translation of unstructured data such as newspaper articles into quantitative data through coding is more or less its defining feature. However, at another level, content analysis does have features of a research method, in the sense that the distinctive coding practices that are involved essentially create data. Official statistics are also not so much a research method as sources of data that social policy researchers seek to draw on in order to tailor to their research questions.

One feature that is also common to all of these methods is the need to 'code' the data that are collected. In their different ways, users of each of the methods must turn the material into a numerical form so that the kinds of statistical analysis covered in Section 4.11 can be implemented. Coding is at once a simple but potentially complex activity. Take, for example, the case of devising a Likert scale of the kind mentioned in Section 4.2. There, it was imagined that we wanted to construct a scale to measure levels of client satisfaction with a service provider. Let us look again at the two items that were presented as possible candidates for inclusion in the scale. Here is the first one:

Staff are always responsive to my needs

Strongly agree	Agree	Neither agree nor disagree	Disagree	Strongly disagree
5	4	3	2	1

A common way of coding items such as these is to allocate numbers to them as has been suggested. Everyone indicating agreement is given a score of 4 for their answers. But what about the next one?

I find the rules for getting the particular service I need difficult to understand

Strongly agree	Agree	Neither agree nor disagree	Disagree	Strongly disagree

A score of 4 could be given to 'Agree' but this would be incorrect. If the direction of scoring is supposed to indicate that a higher score indicates satisfaction, giving a score of 4 for 'Agree' with the second question would be incorrect because someone choosing that answer is really indicating dissatisfaction. Consequently, for an item like this, the direction of scoring needs to be reversed and should go from 1 (Strongly agree) to 5 (Strongly disagree). Thus, although the process of allocating a coding scheme to questions is relatively straightforward, care is still necessary. Further, there is a recognised problem with Likert scales whereby it is known that some respondents will answer all the constituent items in a scale in the same way. This kind of response bias can be addressed by varying the wording to guard against this effect.

Even greater care is necessary when coding materials that are unstructured. This commonly occurs with the following kinds of data:

- *Answers to open questions*. With closed questions, such as the items in a Likert scale, coding is relatively simple, but with open questions, decisions have to be made about which category an answer belongs to before it can be coded. There is always the possibility that the coder will incorrectly allocate an answer to a category. This is a major reason why survey researchers invariably prefer closed questions.
- *Newspaper and magazine articles and television programmes*. The kinds of materials discussed in Section 4.8 are unstructured materials. While some items can be easily coded, such as whether certain words are used, coding in terms of themes requires interpretation and is therefore difficult and potentially prone to error.

- *Behaviour.* Which is the subject of the method covered in Section 4.9, similarly has to be interpreted by the observer before it can be coded. Whether an instance of behaviour is assigned to the correct category also requires interpretation and is potentially a source of error.

Coding is a crucial stage in the processing of data before they can be analysed statistically, but it is one where there is considerable potential for error. In order to keep such errors to a minimum, the researcher needs to spell out the rules for allocating items to a category and if possible to get others to check the allocations that are made.

4.6 Structured interviews and questionnaires in survey research

Alison Park, *Research Director, National Centre for Social Research*

This section explores the range of tasks involved in survey design – from decisions about how a questionnaire will be administered and questionnaire design, to the coding and editing of the data collected.

Once a survey-based approach has been selected, a choice needs to be made about the *mode* in which the survey will be carried out. The most important distinction that exists is between modes that involve an interviewer (who works through the questionnaire to record a respondent's answers) and 'self-completion' methods (where the respondent does this).

Interviewer-mediated surveys

There are two main types of interviewer-mediated surveys – *face-to-face* and *telephone* interviews. In both cases, the interviewer can either use a paper questionnaire or a computer-based questionnaire (often called an interview schedule). The former is often referred to as PAPI interviewing (pen/pencil and paper interviewing) and the latter as CAPI (computer-assisted personal interviewing). See **Box 4c** for an example of the combined use of these two ways of administering a structured interview in a survey.

Box 4c: The British Social Attitudes Survey: data collection

Alison Park, *Research Director, National Centre for Social Research*

The British Social Attitudes (BSA) Survey series was initiated in 1983 by Social and Community Planning Research (SCPR, now the National Centre for Social Research) and has been carried out annually ever since. Its primary purpose is to monitor and interpret changing social values over time (see also **Box 4b** which discusses the sampling technique used on the BSA).

Funding for the survey comes primarily from the main government departments, the ESRC and charitable trusts. All data are deposited at the ESRC Data Archive at Essex University (see Chapter Three, Section 3.13).

The sample

Each year's sample comprises a national probability sample of adults aged 18 and over, living in private households in Great Britain. The sampling frame used is the Postcode Address File (PAF; see also **Box 4b**).

In 1994 and 1998, the BSA Survey was accompanied by a Young Persons' Social Attitudes survey. This involved interviewing all 12- to 19-year-olds living in the same household as an adult BSA respondent (Park, 1999).

From 1999 onwards, the survey has been accompanied by an annual sister survey in Scotland, known as Scottish Social Attitudes. This is because, although Scotland is included in the BSA sample, the number of respondents interviewed there is too small to permit anything but the most cursory analysis (Paterson et al, 2001).

The questionnaire

The survey has covered a wide range of political, social and moral topics over its lifetime. Because the series is designed to examine change (or stasis) over time, many questions are repeated from one year to the next. However, new topics are regularly introduced and even topics that have been covered in the past are refreshed to ensure that their coverage of the issues is as up-to-date as possible. The survey primarily focuses on people's attitudes, but also collects details of their behaviour patterns and household circumstances for analysis purposes.

Examples of topics covered by the series include:

- political trust
- voting behaviour
- marriage and cohabitation
- social security
- devolution
- transport

- poverty
- sex
- racism
- the NHS
- health rationing

- the environment
- national identity
- social capital
- begging

The International Social Survey Programme (ISSP)

This programme is organised by a group of research organisations, each of which agrees to field annually an agreed module of questions on a chosen topic area. Since 1985, an ISSP module has been included on each BSA Survey. Modules are repeated at intervals in order to examine change over time as well as to permit comparison between countries.

Fieldwork

Each BSA interview consists of a face-to-face interview using computer assisted interviewing techniques (CAPI) and a self-completion questionnaire which can be completed by the respondent immediately after the CAPI interview or at a later date. The length of the face-to-face element of the questionnaire varies from year to year, but usually averages at around 60 minutes.

Approximately 3,500 interviews take place each year, most of which are carried out in June and July. Prior to fieldwork all interviewers are personally briefed by a researcher. The response rate in 2001 was 59%.

Analysis

By repeating questions included in previous rounds, the survey series has allowed analysts to build up increasingly detailed pictures as to how British attitudes and values are developing over time and has also enabled the development of theoretical understanding about their implications for policy. Moreover, for any given year, the range of socio-demographic and socio-economic questions included on the survey make it possible to ascertain how far attitudes, expectations and views about particular issues vary from one section of society to another.

Each survey generates an edited book that analyses and tries to explain movements in the British public's beliefs and values (Park et al, 2002). Contributions from a range of authors are included, and a variety of analytic techniques are used, from logistic and multiple regression to factor analysis.

References

Park, A. (1999) 'Young people and political apathy', in R. Jowell, J. Curtice, A. Park and K. Thomson (eds) *British social attitudes: The 16th report – Who shares New Labour values?*, Aldershot: Ashgate.

Park, A., Curtice, J., Thomson, K., Jarvis, L. and Bromley, C. (eds) (2002) *British social attitudes: The 19th Report*, London: Sage Publications.

Paterson, L., Brown, A., Curtice, J., Hinds, K., McCrone, D., Park, A., Sproston, K. and Surridge, P. (2001) *New Scotland: New politics?*, Edinburgh: Edinburgh University Press.

One of the main disadvantages to interviewer-mediated surveys is the fact that they are costly. Put simply; interviewers need to be paid. However, interviewer-mediated interviews also have considerable advantages. In particular, the presence of an interviewer means that these surveys tend to achieve higher response rates than self-completion ones. Moreover, the fact that the interviewer is responsible for administering the questionnaire helps minimise error.

Face-to-face surveys are more expensive than telephone interviews, but tend to achieve higher response rates. They also allow the use of visual aids such as showcards that can be beneficial for respondents. The maximum possible length of a face-to-face interview is longer than that of a telephone survey. The usual rule of thumb is that telephone interviews should last no longer than 30 minutes, whereas face-to-face interviews often exceed this.

Despite these disadvantages, telephone surveys have their advantages. They are cheaper and are ideal when a long interview or visual aids are not required. They can be particularly invaluable when carrying out surveys of employees or employers.

Self-completion methods

Self-completion methods require the respondent to work through and complete a questionnaire on their own. The majority of self-completion formats use paper questionnaires, although there are examples of cases where a self-completion questionnaire is completed on a computer (either as a program on a laptop computer or via the Internet or e-mail; see Internet surveys, Section 4.7).

Clearly self-completion questionnaires can make use of visual cues (unlike telephone surveys). However, they suffer from the fact that, as no interviewer is present, the format of the questionnaire has to be as simple as possible.

Self-completion questionnaires can reach their target respondent in a number of different ways. Perhaps the most common method is the postal survey whereby paper self-completion questionnaires are mailed out to a sample of individuals or addresses. A principal advantage of this method is that it is cheap (particularly when compared with interviewer-mediated methods). However, levels of response to postal surveys tend to be much lower than with interviewer-mediated surveys.

There are a number of ways in which researchers can seek to boost response on postal surveys. These include the use of personalised letters to the respondent, incentives, reminder letters, and making sure that the questionnaires are as attractive, clear and short as possible.

Other self-completion delivery methods include using interviewers to deliver and/or to collect questionnaires (which can boost response) and e-mail.

Identifying the information you want to collect

This stage sounds deceptively simple – identifying the information needed to fulfil the objectives of the research. However, although some requirements will be very evident from the outset, others can be less so. For this reason researchers often spend time considering existing material about the subject – carrying out a literature review, for example, and finding out about other quantitative and qualitative work that has been done.

If the subject matter for the research is particularly new or complex, questionnaire design is often preceded by detailed qualitative work which can help map out the main areas likely to be of interest.

When considering the information that a questionnaire will collect, researchers also have to consider the range of analyses they will want to carry out with the data. It is particularly important to consider the range of 'background' information required about respondents. If a researcher is interested in whether the views of men and women differ, the questionnaire will clearly need to record the sex of the respondent!

Question design

Having identified the topics of particular interest, researchers will then consider how these can be *operationalised*. This is the process by which concepts are translated into concrete, discrete and comprehensible questions.

Before this process can begin, topics of interest need to be broken down into their smallest constituent parts. For instance, if the aim is to explore transport use, the researcher will need to think more precisely about what this means. Is the interest, for example, in what forms of transport people use? Is there a need to find out about both public and private transport?

When designing questions, attention needs to be paid to the tendency of respondents to 'satisfice', that is, to respond in a way that requires the least effort but which they think will suffice (Krosnick, 1991). This makes it important to minimise the difficulty of the task being set respondents. For example, questions should avoid asking people to recall events that happened a long time before, or to count the number of times they have done a common or relatively trivial task over an unrealistically long time period.

Different types of question

Most questions used in questionnaires tend to be *closed* rather than *open*. Closed questions involve the interviewer allocating the respondent's answer to a category in a predetermined list given in the questionnaire. The following is an example of a closed question:

> 'How would you describe the wages or salary you are paid for the job you do   on the low side, reasonable, or on the high side. IF LOW:Very low or a bit low?'

This gives the respondent four different options to choose from, and the interviewer will record one of these as appropriate:

> Very low
> A bit low
> Reasonable
> On the high side

This same question could easily be turned into an open question:

> 'How would you describe the wages or salary you are paid for the job you do?'

In this case, no options are offered to the respondent and the interviewer would simply record what he or she said (usually verbatim). These questions will then need to be 'coded' before they can be analysed. Open questions tend to be used when it is not possible to predict the nature or range of responses that people will give to the question. Some closed questions will also include an open-ended option to record any responses that do not fit into the predetermined list.

While many questions only request one answer from the respondent (a 'single coded' question), some allow more than one response (a 'multi-coded' question).

Question wording

When designing questions the aim should be to arrive at a wording that respondents will interpret in as similar a way as possible. Consequently, the language used should be as simple, clear and unambiguous as possible.

Questions should not be double-barrelled – that is, asking two questions at once. Consider, for example, the following statement:

'How much do you agree or disagree that buses in this area are
unreliable and too expensive?'

This question conflates two distinct and very different aspects of public transport
(reliability and cost), making it hard for many respondents to answer.

Another common problem for respondents, most frequently encountered
on attitudinal surveys, stems from the confusion of knowing how to respond
to statements that contain a negative. For example:

'How much do you agree or disagree that primary school children
are not given enough tests at school?'

Even the most quick-witted respondent might need to pause to consider what
disagreement with this statement actually means. This problem often results
from the desire to include both positive and negative statements when carrying
out attitudinal research. This is because of *acquiescence bias* – the fact that
people are more likely to agree with a statement than disagree. Such bias
means that, if one wants to examine attitudes towards, in this case, school tests
it is important to include a range of questions that express both positive and
negative views about testing. However, careful thought about wording can
usually reveal an alternative wording that makes the same point while avoiding
the use of a negative. For example:

'How much do you agree or disagree that primary school children
should be given more tests at school?'

If a survey's findings are to be seen as credible, it is also important that questions
are not leading – in other words, that they do not push respondents towards
giving a particular answer. Consider, for example, the question:

'What is it that makes you proud to be British?'

This question, assuming it is not preceded by a question asking people *whether*
they are proud to be British, is leading because it makes it difficult for those
who are *not* proud to say so. A less leading (but still flawed) version would be:

'What is it that makes you proud to be British, or are you not
proud of being British at all?'

The leading nature of a question is not always obvious. For example, a question
which alludes to the government's position on an issue will tend to result in a
higher proportion of people endorsing that position than would otherwise be
the case (Hoinville et al, 1978).

Sensitive questions

Some topic areas are seen as particularly sensitive – for example, questions about money, sex, prejudice and wrongdoing. However, it is worth remembering that often respondents are less awkward about answering such questions than researchers (or interviewers) are about asking them. More generally, there are also a number of areas which, although not necessarily sensitive, require careful design in order to avoid people opting for the most 'socially desirable' response. Examples here might include asking people whether they voted in an election, or whether they engage in 'green' recycling behaviour.

There are a number of different techniques used in these sorts of circumstances. Perhaps the most well-known is what Barton (1958) identifies as the 'everybody' approach in which the less socially acceptable option is normalised from the outset. One of his examples follows:

'As you know, many people have been killing their wives these days. Do you happen to have killed yours?'

Barton identifies a range of other question wording formats of use in such situations that are as recognisable now as they were in the 1950s. Other common methods used to ask sensitive questions include self-completion booklets administered during a face-to-face interview and giving the respondent a showcard with numbered options and asking them only to tell the interviewer the number.

Question order and context

The order in which questions are asked during an interview is important. Not surprisingly, it is not advisable to begin an interview with particularly difficult or sensitive questions; these should be introduced once the respondent has got used to the interview and is feeling more comfortable.

It is also important to bear in mind that the context within which questions are asked can affect the responses that are given. Asking, for instance, how much a person gives to charity immediately after a series of questions about attitudes to charitable giving is probably not going to produce the most accurate reading possible. Far better to separate these questions so that respondents will not worry about giving consistent responses.

Question filtering

Some questions are asked of all respondents; others are only asked of a subgroup, usually determined by their responses to previous questions. The instruction used to direct interviewers (or, in the case of self-completion surveys, respondents) to the next relevant question is called a **filter instruction**. In CAPI or CATI surveys, filtering happens automatically as the computer program automatically takes the interviewer to the next correct question.

If filter instructions are being used it is essential that these are clear and concise. If possible, filter questions in self-completion questionnaires should be avoided.

Pre-testing

It is good practice to pre-test new questions to check that they are as clear to respondents and interviewers as they are to researchers. A range of different methods are used, the most common being cognitive tests (which apply intensive qualitative techniques to a small number of questions) and pilot tests (which test out all – or part – of the questionnaire in a more quantitative manner).

Data collection

Once the questionnaire has been designed and tested, and various administrative procedures completed, data collection (or 'fieldwork') can begin.

Response rates – the number of successfully 'achieved' interviews as a proportion of the interviews 'possible' – need to be monitored throughout the fieldwork period in order to identify problems as early as possible and take remedial action. Other means of helping ensure a good response rate include sending out letters in advance to the selected respondents and the use of incentives.

If interviewers are being used to carry out data collection, it is important that they all have a clear, and similar, view as to the purpose of the survey and the mechanics that they should follow in carrying out their interviews. For this reason, it is common practice to have interviewer 'briefings' at which the survey and its various administrative requirements are introduced. Briefings can also play an important role in boosting interviewer morale and helping ensure that they achieve a good response rate (Campanelli et al, 1997).

Data preparation

Once a questionnaire has been completed and received back at the office, the data can enter the next stage of the survey process – data preparation. The two main features of data preparation are *editing* and *coding*.

If paper questionnaires have been used, the results will have to be keyed or scanned so that it is in electronic form.

Editing

Data editing involves checking the quality of the data and, where possible, correcting any errors. This process is usually more laborious when the data were collected using PAPI techniques; with CAPI or CATI methods, the scope for errors in data entry can be limited by the computer program.

A number of common editing checks are usually made. These include: checking that questions have been asked only of those who should have been asked them (*filter checks*); checking that responses lie within an appropriate range – for example, that people do not have 30 children (*range checks*); and checks to ensure logical consistency between different answers (*logic checks*). In all cases, the editing process can only correct identifiable errors where there is a clear clue as to their resolution.

Coding

Most survey questions are 'closed', that is, respondents and interviewers choose from a range of specified options. Otherwise a respondent's answer has to be recorded and the information collected then has to be reduced to a numeric form before it can be analysed. To do this, the researcher examines a number of responses to the question and develops a 'code frame' that lists a number of possible answers and allocates a numeric code to each. This code frame is then used to code all subsequent responses to this question.

Question for discussion

* What are the main advantages of face-to-face surveys over other modes of interview?

References

Barton, J.A. (1958) 'Asking the embarrassing question', *Public Opinion Quarterly*, vol 22, pp 67-8.

Campanelli, P., Sturgis, P. and Purdon, S. (1997) *Can you hear me knocking? An investigation into the impact of interviewers on survey response rates*, London: National Centre.

Hoinville, G., Jowell, J. and Associates (1978) *Survey research practice*, London: Heinemann Educational Books.

Krosnick, J.A. (1991) 'Response strategies for coping with the cognitive demands of attitude measures in surveys', *Applied Cognitive Psychology*, vol 5, pp 213-36.

Further reading

Thomas, R. and Lynn, P. (eds) (2004, forthcoming) *Survey research practice II*, London: Sage Publications.

Park, A., Curtice, J., Thomson, K., Jarvis, L. and Bromley, C. (eds) (2001) *British social attitudes: Public policy, social ties*, London: Sage Publications.

Schuman, H. and Presser, S. (1981) *Questions and answers in attitude surveys: Experiments on question form, wording and context*, New York, NY: Academic.

Relevant organisations

National Centre for Social Research:
35 Northampton Square, London EC1V 0A
www.natcen.ac.uk
Office for National Statistics
1 Drummond Gate, London SW1V 2QQ
www.statistics.gov.uk

Website resources

ESRC Data Archive: www.data-archive.ac.uk
International Social Survey Programme: www.issp.org

4.7 Internet surveys

David de Vaus, *Professor of Sociology, La Trobe University, Australia*

Survey research has been transformed by the use of Computer-Assisted Interviewing (CAI). Computer-based interviewing is well established in telephone surveys and since the mid-1990s has been used to administer surveys using the Internet. The early use of the Internet for collecting quantitative survey data relied on primitive e-mail-based methods but the web with its graphical interface and interactive abilities has led to the rapid growth of sophisticated web-based surveys that make use of CAI features.

Web surveys

While market researchers were early users of web surveys, they are now being used for serious social science research. An example is *Survey2000*, a survey of over 80,000 people from many nations administered by US-based university researchers in conjunction with the National Geographic Society (Witte et al, 2000).

While early Internet surveys were e-mail-based the best Internet surveys now use the WWW. E-mail is used mainly as a means of recruiting and following up samples rather than for distributing questionnaires. Web surveys are distributed by making a questionnaire accessible via a web page or web address (URL). Depending on the type of web survey used, respondents might download a questionnaire, answer it and submit responses to the researcher. Alternatively, the questionnaire may be completed online. These online surveys can use interactive questionnaires that take advantage of the computer-based format to deliver complex questionnaires that are easy and enjoyable to answer. Among other things web-based questionnaires can:

- automatically skip questions depending on answers to earlier questions as well as selectively give modules of questions to selected individuals;
- create a dynamic questionnaire in which questions are created 'on the fly' based on earlier responses. For example, in the food tastes section of *Survey2000* the list of foods delivered to each respondent was custom-built based on the various locations the respondent had previously reported living in;
- check for errors and prompt the respondent to double-check their answers;
- ensure that question answering instructions are followed;
- ensure that questions are answered in the order in which the research intended;
- automatically code responses and compile these into a database;
- automatically conduct some preliminary analysis of the data and provide respondents with feedback.

In addition to computerising the questionnaire and its administration, web surveys can be implemented quickly and at low cost. Once the questionnaire has been developed increasing the sample size is simple and cheap. Where sample members are invited using e-mails the task of following up non-responders is simple, quick and inexpensive.

Internet samples

Samples for Internet surveys are constructed in a number of ways. These include:

- *using lists of e-mail addresses* to invite participation;
- *advertising* for volunteers on specific websites, listservers and chat groups;
- *pop-up web page questionnaires* that can be answered by anyone visiting the specific web page;

- *commercial Internet panels* are used to provide a sample of cases with specific characteristics. These panels or pools of potential respondents are recruited by commercial agencies which reward survey participants in one way or another.

These samples are of no value if you want to generalise your results beyond the specific group of respondents. However, some Internet sampling strategies have been developed to try to obtain more representative samples. These methods include:

- Recruiting a representative sample using normal random sampling methods and then *pay to connect all the sample members to the Internet* in return for their participation in surveys for a set period (see Knowledge Networks website listed below).
- *Using quota Internet samples*. A sample can be made representative of a population *in specific respects* by establishing representative quotas and filling these from commercial sample panels.
- *Weighting Internet samples* so that the sample reflects the population in specific respects. This is the solution adopted in *Survey2000* to ensure that their sample represented the general population in specific respects.

Problems with Internet samples

While Internet surveys can collect information from large numbers of people relatively quickly and cheaply, the quality of the samples on which they rely is a major focus of criticism. These samples encounter three main difficulties.

First, they *lack a sampling frame*. Probability samples require an unbiased sampling frame that contains all the elements of the population from which the sample is to be drawn. Since there is no list of all Internet users it is very difficult to obtain general population samples using Internet surveys. Second, they encounter *coverage bias* – that is, even a representative sample of Internet users cannot easily be used for generalisation to the broader population. Young, educated, wealthy American males are over-represented among Internet users. Third, Internet samples are subject to *response bias* due to their generally low response rates.

In addition to sample problems Internet surveys face other practical difficulties. They are subject to low response rates that may stem from various sources, including fear of viruses, privacy concerns and a lack of credibility of Internet surveys due to overuse by marketing groups. Internet surveys also face difficulties due to lack of standardisation of software and hardware. Since these surveys partly rely on the respondent's computer and software, as well as their level of computer literacy, widespread difficulties can be encountered due to software incompatibilities and hardware inadequacies.

Setting up a web survey

Apart from recruiting a sample an Internet survey involves developing an electronic questionnaire and establishing systems for distributing the questionnaire electronically, receiving electronic responses and compiling these for data analysis. This process has been greatly simplified by the production of dedicated software for the production and deployment of Internet surveys. A listing and reviews of some of this software is available at Tim Macer's website.

There are two main ways in which web-based surveys are designed and implemented. They can be designed, distributed, returned and analysed *entirely online*. All the work for fully online surveys is conducted on an Internet server. The Electronic sources (below) lists some sites at which you can create and administer fully online web surveys.

An alternative way of setting up a web survey is to use a *mixture of online and offline* stages. Using special software on your own computer (see Tim Macer's website) you can develop an electronic questionnaire for web deployment. This is then uploaded to an Internet server and made available to your sample. Responses are then electronically returned to the server or directly to you by e-mail. Your Internet survey software on your desktop computer can automatically create a database from these responses and set up your data for analysis using specialised data analysis software.

Question for discussion

- What are the main advantages and sampling problems when using the Internet to conduct a survey?

Reference

Witte, J.C., Amoroso, L.M. and Howard, P.E.N. (2000) 'Research methodology: method and representation in Internet-based survey tools – mobility, community, and cultural identity in survey2000', *Social Science Computer Review*, vol 18, no 2, pp 179-95.

Further reading

Couper, M.P. (2000) 'Web surveys: a review of issues and approaches', *Public Opinion Quarterly*, vol 64, pp 464-94.
Dillman, D.A. (2000) *Mail and Internet surveys: The total design method*, New York, NY: Wiley.

Witte, J.C., Amoroso, L.M. and Howard, P.E.N. (2000) 'Research methodology: method and representation in Internet-based survey tools – mobility, community, and cultural identity in survey2000', *Social Science Computer Review*, vol 18, no 2, pp 179-95.

Website resources

Knowledge Networks [representative Internet sampling methods, password required]: www.knowledgenetworks.com/ganp/safe/surveymethod.html
Web Survey Methodology: www.websm.org/topics.html
Web survey software: Tim Macer Services – Research Software Central: www.macer.co.uk/rscentral/rscentral.html
Online survey sites
Response-O-matic: www.response-o-matic.com/home.htm
Instant Survey: www.instantsurvey.com/settings/fstPage.asp
SurveyTracker: www.surveytracker.com/
Zoomerang: www.zoomerang.com/Login/index.zgi
SurveyWriter: www.surveywriter.com/site/index.html
Student researcher: www.studentresearcher.com

4.8 Content analysis

David Deacon, *Senior Lecturer in Communication and Media Studies, Loughborough University*

Content analysis is used to quantify the manifest features of texts. In the past, some have claimed that it represents an objective form of textual analysis, but these sorts of claims need to be treated sceptically. As such, it can provide insights into issues such as how the media (or others) report homelessness or domestic violence. Such information can be useful to contextualise the ways in which policy issues surface and become discussed.

There are various stages involved in deploying this method and these are outlined below. An example of its application is set out in **Box 4d**. Before applying the method, you need to consider whether it is appropriate for your research objectives. Content analysis is a method that aims to produce 'a big picture': delineating manifest trends, patterns and absences over large aggregations of texts. But by looking at meaning making *across* texts, the method skates over complex processes of meaning making *within* texts: the latent levels of form and meaning.

Sampling

Sampling considerations in relation to content analysis are essentially the same as those that concern any attempt to generate a representative sample. You first need to identify your research population (which is determined by your research objectives) and then decide on a sampling strategy that will produce an adequate representation of that population (see Section 4.4). As a general rule, the bigger your sample is, the better. Issues regarding representativeness operate in two ways: *horizontally* – how far backwards or forwards in time should sampling extend your sampling period? – and *vertically* – how extensively should you sample across the component elements of your 'population'? For example, if you are interested in examining media representations of disability, should you concentrate on news reporting or extend your analysis to include other fictional and actuality forms?

You also need to decide on your sampling unit. Some content analysis studies have a very precise focus, taking individual words as their sampling units to explore "the lexical contents and/or syntactic structures of documents" (Beardsworth, 1980, p 375). Other studies provide a more generalised analysis that involves coding themes and features in texts. The second form is the most widely adopted in social research and the basic sampling unit tends to be an entire text (for example, a TV programme) or clearly identifiable component elements of a text (for example, separate news items within a TV programme). Once chosen, the selected sampling unit becomes the 'host' to all textual elements that are subsequently quantified.

What to count?

What you count is determined by your research objectives and these decisions require the production of:

- *a coding schedule*, which lists the variables of your analysis;
- *a coding manual*, which sets out the coding values for each of the variables.

Their design requires a lot of careful deliberation, as some things are easier to categorise than others. Piloting is essential at this stage, to discern how readily the variables and values can be operationalised, and to gain some sense of their comprehensiveness. As a general rule, content analysis works most reliably in the coding of manifest features of texts.

Qualifying criteria

You need to define what criteria will be used to decide which sample units fall within your study's remit. Sometimes this is quite straightforward. Imagine you wanted to conduct an analysis of media reporting of a specific social policy initiative. For this study, your qualifying criteria could simply be any explicit reference made to the policy in a sampled item or programme. Other topics are more problematic. For example, the case study in **Box 4d** describes a content analysis of media coverage of the voluntary sector (Deacon, 1999). As there is no consensus as to how to define the voluntary sector, careful thought needs to be given to identifying 'when a voluntary sector item is a voluntary sector item'. Should the study include items that mention trades unions and political parties, or solely focus on registered charities? In the case described, neither strategy was adopted – in the former instance, because it would have made the study too inclusive (in Britain, the voluntary sector is generally seen as separate from unions and political parties); in the latter, because it would have been too restrictive (many voluntary organisations do not have charitable status).

Box 4d: Media reporting of the voluntary sector

David Deacon, *Senior Lecturer in Communication and Media Studies, Loughborough University [This illustration is based on a study by Deacon (1999)]*

Sampling
Horizontal dimensions
A composite sample of four week's British local and national broadcast and press coverage was analysed. Sampling began on Monday 26 October 1992 and from that date every eighth day was sampled, for 27 further days.

Vertical dimensions (national media)
All national daily and Sunday newspapers for each sample day were analysed. For the national broadcast sample, recording on each sample day began at 9.00am and concluded at 12.00pm, and included all actuality coverage on BBC1, BBC2, ITV, Channel 4 and BBC Radio 4 that could be categorised as one of the following: news, current affairs, entertainment, general information or social action programming. BBC Radio 2's 'Jimmy Young' show and BBC Radio 1's, 'News '92/3' were also added to the sample.

Vertical dimensions (local media)
Four counties were purposively selected for their regional and demographic variation. All newspapers published in these areas on the sampling days were analysed. The local television sample comprised the main early evening regional news programmes broadcast in each of the local sample areas, for both BBC1 and ITV, on each of the sample weekdays. Local radio was not sampled due to logistical difficulties.

Sampling unit

In the main, the sampling units were individual items within programmes and newspapers (that is, separate news and feature items). Where broadcast programmes were not segmented, the entire programme was taken as the sampling unit.

What was counted?

Up to five 'voluntary sector' organisations could be coded per item (more, if the sample unit was an entire programme). These codes indicated the area of activity of each organisation, the nature of its presentation, and the role it fulfilled in the item. These roles were organised under two broad categories – 'Doing' (for example, fund-raising, providing services, and so on) and 'Commenting' (for example, criticising other organisations, highlighting issues, and so on). Each voluntary sector source could be assigned up to two roles per item (if appropriate). Assorted other descriptive details related to each item were also coded (for example, length of item, its location and position).

Qualifying criteria

An item or programme was deemed relevant if it either: (a) mentioned any organisation that was (1) non-profit making, (2) non-statutory, (3) non party political, (4) not affiliated to a professional group and (5) had a formal structure; or (b) referred to broader issues concerning the voluntary sector.

Coding and analysis

More than 4,500 items and programmes were included in the analysis. Coverage was found to cluster around general and non-contentious areas of voluntary activity (for example, children, animals and health) and neglected organisations working in minority or contentious issue domains. Voluntary organisations received more coverage for their deeds (fund-raising, doing good works, and so on) than for their political interventions (raising topics, adjudicating upon the views or actions of others). When voluntary sector sources were included as commentators, their most common role was a 'signalling' one: highlighting issues and concern for public debate rather than directly engaging in the cut and thrust of political argument. Instances of direct media criticism of voluntary agencies were rare, but scant attention was paid to the broader political questions raised by the expanding role and importance of the voluntary sector in Britain.

Reference

Deacon, D. (1999) 'Charitable images: the construction of voluntary sector news', in B. Franklin (ed) *Social policy, the media and misrepresentation*, London: Routledge, pp 51-68.

Coding

The key principle in coding is to be very systematic in applying the research instruments. Even with well-piloted coding schedules and manuals, you may encounter examples that do not fit neatly within your categories. Once you have decided on a coding solution, you should note down the decision, and repeat it studiously for similar cases.

The issue of consistency is particularly significant when more than one person is involved in the coding, as there may be inconsistencies *between* the interpretations of coders. Various statistical procedures can be used to test for inter-coder reliability.

Analysis

Some people refer irreverently to this stage as 'number crunching', which implies it is a mechanistic, self-evident process. This is a misconception. In data analysis you need both to describe your findings and interpret their significance. The first task is straightforward, but the second requires considerably more imagination and reflexivity. Be directive in your analysis of the results at the start. Avoid the temptation of indiscriminately trawling for numbers, as this is a recipe for confusion.

Conclusion

Content analysis provides an extensive rather than intensive analysis of texts and only offers answers to the questions you pose. It requires care and rigour in design and implementation and does not offer much opportunity to explore textual aspects to develop new insights. Nor can it be said to provide an 'objective', value-free perspective. Arbitrary decisions are involved in all stages of the research process: what you count, how much you sample, how you categorise, and so on; and all of these decisions ultimately depend on the researcher's judgement of what is significant. Therefore, findings produced by this method do not represent incontrovertible facts. They are 'constructs' and when presenting them you must be open about the construction process.

Question for discussion

- Is the coding process both central to content analysis and its defining feature?

References

Beardsworth, A. (1980) 'Analyzing press content: some technical and methodological issues', in H. Christian (ed) *The sociology of journalism and the press*, Keele: University of Keele, pp 371-95.

Deacon, D. (1999) 'Charitable images: the construction of voluntary sector news', in B. Franklin (ed) *Social policy, the media and misrepresentation*, London: Routledge, pp 51-68.

Further reading

Weber, R. (1990) *Basic content analysis*, London: Sage Publications.

4.9 Structured observation

Structured observation is a somewhat underutilised technique for gathering data on people's behaviour. Unlike the kind of participant observation in which ethnographers engage, the observer is typically on the sidelines of the aspect of social life he or she is studying. The idea is to use an *observation schedule*, which is similar to a structured interview schedule of the kind used in survey research, to observe people and their behaviour in terms of already established categories. The researcher will usually be interested in several variables and for each variable there will be at least two categories in terms of which behaviour needs to be coded. Imagine that we are interested in the way social security claimants are treated by social security staff. An observer might want to categorise the behaviour of both claimants and the member of staff concerned. Regarding the member of staff, the focus of interest may be issues such as: 'does the member of staff greet the claimant?', 'how long does he or she spend checking through the claimant's application form?', 'does the member of staff provide help with any aspects of the form that have not been fully completed?', and so on. Many of these issues are relatively straightforward for an observer to assess. More difficult to code, because they require some interpretation on the part of the observer, might be more impressionistic issues in which the researcher might be interested, such as whether the member of staff is friendly, whether he or she is helpful, whether he or she becomes aggressive towards a claimant, and so on. In order to devise indicators of such issues, the researcher needs to make the observation schedule as straightforward as possible so that the observer has very little interpretation to do. The problem with interpretation of what is going on (such as whether the member of staff is being friendly) is that observers may not be consistent in their application of criteria and if there is more than one observer, they may not be consistent with each other.

A further issue that requires consideration in connection with structured observation is the issue of sampling. Bearing in mind that there may be several members of staff helping claimants at any one time, is each member of staff continuously observed over several days or is there some attempt to sample members of staff and the times they are observed? Observing all members of staff continuously would require a large research team and would be very wearying for the members of staff. Accordingly, a researcher might want to observe just one or two members of staff at any one time. Alternatively, one may want to video record interactions. But this still leaves open the questions: how are they chosen and when are they observed? A random sampling approach is the most desirable strategy, but with structured observation further issues are thrown up. First, should each staff member be observed for a whole day? If the answer is that this is undesirable because it might be exhausting for them, when should they be observed? This second issue is important because we should not always observe a particular member of staff at the same time each day because his or her behaviour may vary considerably over the course of the day and this would not be captured if, for example, he or she was always observed between 9.00am and mid-morning. In the morning members of staff may feel friendlier and more helpful than late in the day when they may have experienced some difficult claimants. Consequently, it is likely to be necessary to ensure that the observation of members of staff takes place at different times of the day. Other sampling techniques that are fairly specific to structured observation are discussed in Bryman (2004, Chapter 8).

An American study of meetings between family care staff and parents of children with emotional and behavioural disorders illustrates the use of an observation schedule to examine the degree to which the family care team were family-friendly (Singh et al, 1997). This meant assessing whether each of several things happened in the meeting, such as:

- A statement is made to the parent that all information will be kept confidential.
- The parent is asked what treatments or interventions he/she felt worked/ didn't work in the past.
- The parent's ideas are elicited about the types of service he/she would prefer.
- The parent is involved in designing the service plan.

In each case, the item could be recorded by observers on a yes/no/not applicable basis. The foregoing items are all relatively straightforward to record but one requiring more interpretation was:

- Family members are attended to in a courteous fashion at all times.

A total of 79 meetings were observed, although we are not told how they were sampled. A crucial issue for research of this kind is obtaining consent and in this case we are told that permission was obtained from all those involved in the meetings, including children. This point is very important since structured observation is a rather invasive technique, especially in emotionally charged situations of this kind. In fact, the research shows that the family–friendliness of the meetings was variable, although overall it is described by the authors as reasonably good.

The main advantage of structured observation is that it allows the researcher to study behaviour directly rather than indirectly by asking people about their behaviour through a questionnaire or interview. Asking people questions about their behaviour is vulnerable to such things as misrepresentation, inaccurate reporting and memory loss. On the other hand, with structured observation there is always the risk that people adjust their behaviour to the observer's presence. However, it is extremely difficult to determine how far and in what ways behaviour is affected by being observed.

Question for discussion

- For what kinds of research questions might structured observation be a useful research method in social policy research?

References

Bryman, A. (2004) *Social research methods* (2nd edn), Oxford: Oxford University Press.

Singh, N.N., Curtis, W.J., Wechsler, H.A., Ellis, C.R. and Cohen, R. (1997) 'Family friendliness of community-based services for children and adolescents with emotional and behavioral disorders and their families: an observational study', *Journal of Emotional and Behavioral Disorders*, vol 5, no 2, pp 82-92.

Further reading

McCall, G.J. (1984) 'Systematic field observation', *Annual Review of Sociology*, vol 10, pp 263-82.

4.10 Official statistics

David Gordon, *Professor of Social Justice, and Director of the Townsend Centre for International Poverty Research, University of Bristol*

> In the original sense of the word, 'Statistics' was the science of Statecraft: to the political arithmetician of the eighteenth century, its function was to be the eyes and ears of the central government. (Sir Roland Fisher, cited in Gaither and Cavazos-Gaither, 1996, p 243)

The word statistics is derived from the Italian word for *state*. Therefore all *statistics* were originally 'official statistics' as they were literally information collected for and by the state. However, in modern societies statistics are collected and published by a wide range of organisations, including governmental organisations. Nevertheless it is always important to remember that no statistics can be considered to be 'objective facts', they are all paid for and collected by some organisation for a specific purpose (often a policy purpose).

Many textbooks claim that statistics were founded by John Graunt of London, a 'haberdasher of small wares' in a tiny book called *Natural and political observations made upon the Bills of Mortality*, published in 1672. However, policy relevant statistics collected during population and housing censuses have a much longer history than this, with records dating back to early Babylonian, Egyptian and Chinese civilisations. These innovative early Asian and African censuses were undertaken primarily for military, tax and land allocation purposes (Nissel, 2001). The first censuses in Europe were conducted by the Roman Empire, usually on a quinquennial basis (the word *census* is Latin in origin) but, after the empire's collapse, census-taking declined with only a few sporadic and usually incomplete, population counts occurring until the 1800s (for example the Gaelic *Senchus fer n'Alba* in 7th-century England, the *Doomsday Book* in 1086 and the 'Hearth Tax' counts in 14th-century France). Censuses in Quebec in 1666, in Iceland in 1703, China in 1711 and Sweden in 1749 were influential in promoting the idea of 'modern' census-taking and by the beginning of the 19th century many countries had instituted a regular national census programme (Eurostat, 1992; Dale and Marsh, 1993).

National census information plays a central part in any assessment of social conditions in the world. They are the only source of reliable and comprehensive data on the socio-demographic and economic situation of the world's populations. For example, only census data provide high quality estimates of such basic factors as the number of children and the number of families and households. They are similarly the only high quality source of basic employment information such as employment status, occupation, industry, place of work, current activity status, and so on. It cannot be overemphasised that census data are always much more reliable than survey-based data and should always be used in preference to survey data when they are available for the time frame in question. The main problem with census data is that they are only collected every 10 years in most countries (some countries carry out a census every five years), and only a limited amount of basic information is collected.

Apart from the National Census there are two other main sources of 'official' statistics: *sample survey data* and *administrative statistics*. In the UK most of these government statistics are catalogued in the Office for National Statistics (ONS) *Guide to official statistics* (available free at http://www.statistics.gov.uk/downloads/theme_compendia/GOS2000_v5.pdf). A lot of statistical data are available free of charge from the ONS website (http://www.statistics.gov.uk) at both national and small area level (see neighbourhood statistics at http://www.neighbourhood.statistics.gov.uk/home.asp).

Most of the data described in the *Guide to official statistics* are administrative statistics relating to the specific functioning of national and local government departments. Many are very specialised (for example, the Turkey Census, Ship Arrivals, General Ophthalmic Services – Vouchers, and so on) and of limited interest to most social policy researchers. However, some, like the unemployment claimant count, are of both considerable academic and political interest and sometimes a subject of controversy. During the 1980s, thirty changes were made to the way the unemployment count was measured, many of which resulted in a reduction in the number of unemployed. These changes, during a period of high unemployment, led to a widespread belief that the unemployment statistics were being 'fiddled' (Royal Statistical Society, 1995; Levitas, 1996; Taylor, 1999).

The UK government typically commissions 10-20 social surveys each year, five large-scale continuous surveys and a range of one-off issue specific surveys that vary in content from year to year (for example, the *Psychiatric Morbidity Survey*). The five continuous surveys are shown in **Table 4.2**.

Similar surveys are also carried out in Northern Ireland, as are a range of country specific surveys, for example, Health Survey of England, Welsh Health Survey and the Scottish Household Survey. Academic researchers can obtain the raw data from all these (and many other) surveys from the ESRC UK Data Archive (http://www.data-archive.ac.uk/). Most datasets can be downloaded via the Internet once the relevant forms have been completed.

Table 4.2: Major continuous household sample surveys in Britain

Survey	Earliest national data	Approximate annual sample size	Main topics
Expenditure and Food Survey (EFS)[a]	1950 NFS/ 1957 FES	7,000 households	Annual survey of income, expenditure and food consumption
Family Resources Survey	1993	25,000 households	Annual survey of income, earnings and social security
General Household Survey	1971	10,000	Annual multi-purpose households survey with data on housing, employment, education and health
Labour Force Survey	1973	95,000 households	Quarterly labour market data on employment, education and training
Omnibus Survey	1990	24,000 individuals (one adult per household)	Multi-purpose monthly survey of about 2,000 adults

Note: [a] The EFS began in 2001 and replaces both the National Food Survey (NFS) and the Family Expenditure Survey (FES).

International statistics

Until the 1990s, virtually all official statistics produced by international organisations were simple compilations of data collected from the countries' national statistical offices. However, the end of the 20th century witnessed a revolution in the collection and availability of high quality statistical information, particularly from countries in the developing world (see **Box 4e** for an examination of the comparison of such statistics in Europe). Data from three main harmonised surveys are now available:

• *Demographic and Health Surveys (DHS):* since the mid–1980s, the DHS programme has assisted countries in conducting national surveys on fertility, family planning, and maternal and child health. Since 1997, DHS data from over 100 surveys has been made available, free of charge, over the WWW (www.measuredhs.com).

- *Living Standards Measurement Study (LSMS):* since 1985, over 265 LSMS and other similar national sample surveys have been conducted in 83 countries (Grosh and Muñoz, 1996; Chen and Ravallion, 2000; www.worldbank.org/lsms/).
- *Multiple Indicator Cluster Surveys (MICS):* these household surveys are specifically designed to help countries accurately assess progress for children in relation to the 1990 *World Summit for Children* goals. By 1996, 60 developing countries had carried out stand-alone MICS, and another 40 had incorporated some of the MICS modules into other surveys (www.childinfo.org/MICS2/Gj99306k.htm).

It is now possible to download over the Internet and analyse comparable social survey microdata from over 100 countries. Few such global analyses have yet been produced but high quality statistical data are now readily available to social policy researchers for the first time in history.

Box 4e: International statistical comparisons in Europe

David Gordon, *Professor of Social Justice, and Director of the Townsend Centre for International Poverty Research, University of Bristol*

Many researchers want to compare statistical information about different countries. However, statistics are social constructs that were developed for specific historical and cultural purposes. Since countries have had different cultural and economic histories it is unsurprising that there are many differences between their social statistics. This is not problematic for analysis within countries but it raises substantial problems when trying to compare countries (see also Chapter Three, Section 3.9).

Although there are United Nations and European Union conventions regarding the collection of social statistics and the calculation of indices, there are no international agreements on socio-demographic data comparable, for example, to the International Classification of Causes of Death developed by the World Health Organisation (WHO), according to the rules of which most countries now report their mortality data (Colman, 1999). International compilations of social indicators, therefore, either have to take as read the differences in definition and usage employed by participating countries, and present them with appropriate warnings, as does the Council of Europe and the Organisation for Economic Co-operation and Development, or instead attempt to harmonise them by re-computing indices from raw data, as Eurostat (European Statistical Office) does for EU member states. Harmonisation by Eurostat improves comparability but after such processing, some data will no longer be identical to that reported by the national statistics offices in question.

For example, results from the same Labour Force Survey produced by Eurostat, the Luxembourg Employment Study and the national statistical office of an EU member state may often differ, even though the same dataset is being analysed. It is therefore important to make clear which source is being used in any report (for example, Labour Force Survey unemployment rate according to Eurostat or the national statistical office).

The major problem with many comparative studies that make use of social statistics is that many simple concepts appear to be unambiguous and not open to the possibility of measurement differences (see also Chapter Three, Section 3.9). This is an illusion; there is not a single social indicator that is measured in the same way in every country even within the EU. For example, anthropological studies indicate that all societies have a concept of 'age' and the concept of age seems simple and not open to definitional differences. Unfortunately this is not the case: two definitions of 'age' are in use in different countries of the EU. The first is 'age in completed years' (in other words, a given birthday having been reached). The second is 'age achieved during the calendar year in question', even when the birthday has not been reached. For every one year of birth there are two years of completed age, and vice-versa. With classification by completed years, events at a given age apply to persons on average half a year older compared with age reached during the year. That makes a difference to statistics on mean age of the workforces, mean age of mother at first birth, and so on.

Harmonised statistics produced by Eurostat
Eurostat produces a range of statistical analyses from member states which are mainly based on the:

1) *Labour Force Surveys (LFS):* which are required by the Treaty of Rome;
2) *Household Budget Surveys (HBS):* which are needed to produce the United Nations System of National Accounts, particularly inflation estimates.

More recently, Eurostat has begun to harmonise Time Use Survey (TSU) data from member states. Unfortunately, it is very difficult for academic researchers to gain access to the Eurostat harmonised datasets. Consequently, a much more limited set of member states' HBS and LFS data have been extensively analysed by the Luxembourg Income Study (LIS) and Luxembourg Employment Study (LES) (see www.lis.project.org).

In 2000, a list of core 'variables' for use in the EU was agreed. The 17 core variables for harmonisation by Eurostat are (Everaers, 2000) as follows:

Core variables
- Place of usual residence (Census)
- Sex (Census)
- Age (Census)
- Private household
- Educational attainment
- Labour status
- Economic activity
- Hours worked (Census)
- Disposable income
- Main activity status
- Health status
- Current education/training
- Country of birth (Census)
- Tenure status of household (Census)
- Country of citizenship (Census)
- Number of rooms (Census)
- Socio-economic status

In addition to the harmonised variables from existing data collected by countries, statistical information in Europe is available from three main EU-wide surveys:

- European Community Household Panel Survey (ECHP): http://forum.europa.eu.int/irc/dsis/echpanel/info/data/information.html and www.iser.essex.ac.uk/epag/index.php
- European Surveys on Working Conditions (ESWC): www.eurofound.ie/working/surveys.htm
- Eurobarometer: http://europa.eu.int/comm/public_opinion/

The longitudinal ECHP will be replaced in 2003 by a new survey EU-SILC (Survey of Income and Living Conditions).

Metadata and high quality information sources
One of the major problems with trying to compare employment statistics in different EU member states is where to find the necessary metadata on definitions, concepts and survey methods, for example, does the Labour Force Survey in Portugal and Finland use the same concept of a household?

Fortunately, the University of Mannheim (MZES) has for many years provided help with these issues via their excellent website for the Eurodata Research Archive (www.mzes.uni-mannheim.de/eurodata/index.html).

Conclusion
Comparative studies and social policies have often failed to achieve their aims due to inadequate knowledge of the contexts in which state intervention and statistical measurement have taken place and due to inadequate comparative data to aid policy development. Out of necessity, policy decisions at European level have often been based on simplistic assumptions concerning the

disappearance of national differences and the belief that European integration will emerge quite naturally from the harmonisation of social policies (Affichard et al, 1998). Social policy researchers in the 21st century need a greater awareness of these theoretical and statistical problems, if the promise of effective international social policy development is to be realised.

References

Affichard, J. with Hantrais, L., Letablier, M.-T. and Schultheis, F. (1998) *Social situation in member states of the European Union: The relevance of quantitative indicators in social policy analysis*, Dublin: European Foundation for the Improvement of Living and Working Conditions.

Colman, D. (1999) 'Demographic data for Europe: a review of sources', *Population Trends*, vol 98, pp 42-52.

Everaers, P. (2000) 'Comparable results in European social statistics: key social indicators, harmonisation, integration and core variables', Paper presented to the *Siena Group Meeting 2000*.

Gaither, C.C. and Cavazos-Gaither, A.E. (1996) *Statistically speaking: A dictionary of quotations*, Bristol: Institute of Physics Publishing.

Question for discussion

• Are official statistics 'objective' facts about the world?

References

Chen, S. and Ravallion, M. (2000) *How did the world's poorest fare in the 1990s?*, New York, NY: World Bank Occasional Paper.

Dale, A. and Marsh, C. (1993) *The 1991 Census user's guide*, London: HMSO.

Eurostat (1992) *1990/91 Community Programme of Censuses of Population Comparative Analysis*, Luxembourg: Office des Publications Officielles des Communautés Européennes.

Grosh, M.E. and Muñoz, J. (1996) *A Manual for planning and implementing the Living Standards Measurement Study Survey*, Living Standards Measurement Study Working Paper no 126, Washington DC: World Bank.

Levitas, R. (1996) 'Fiddling while Britain burns? The "measurement" of unemployment', in R. Levitas and W. Guy (eds) *Interpreting official statistics*, London: Routledge, pp 45-65.

Nissel, M. (2001) '200 years of the Census of Population', *Social Trends*, no 31, London: The Stationery Office.

Royal Statistical Society (1995) 'The measurement of unemployment in the UK', *Journal of the Royal Statistical Society A*, vol 158, pp 363-417.

Taylor, D. (1990) *Creative counting*, London: Unemployment Unit.

Further reading

Dorling, D. and Simpson, L. (1998) *Statistics in society*, London: Arnold.

Kerrison, S. and Macfarlane, A. (eds) (2000) *Official health statistics: An unofficial guide*, London: Arnold.

Levitas, R. and Guy, W. (eds) (1996) *Interpreting official statistics*, London: Routledge.

Website resources

Demographic and health surveys: www.measuredhs.com/

Department for Work and Pensions National Statistics: www.dwp.gov.uk/asd/statistics.asp

ESRC Data Archive: www.data-archive.ac.uk/

Guide to official statistics: www.statistics.gov.uk/downloads/theme_compendia/GOS2000_v5.pdf

Living Standards Measurement Study: www.worldbank.org/lsms/

Multiple indicator cluster surveys: www.childinfo.org/MICS2/Gj99306k.htm

Office for National Statistics (ONS): www.statistics.gov.uk/

See also Section 4.9 and **Box 4e**.

PART THREE: THE ANALYSIS OF QUANTITATIVE DATA

4.11 Analysing data

Duncan Cramer, *Reader in Psychological Health, Department of Social Sciences, Loughborough University*

Qualitative and quantitative variables

When analysing numerical data statistically, it is necessary to make a distinction between two kinds of variable that the data may represent, because the appropriate procedures for analysing these two kinds of variable differ. A variable is a quality that consists of two or more categories. For example, the variable of *biological sex* generally consists of the two categories of female and male. The variable of *marital status* may comprise the five categories of the never married, the married, the separated, the divorced and the widowed. The categories that make up these variables are qualitatively distinct. Females differ from males in various ways. The never married may differ from the married in numerous ways. Variables consisting of qualitatively distinct categories are variously known as *qualitative, categorical* or *nominal* variables. Numbers may be used to name or to represent these qualitative categories. For example, females may be coded as 1 and males as 2. The never married may be coded as 1, the married as 2, the separated as 3, and so on. Numbers are simply used to indicate a particular category but do not reflect any other characteristic of that quality. Other qualitative variables include whether one is employed, holds a particular religious belief, belongs to a particular ethnic group, has a particular occupation, and so on.

Qualitative variables need to be distinguished from quantitative variables in which the categories are quantitative and represent increasing size. For example, the quantitative variable of age may consist of categories that refer to whole years. Someone who is 40 is older than someone who is less than 40. In other words, the categories can be ordered in terms of their size. Attitudes towards issues, such as mothers working outside their home, are considered to be quantitative variables in that higher scores on the attitude scale may represent a more positive attitude to that issue. Similarly the rank ordering of possibilities, such as from whom one is likely to seek help, is a quantitative variable in which smaller numbers such as 1 and 2 generally indicate a higher ranking.

Having made this distinction between qualitative and quantitative variables, and at the risk of inviting some confusion, it is important to point out that some variables may be treated as either a qualitative or a quantitative variable. For example, the variable of biological sex may be viewed as a quantitative variable in that females may be seen as having more femaleness than males. To the extent that the categories of a variable can be ordered in this way, these variables can be treated as if they were quantitative. The variable of social class is one that can be dealt with as either a qualitative variable in which the classes are seen as being qualitatively distinct or a quantitative variable in which higher social classes are viewed as representing greater social status.

Descriptive statistics

Tables and charts

In order to make sense of the data collected in a study it is usually necessary to summarise the results for the main variables. Such summaries are often referred to as *descriptive statistics* in that they simply describe the main features of the results and no attempt is made to draw any inferences from them, as is the case with inferential statistics. The only way of summarising qualitative variables is to count the number of cases that fall into a particular category and to present these frequencies as they are or as a percentage of the total number of cases.

These figures may be displayed in the form of a table such as that shown in *Table 4.3*. This table presents the number and percentage of cases in five categories of employment status for a sample of 140 people. The percentages have been rounded to a whole figure following the usual rounding convention. The number is rounded up by one if the first decimal place is 0.5 or more (for example, 40/140 x 100 = 28.57 = 29) and is left as it is if the first decimal place is less than 0.5 (for example, 10/140 x 100 = 7.14 = 7). This procedure results in this instance in the total percentage being slightly greater than 100.

Table 4.3: *Frequency of employment status*

Employment status	Number (*n*)	Percentage (%)
Full-time paid work	50	36
Part-time paid work	40	29
Unemployed, looking for work	15	11
Looking after the home	25	18
Other	10	7
Total	**140**	**101**

These frequencies may be broken down with respect to further qualitative variables such as biological sex. A table showing the frequency of cases broken down in terms of two or more qualitative variables is known as a *contingency table*, in that the frequency of cases in the category of one variable (for example, employment status) is dependent or contingent on the category of the other variable (for example, sex). It is also known as a *cross-tabulation*, in that one variable (for example, employment status) is tabulated across the other variable (for example, sex). A contingency table of employment status in women and men is presented in *Table 4.4*. Where the number of cases in the categories of the second variable is not the same as in this example, the relative sizes of the categories are easier to grasp if percentages rather than the number of cases is used. For example, although the number of women and men who are unemployed is the same at 10, because the sample of women is almost twice as big as that of men, the percentage of unemployed women (11%) is almost twice as small as that of unemployed men (20%).

It is worth introducing a note of caution here on how to read *Table 4.4* and other tables like this. It is important to realise that the percentages are 'column' percentages, in other words, they provide the percentage of men or women who are in each category of employment status. They do *not* indicate the percentage in each category of employment status who are men or women. To make such a calculation you would need 'row' percentages. So, for example, there are 20 people who are unemployed and looking for work. Of these, 10 are women and 10 are men. These represent 50% and 50% of those unemployed.

These are row percentages and represent a different way of reading the table. By contrast, 11% of all women and 20% of all men are unemployed and looking for work.

Table 4.4: *Frequency of employment status in women and men*

	Women		Men	
Employment status	*n*	%	*n*	%
Full-time paid work	20	22	30	60
Part-time paid work	30	33	5	10
Unemployed, looking for work	10	11	10	20
Looking after the home	25	28	0	0
Other	5	6	5	10
Total	**90**	**100**	**50**	**100**

The figures in tables may be turned into diagrams in order to provide further information about the relative size of the groups, thereby making it easier for some people to understand what is being conveyed. For example, the contingency table in **Table 4.4** can be converted into the clustered bar chart in Figure 4b, where the height of the bar corresponds to the percentage and where the bars for women and men are clustered together to make their comparison easier.

Measures of central tendency

Quantitative variables, such as the number of children a women has, may also be presented in terms of a frequency table. **Table 4.5** shows the number of children that a sample of 10 women have. For instance 2 women have no children, 3 women have 1 child, and so on. Quantitative variables are not usually presented as frequency tables for two main reasons. First, these tables would take up considerable space, particularly the more categories and variables there are. And second, there are useful descriptive statistics that can summarise in a few numbers the main characteristics of the distribution of the values in these categories.

Figure 4b: A bar chart of the employment status of women and men

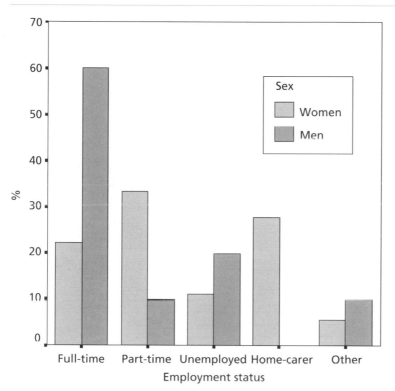

Table 4.5: *Number of children per woman*

Number of children	Number of women
0	2
1	3
2	2
3	1
4	1
5	0
6	1

In describing a distribution of values such as those in ***Table 4.5***, it is useful to know what value characterises the centre or central tendency of the distribution of values (in this case the number of children). There are three main measures of central tendency. These are the *mode*, the *median* and the *arithmetic mean* (*M*), the last of which is generally referred to as the mean and which differs from other means such as the geometric or harmonic mean. The mode is the most common value that in this case is 1. Women with one child is the most frequent category. The median is the value that divides the values arranged in order of size into two equal halves. There are 10 values. So the median lies midway between the 5th and the 6th value. The 5th value is 1 and the 6th value is 2 so the median is 1.50. Fifty per cent of the women have two or more children and 50% have less than two children. The mean is the sum of all the values divided by the number of cases (N). The total number of children is 20 (0 + 0 + 1 + 1 + 1 + 2 + 2 + 3 + 4 + 6 = 20) which divided by 10 gives a mean of 2.00 (20/10 = 2.00). Women on average have 2.00 children each.

When the distribution of values is bunched towards the lower values as it is here, the mode will be the lowest value (1) followed by the median (1.50) and then the mean (2.00). Conversely, when the distribution of values is skewed towards the higher values, the lowest value will be the mean, followed by the median and then the mode. When the distribution of scores is symmetrical, the mode, median and mean will have the same value. The mean is usually reported because it is often used in the calculation of other statistics particularly when values are normally distributed. A normal distribution is bell-shaped.

Measures of dispersion

Statistical measures of central tendency do not provide any information about the spread or dispersion of the values in the distribution. It is useful to know how much the values vary. The simplest measure is the range of values, that is the difference between the highest and the lowest value. The range in the number of children per woman in this sample is 6 (6 − 0 = 6). A more complicated and widely used measure of dispersion is the *standard deviation* (*SD*). There are three main reasons for its popularity. First, unlike the range that is based on only the extreme values of the distribution, every value in the distribution contributes to the calculation of the standard deviation. Second, when the distribution of values is normally distributed, the standard deviation together with the mean provides information about the percentage of values that fall between various values of the distribution. For example, about 34% of the values will fall between the mean and one standard deviation either above or below the mean. And third, the standard deviation is used in calculating many other useful statistics.

The standard deviation is the square root of the variance. The variance is the mean of the sum of the squared deviations or differences between each value and the mean of the values. In other words, the variance is the mean squared deviation. Unsquaring the variance (or mean squared deviation) by taking its square root gives the standard deviation that is similar to, but not exactly the same as, the mean deviation. There are two kinds of standard deviation and variance. One is sometimes known as the sample standard deviation or variance because this describes the standard deviation and variance for the sample. In this measure the sum of squared deviations is divided by the number of cases, that is 10 in our example.

The other measure is often referred to as the estimated population standard deviation and variance. In this measure the sum of squared deviations is divided by the degrees of freedom (*df*) that for this statistic is the number of cases minus 1 ($N - 1$). This slight adjustment provides an unbiased estimate of the population standard deviation and variance and has the effect of making the standard deviation and variance larger. This effect will be greater for small samples. The estimated population standard deviation and variance is used in calculating other kinds of statistics and so is more widely used than the sample standard deviation and variance. The calculation of the standard deviation and variance is shown in ***Table 4.6***.

Correlation

The straight-line or linear relationship between two quantitative variables may be expressed as a Pearson correlation coefficient (*r*). For example, we could use Pearson's correlation to see whether families with bigger household incomes generally have fewer children. A Pearson's correlation has two characteristics. The first characteristic is the sign of the correlation. The sign can be positive

Table 4.6: *Calculations for the variance and standard deviation*

Values		Mean – values	Squared deviations
	0	$2 - 0 = 2$	$2^2 = 4$
	0	$2 - 0 = 2$	$2^2 = 4$
	1	$2 - 1 = 1$	$1^2 = 1$
	1	$2 - 1 = 1$	$1^2 = 1$
	1	$2 - 1 = 1$	$1^2 = 1$
	2	$2 - 2 = 0$	$0^2 = 0$
	2	$2 - 2 = 0$	$0^2 = 0$
	3	$2 - 3 = -1$	$-1^2 = 1$
	4	$2 - 4 = -2$	$-2^2 = 4$
	6	**$2 - 6 = -4$**	**$-4^2 = 16$**
Sum	20		32
N	10		
Mean	2		
Variance		Sample	$32/10 = 3.20$
		Estimate	$32/(10 - 1) = 3.56$
Standard deviation		Sample	$\sqrt{3.20} = 1.79$
		Estimate	$\sqrt{3.56} = 1.89$

or negative. A positive correlation means that high values on one variable (for example, household income) go with high values on the other variable (for example, number of children). A negative correlation means that high scores on one variable (for example, household income) go with low values on the other variable (for example, number of children). If we thought that families with bigger incomes had fewer children we would expect a negative correlation. Negative values and correlations have a negative sign whereas positive values and correlations usually have no sign.

The second characteristic of a correlation is its size or value which can vary from 0 to ±1. A correlation of 0 or close to 0 means that there is no linear relationship between the two variables but there may be a non-linear relationship between them. A correlation of ±1 means that there is a perfect relationship between the two variables. The bigger the correlation, the stronger the linear relationship is between the two variables. The size of a correlation may be described verbally as follows: 0.19 or less is very low (small or weak); 0.20 to 0.39 is low; 0.40 to 0.69 is moderate; 0.70 to 0.89 is high (big or strong); and 0.90 or more is very high. These ranges are approximate and not definitive. The proportion of the variance that is shared between two variables is given by squaring the correlation. So, a correlation of 0.50 means that 0.25 ($0.50^2 = 0.25$) or 25% ($0.25 \times 100 = 25$) of the variance is common to the two variables. This means that 25% of the variance in one variable is attributable to the other variable and that 75% of the variance that they share is due to other variables. This squared correlation is known as the *coefficient of determination*.

The estimated population standard deviation (*SD*) or variance of the two variables can be used to calculate Pearson's correlation as shown in the following two formulae:

$$r = \frac{\text{covariance estimate of variables A and B}}{\sqrt{\text{variance estimate of A}} \times \sqrt{\text{variance estimate of B}}}$$

$$= \frac{\text{covariance estimate of variables A and B}}{SD \text{ estimate of A} \times SD \text{ estimate of B}}$$

This is one example of the usefulness of these two measures of dispersion.

Tests of statistical significance

When collecting data we usually want to know the extent to which we can generalise the findings from our sample to the population in which we are interested. For example, we may wish to know to what extent the correlation we have found in our sample is likely to be true of the population from which we have drawn our sample. To do this, we need to ideally select a sample at random from the population of values although it is not always possible to do this. We then need to test the statistical significance of our finding that is based on the probability of it occurring by chance. Findings that have a probability of occurring 1 or fewer times out of 20 are considered not to have happened by chance and are called statistically significant. Findings which have a probability of occurring more than 1 times out of 20 are judged to have happened by chance and are referred to as being statistically non-significant.

This probability level is usually expressed as a proportion 0.05 (1/20 = 0.05) but may also be referred to as a percentage 5 (0.05 x 100 = 5). Findings are more likely to be statistically significant the bigger the sample. For instance, a weak correlation of 0.10, which is very small, is statistically significant at the 0.05 level with a sample of 385 or more when there are no sound reasons for predicting the direction of the correlation. Much of statistical analysis in the social sciences is concerned with establishing the size and statistical significance of findings.

Computer analysis

Carrying out data analysis through handwritten calculations can be very time consuming and prone to error, both of which increase the greater the dataset. For those who intend or have to conduct several statistical analyses of data, it is generally advisable to learn how to use one of a number of computer packages of programs that have been developed for these purposes. One of the most widely available and used packages is referred to as *SPSS*. SPSS is both the abbreviation for the Statistical Package for the Social Sciences and the name of the company responsible for this package. This package was first produced in 1965 and is regularly revised. The latest version at the time of writing is *SPSS Release 12 for Windows.*

Question for discussion

• What is the distinction between a qualitative and a quantitative variable?

Further reading

Bryman, A. and Cramer, D. (2001) *Quantitative data analysis with SPSS Release 10 for Windows: A guide for social scientists*, Hove: Routledge.
Cramer, D. (1998) *Fundamental statistics for social research: Step-by-step calculations and computer techniques using SPSS for Windows*, London: Routledge.

Howitt, D. and Cramer, D. (2000) *An introduction to statistics in psychology: A complete guide for students* (2nd edn), Hemel Hempstead: Prentice Hall.

Website resource

Some useful help with analysing variables can be found at: http://trochim.human.cornell.edu/selstat/ssstart.htm

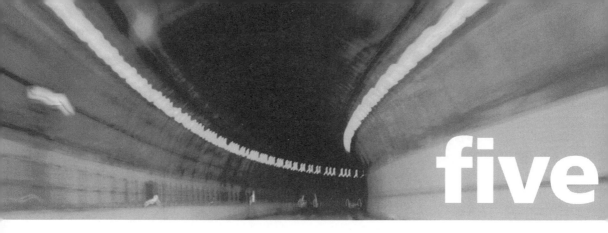

Qualitative research

Detailed contents

5.1 Introduction

In this chapter we address the main aspects of conducting qualitative research. The chapter is divided into three parts:

Part One: Fundamentals of qualitative research: this section begins by addressing the nature of qualitative research and the quest among some practitioners for alternative criteria of quality from those employed by quantitative researchers (described in Chapter Four, Section 4.2). It then moves on to discuss two aspects of quantitative research that are fundamental aspects of social policy research associated with this strategy: the different kinds of research design employed by quantitative researchers (including cross-sectional, longitudinal and case study designs) and the approaches to sampling that they use.

Part Two: Qualitative research methods and sources of qualitative data: this section explores the main methods for the collection of qualitative data and covers:

- semi-structured and unstructured interviewing;
- ethnography;
- focus groups;
- documents; and
- the use of the Internet for collecting qualitative data.

Part Three: The analysis of qualitative data: this final section deals with the basic elements of conducting an analysis of qualitative data. Several important approaches are covered:

- grounded theory and analytic induction (this section also addresses the way in which qualitative researchers typically code their data);
- discourse analysis;
- conversation analysis; and
- narrative analysis.

PART ONE: FUNDAMENTALS OF QUALITATIVE RESEARCH

5.2 Qualitative research

We have already encountered qualitative research in Chapter Three as an approach to social policy research that employs principles that are not only different from those operating in the natural sciences but that also in many respects entail a rejection of those principles. The main concerns and preoccupations of qualitative researchers can be viewed as stemming from this commitment to alternative criteria. The four main concerns and preoccupations were described as being: a focus on actors' meanings and description, along with an emphasis on context, process and flexibility. Therefore, although the term *qualitative* research seems to imply that the absence of quantification is the chief distinguishing characteristic of this research strategy, it is clear that there is more to it than the mere lack of numbers.

As Bryman (2004) points out, in addition to its epistemological roots in a view of the research process that seeks out an alternative to a natural scientific approach, qualitative research tends to have two important features that further distinguish it from quantitative research. First, the approach taken by qualitative researchers typically involves an *inductive* approach to the relationship between theory and research. This term was encountered in Robert Pinker's discussion of the role of theory in social policy research in Chapter Two, Section 2.5. An inductive approach entails generating concepts and theory out of data rather than the quantitative research approach in which concepts and theoretical ideas guide the collection of data.

Second, qualitative research adopts a *constructionist* position with respect to the nature of social reality. This means that social phenomena and social reality generally are taken as created out of the actions and interpretations of people during their social interactions. To take the example of a social network suggested in Chapter Four, a constructionist position would pay greater attention to the role that individuals play in constructing a network and having an influence over it. In treating social reality in a constructionist mode, qualitative researchers are inclined to treat it not as something that exists beyond the reach and influence of people but as something that they are in a continuous process of forming and revising.

Quality criteria in qualitative research

One of the ways in which the tendency of qualitative researchers to associate themselves with principles that are different from those of the natural scientist (and indeed the quantitative researcher) is in their discussions of the criteria that are employed for assessing the quality of research. Whereas quantitative researchers have developed a well understood and clear set of criteria that influence the way research is done and written about (see Chapter Four, Section 4.2), in qualitative research no such generally agreed criteria exist.

Two basic stances exist with regard to the suitability and relevance of the four criteria outlined in Chapter Four, Section 4.2, which we call *adaptation* and *replacement* stances. An **adaptation stance** essentially argues that the conventional criteria (validity, reliability, generalisability and replication) are relevant but need to be adapted to the nature and orientation of qualitative research. One reason for this preference is that to suggest that criteria such as validity and reliability are not relevant could be taken to imply that qualitative research is *in*valid and *un*reliable, or at least that qualitative researchers are not concerned about the possibility that they might be invalid and unreliable. This may not be a sound public relations strategy so some writers on qualitative research criteria have preferred to adapt the quantitative research criteria.

Adaptation position

An example of an adaptation position has been provided by LeCompte and Goetz (1982), who propose the following criteria:

- *External reliability:* can the study be replicated? This is difficult to achieve because it is difficult to freeze a situation so that different researchers can approach the same situation in the same way. High profile re-studies of small-scale societies by ethnographers often give rise to very contrasting findings (Bryman, 1994). In particular, there is the problem of alternative reasons for differences, such as the gender, age and social position of the qualitative researcher (for example, whether accompanied by a spouse), whether exactly the same kind of context is being studied, and the significance of different time periods for the findings. However, as with the quantitative research criterion of replication, it is possibly the *ability* to replicate, so that procedures are fully set out, that is crucial, rather than whether a replication takes place and what its findings are.
- *Internal reliability:* do different researchers in a team agree over their observations and what they are told? This is an interesting criterion but holds little relevance to lone researchers, although some might wish to seek confirmation from others of their interpretations.

- *Internal validity:* is there a good match between researchers' observations and their theoretical ideas? This is a great strength of qualitative research because concepts and theories emerge inductively out of the data, so that there is likely to be a good correspondence between the data and concepts unless the researcher draws unwarranted inferences from the data. However, it is difficult to come up with clear-cut standards to assess this feature.
- *External validity:* can findings be generalised to other settings/populations? This criterion is often regarded as a problem for qualitative research because it does not usually draw on probability and random sampling procedures for selecting research participants and often employs a case study research design that does not readily permit generalisation to a wider population. On the other hand, for qualitative researchers, the goal is not to generalise to populations but to provide a theoretical understanding that can be taken up by other researchers. Williams (2002, p 131) takes a somewhat different position when he argues that in qualitative research, generalisations frequently take the form of *moderatum* generalisations whereby aspects of a situation "can be seen to be instances of a broader recognizable set of features". In fact, Williams suggests, it is not that he is recommending that qualitative researchers should seek to forge such generalisations, but that they frequently do so anyway, but do not recognise that this is what they are going.

Replacement position

As an example of a replacement position, there is the work of Lincoln and Guba (1985) who propose four criteria that are analogous to but different from quantitative research criteria. The criteria are concerned with whether findings are *trustworthy*. To a large extent, their work reflects a concern about whether it is ever possible to arrive at a single, definitive account of social reality. This is often referred to as an *anti-realist* position that has strong affinities with the postmodernist standpoint described in Chapter Three, Section 3.10 and **Box 7a**, Chapter Seven. In many respects, their criteria are to do with making research *appear* trustworthy rather than with whether following their suggestions will actually make it trustworthy. By contrast, criteria such as reliability and validity assume a realist position, which assumes that there is an external reality that can be described and represented by the social policy researcher.

Table 5.1: *Lincoln and Guba's alternative criteria and their equivalent conventional criteria terms*

Alternative criteria	Quantitative research criteria
Credibility	Internal validity
Transferability	External validity
Dependability	Reliability
Confirmability	Objectivity

Table 5.1 presents Lincoln and Guba's alternative criteria (1985) and what they take to be the equivalent terms associated with the conventional criteria employed in quantitative research. While their ideas are controversial and by no means have the hold that conventional criteria have among quantitative researchers, their ideas are interesting.

Credibility is concerned with the question of whether a set of findings are believable. Lincoln and Guba stipulate a variety of activities and practices that can enhance the believability of findings. These include: triangulation (see Chapter Three, Section 3.4); negative case analysis, whereby the researcher seeks out cases that go against the grain of an emerging finding, so that the findings may be revised in the light of the new information (a strategy associated with analytic induction; see Section 5.14); and what they call 'member checks'. Member checks, often also called *respondent validation*, and *member validation* is an increasingly commonly used procedure whereby the researcher provides research participants with some of his or her research materials and asks them to comment on them. Different kinds of materials might be, and have been, used by researchers, such as: transcripts or summaries of interviews; short reports of findings; and drafts of articles or chapters. The idea is to make the research findings more credible by being able to state that aspects of them have been verified by the very people on whom the research was conducted. For researchers of a less anti-realist persuasion than Lincoln and Guba, member checks are often a useful way of increasing the accuracy of their findings.

Transferability is concerned with the issue of whether a set of findings is relevant to settings other than the one or ones in which it was conducted. In order to enhance transferability, Lincoln and Guba recommend detailed accounts of research settings (often referred to as *thick descriptions*). Such accounts allow other researchers to establish whether findings hold up in other contexts. For Lincoln and Guba, whether a set of findings are transferable to other contexts is entirely an empirical question and not something that is intrinsic to an investigation. What the qualitative researcher can do is to provide someone wishing to consider the generalisability of findings the material which are required for determining whether findings apply to another context. There are affinities here with Yin's (1984) notion of a *replication logic*, which was discussed in Chapter Four, Section 4.3, and Williams's (2002) idea of *moderatum* generalisations (see discussion above).

Dependability is concerned with the question of how far we can rely on a set of findings. To this end, Lincoln and Guba advocate an auditing approach using an 'audit trail'. This means that records must be kept of all stages of the research process, including minutes of meetings and details of decision making during each phase of a project, so that questions such as the following can be addressed: 'have correct procedures been followed?', 'have records been kept of how people were sampled?', 'were they properly briefed in terms of ethics?', 'do the data warrant the conclusions generated?'. This is potentially very demanding for the auditors who are likely to be peers. Such a procedure would involve going through transcripts of interviews, fieldnotes, minutes of meetings, draft reports, and so on in order to establish dependability. It is not surprising, therefore, that there are very few examples of an audit trail approach being used in practice (Bryman, 2004, pp 275-6).

Confirmability is concerned with issues such as whether the researcher allowed personal values to intrude excessively or in an unwarranted way. To assess confirmability, Lincoln and Guba advocate an audit trail approach for this criterion as well. A puzzling feature of this criterion is its use of objectivity as a parallel criterion in quantitative research. In fact, it is not entirely clear that quantitative researchers nowadays typically accept this as a criterion. Most recognise that values and biases intrude into the research process but take the view that the crucial issue is to keep these to a minimum, although some writers, working from the vantage point of specific commitments argue that the social researcher should *not* attempt to be value-free (Temple, 1997). As Seale (1999, p 45) suggests, in juxtaposing confirmability against objectivity, Lincoln and Guba have set up a somewhat overdrawn contrast.

In adopting a position that largely depicts qualitative researchers as engaged in a game of persuading readers and others that their version of an aspect of social reality is more credible and authoritative than other possible accounts, Lincoln and Guba are at variance with quantitative research *and* with much qualitative research. By no means would all qualitative researchers subscribe to Lincoln and Guba's implicit view that there can be many different versions of reality, and that the key feature for a researcher is that of persuading others of his or her version. Indeed, there has been some evidence in recent years of a return to traditional ways of thinking about issues such as validity and reliability in qualitative research (see for example, Armstrong et al, 1997). Nonetheless, Lincoln and Guba's suggestions are interesting and some of their ideas about features such as an auditing approach are intriguing if difficult to implement.

Question for discussion

*   Why do quality criteria in qualitative research appear to be so controversial?

References

Armstrong, D., Gosling, A., Weinman, J. and Marteau, T. (1997) 'The place of inter-rater reliability in qualitative research: an empirical study', *Sociology*, vol 31, pp 597-606.

Bryman, A. (1994) 'The Mead/Freeman controversy: some implications for qualitative researchers', in R.G. Burgess (ed) *Studies in qualitative methodology*, vol 4, Greenwich, CN: JAI Press, pp 1-27.

Bryman, A. (2004) *Social research methods* (2nd edn), Oxford: Oxford University Press.

LeCompte, M.P. and Goetz, J.P. (1982) 'Problems of reliability and validity in qualitative research', *Review of Educational Research*, vol 52, pp 31-60.

Lincoln, Y. and Guba, E. (1985) *Naturalistic Inquiry*, Beverly Hills, CA: Sage Publications.

Seale, C. (1999) *The quality of qualitative research*, London: Sage Publications.

Temple, B. (1997) '"Collegial authority" and bias: the solution or the problem?', *Sociological Research Online*, vol 2 (www.socresonline.org.uk/socresonline/2/4/8.html).

Williams, M. (2002) 'Generalisation in interpretive research', in T. May (ed) *Qualitative research in action*, London: Sage Publications, pp 125-43.

Yin, R.K. (1984) *Case study research: Design and methods*, Beverly Hills, CA: Sage Publications.

Further reading

Lincoln, Y. and Guba, E. (1985) *Naturalistic inquiry*, Beverly Hills, CA: Sage Publications.

Seale, C. (1999) *The Quality of qualitative research*, London: Sage Publications.

5.3 Research design: an overview

In Section 4.3, a research design was referred to as a structure or framework within which data are collected. This notion, which was framed within the context of quantitative research, is equally applicable to qualitative research. As with quantitative research, a research design is a *mechanism for linking research questions and evidence*. Understanding the principles of research design is therefore as important for qualitative researchers as it is for quantitative researchers. Moreover, the basic forms of research design introduced in Section 4.3 are equally applicable to a qualitative research strategy, although the experimental design is rarely, if ever, found in such a context. The next two sections discuss the three research designs that were introduced – the *case study*, which is frequently extended into a multiple case study approach (Eisenhardt, 1989), the *cross-sectional design* and the *longitudinal design*. While the implementation of these designs in qualitative research differs somewhat from their use in quantitative research, the methodological issues involved are fundamentally the same.

Reference

Eisenhardt, K.M. (1989) 'Building theories from case study research', *Academy of Management Review*, vol 14, no 4, pp 532-50.

5.4 Case study

Martyn Hammersley, *Professor of Educational and Social Research, The Open University*

The term *case study* is not used in a standard way, and at face value it can be misleading, since there is a sense in which all research studies are cases. Nevertheless, we can identify a core meaning of the term as referring to research that investigates a small number of cases, possibly even just one, in considerable depth.

Case study is often contrasted with two other influential kinds of research design: the *social survey* and the *experiment*. The contrast with the survey relates to dimensions already mentioned: the number of cases investigated, and the amount of detailed information the researcher collects about each case studied. Other things being equal, the less cases investigated the more information can be collected about each of them. *Social surveys* study a large number of cases but usually gather only a relatively small amount of data about each one, focusing on specific features of it (cases here are usually, although not always, individual respondents). By contrast, in case study, large amounts of information are collected about one or a few cases, across a wide range of features. Here the case may be an individual (as in life history work), an event, an institution, or even a whole national society or geographical region. The case study is a design that can and frequently does draw on both quantitative and qualitative research methods.

Case study can also be contrasted with *experimental research*. While the latter also usually involves investigation of a small number of cases compared to survey research, what distinguishes it from case study is the fact that it involves direct control of variables. In experiments, the researcher creates the case(s) studied, whereas case study researchers identify cases out of naturally occurring social phenomena.

The term case study is also often taken to carry implications for the *kind* of data that are collected, and perhaps also for *how these are analysed*. Frequently, but not always, it implies the collection of unstructured data, and qualitative analysis of those data. Moreover, this relates to a more fundamental issue about the purpose of the research. It is sometimes argued that the aim of case study research should be to capture cases in their uniqueness, rather than to use them as a basis for wider empirical or theoretical conclusions. This, again, is a matter of emphasis: it does not necessarily rule out an interest in coming to general conclusions, but it does imply that these are to be reached by means of inferences from what is found in particular cases, rather than through the cases being selected in order to test a hypothesis. In line with this, it is frequently argued that case study adopts an inductive orientation.

Another question that arises in relation to case study concerns objectivity, in at least one sense of that term. Is the aim to produce an account of each case from an external or research point of view, one that may contradict the views of the people involved? Or is it solely to portray the character of each case 'in its own terms'? This contrast is most obvious where the cases are people, so that the aim may be to 'give voice' to them rather than to use them as respondents or even as informants. However, while this distinction may seem to be clear-cut, in practice it is more complicated. Where multiple participants are involved in a case, they may have different views. And even the same person may present different views on different occasions. Furthermore, there are complexities involved in determining whether what is presented can ever 'capture' participant views rather than presenting an 'external' gloss on them.

However, some commentators point out that a case is always a 'case of' something, so that an interest in some general category is built in from the beginning, even though definition of that category may change over the course of the research. In line with this, there are approaches to case study inquiry that draw on the comparative method in order to develop and refine theoretical categories. Examples include grounded theorising (Glaser and Strauss, 1967), historical approaches employing John Stuart Mill's methods of agreement and difference (see Skocpol, 1979), and analytic induction (Cressey, 1953).

Another area of disagreement concerns whether case study is a method – with advantages and disadvantages, and to be used as and when appropriate, depending on the problem under investigation – or a paradigmatic approach that one simply chooses or rejects on philosophical or political grounds. Even when viewed simply as a method, there can be variation in the specific form that case studies take:

- in the number of cases studied;
- in whether there is comparison – and, if there is, in the role it plays;
- in how detailed the case studies are;

- in the size of the case(s) dealt with;
- in what researchers treat as the context of the case, how they identify it, and how much they seek to document it;
- in the extent to which case study researchers restrict themselves to description, explanation, and/or theory, or engage in evaluation and/or prescription.

Variation in these respects depends to some extent on the purpose that the case study is intended to serve. Where it is designed to test or illustrate a theoretical point, then it will deal with the case as an instance of a type, describing it in terms of a particular theoretical framework (implicit or explicit). Where it is concerned with developing theoretical ideas, it is likely to be more detailed and open-ended in character. The same is true where the concern is with describing and/or explaining what is going on in a particular situation for its own sake. Where the interest is in some problem in the situation investigated, then the discussion will be geared to diagnosing that problem, identifying its sources, and perhaps outlining what can be done about it.

Many commentators, however, regard case study as more than just a method – they regard it as involving quite different assumptions about how the social world can and should be studied from those underlying other approaches (see, for example, Hamilton, 1980; Simons, 1996). Sometimes, this is formulated in terms of a contrast between positivism, on the one hand, and naturalism, interpretivism or constructionism, on the other. At the extreme, case study is viewed as more akin to the kind of portrayal of the social world that is characteristic of novelists, short story writers and even poets. Those who see case study in this way may regard any comparison of it with other methods in terms of advantages and disadvantages as fundamentally misconceived.

Question for discussion

- What are the arguments for case study as a methodological approach, and for it being just one method among others?

References

Cressey, D. (1953) *Other people's money*, Glencoe, IL: Free Press.
Glaser, B.G. and Strauss, A. (1967) *The discovery of grounded theory*, Chicago, IL: Aldine.
Hamilton, D. (1980) 'Some contrasting assumptions about case study research and survey analysis', in H. Simons (ed) *Towards a science of the singular: Essays about case study in educational research and evaluation*, Norwich: Centre for Applied Research in Education, University of East Anglia, pp 78-92.
Simons, H. (1996) 'The paradox of case study', *Cambridge Journal of Education*, vol 26, no 2, pp 225-40.

Skocpol, T. (1979) *States and social revolutions: A comparative analysis of France, Russia, and China*, Cambridge: Cambridge University Press.

Further reading

Gomm, R., Hammersley, M. and Foster, P. (eds) (2000) *Case study method*, London: Sage Publications.
Yin, R. (1994) *Case study research* (2nd edn), Thousand Oaks, CA: Sage Publications.

5.5 Cross-sectional design and longitudinal design

The cross-sectional design and the longitudinal design, which were introduced in Chapter Four, Section 4.3, in the context of quantitative research, are equally relevant to qualitative research. The first of these two designs is especially frequently employed in connection with qualitative research using semi-structured interviewing and unstructured interviewing. In these cases, the researcher interviews a cross-section of people at a particular moment in time. Of course, they can never be interviewed at precisely the same point in time, any more than the interviewees in a social survey conducted by structured interview can be interviewed simultaneously. What the researcher attempts to do is to interview a variety of people within the time frame of his or her investigation.

It is not common to write about qualitative researchers as users of a cross-sectional design, but that is essentially what is involved in most qualitative interview studies. For example, in an article discussing her research on pension planning, which was referred to in **Box 2b**, Chapter Two, Rowlingson (2002, p 632) writes that "41 people were interviewed in depth from a cross-section of the public. Quotas were set to ensure a reasonable mix of: men and women; different employment/social class groups; and different life-cycle/age groups". There is next to nothing to distinguish this design from one that a survey researcher using a structured interview or postal questionnaire might use to examine the same kind of issue. Rowlingson notes that because she did not use random sampling she is unable to generalise from her sample of 41 to a wider population. However, the same point could be made of many surveys in social policy research that are not based on random sampling or even quota sampling (see Chapter Four, Section 4.4, on this kind of point). Similarly, Dean and Shah (2002) report the results of a qualitative investigation using semi-structured interviews with 47 recipients of Family Credit. The research was conducted in September 1999 – one month before Family Credit was due to be replaced by Working Families Tax Credit. The sample was compiled through three sources: the then Department of Social Security, snowball sampling and advertisements for interviewees. Once again, this would appear to be a cross-sectional design which allows the authors, in much the same way as Rowlingson, to glean "a much richer understanding of processes, motivations, beliefs and attitudes than can be gleaned from quantitative research" (Rowlingson, 2002, p 632).

Unsurprisingly, the cross-sectional design can be extended into a longitudinal design. Extending a cross-sectional design into a longitudinal design is particularly valuable for charting changes in experiences and views following a change of some sort. For example, Arksey's (2002) research on the support needs of informal carers, which was referred to in Chapter Two, Section 2.2, was conducted in four social services departments in the North of England. These were chosen to reflect a 'cross-section of authorities'. In addition to interviewing a senior manager in each authority and some practitioners, Arksey interviewed 51 carers. She writes:

> Semi-structured interviews with carers were held at two points in time: as soon as possible after they had been assessed under the Carers Act ... and six months after the first interview.... The first interview focused on the process and form of assessment, and any associated service provision. The second interview concentrated on changes during the six-month interval, and the perceived outcome of assessment for carers. (Arksey, 2002, p 85)

Box 5a provides a more detailed illustration of the way in which a longitudinal design can be employed in relation to qualitative research.

Box 5a: Longitudinal qualitative research

Noel Smith, *Research Fellow*, Ruth Lister, *Professor of Social Policy and* Sue Middleton, *Director, all at Centre for Research in Social Policy, Loughborough University*

Although social policy has a history of using longitudinal qualitative research (LQR), there is growing interest in its effectiveness for examining dynamic social processes, and greater recognition that it involves a distinct methodology. LQR involves repeat observations of, ideally, the same research subjects over time, to research the holistic dynamics of change. Qualitative approaches enable social policy research to draw out participants' own interpretations of the processes underlying social change. Whereas longitudinal quantitative research identifies who and what changes, and the explanations for such change, LQR identifies 'how' and 'why' change takes place, grounded in the participants' own understandings.

An example of LQR is 'Negotiating Transitions to Citizenship', funded by the Economic and Social Research Council. This study examined young people's experiences and understandings of the meanings of citizenship and their changing perceptions of themselves as citizens. A longitudinal qualitative methodology was chosen to enable a focus on individual change and perceptions of change rather than on aggregate differences from one point of data collection to the next.

In 1999, 110 young people in Leicester were recruited to the study and completed a baseline questionnaire, outlining their personal histories. Each participant then took part in an in-depth, face-to-face interview, once a year for three years (64 took part in all three waves). Interviews followed topic guides, individually tailored for each participant. Participants were asked to reflect back on previous experiences, to consider present lifestyles, feelings and views, and to discuss future expectations and aspirations. Each interview was tape-recorded and transcribed verbatim. Initial thematic analysis of first and second wave data, assisted by Nud*ist (a software program for computer-assisted qualitative data analysis), produced profiles of views and activities which informed the topic guides for subsequent waves. To develop a consistent focus on areas of change, interviews were increasingly structured and narrowed down at each successive wave. The cross-sectional data from the three waves were used to analyse change at the group level, and provided a framework for analysis of change at an individual level. In this way, longitudinal analysis was built on cross-sectional analysis.

The longitudinal qualitative approach resulted in findings that could not have been achieved by other designs. For example, it found that:

- citizenship identity development was not simply a linear process, something only achieved with age: the extent to which participants identified themselves as citizens varied in relation to their recent employment status or level of community involvement;
- attitudes towards voting changed markedly in ways that could not be explained simply by aging; and
- family and community networks were key to young people's constructive social participation, such as voluntary work, campaigning and neighbourliness, for example, going to university was associated with a decline in participation.

LQR generates enormous quantities of material and is unavoidably resource-intensive. The likelihood of participant attrition must be acknowledged, for example, by over-sampling when recruiting, and by limiting the depth of analysis of first wave participants to thereby limit unnecessary analysis of those who then exit the study. Despite such challenges, the systematic treatment of voluminous, rich, longitudinal qualitative data offers fascinating and invaluable insights into the complex dynamics of social change in the context of individuals' everyday lives.

Question for discussion
• What are the particular gains and challenges of combining longitudinal and qualitative methodologies?

Further reading
Huber, G.P. and Van de Ven, A.H. (eds) (1995) *Longitudinal field research methods: Studying processes of organisational change*, London: Sage Publications.

Saldaña, J. (2003) *Longitudinal qualitative research: Analyzing change through time*, Walnut Creek, CA: AltaMira Press.

Relevant organisations
Centre for Research in Social Policy
Department of Social Sciences, Loughborough University, Leics, LE11 3TU
www.lboro.ac.uk/departments/ss/centres/crsp

Website resource
Economic and Social Research Council's programme of research on young people, *'Youth, Citizenship and Social Change'*: www.tsa.uk.com/YCSC/index.html

These examples help to underline the point made in Chapter Four, Section 4.3, that research designs can be associated with different research methods. Where qualitative research in the area of social policy and other fields of social research may differ from the use of cross-sectional design and longitudinal design in quantitative research is in respect of the range of interviews involved. In the case of Arksey's research, it is not just the carers who were interviewed, since, as noted above, she also interviewed a small number of senior managers and front-line practitioners. Quantitative researchers often compare samples of respondents, for example, samples of both practitioners and clients of social services departments, but they would not normally interview very small numbers of senior managers, as Arksey did, because they would not constitute a big enough sample. Purposive sampling of the kind frequently practiced by qualitative researchers (see Section 5.6) sometimes results in very small numbers of people in a particular category that would not form the basis for a sample in a survey. However, the basic point being made in this section is that cross-sectional designs and longitudinal designs often form viable frameworks for the collection of qualitative data, especially in interview-based research.

Question for discussion

• How similar is the cross-sectional design in qualitative research to the cross-sectional design in quantitative research?

References

Arksey, H. (2002) 'Rationed care: assessing the support needs of informal carers in English social service authorities', *Journal of Social Policy*, vol 31, pp 81-101.
Dean, H. and Shah, A. (2002) 'Insecure families and low paying labour markets: comments on the British experience', *Journal of Social Policy*, vol 31, pp 61-80.
Rowlingson, K. (2002) 'Private pension planning: the rhetoric of responsibility, the reality of insecurity', *Journal of Social Policy*, vol 31, pp 623-42.

Further reading

de Vaus, D. (2001) *Research design in social research*, London: Sage Publications.

5.6 Sampling in qualitative research

Clive Seale, *Research Professor, Department of Human Sciences, Brunel University*

Qualitative researchers are often interested in generalising their findings to other settings in much the same way as researchers who use quantitative methods. Because of this, all of the considerations outlined in Chapter Four with regard to the principles of probability sampling, quota sampling and the rest are also relevant for qualitative designs. This can get forgotten if qualitative researchers become excessively attached to the notion of difference between their own approaches and those of their quantitatively minded colleagues. Nevertheless, there are some sampling techniques developed to further the particular aims of qualitative researchers, the application of which may involve dispensing with quantitative sampling logic on certain qualitative projects, and these are outlined in this section.

One of the characteristics of much qualitative research is that it is devoted to discovering, in the words of John Lofland, "what kinds of things are happening, rather than to determine the frequency of predetermined kinds of things that the researcher already believes can happen" (1971, p 76). Thus, instead of seeking to describe how many red, or black, or oval pebbles there are on a beach, the qualitative researcher may be searching for the pebble that stands out from the rest. This can require looking in unusual places, perhaps using geological knowledge and quantitative data about the existing distribution of shapes and colours to direct the search to the most likely spot. Thus theory and ongoing data analysis – in short, brain work – may direct the hunt. Once found, the new phenomenon is studied intensively because it is likely to change current theories of how pebbles are formed. Thus qualitative sampling may concentrate on the search for theoretically rich examples, so that many have said its purpose is to create *theoretical generalisations* rather than the *empirical generalisations* of quantitative researchers (Mitchell, 1983).

Sampling in qualitative research, then, may take forms that are unpredictable, being close in character to the operations used by the scholar in an archive wishing to select which file to investigate next. This will depend in part on what was found in the last file, in part on the investigator's own perspective of the relevant literature on his or her subject, and on the emerging shape of the project which will usually take the form of a story that the investigator wishes to tell. Perhaps the best attempt at conveying this spirit of open-ended, yet intellectually directed, inquiry is the account of 'theoretical sampling' given by Glaser and Strauss, arising from their observational study of hospital wards in the 1960s (see **Box 5b** for a full example). Here, the researcher's emerging theory influences sampling decisions.

Box 5b: Theoretical sampling

Clive Seale, *Research Professor, Department of Human Sciences, Brunel University*

Theoretical sampling, proposed originally by Glaser and Strauss (1967), involves a researcher sampling to extend and broaden the scope of an emerging theory. Cases, settings or people are chosen to study with a view to finding things that might challenge and extend the limitations of the existing theory, which may not incorporate sufficiently the range of phenomena that can occur:

> Theoretical sampling is the process of data collection for generating theory whereby the analyst jointly collects, codes, and analyzes his data and decides what data to collect next and where to find them, in order to develop his theory as it emerges. This process of data collection is *controlled* by the emerging theory.... The basic question in theoretical sampling ... is: *what* groups or subgroups does one turn to *next* in data collection? And for *what* theoretical purpose? In short, how does the sociologist select multiple comparison groups? The possibility of multiple

comparisons are infinite, and so groups must be chosen according to theoretical criteria. (1967, pp 45-7)

Glaser and Strauss illustrate theoretical sampling from their own work among dying people, in which the concepts of 'awareness contexts' and 'dying trajectories' were developed:

Visits to the various medical services were scheduled as follows: I wished first to look at services that minimized patient awareness (and so first looked at a premature baby service and then a neurosurgical service where patients were frequently comatose). I wished then to look at dying in a situation where expectancy of staff and often of patients was great and dying was quick, so I observed on an Intensive Care Unit. Then I wished to observe on a service where staff expectations of terminality were great but where the patient's might or might not be, and where dying tended to be slow. So I looked next at a cancer service. I wished then to look at conditions where death was unexpected and rapid, and so looked at an emergency service. While we were looking at some different types of services, we also observed the above types of service at other types of hospitals. So our scheduling of types of service was directed by a general conceptual scheme – which included hypotheses about awareness, expectedness and rate of dying – as well as by a developing conceptual structure including matters not at first envisioned. Sometimes we returned to services after the initial two or three or four weeks of continuous observation, in order to check upon items, which needed checking or had been missed in the initial period. (1967, p 59)

Unlike a statistical sample whose size is limited by setting the degree of confidence with which the researcher wishes to generalise from sample to population, theoretical sampling is potentially endless, since the researcher can never be certain that a further case will exhibit properties that force some further changes in a theory. Glaser and Strauss propose a pragmatic solution to this in their idea of 'theoretical saturation'. This point is said to be reached when new data generates no further theory development, with categories and their properties therefore appearing fully developed. Of course, the researcher must try very hard to seek out diverse groups and settings before concluding that a theory is saturated. This means that rather different criteria apply in judging a statistical versus a theoretical sample. The statistical sample is judged adequate according to underlying laws of probability, on the basis of which the likelihood of sample results holding true in the population is estimated. The theoretical sample is judged adequate if no obvious exceptions to the theory are evident to the critical reader, who may use human judgement and imagination to make this assessment, and deem a theory empirically 'thin' or unconvincing if the existence of plausible exceptions has not been investigated.

Reference

Glaser, B.G. and Strauss, A.L. (1967) *The discovery of grounded theory: Strategies for qualitative research*, Chicago: Aldine.

While **Box 5b** suggests a continuing interaction between data collection and analysis throughout the life of a project, it is also the case that sampling decisions made at the outset of a study, and then more or less followed through regardless of what emerges, can be theoretically informed. Thus, a researcher may seek to maximise the chances of generating insights by choosing comparison groups carefully. Qualitative studies quite often begin by wishing to explore the unique position of some marginalised or oppressed group of people (for example, women, or a group with a self-defined sexual, ethnic or religious identity). The case for uniqueness, however, may be hard to prove in the absence of a comparison group (for example, men, or those with a different sexual, ethnic or religious self-identification). This was demonstrated in a study of breast cancer narratives in newspapers (Seale, 2002). Previous studies (for example, Lupton, 1994) had focused on the portrayal of women, arguing that their responses to cancer were shown in ways likely to intimidate and disadvantage women readers with the disease. Seale's study compared portrayals of men with cancer as well as women, showing that stereotypes of masculinity were also present, and pointing to both differences and similarities in the way each gender was depicted.

An essential conceptual tool for the researcher interested in sampling for theoretical richness is the idea that sampling ought to be devoted, in part, to searching for a 'negative instance' or 'deviant case' that, by contradicting an emerging theory, may in the end extend or deepen it. In quantitative research such instances are conceived of as threats to a study's validity, and the attempt to rule out alternative explanations (for example, spurious variables) can lead to some very creative approaches to research design and analysis (see, for example, Campbell and Stanley, 1966). In qualitative research the deviant case may be actively sought out, because it is likely to generate a more robust theory. Thus, Dingwall and Murray (1983) extended the sampling of an earlier study of hospital casualty departments so that children as well as adults were sampled. Although children sometimes came to casualty with mild problems, or having self-inflicted injuries, they were not stigmatised for this, in contrast to adults. The initial theory that staff stigmatised people for doing these things had to be modified to state that staff, before doing this, assessed how free patients were to make choices. Children were deemed not to be free, so were not blamed for their acts, and a few adults were eventually found who fulfilled this criterion as well, thus making for a better theory.

Snowball, volunteer and convenience sampling are also methods used by qualitative researchers. A sampling frame is not always available, and some members of the relevant group may be hard to approach. In the *snowball approach*, the researcher asks each interviewee who else might be relevant and willing to be interviewed, so that a network of contacts is built up. *Volunteers* may be recruited through advertisements in a variety of sites – newspapers, notice boards or word of mouth. Or the research may simply begin with whoever is *conveniently available* – a friend or a passer-by – and continue that way until sufficient insights are judged to have been generated. These methods, of course, may be somewhat theoretically informed, and may themselves be applied in a mixed fashion, the research using elements of each on any one project. The method is unlikely to be adequate in terms of representativeness, since volunteers are usually different from non-volunteers, and people who are part of social networks are likely to be different from the socially marginalised. None of this matters if the aim of the project is solely to generate theoretical insights rather than to generalise empirically. In practice, however, it is rare for qualitative researchers to maintain exclusive focus on theoretical generalisation, and they very frequently slip into statements that require consideration of the empirical representativeness of their sample for a wider population.

At this point, it may become relevant to conduct some checks in order to become more aware of how accidents of sampling may have been responsible for the story told. Sieber (1979) gives an example of this and shows, incidentally, that numbers also have a role to play in qualitative research. He was concerned in the course of his study of school districts that he had interacted more with education officials than rank and file teachers, thus distorting his estimates of job satisfaction. He conducted a small survey of randomly sampled teachers, asking them fixed-choice questions about their levels of satisfaction. Beforehand, he had tried to predict what results he would get, using his knowledge derived from the qualitative case study material he had collected. He found that his predictions of satisfaction were too optimistic when compared with the survey results, and concluded that he had "fallen prey to … elite bias, despite recent training in the dangers of giving greater weight to prestigious figures as informants" (1979, p 1353). Sieber suggests that such checking exercises can be done during fieldwork so that sampling can be adjusted if need be. More examples showing the use of quantitative data to check the representativeness of qualitative samples can be found in Seale (1999).

Sampling in qualitative research, then, is quite various, and sometimes departs in its purpose from quantitative sampling. It is important to be aware of the different consequences that sampling decisions may have for the kind of arguments one wishes to sustain, as these are often quite fundamental. In this respect, sampling in both quantitative and qualitative research is exactly the same.

Questions for discussion

- When is it appropriate to sample without regard to representativeness?
- What sampling methods are appropriate for researching 'hidden' populations (that is, groups concerned to hide their activities from official surveillance)?
- Why might random sampling from a list of a population be relevant in a research project involving qualitative data and analysis that you are planning? How would you go about achieving this?

References

Campbell, D.T. and Stanley, J.C. (1966) *Experimental and quasi-experimental design for research*, Chicago, IL: Rand McNally.

Dingwall, R. and Murray, T. (1983) 'Categorisation in accident departments: "good" patients, "bad" patients and children', *Sociology of Health and Illness*, vol 5, no 2, pp 121-48.

Lofland, J. (1971) *Analysing social settings: A guide to qualitative observation*, Belmont, CA: Wadsworth.

Lupton, D. (1994) 'Femininity, responsibility, and the technological imperative: discourses on breast cancer in the Australian press', *International Journal of Health Services*, vol 24, no 1, pp 73-89.

Mitchell, J.C. (1983) 'Case and situational analysis', *Sociological Review*, vol 31, no 2, pp 187-211.

Seale, C.F. (1999) *The quality of qualitative research*, London: Sage Publications.

Seale, C.F. (2002) 'Cancer heroics: a study of news reports with particular reference to gender', *Sociology*, vol 36, no 1, pp 107-26.

Sieber, S. (1979) 'The integration of fieldwork and survey methods', *American Journal of Sociology*, vol 78, no 6, pp 1135-59.

Further reading

Glaser, B.G. and Strauss, A.L. (1967) *The discovery of grounded theory: Strategies for qualitative research*, Chicago, IL: Aldine.

Seale, C.F. (1999) *The quality of qualitative research*, London: Sage Publications, Chapter 7.

Strauss, A.L. and Corbin, J. (1990) *Basics of qualitative research: Grounded theory procedures and techniques*, Newbury Park, CA: Sage Publications.

Grounded Theory Institute: www.groundedtheory.com/

Grounded theory: a thumbnail sketch: www.scu.edu.au/schools/gcm/ar/arp/
  grounded.html

National Centre for Social Research, Qualitative Research Unit:
  www.natcen.ac.uk/units/qru/

Qualitative Research in Health Care: www.bmjpg.com/qrhc/subjind.html

Sampling and qualitative research: www.rdg.ac.uk/ssc/dfid/booklets/
  tp2_samp.pdf

PART TWO: QUALITATIVE RESEARCH METHODS AND SOURCES OF QUALITATIVE DATA

5.7 Overview of the main research methods and sources of data in qualitative social policy research

In this section, the main methods for collecting qualitative data are examined. Five main research methods and sources of data are examined:

- unstructured interviews and semi-structured interviewing;
- ethnography;
- focus groups;
- documents – both historical and contemporary;
- using the Internet for the collection of qualitative data.

Each of these methods and approaches to the collection of data is underpinned by the preoccupations outlined in relation to qualitative research in Sections 5.2 and 5.3.

Some of the analytic styles that appear in the sections on the analysis of qualitative data are difficult to distinguish from methods of data collection. This point applies to *discourse analysis* (Section 5.15), *conversation analysis* (Section 5.16), and *narrative analysis* (Section 5.17). In each case, while they represent styles of analysis, they are not exclusively that because the data have to be prepared in such a way as to enable the analysis to take place. With conversation analysis, for example, the analyst records conversations and transcribes in precise detail (including such things as the length of pauses in conversation) in order to enable the analysis to take place. Similarly, narrative analysis can be thought of as an approach to the analysis of qualitative data that takes the uncovering of narratives in people's interview replies as its central feature. However, increasingly those researchers adopting the approach carry out interviews that are specifically designed to elicit narratives.

In qualitative research, therefore, there is less of a sharp distinction between research methods and sources of data, on the one hand, and analysis on the other. In grounded theory, for example, the collection and analysis of data are depicted as intertwined and constantly revised in the light of each other.

5.8 Semi-structured and unstructured interviewing

Hilary Arksey, *Research Fellow, Social Policy Research Unit, University of York*

Interviewing is a primary mode of data collection in qualitative research; semi-structured and unstructured interviews are labels used to describe two types of interview. Other terms include *in-depth interviews, qualitative research interviews, informant interviews, focused interviews* and *non-directive interviews*. These names tend to be used loosely, and sometimes interchangeably, which can be confusing. For present purposes, we will use the terms *semi-* and *unstructured interviews*.

Social science researchers employ semi- and unstructured interviews when eliciting people's views, opinions, attitudes and experiences. These non-factual phenomena are often complex and multidimensional; they are not easily captured through, say, survey questionnaires or fully structured/standardised interviews. Semi-structured and unstructured interviews may be done on a one-time basis, or repeated over time. Interviews can be conducted with one person at a time, or with couples (for fuller information about joint interviewing, see Seymour et al, 1995; Arksey, 1996). They may be face-to-face encounters, or conducted over the telephone. (For a useful account of telephone interviews see Halfpenny et al, 1998.) The information generated through semi-structured and unstructured interviews is generally rich, in-depth material that gives the researcher a fuller understanding of the informant's perspective on the topic under investigation.

What is the difference between a semi-structured interview and an unstructured interview? Both employ open-ended questions but differ in the degree of standardisation and the amount of latitude accorded the person being interviewed. In a *semi-structured interview*, the interviewer uses an interview guide organised around key areas of interest (see the example given in **Box 5c**). However, there is freedom to make ongoing adjustments to the guide in response to the way the interview is progressing. This might mean the interviewer modifies the order in which the questions are asked; changes the wording of questions; clarifies the meaning of questions; adds or omits questions according to their relevance to the particular interviewee; or extends or reduces the amount of time given to different topics. It is customary for interviewers to probe and/or prompt for more detailed responses, specific examples, clarification and so on. Social policy research projects that have used semi-structured interviews include studies examining the process and outcomes of assessments carried out under the auspices of the 1995 Carers (Recognition and Services) Act (Seddon and Robinson, 2001); the experiences of elderly people on discharge from inpatient care (Roberts, 2001); and equal opportunities for minority ethnic women within an NHS hospital trust (Bagilhole and Stephens, 1999).

Box 5c: An example of semi- and unstructured interviews
Hilary Arksey, *Research Fellow, Social Policy Research Unit, University of York*

I am conducting interviews for an ongoing study examining life in local communities in deprived areas, particularly the effects on residents' quality of life as a result of the process of regenerating disadvantaged estates. The research design involves conducting a series of three semi-structured interviews, nine months apart, with two generations in ten households. As an incentive to take part in the research, the 20 study participants receive a gift of £15 per interview; children and young people under the age of 18 are offered a voucher from a retailer of their choice.

To be a credible interviewer, it is important to demonstrate some degree of familiarity with the topic of interest. As part of my preparations, I drove round the neighbourhood at different times of day (but not once darkness fell, on personal safety grounds). There is a Regeneration Project office on the estate, which I use as my base. This is also valuable as a source of up-to-date information, either from staff, newsletters or leaflets.

The interviews are semi-structured, last an average of 45 minutes and are audiotaped (with permission). They are organised around an interview guide; extracts from the Time 1 interview guide are shown below. At this very first interview, it was important to collect standardised factual biographical information. I then explored how people viewed their neighbourhoods, and the perceived effects of regeneration. I concluded by asking how people saw the area in nine months' time. It was anticipated that these responses would be a useful starting point for their Time 2 interview. I used printed street maps of the estate and photographs of different places and spaces. The photographs provided a visual stimulus that aroused people's interest, facilitated more detailed descriptions and generated concrete examples of key issues.

Time 1 interview guide: background information
- Brief social and personal characteristics of: interviewee; others in the household; family members living locally (*probe on: employment status; marital status; health; age; family; social networks*)

Living on the estate
- Neighbourhood resources and facilities (*probe on: shops; entertainment and recreation; healthcare; transport; environment; police, security and safety; church; clubs*)
- Perceived problems (*probe on: crime; vandalism; drugs; troublesome residents; harassment; physical appearance of area*)
- Recent changes (*probe on: improvements/deteriorations; effect on interviewee [and family]*)

Results of regeneration
- Expectations of changes in next nine months (*probe on: what might change; why changes will/will not happen; approving or disapproving*)

Eight weeks before the second round of interviews took place, I gave each participant a disposable camera and asked them to photograph places in the neighbourhood that they liked and disliked. As cameras were returned, I had two copies of each film developed. One set was returned, and I retained the second set for use in the Time 2 interviews. A large part of these interviews centred on why informants had chosen to photograph each specific location, a technique that again elicited a wealth of detailed information.

Research methods textbooks tend to depict the ideal interview scenario. However, at least three of the second interviews were done in quite chaotic circumstances. Not only were televisions on in the background, but other family members and/or neighbours were present in the room. Having checked whether privacy was an issue – and it never was – the interview would continue. One interview transcript shows that six people contributed to the conversation! It can be difficult to keep the questions focused in these circumstances, but saying "Can we come back to the question of ...", and including the name of the principal interviewee in a question can be helpful. These 'interviews' were not straightforward and I had to 'think on my feet' as people in the room interacted with one another and spoke their minds. The data that was generated, however, is a rich resource for the research as some people expressed views contrary to prevailing opinions, and issues came to light that might otherwise not have done.

The Time 3 interviews, which took place in August 2002, completed the data collection. A month or so beforehand, I wrote to participants asking them whether they would like to take another set of photographs for us. I knew from comments made during the second round of interviews that quite a number of people had felt intimidated – frightened, even – when they were walking round the estate taking pictures. I was not at all surprised that only a small minority volunteered. One thing I did want to know about, however, was people's use of space on the estate. To this end, I again used printed street maps which interviewees drew on in different colours to show me: the area they considered to be where their 'neighbours' lived; whereabouts on the estate any friends they had lived; how far from their own house they might travel on foot (on their own; with a friend; after dark); and any part of the area that they just would not consider walking around.

Altogether, the fieldwork generated huge amounts of different types of data: interview transcripts, drawings, photographs and maps. Making full use of it, in particular the photographs, has given rise to unexpected ethical dilemmas. This is because I promised the research participants anonymity and confidentiality in any report writing. However, including photographs of the estate in the published report might prompt curious readers to try to trace the exact location of the research. The issue of how photographs of fieldwork sites are later used seems to me to be an issue that researchers need to consider in some depth when first planning their study.

In comparison, an *unstructured interview* is far more informal and 'unorganised' (but see the critique by Collins, 1998, in which he argues that even the most 'unstructured' interview is actually structured at a number of levels). In an unstructured interview, the interviewer's role is to be as unintrusive as possible. The person being interviewed, therefore, has more control than the interviewer, determining the content and flow of the discussion. Reflecting the relative lack of control on the interviewer's part, there is more scope for these interviews to take off at a tangent and not cover key areas for the research questions and/ or be prolonged if the interviewee takes the opportunity to enlarge upon what might be burning issues for them. Measor (1985) discusses the problem of people 'rambling', while pointing out that at the same time the information generated is clearly central to the person being interviewed. There are very few examples of the use of unstructured interviews in social policy research (exceptions include Ely, 1991; Tighe, 2001), but in any case it is reasonable to think of semi- and unstructured interviews as on a continuum (Denscombe,

1998). It is feasible that occasionally what was planned to be a semi-structured interview might proceed more informally and in the process recast itself as an unstructured interview.

Semi- and unstructured interviews have been likened to "conversations with a purpose" (Burgess, 1984, p102). This is not to imply that as a data collection technique they are the 'soft' option. Quite the reverse in fact, they require particular skills of the researcher. Effective interviewing is characterised by the extent to which the researcher can: establish rapport; ask questions and/or elicit information; listen; and record the data accurately. We will look at each area in turn.

Establishing rapport: rapport refers to the degree of understanding, trust and respect that develops between the interviewer and the interviewee. The time to start creating these ties is as soon as the relationship begins, which may be over the telephone when negotiating and arranging access. Likewise, what happens in the opening stage of the interview itself is important to the success of what follows, as many interviews are 'one-off' events and completed within a relatively short space of time. Essentially, be friendly, polite and open. During the interview, listen (see below), make eye contact, and offer encouraging comments; avoid conveying a sense of urgency or impatience. Leave people with a feeling of success, and after the interview write to thank them for taking part in the study.

Asking questions and eliciting information: use open-ended questions that are clearly understandable and appropriate for the particular social/cultural group being interviewed. Try not to use prejudicial language, and words or terms that are ambiguous or imprecise. Leading questions, assumptive questions and double-barrelled questions are to be avoided. Use prompts if necessary, but give people time to think and reflect so do not intervene too quickly. As you work through the different stages of the questioning, summarise and/or recap to make sure you are getting the story right. Check out the chronology and timing of events if you get confused. It can be quite hard for people to recall the order in which things happened. Using photographs and/or documents in an interview adds a further dimension. Photographs, for instance, can provide visual images of the issues being discussed, and asking people to respond to questions about them stimulates the conversation. See Harper (1994, 2000) for a discussion of the photo-elicitation interview.

Listening: interviewers must be competent active listeners. This involves attentive listening, both to the words being spoken by the interviewee, but also to how they are being said, for instance emphases and the emotional tone used. By listening carefully, you can ask new questions generated by a hunch as unexpected topic areas emerge. Make sure that during an interview you listen more than you speak. Check this by reviewing any tape recording and/or reading through the verbatim transcripts looking for how much and how often you actually speak yourself.

Recording data: it is essential to have a full record of the interview. This can be an audiotape recording and/or notes made at the time, and supplemented later. In either case, note down key words, important issues and turning points as the narrative unfolds. This is because (a) the tape recording might fail; (b) you might want to refer back to points raised later in the interview, so it helps with recall; and (c) it values interviewees' comments. If tape recording the interview, check beforehand that the equipment is working properly; make sure you take spare batteries/tapes with you.

After the interview, write up brief fieldnotes: points noted might include: how you felt the interview went; issues from the topic guide that were not covered and why; and any comments said off the tape. These notes can be added to whatever format you use to make a written record of the interview. If the interview has been audiotaped, the commonest procedure is to produce a typed version of the words on the tape. Transcription is time consuming and can be expensive if a transcription agency is used. On the other hand, transcription is desirable as it provides: a complete record of the interview; a springboard for analysis, and accurate, verbatim quotes that can be used to illustrate key points being made in the research report.

Throughout interviews, it is important to be sensitive to the interviewee, and how they are responding to the questions you are posing. Possible harms include undue intrusion into private and personal spheres, embarrassment, distress, nervous strain or a sense of failure or coercion. There may also be costs in terms of time spent in taking part in the interview and/or any expenses involved in travelling to the venue. However, it is known (Oakley, 1981; Maynard and Purvis, 1994) that for some people interviews can be cathartic; they welcome the opportunity to have a ready and willing 'listening ear'. Likewise, there are individuals who find it gratifying to contribute to a worthwhile endeavour; taking part in a research study can boost confidence and self-esteem. In the past, financial incentives for taking part in a study have been frowned upon on the basis that people would be participating for the wrong reasons. This argument has been questioned in recent years, and there are increasing examples of study participants receiving a small monetary or other type of gift in return for help with a research project (SCPR, 1998; Hughes, 1999).

To conclude, semi- and unstructured interviews can be challenging. Not only are they demanding in listening, communication, practical and social skills, they are time consuming to arrange and conduct. Even relatively short interviews generate a large volume of data that have then to be analysed. There may be concerns about the quality of the data, for instance the lack of standardisation that this type of interview implies raises concerns about reliability, and biases can be hard to rule out (Robson, 2002). Having said that, semi- and unstructured interviews are one of the most widely used methods of data collection in qualitative research (Mason, 1996). For many researchers, they are the most appropriate way to generate data that are rich and insightful. **Box 5c** provides an example of how semi-structured interviews are being used in a current study, and some of the issues that have arisen.

Question for discussion

• What are the strengths, limitations and challenging aspects of conducting semi- and unstructured interviews?

References

Arksey, H. (1996) 'Collecting data through joint interviews', *Social Research Update*, issue 15, Guildford: Department of Sociology, University of Surrey.

Bagilhole, B. and Stephens, M. (1999) 'Management responses to equal opportunities for ethnic minority women within an NHS hospital trust', *Journal of Social Policy*, vol 28, no 2, pp 235-48.

Burgess, R.G. (1984) *In the field: An introduction to field research*, London: Allen and Unwin.

Collins, P. (1998) 'Negotiating selves: reflections on 'unstructured' interviewing', *Sociological Research Online*, vol 3, no 3 (www.socresonline.org.uk/socresonline/3/3/2.html).

Denscombe, M. (1998) *The good research guide for small-scale research projects*, Buckingham: Open University Press.

Ely, M. with Anzul, M., Friedman, T., Garner, D. and McCormack Steinmetz, A. (1991) *Doing qualitative research: Circles within circles*, London: Falmer Press.

Halfpenny, P., Hudson, S. and Jones, J. (1998) 'Researching small companies' charitable giving through telephone interviews', *International Journal of Social Research Methodology*, vol 1, no 1, pp 65-74.

Harper, D. (1994) 'On the authority of the image: visual methods at the crossroads', in N.K. Denzin and Y.S. Lincoln (eds) *Handbook of qualitative research*, London: Sage Publications, pp 403-12.

Harper, D. (2000) 'Reimaging visual methods: Galileo to Neuromancer', in N.K. Denzin and Y.S. Lincoln (eds) *Handbook of qualitative research* (2nd edn), London: Sage Publications, pp 717-32.

Hughes, R. (1999) 'Why do people agree to participate in social research? The case of drug injectors', *International Journal of Social Research Methodology*, vol 1, no 4, pp 315-24.

Mason, J. (1996) *Qualitative researching*, London: Sage Publications.

Measor, L. (1985) 'Interviewing: a strategy in qualitative research', in R.G. Burgess (ed) *Strategies of educational research: Qualitative methods*, London: Falmer Press, pp 55-77.

Maynard, M. and Purvis, J. (eds) (1994) *Researching women's lives from a feminist perspective*, London: Taylor and Francis.

Oakley, A. (1981) 'Interviewing women: a contradiction in terms', in H. Roberts (ed) *Doing feminist research*, London: Routledge and Kegan Paul, pp 30-61.

Roberts, K. (2001) 'Across the health-social care divide: elderly people as active users of health care and social care', *Health and Social Care in the Community*, vol 9, no 2, pp 100-7.

Robson, C. (2002) *Real world research: A resource for social scientists and practitioners-researchers* (2nd edn), Oxford: Blackwell.

Seddon, D. and Robinson, C.A. (2001) 'Carers of older people with dementia: assessment and the Carers Act', *Health and Social Care in the Community*, vol 9, no 3, pp 151-8.

Seymour, J., Dix, G. and Eardley, T. (1995) *Joint accounts: Methodology and practice in research interviews with couples*, York: Social Policy Research Unit, University of York.

SCPR (Social and Community Planning Research) Survey Methods Centre Newsletter (1998) Special Issue on Respondent incentives in surveys, vol 18, no 2.

Tighe, C.A. (2001) '"Working at disability": a qualitative study of the meaning of health and disability for women with physical impairments', *Disability & Society*, vol 16, no 4, pp 511-29.

Further reading

Arksey, H. and Knight, P. (1999) *Interviewing for social scientists: An introductory resource with examples*, London: Sage Publications.

Gubrium, J.F. and Holstein, J.A. (eds) (2002) *Handbook of interview research: Context and method*, London: Sage Publications.

Robson, C. (2002) *Real world research: A resource for social scientists and practitioners-researchers* (2nd edn), Oxford: Blackwell.

Relevant organisations

For further information about ethical issues, including informed consent and maintaining confidentiality, see Chapter Three, Section 3.14 and **Box 3j**, Chapter Six, Sections 6.3 and 6.7, and the professional codes and guidelines of organisations such as:

American Psychological Association: www.apa.org/
American Sociological Association: www.asanet.org/
British Sociological Association: www.britsoc.org.uk/
Social Research Association: www.the-sra.org.uk/

5.9 Ethnography

John D. Brewer, *Professor of Sociology, Queen's University, Belfast*

Ethnography is a style of research rather than a single method and can be defined as: "the study of people in naturally occurring settings or 'fields' by means of methods which capture their social meanings and ordinary activities, involving the researcher participating directly in the setting, if not also the activities, in order to collect data in a systematic manner but without meaning being imposed on them externally" (Brewer, 2000, p 10). It is commonly confused with participant observation, but ethnography does not necessarily require participation and its repertoire of techniques includes in-depth interviews, discourse analysis, personal documents and vignettes (see **Box 5d** for an example). Visual methods, such as video, photography and film are now also popular (see Pink, 2001; and **Box 5e**). These methods are used in other research but what distinguishes their application in ethnography is that they are employed to meet the objectives that distinguish this style of research; namely, the exploration of the social meanings of people by close involvement in the field.

Box 5d: An example of ethnography

John Brewer's discussion of ethnography brings out two points, which will be followed up in this box, that point to its distinctiveness: its emphasis on people's meanings and the tendency for ethnographies to be connected with a case study research design. Sainsbury (2002) was interested in the operation of community care policies and particularly in the way in which such policies are worked through for people with learning disabilities. The emphasis on meanings was especially relevant to the question of what we mean by *community* when we talk or write about community care. The issue of what people mean by community and whether there is a common understanding of the term, along with the issue of how far those understandings of the term tally with those of social policy researchers and practitioners, was of particular significance.

To explore these issues and concerns, Sainsbury took up residence in a small town in Wales for four months. In this way, Sainsbury employed ethnography within the context of a case study research design. This afforded her the opportunity to engage with a wide variety of people and groups in a diversity of contexts. Among the activities she mentions are:

- observing the work of the Local Community Mental Handicap Team;
- some involvement in some of the team's formal and informal meetings and activities;
- observation in a special school, the Adult Training Centre and self-help and voluntary groups, which presented opportunities to discuss the work involved;
- usage of the town's facilities (such as its shops, pubs, library and public transport) to gain an appreciation of residents' perceptions of their town.

In addition, Sainsbury conducted 100 semi-structured interviews, whose average duration was one-and-a-half hours. The interviews were conducted with people with a learning difficulty, their families, service providers and some residents of the town. These interviews were important in providing information about the experiences of community care with regard to learning disability and about the senses of community among people in general. In addition, Sainsbury writes that she drew on additional information from "local census data, town council meeting minutes, local newspapers, histories of the area, and written material provided by the social services department" (2002, p 3).

One feature that is striking about the evidence Sainsbury compiled is that it is based on a diversity of sources: observation, informal discussions, somewhat more formal discussions in semi-structured interviews, census data, various documents, and so on. We see here a striking feature of ethnography, namely, that it often entails a variety of sources of data, some of which are primary data collected by the researcher (in Sainsbury's case, the data gleaned from observation and interviews) and secondary information and documents. As John Brewer observes, ethnography is often mistakenly equated with participant observation and we see here why that is the case, for ethnography entails considerably more than observing. It frequently entails several methods of data collection or sources of data and information.

Sainsbury's study shows how community care is worked through in practice. It shows, for example, how members of the Local Community Mental Handicap Team were often at loggerheads, or at the very least experienced differences of opinion, with parents of children with learning disabilities and often with others in this field of service provision. These differences of opinion often revolved around contrasting views about the nature of the town as a community and around their seeking to work with an ideology of normalisation to which others involved with people with learning disabilities could not relate. This ideology was one that sought to make the lives of people with learning disabilities as normal as possible through independent living in the community. Many members of the community found this a difficult set of principles to work with because they tended to favour greater involvement of relatives and others in the lives of those with learning disabilities.

Reference

Sainsbury, S. (2002) *People, politics and professionals: A study of learning disability in a small town*, Aldershot: Ashgate.

Ethnography has endless application. There are few topics after all that cannot be approached in terms of the social meanings and behaviours of the participants involved, although the boundaries of every topic are not necessarily always satisfactorily covered this way. The focus on social meanings ensures that ethnographic research is based on case studies (see Travers, 2001). The case can comprise single individuals or a group, particular events or situations, a specific organisation, a social institution, neighbourhood, national society or global process, but what distinguishes an ethnographic approach is that the case permits detailed, rich and in-depth study. This often restricts ethnography to a specific locality, although it is possible to examine variations within a case or across cases in space and time, thereby engaging in comparative research and generalisations. Proper sampling of cases, primarily through non-probabilistic forms of sampling, extends the possibility of making generalisations. Its critics usually present ethnography as being very unsystematic, but rigorous practice has been introduced through the development of qualitative forms of sampling, computer-assisted qualitative data analysis packages, team-based ethnographies that permit geographical spread, and close attention to research practice in the field, amongst other things.

Box 5e: Visual ethnography

Sarah Pink, *Senior Lecturer in Sociology, Loughborough University*

Visual images form a key part of our everyday lives, the way we communicate with others, our memories and our goals. The image is a real and important part of the contemporary cultures, societies and individual lives that we research. It therefore follows that ethnographic research about lives and experiences would benefit from attention to the visual. In recent years technological developments and a new acceptance of the idea that ethnographic research is an inevitably subjective enterprise have meant that increasingly sophisticated visual media and technologies have become both available and acceptable for use in ethnographic research. Along with this a number of new texts on visual research (Banks, 2001; Pink, 2001; Rose, 2001) have been published outlining these methods for students and researchers. As the authors of these recent texts argue, visual ethnography should be: *reflexive* – researchers should maintain awareness of both how the intersubjectivity between themselves and informants impacts on the visual materials produced and how their own subjectivity affects their interpretations of these materials; *collaborative* – it would be difficult, and usually unethical, to produce images of other people without their agreement and participation; and should recognise that the meanings of visual images are not fixed and static, but arbitrary and open to new interpretations in new contexts. As part of a visual ethnographic project a researcher might include a range of methods and often a visual ethnographer will combine different visual and other methods in the same project.

The main methods a visual ethnographer might use are:

1 *Analysing existing visual texts:* including art, advertisements or media texts (see Rose, 2001), family or personal photograph collections or home movies (see Chalfen, 1987), exhibitions or home image displays (see Pink, 1997). Through such analysis we can hope to learn about the themes and patterns that are represented visually in the images that form part of the visual worlds informants create and inhabit. This method is used in combination with also working with informants to explore how and why these images are meaningful to them, and how they use them in their everyday lives.

2 *Photographing or video recording events or informants engaging in activities:* including family celebrations, public events, or everyday activities such as cooking, everyday interaction or housework. Visual ethnographers use this method to produce their own subjective visual representations of particular events and activities, usually in collaboration with informants. It is usually used in combination with methods such as keeping fieldnotes and diaries, and interviewing informants about the activities and events they are engaged in. This method also often forms part of participant observation: a visual ethnographer who is photographing or video recording is rarely a mere observer, but will become involved with her or his camera in the research situation in some way. Indeed her or his involvement in the research context may become as an unofficial video-maker or photographer (see Pink, 2001).

3 *Photographing or video recording individuals, objects or activities as directed by informants:* including when attending public performances or observing processes or activities with informants. Visual ethnographers have found this method can develop either intentionally as planned by themselves or by chance as part of their interaction with informants. For example, a researcher might invite one or more informants to attend an event with her or him, and brief them by asking them to direct their visual coverage of the event, pointing out what, when and whom should be photographed. However, in research at an Indian celebration (Banks, 2001) and at the Spanish bullfight (Pink, 2001) visual ethnographers have found that informants often direct their photography without being asked to.

4 *Using photographs or video as part of an informal interview:* including use of any of the sets of images that have been analysed or produced through the methods described above, or introducing new images for the purpose.

This method, often called 'photo-elicitation' (see Harper, 1998) explores informants' interpretations of images.

Visual ethnography raises new ethical issues. Whereas in written ethnography informants' anonymity can be guaranteed if necessary, photographs and video recordings make identities explicit. Clear agreements should be made with both informants and any stakeholders in the project about the eventual use of images and the level of confidentiality of the research before work begins.

As we have seen, visual ethnography is never purely visual – in fact, it is concerned with the relationship between the visual and the verbal, both in producing data and in analysing and writing about these data.

Question for discussion
• How might a researcher integrate the visual into an ethnographic project using two or more visual methods?

References
Banks, M. (2001) *Visual methods in social research*, London: Sage Publications.

Chalfen, R. (1987) *Snapshot versions of life*, Bowling Green, OH: Popular Press.

Harper, D. (1998) 'An argument for visual sociology', in J. Prosser (ed) *Image-based research: A sourcebook for qualitative researchers*, London: Falmer Press, pp 24-41.

Pink, S. (1997) 'Visual histories of success', in E. Edwards (ed) *History of photography*, London: Taylor & Francis, pp 54-9.

Pink, S. (2001) *Doing visual ethnography: Images, media and representation in research*, London: Sage Publications.

Rose, G. (2001) *Visual methodologies*, London: Sage Publications.

Further reading
Banks, M. (2001) *Visual methods in social research*, London: Sage Publications.

Pink, S. (2001) *Doing visual ethnography: Images, media and representation in research*, London: Sage Publications.

Website resource
The *Visualising Ethnography* website: www.lboro.ac.uk/departments/ss/visualising_ethnography/

Two features of contemporary ethnographic practice are worth stressing here. The first is angst over methodology, the second is the development of applied ethnography. Method and methodology are interpolated in ethnography in a problematic manner. Ethnography became closely associated with a particular methodology, known as *naturalism*, within which it was privileged as the principal method and its weaknesses overlooked. Critics of naturalism meanwhile rejected ethnography outright. This has prevented ethnography from assuming the dominant mantle in post-positivist social research, and allowed hoary complaints to resurface. Goldthorpe attacked ethnography for failing the 'logic of inference' in social science, which demands that the social world exist independently of our ideas about it and information about it permit inferences beyond the data at hand (2000, p 67). While this reifies one approach to research – and suggests that the ethnographic perspective could usefully be applied to quantitative researchers' notions of science – it rules out the possibility of ethnography except with probabilistic samples. Unfortunately, whatever defence ethnography might mount is undermined by the 'principled irrationalism' of postmodernism (Goldthorpe, 2000, p 69), which so bedevils ethnography.

It was inevitable that ethnography would be a battleground on which post-structuralists and postmodernists fought the conflict against the Enlightenment ethos of *rational social science*. Ethnography had such a tenuous link to this ethos anyway, often being presented as an alternative to more scientific models of social research, that ethnography was always susceptible to criticisms of its methodological foundation and the technical reliability of its practice. What was surprising was that it should be ethnographers themselves who potentially undermined their own practice. First, in social and cultural anthropology in the 1980s, and then in sociology, ethnographers themselves criticised ethnographic representations of social reality and queried the criteria by which ethnographic data could be evaluated. Denzin and Lincoln (1998, pp 21-2) famously described such doubts as ethnography's dual crises and no substantive ethnographic study or methodological account was free from agonising about the status of the method, the data, the text and the author's presence and voice.

The 'crisis of representation' challenges that ethnography can produce universally valid knowledge by accurately capturing the nature of the social world 'as it is' – a view described as 'naïve realism' by Hammersley (1990, 1992). All accounts are constructions and the whole issue of which account more accurately represents social reality is meaningless (see Denzin, 1992). In as much as ethnographic descriptions are partial, selective, even autobiographical, in that they are tied to the particular ethnographer and the contingencies under which the data were collected, the traditional criteria for evaluating ethnography become problematic, as terms like 'validity', 'reliability' and 'generalisability' lose their authority. Hence the 'crisis of legitimation'. These crises have implications for how we understand ethnographic accounts:

ethnography does not neutrally represent the social world (but, then in this view, nor does anything else). There are implications for the claims ethnographers are able to make about their account: ethnography is no longer a privileged description of the social world from the inside (once called 'thick description' in order to emphasise its richness and depth). And there are implications for the written text, for ethnographers should no longer make foolish authority claims in order to validate the account as an accurate representation of reality.

However, many have tried to rescue ethnography from the worst excesses of postmodernism. Sets of guidelines exist by which the practice of ethnography is codified (Silverman, 1989, 2001; Hammersley, 1990, 1992; Stanley, 1990; Brewer, 2000). What one might call 'post-postmodern ethnography' advocates the possibility and desirability of systematic ethnography and remains rooted in realism, albeit weaker versions. Hammersley's account of subtle realism (1990, 1992), for example, makes clear that he believes in independent truth claims that can be judged by their correspondence to an independent reality. 'Post-postmodern ethnography' contends that, while no knowledge is certain, there are phenomena that exist independent of us as researchers and knowledge claims about them can be judged reasonably accurately in terms of their likely truth. This shares with realism the idea that research investigates independently knowable phenomena but breaks with it in denying that we have direct access to these phenomena. It shares with anti-realism recognition that all knowledge is based on assumptions and human constructions, but rejects that we have to abandon the idea of truth itself. A similar argument has been mounted to enable us to preserve the idea of bias as a way of distinguishing good and bad research (Hammersley, 2000).

Another motif of contemporary ethnographic practice is its growing application to policy making in areas such as law, education, healthcare and social work. There are textbooks directed towards the practice of applied qualitative research (Walker, 1985) and other programmatic claims (see Rist, 1981; Bulmer, 1982; Finch, 1986; Wenger, 1987). The popularity of applied ethnography among ethnographers and policy makers conceals a tension between ethnographic research designed with the express purpose of addressing policy and that whose findings are used coincidentally as part of a body of knowledge drawn on to inform policy decisions. The former is genuinely 'applied' research; the latter is 'pure' or 'basic' research that has an intended or unintended policy effect. In either respect, ethnography can offer the following to policy makers (taken from Brewer, 2000, p 164):

- it can help provide the worldview and social meanings of those affected by some policy or intervention strategy;
- it can help to provide the views of those thought to be part of the problem that the policy or intervention strategy is intended to address;

- it can be used to evaluate the effects of a policy or intervention strategy as these effects are perceived and experienced by the people concerned;
- it can be used to identify the unintended consequences of policy initiatives and strategies as they manifest in the experiences of people;
- it can be used to provide cumulative evidence that supplies policy makers with a body of knowledge that is used to inform decision making; and
- it can be used to supplement narrow quantitative information and add flesh to some of the statistical correlations and factual data used to inform decision making.

Ethnography has long been recognised as complementing survey research, but the use of ethnography as the principal source of evidence is appropriate given certain research topics or subjects (taken from Brewer, 2000, pp 164-5):

- when the information is new and unfamiliar and 'closed questions' in surveys cannot be formulated;
- when the information requested is too subtle or complex to be elicited by questionnaires and other quantitative techniques;
- when actors' social meanings are required in order to illuminate the causal explanations derived from statistical explanations;
- when a longitudinal element is required in order to study social processes over time;
- when the subjects of the research are not amenable to study by quantitative means because they are inarticulate, elitist, resistant or sensitive to research, small in number or difficult to locate geographically.

Question for discussion

- How concerned should practising ethnographers be about methodological issues and disputes?

References

Brewer, J.D. (2000) *Ethnography*, Buckingham: Open University Press.
Bulmer, M. (1982) *The uses of social research*, London: Allen and Unwin.
Denzin. N. (1992) 'Whose Cornerville is it anyway?', *Journal of Contemporary Ethnography*, vol 21, pp 120-32.
Denzin, N. and Lincoln, Y. (1998) 'Entering the field of qualitative research', in N. Denzin and Y. Lincoln (eds) *Collecting and interpreting qualitative materials*, London: Sage Publications, pp 1-34.
Finch, J. (1986) *Research and policy*, Brighton: Falmer Press.

Goldthorpe, J. (2000) 'Sociological ethnography today: problems and possibilities', in J. Goldthorpe, *On Sociology*, Oxford: Oxford University Press, pp 65-93.

Hammersley, M. (1990) *Reading ethnographic research*, London: Longman.

Hammersley, M. (1992) *What's wrong with ethnography?*, London: Routledge.

Hammersley, M. (2000) *Taking sides in social research*, London: Routledge.

Pink, S. (2001) *Doing visual ethnography*, London: Sage Publications.

Rist, R. (1981) 'On the utility of ethnographic research for the policy process', *Urban Education*, vol 15, pp 48-70.

Silverman, D. (1989) 'Six rules of qualitative research: a post-Romantic argument', *Symbolic Interaction*, vol 12, pp 215-30.

Silverman, D. (2001) 'The potential for qualitative research: eight reminders', in D. Silverman, *Interpreting qualitative data*, London: Sage Publications.

Stanley, L. (1990) 'Doing ethnography, writing ethnography: a comment on Hammersley', *Sociology*, vol 24, pp 617-28.

Travers, M. (2001) *Qualitative research through case studies*, London: Sage Publications.

Walker, R. (1985) *Applied qualitative research*, Aldershot: Gower.

Wenger, C. (1987) *The research relationship: Practice and politics in social policy research*, London: Allen and Unwin.

Further reading

Atkinson, P., Coffey, A., Delamont, S., Lofland, J. and Lofland, L. (2001) *Handbook of ethnography*, London: Sage Publications.

Brewer, J.D. (2000) *Ethnography*, Buckingham: Open University Press.

Website resources

Computer Assisted Qualitative Data Analysis Software network, University of Surrey: http://caqdas.soc.surrey.ac.uk

Economic and Social Research Council, Qualitative Data Archive, University of Essex: www.essex.ac.uk/qualidata

5.10 Focus groups

Barbara Dobson, *formerly Research Fellow, Centre for Research in Social Policy, Loughborough University*

Focus groups are discussions that are organised to explore a specific set of issues and involve some kind of collective activity (Kitzinger, 1990, 1994;

Edwards and Talbot, 1994). They are appropriate when the researcher wishes to explore people's experiences, opinions and concerns (Barbour and Kitzinger, 1999). The fact that participants engage in discussion with each other on a specified topic differentiates focus groups from other group interviewing techniques. The emphasis is on the interaction within the group based on topics that are of interest to the researcher (Morgan, 1993, 1995). Catterall and Maclaran (1997) also stress the importance of the dynamic and interactive aspects of focus groups.

There are a number of advantages to using focus groups. For example, they provide an opportunity to observe a large amount of interaction on a topic over a short period of time (Bloor et al, 2001). Discussions in a group setting should generate rich data as respondents rise to challenges and defend views. Indeed, it has been noted that conversations between participants may help them to clarify for themselves what is their opinion or what factors may influence behaviour (Morgan and Krueger, 1993). Focus groups encourage people to theorise, elaborate and possibly think about a topic for the first time.

A criticism levelled at focus groups is that the data they generate are limited in generalisability (Stewart and Shamdasani, 1990). Since focus groups do not usually involve individuals who have been randomly selected, the results produced are not generalisable to the population. However, the results from focus groups can be heuristic and, in this sense, the findings will apply beyond the individuals who participated.

Also, those who are willing to travel and participate in focus groups may be quite different to those who are unwilling to do so. This highlights the need for rigorous recruitment procedures to avoid such bias.

As with other types of qualitative research there exists the problem of interviewer bias, whereby the respondent may be influenced by the presence of the researcher and their perceptions of him or her. Focus groups can be run with little intervention from the researcher thus minimising this effect. However, most research methods and situations involve the researcher and, rather than sanitising the research process by trying to avoid any researcher effect, the researcher should be reflexive and reflective about their role and influence and their involvement should be clearly and rigorously documented (Thomas, 1999).

Conducting focus groups

Within market research, focus groups generally involve 8-12 individuals, although Barbour and Kitzinger (1999) suggest that this number is often too large for many sociological studies. They advocate approximately six participants, but stress that the nature of the topics to be discussed should determine the size of the group.

Focus groups usually last between one and two hours. Participants are assured confidentiality and, with their permission, the discussion is tape-recorded. Careful and creative consideration of the composition of the focus group is essential and, for example, the aims of the research should determine how participants are recruited. A decision has to be made whether to recruit individuals who are strangers or to use pre-existing networks and groups. Thought also needs to be given to whether the focus group should consist of people who share similar experiences or whether the aims and purposes of the research require people with different views to be brought together. Recent developments in focus group research have seen this method extended to include children and the use of virtual focus groups (Bloor et al, 2001).

The amount of direction given by the moderator affects the quality and type of data generated by the focus group. There needs to be balance between the researcher's agenda and that of the participants so that those attending the group are able to enjoy the discussion and explain and contextualise their replies. Those conducting focus groups need to be aware that it takes time for participants to relax and become comfortable and to interact with each other and the moderator must allow and encourage this process (Bales, 1950). A list of the issues to be covered within the focus group (topic guide) should also be drawn up creatively and tested.

The number of focus groups to be conducted should be determined by the complexity of the research questions and should reflect the type and number of any subgroups included in the study (Bloor et al, 2001). Time and money are also crucial factors to be borne in mind as recruiting, hosting, transcribing and analysing focus groups is an expensive business.

All research methods have strengths and weaknesses and in this sense focus groups are no different. The key to using focus groups successfully is in ensuring that their use is consistent with, and appropriate for, the objectives and purpose of the research. **Box 5f** provides an illustration of the use of focus groups with parents of disabled children.

Box 5f: Using focus groups with parents of children with severe disabilities

Barbara Dobson, *formerly Research Fellow, Centre for Research in Social Policy, Loughborough University*

The aim of this study was to explore the additional financial costs of childhood disability and to develop minimum essential budget standards. The budget standards were drawn up by parents of children with severe disabilities during a total of 36 focus groups. In the standard focus groups participants are usually asked only to express their opinions and to share their experiences. However, the focus groups in this study were different in that the participants had to work through lists of items then negotiate and agree as a group those items that they deemed essential to maintain a minimum standard of living for a disabled child. To facilitate this process, the groups lasted two hours, which is slightly longer than the average focus group discussion.

The focus groups were divided into three stages: orientation, task and check back groups. The topic guide for each stage was amended to reflect the aims of the focus groups.

The orientation stage (nine groups), aimed to ensure that the ideas and concepts employed in later stages of the research were informed and understood by parents. Parents also developed the case studies for three children for whom budget standards were to be constructed by the task groups.

Questionnaires and other instrumentation was completed by parents prior to attending the task groups. During the task groups (18 groups) each area of the budget was considered and parents negotiated and agreed lists of minimum essential items. The group moderator intervened in the discussions and negotiations as little as possible: recording decisions reached on a flip chart and moving the negotiations along. Once each list was complete, groups were asked to consider whether it was too restrictive or overgenerous. Issues such as the ratio of new to second-hand, durability and where items should be costed were all discussed.

After this stage, the lists were costed by researchers at outlets agreed by the groups. Lists were prepared of outstanding matters that needed to be resolved in the final phase of the groups.

The check back groups (nine groups), were in some ways the most important since, as well as resolving outstanding issues, the financial implications of the budgets were considered and the strength of the consensus tested. Parents were given uncosted lists of items compiled by the task groups and asked whether they agreed with them (or not), and if they should be amended in any way. Once changes had been negotiated, agreed and incorporated into the budgets, parents were told how much it would cost to provide the agreed list and asked if, in the light of this, they would change the lists. Any changes were noted and the budgets revised accordingly. Parents were then asked to think about the public expenditure implications of their minimum essential budgets by imagining that the moderator was the Chancellor of the Exchequer. They were asked if and how they would amend the minimum essential budgets if they were told that the country could not afford to meet the costs involved in providing children with all the items on their lists. Following the check back groups the budgets were re-costed and finalised and the minimum essential budget standards were drawn up.

The purpose of the focus groups conducted as part of this study was to provide a forum within which parents could discuss the financial, practical and emotional aspects of bringing up a child with a severe disability. They were the most suitable method because they offered parents the opportunity to share their experiences, and the interaction between parents in the groups generated a wealth of data while at the same time being enjoyable and useful.

Question for discussion

- What are the ethical and practical considerations that researchers need to be aware of when planning to conduct focus groups around sensitive and personal issues?

Further reading

Baldwin, S. (1985) *The costs of caring: Families and disabled children*, London: Routledge and Kegan Paul.

Baldwin, S. and Carlisle, J. (1994) *Social support for disabled children and their families: A review of the literature*, Edinburgh: HMSO.

Baldwin, S. and Glendinning, C. (1981) 'Children with disabilities and their families', in A. Walker and P. Townsend (eds) *Disability in Britain: A manifesto of rights*, Oxford: Martin-Robinson.

Dobson, B. and Middleton, S. (1998) *Paying to care: The cost of childhood disability*, York: York Publishing Services.

Dobson, B., Middleton, S. and Beardsworth, A. (2001) *The impact of childhood disability on family life*, York: York Publishing Services.

Marks, D. (1999) *Disability: Controversial debates and psychological perspectives*, London: Routledge.

Read, J. (2000) *Disability, the family and society: Listening to mothers*, Buckingham: Open University.

Smyth, M. and Robus, N. (1989) *The financial circumstances of disabled children living in private households*, London: HMSO.

Website resources

Department for Work and Pensions: www.dwp.gov.uk/
Centre for Disability Studies: www.leeds.ac.uk/disability-studies/
Joseph Rowntree Foundation: www.jrf.org.uk/home.asp
Norah Fry Research Centre: www.bris.ac.uk/Depts/NorahFry/

Question for discussion

- The aims of a research project are to explore the knowledge and beliefs of healthy eating for children among parents. What are the issues for the recruitment strategy and for the development of the topic guide?

References

Bales, R.F. (1950) *Interaction process analysis: A method for the study of small groups*, Cambridge, MA: Addison-Wesley.

Barbour, R.S. and Kitzinger, J. (1999) *Developing focus group research: Politics, theory and practice*, London: Sage Publications.

Bloor, M., Frankland, J., Thomas, M. and Robson, K. (2001) *Focus groups in social research*, London: Sage Publications.

Catterall, M. and Maclaran, P. (1997) 'Focus group data and qualitative analysis programs: coding the moving picture as well as the snapshots', *Sociological Research Online*, vol 2, no 1 (www.socresonline.org.uk/socresonline/2/1/6.html).

Edwards, A. and Talbot, R. (1994) *The hard-pressed researcher: A research handbook for the caring professions*, London: Longman Group.

Kitzinger, J. (1990) 'Audience understandings of AIDS media messages: a discussion of methods', *Sociology of Health and Illness*, vol 12, no 3, pp 319-35.

Kitzinger, J. (1994) 'The methodology of focus groups: the importance of interaction between research participants', *Sociology of Health and Illness*, vol 16, no 1, pp 103-21.

Morgan, D.L. (1993) *Successful focus groups: Advancing the state of the art*, Newbury Park, CA: Sage Publications.

Morgan, D.L. (1995) 'Why things (sometimes) go wrong in focus groups', *Qualitative Health Research*, vol 5, no 4, pp 516-23.

Morgan, D.L. and Kreuger, R.A. (1993) 'When to use focus groups and why', in D.L. Morgan (ed) *Successful focus groups*, London: Sage Publications, pp 1-19.

Stewart, D. and Shamdasani, P. (1990) 'Focus groups: theory and practice', *Applied Social Research Methods Series*, vol 20, London: Sage Publications.

Thomas, M. (1999) 'Foreign affaires: a sociological exploration of "holiday romance"', Unpublished doctoral thesis, University of Cardiff.

Further reading

Barbour, R.S. and Kitzinger, J. (1999) *Developing focus group research: Politics, theory and practice*, London: Sage Publications.

Bloor, M., Frankland, J., Thomas, M. and Robson, K. (2001) *Focus groups in social research*, London: Sage Publications.

Website resource

Forum for Qualitative Social Research (FQS): http://qualitative-research.net/fqs/fqs-eng.htm

NOP Research Group: www.nop.co.uk/techniques/
  tech_inter_qual_meth_groupdiscuss.shtml
Surrey University: www.soc.surrey.ac.uk/sru/SRU19.html
Social Research Organisation: www.the-sra.org.uk/safe.htm
The qualitative report: www.nova.edu/ssss/QR/

5.11 Documents in qualitative research

Jane Lewis, *Barnett Professor of Social Policy, Oxford University*

Documentary sources are possibly the most taken-for-granted in any research project; after all, we can all read a document and take notes. However, most first year undergraduates are familiar with the problem of what to take notes on, and the danger of ending up with a sheaf of notes that approaches book-length. This problem often re-emerges at the beginning of a piece of original research, and much depends on approaching documents with good research questions.

Documents take many forms and many researchers do not get beyond published sources, in the form of books or government reports and policy papers, together with press comment, which gives an indication as to how a policy was received and debated. Diaries and memoirs of political figures can also be useful for understanding the debates and position of actors. Personal documents also exist for ordinary people, which may sometimes give an idea as to how policies were received. However, these are relatively rare and difficult to trace. The Mass Observation Archive at Sussex University has collected written observations from a large number of people for the whole of the post-war period. These are unpublished, archival sources. The unpublished records of government departments exist in the archives of the Public Record Office (PRO) (see Land et al, 1992; Bridgen and Lowe, 1998, for a guide to these). There is, usually, a '30-year rule' on these documents, meaning that they only become publicly available after 30 years have elapsed.

It is also important to think about the order in which to read documentary materials: for example, newspapers before or after government documents? There are no rules to be followed here and a lot depends on how much knowledge the researcher has about the subject. It is often a good idea to begin with source materials that are more generally focused and that therefore provide more context (thus, newspapers before government documents). But, if the research is relatively small and tightly focused, it may be better to plunge into policy documents that are precisely related to the topic, establish which ones are particularly important, and then read 'around' those in particular to get more of an idea of how they have been received (thus, documents before newspapers). Given that researchers are likely to begin many investigations with some form of documentary research (it is always necessary to acquire a good substantive knowledge of the topic before interviewing, for example), it is also important to keep detailed references. This is crucial for footnoting and endnoting, but also, as interpretations of the material mature, it is inevitable that notes on a particular point will have to be rechecked.

Historical documents

Historical documents are by no means easy to define. Most historians believe that it is not possible to write good history without the perspective that comes only with a certain amount of distance from the events. Those interested in social policy issues rarely venture beyond the point at which archival sources cease to become available. The main archival sources for social policies are the records of government departments, in the form of memoranda, correspondence, minutes of meetings and the like, which in the UK are held at the PRO. Local record offices, which may hold personal papers as well as local government archival materials, operate a similar rule. Researchers may also want to pursue the records of important actors. Voluntary organisations, for example, may keep their own archival records, or may have deposited them elsewhere (for example, the records of the Family Planning Association are kept by the Wellcome Library for the History of Medicine; see Cook et al, 1984, for a guide to post-war historical documents).

Archival records provide very detailed data and are usually very time consuming to use. Nevertheless, they provide close insights into policy making. Printed and published documents may provide a variety of competing explanations for the introduction of a particular policy. The records of the government department involved will usually contain documents and correspondence (including reference to major actors outside government) that discuss the various options and enable the researcher to see how a decision was reached. Thus John Macnicol (1980) was able to conclude that the introduction of family allowances in 1944 had much more to do with the aim of keeping down wages than with any desire to do something about the falling birth rate, child poverty or rewarding women's domestic work (all issues in the preceding debate). To work with this level of data is very different from working with a Green or White Paper. It is easy to become submerged in the detail, and once again, the researcher needs to keep a firm grasp of both the research questions and the larger picture. Unless the research topic is explicitly historical, it is unlikely that the researcher will be able to explore every avenue offered by archival sources or extensively cross-check what is said by one government department with another.

There are also what are often referred to as *primary printed documents*. Historians often divide their bibliographies into 'primary' and 'secondary' sources. While secondary sources provide a commentary on a particular historical event and usually offer an interpretation of it, a primary source is something written by a contemporary and published at the time. It is important to put such source material, which may take the form of books, pamphlets or articles published in newspapers and magazines, alongside the archival material; wherever possible evidence should be 'triangulated', that is, examined in three different types of source material.

Finally, it is important that the researcher is clear about why it is necessary to look at historical documents. Many doctoral theses in social policy have an 'historical chapter', in which the author traces the evolution of a particular policy, usually in the post-war period. If the researcher is working with the idea of *path dependence*, for example, which stresses the importance of the role that historical experience plays in forming mutually consistent expectations on the part of actors in the absence of central guidance, then history (and institutions) obviously 'matters'. But all too often there is no clear justification for the historical chapter, and at worst it is implied that somehow, knowing about the past will explain the present. However, mere chronology cannot explain. The researcher must have a particular reason for investigating the past. Thus Bridgen and Lewis (1999) sought to investigate how the boundary between health and social care, which is particularly striking in the UK context, had been constructed over time; archival documents revealed the extent to which this had been a struggle over the respective responsibilities of health and local authorities.

Contemporary documents

Contemporary documents may appear somewhat easier to deal with; at least the researcher does not have to pay so much attention to the different levels of data and how to integrate them. However, there may be greater problems to do with selection and decisions about the weight to attach to a particular document. The interrogation of contemporary material also presents particular challenges in respect of meaning and context. It will be rare that a document that is agreed by several key actors to be important has not already been analysed by an academic or policy analyst. However, a researcher pursuing an original piece of research must go back to the original document because his or her research questions will in all likelihood be different to those informing existing commentaries.

Any government document must first be located in terms of the debates giving rise to it, inside and outside Parliament and the civil service. Thus, for example, a researcher investigating family policies under the Labour government and reaching first for what appears to be the most relevant document – the 1998 Home Office's Green Paper, *Supporting families* – has to know something about the debates about family change, before he or she can even begin to appreciate the significance of the title, with its reference to 'families' rather than 'the family'. The researcher will come to the document with particular research questions, but he or she also needs to be able to assess the document on its own terms: what is included and excluded, where does the emphasis fall and why, what does it reveal about the role of the state in this difficult policy arena? *Grey literature* – that is, ephemeral pamphlet material from 'think tanks' and campaign groups, now often available on the Internet – will help to elucidate the position adopted by key actors, just as Parliamentary Debates will help to refine the researcher's understanding of the position of politicians active in the debate. Thus, if the document *Supporting families* proves material in answering the questions the researcher has about family policies, reading it is only to begin the process of understanding what it contains. If the researcher wanted to look at family policies in the early and mid-1990s, there would be no such explicitly titled document to go to. But this does not mean that there were no family policies. Indeed, the researcher interested in early 21st-century family policies would miss much of the most important material if his or her attention were to be confined to the 1998 Home Office document. An exploration of social policy development must pay attention to the process of problem definition and to the theoretical literature on the way in which policy gets made (Ham and Hill, 1997; Stone, 1997; Sabatier, 1999; see also Chapter One, this volume) if the researcher is to be successful in tracking down documents that might be relevant.

Researchers are likely to face an overwhelming amount of documentary evidence. Finding an entry point, a logical way of proceeding and reaching a judgement about how to weigh the evidence are crucial. In respect of the latter, a basic appreciation of who is speaking (and why that person or organisation), when they are speaking (and why then), how they are defining the problem and where they are looking for solutions (and why) will always serve the researcher well in terms of placing the text and evaluating its claims.

Question for discussion

- What kinds of documents are useful for the study of social policy and why?

References

Bridgen, P. and Lewis, J. (1999) *Elderly people and the boundary between health and social care 1946-1991*, London: Nuffield Trust.

Bridgen, P. and Lowe, R. (1998) *Welfare policy under the Conservatives, 1951-1964. A guide to documents in the public record office*, London: PRO.

Cook, C., Waller, D., Leonard, J. and Leese, P. (1984) *The Longman guide to sources in contemporary British history*, London: Longman.

Ham, C. and Hill, M. (1997) *The policy process in the modern state* (3rd edn), London: Prentice Hall.

Home Office (1998) *Supporting families*, London: Home Office.

Land, A., Lowe, R. and Whiteside, N. (1992) *The development of the welfare state 1939-51: A guide to documents in the public record office*, London: PRO.

Macnicol, J. (1980) *The movement for family allowances 1918-45*, London: Heineman.

Sabatier, P.A. (1999) *Theories of the policy process*, Boulder, CO: Westview Press.

Stone, D. (1997) *Policy paradox: The art of political decision-making*, New York, NY: W.W. Norton.

Further reading

Scott, J. (1990) *A matter of record*, Cambridge: Polity Press.

5.12 Using the Internet for the collection of qualitative data

Henrietta O'Connor, *Lecturer in the Centre for Labour Market Studies, and* Clare Madge, *Lecturer in the Department of Geography, both at the University of Leicester*

Fitzpatrick (2000) has recently argued that those interested in welfare theory and policy cannot afford to overlook the emerging interactions between online and offline environments. Indeed, it is now widely acknowledged that *Information and Communication Technologies* (ICT) present researchers with new potentials for collecting social policy data. Internet methodologies thus offer interesting possibilities for interacting with participants in innovative ways through administering electronic surveys (Roberts and Parks, 2001; see also Chapter Four, Section 4.7), reconsidering sampling strategies (Litvin and Kar, 2001) and conducting qualitative research (Chen and Hinton, 1999; Mann and Stewart, 2000). Qualitative research techniques such as participant observation, discourse analysis and ethnographic research have been used in a virtual setting to study online communities, specialised websites and listservers

(Herring, 1996; Sharf, 1997; Soukup, 1999; Ward, 1999; Hine, 2000; Miller and Slater, 2000). The suitability of cyberspace as an interview venue has also been explored and it is asynchronous interviews, characterised by the fact that they do not take place in 'real time', which have received the most attention to date. These are usually facilitated by e-mail (Kennedy, 2000), bulletin board services (Ward, 1999) or in a listserv environment (Gaiser, 1997). Synchronous or 'real time' online interviewing has received less attention but is nonetheless a valuable way of using the Internet to collect qualitative data.

An example of a recent Internet–based research project, 'Cyberparents' (O'Connor and Madge, 2001), is discussed below to highlight some of the issues involved when collecting data through virtual synchronous interviewing. For this particular project, which was initiated to examine how new parents use the Internet as an information source and as a form of social support, data were collected using online synchronous interviews. During the interview process a number of interesting differences emerged between online and offline interviews, raising a series of questions about this methodological approach: 'does the electronic interviewer require different skills to engage the interviewees and build up rapport than the 'real world' interviewer?'; 'what impact does the virtual setting have on the researcher's role in the research process?'; and 'does the disembodying quality of online research alter the interview process?'.

It is to this final question we now turn (see Madge and O'Connor, 2002, for discussion of the other questions).

The online interview is a process that removes the tangible presence of the researcher, so bodily presence (age, gender, hairstyle, clothes) become invisible. According to Chen and Hinton (1999, 13.2) this results in the potential of the virtual interview to become the 'great equaliser' with the interviewer having less control over the interview process. This we feel is a rather utopian vision. In our case we posted photographs of ourselves on our dedicated project web pages and shared our background interests with the women, both important processes in creating rapport and breaking down the researcher–researched relationship, giving 'clues' to our bodily identities. This may have influenced the interview process with white, 30-something women feeling more comfortable talking to us than other groups. Additionally, in the situation of a virtual interview, the speed of typing dominates the interaction rather than the most vocal personality, which, although having the potential to disrupt power relations among groups, has the possibility of marginalising people with poor or slow keyboard skills. Moreover, the 'equaliser' argument glosses over the structural power hierarchies that enable researchers to set the agenda, ask the questions and benefit from the results of the interview process.

Nevertheless, we must acknowledge that for the interviewees, the ability to mask their identity changed some accepted norms of behaviour and probably allowed them a more active voice in shaping the tone and atmosphere of the interview. Despite Gaiser's (1997, p 142) warning that virtual interview discussion may be "... superficial and playful" with interviewers finding it more difficult to persuade participants to "... reconceptualise their behaviour ... to participate in substantive discussion", we found that the relaxed and informal atmosphere created a platform for successful interviewing. Indeed, as is common in conventional situations when women interview other women, the interviews all provided high levels of self-consciousness, reflexivity and interactivity. Whether this was owing to the nature of the interviewees (self-selected, motivated, frequent online users), or owing to the nature of the subject matter, clearly being very close to the hearts of the women involved, it is difficult to judge. In our virtual interviews we did not encounter the much written about "... aura of suspicion" surrounding "... stranger-to-stranger communication in cyberspace" (Smith, 1997, p 40).

From this example, it is clear that the advantages of conducting synchronous online interviews in an environment without the temporal or spatial restrictions of 'real world' interaction are many. For example, the Internet offers the potential for interfacing with groups of people who are widely geographically distributed or those difficult to reach via conventional research approaches (Mann and Stewart, 2000; Reeves, 2000; Pendergrass et al, 2001). The indicative data gained from online research may also be useful for research on population subgroups and for exploratory analysis (Lamp and Howard, 1999; Burrows et al, 2000). Savings of time and money, for example the elimination of costs associated with the transcription process, are also to be recommended. As online research is still in its infancy, many of its potentials are still to be discovered and evaluated. Indeed it is actually unlikely that there will be a radical transformation of social policy research through ICT but rather it offers some interesting new potentials in terms of making visible "... arenas of social life previously distant and concealed" (Crang et al, 1999, p 11).

Despite its promise, the limitations of online research are also coming to light. Virtual interviews are still fairly novel techniques, and while some of their limitations may therefore be solved in time, others may never be remedied. As Smith (1997, p 4) concludes: "The new technology offers a spate of problems layered over the old". Indeed although the data collected by virtual interviews, in particular, can be rich and valuable to the researcher, the potential of online research should not be exaggerated: many of the issues and problems of conventional research methods still apply in the virtual venue. Caution should be stressed in an attempt to avoid the 'cyberbole' (Imken, 1999) and overdrawn opposition between 'real' and virtual techniques. This research is just beginning to show its potential as a useful adjunct to existing methods but much still remains to be done to assess its usefulness.

Question for discussion

• What are the potentials and limitations of online synchronous interviews for social policy research?

References

Burrows, R., Nettleton, S., Please, N., Loader, B. and Muncer, S. (2000) 'Virtual community care? Social policy and the emergence of computer mediated social support', *Information, Communication and Society*, no 3, pp 1-16.

Chen, P. and Hinton, S.M. (1999) 'Realtime interviewing using the World Wide Web', *Sociological Research Online*, vol 4, no 3 (www.socresonline.org.co.uk/socresonline/4/3/chen.html).

Crang, M., Crang, P. and May, J. (1999) *Virtual geographies*, London: Routledge.

Fitzpatrick, T. (2000) 'Critical cyberpolicy: network technologies, massless citizens, virtual rights', *Critical Social Policy*, no 20, pp 357-407.

Gaiser, T. (1997) 'Conducting online focus groups: a methodological discussion', *Social Science Computer Review*, vol 15, no 2, pp135-44.

Herring, S. (1996) 'Posting in a different voice: gender and ethics in computer-mediated communication', in C. Ess (ed) *Philosophic perspectives in computer-mediated communication*, Albany, NY: State University of New York Press, pp 115-46.

Hine, C. (2000) *Virtual ethnography*, London: Sage Publications.

Imken, O. (1999) 'The convergence of virtual and actual in the global matrix: artificial life, geo-economics and psychogeography', in M. Crang, P. Crang and J. May (eds) *Virtual geographies*, London: Routledge, pp 92-106.

Kennedy, T.L.M. (2000) 'An exploratory study of feminist experiences in cyberspace', *Cyberpsychology and Behavior*, no 3, pp 707-20.

Lamp, J.M. and Howard, P.A. (1999) 'Guiding parent's use of the Internet for newborn education', *Maternal-Child Nursing Journal*, no 24, pp 33-6.

Litvin, S.W. and Kar, G.H. (2001) 'E-surveying for tourism research: legitimate tool or a researcher's fantasy?', *Journal of Travel Research*, no 39, pp 308-14.

Madge, C. and O'Connor, H. (2002) 'On-line with e-mums: exploring the Internet as a medium for research', *Area*, no 34, pp 92-102.

Mann, C. and Stewart, F. (2000) *Internet communication and qualitative research*, London: Sage Publications.

Miller, D. and Slater, D. (2000) *The Internet: An ethnographic approach*, Oxford: Berg.

O'Connor, H. and Madge, C. (2001) 'Cyber-Mothers: online synchronous interviewing using conferencing software', *Sociological Research Online*, vol 5, no 4 (www.socresonline.org.uk/5/4/o'connor.html).

Pendergrass, S., Nosek, M.A. and Holcomb, J.D. (2001) 'Design and evaluation of an Internet site to educate women with disabilities on reproductive health care', *Sexuality and Disability*, no 19, pp 71-83.

Reeves, P.M. (2000) 'Coping in cyberspace: the impact of Internet use on the ability of HIV-positive individuals to deal with their illness', *Journal of Health Communication*, no 5, pp 47-59.

Roberts, L.D. and Parks, M.R. (2001) 'The social geography of gender switching in virtual environments on the Internet', in E. Green and A. Adam (eds) *Virtual gender: Technology, consumption and gender*, London: Routledge, pp 265-85.

Sharf, B. (1997) 'Communicating breast cancer online: support and empowerment on the Internet', *Women and Health*, no 26, pp 65-84.

Smith, C. (1997) 'Casting the net: surveying an Internet population', *Journal of Computer Mediated Communication*, vol 3, no 1 (http://jcmc.huji.ac.il/vol3/issue1/smith.html).

Soukup, C. (1999) 'The gendered interactional patterns of computer-mediated chatrooms: a critical ethnographic study', *The Information Society*, no 15, pp 169-76.

Ward, K.J. (1999) 'The cyber-ethnographic (re)construction of two feminist online communities', *Sociological Research Online*, vol 4, no 1 (www.socresonline.org.uk/socresonline/4/1/ward.html).

Further reading

Mann, C. and Stewart, F. (2000) *Internet communication and qualitative research*, London: Sage Publications.

Woolgar, S. (ed) (2002) *Virtual society? Technology, cyberbole, reality*, Oxford: Oxford University Press.

Website resources

Centre for Research into Innovation, Culture and Technology at Brunel University: www.brunel.ac.uk/depts/crict/vmesrc.htm
Cyberparents research project: www.geog.le.ac.uk/baby/
ESRC Research Programme: Virtual Society? The social science of electronic technologies (home page): http://virtualsociety.sbs.ox.ac.uk/
Mapping Cyberspace: www.MappingCyberspace.com

PART THREE: THE ANALYSIS OF QUALITATIVE DATA

5.13 Analysing qualitative data: an overview

The next four sections address different approaches to the analysis of qualitative data. Sometimes, *content analysis* (Chapter Four, Section 4.8) is considered to be an approach to the analysis of qualitative data. It does indeed do this, in that the technique can be employed to analyse unstructured data such as newspaper articles, semi-structured interview transcripts, diaries and novels. However, content analysis draws on a quantitative research strategy in order to analyse such data.

The approaches to qualitative data analysis covered in this section are:

- grounded theory;
- analytic induction;
- discourse analysis;
- conversation analysis;
- narrative analysis.

Unlike content analysis, each of these approaches to analysing qualitative data seeks to preserve the nature of the data, albeit in different ways and degrees. That is to say, they aim for an analytic approach that is consistent with the underling principles of qualitative research. Grounded theory and analytic induction are best thought of as general strategies that can be applied to a wide range of qualitative data. Narrative analysis is typically employed as a means of unpacking the underlying themes that run through such sources of data as interview transcripts. Discourse analysis and conversation analysis take the detailed examination of language use as their point of departure. For the social policy researcher these two approaches offer new ways of understanding interactions and pose new challenges. For example, discourse analysts and conversation analysts might analyse the transactions between a benefit claimant and personal adviser, or between a social worker and someone requiring an assessment of their needs. Here, the focus of analysis is not on the content specifically, but on the ways in which talk is used to construct the interaction and to confer roles on each party. Understanding the process of these and similar interactions adds an additional dimension to an appreciation of what goes on in the delivery and implementation of social policies.

Section 5.14 also covers coding and computer-assisted qualitative data analysis. Coding was also encountered in the previous chapter, but, as Section 5.14 shows, the goals of coding in qualitative data analysis are somewhat different in that the links between data and concepts are somewhat less fixed and more fluid there than they are in connection with quantitative data (see Chapter Four, Sections 4.3 and 4.5). In qualitative research, codes are often revised and are a way of leading to concepts rather than being quantitative markers of pre-existing concepts. Whereas the quantitative researcher typically devises a number of categories for each variable and each category is then allocated a code according in terms of which the researcher then allocates people, newspapers, behaviour or whatever, in qualitative research the codes are gradually built up out of the data. Indeed, in some approaches to analysing qualitative data, there is a very flexible relationship between data collection and analysis, as in grounded theory, where data are often analysed in the course of data collection to give the researcher ideas about which cases or contexts should be focused upon in later stages of the enquiry. Coding in this kind of environment needs to be flexible to accommodate changes in the direction of the research that might be suggested by further data collection. **Box 5h** describes such an approach that draws on standard techniques like coding and brings them together into a coherent analytic strategy.

Coding is sometimes a controversial activity in qualitative data analysis: narrative analysts, for example, sometimes argue that it undermines the underlying coherence of what people say in interviews. However, it is a common way of handling qualitative data and beginning the process of qualitative data analysis, and moreover, it is increasingly conducted using computer software. This development and some of the issues involved in its use is also covered in Section 5.14.

5.14 Grounded theory, analytic induction, coding and computer-assisted analysis

Nigel Fielding, *Professor of Sociology, University of Surrey*

Qualitative research is committed to the idea that an adequate analysis of social reality requires that we understand the 'symbolic world' of those we study, the meanings people apply to their experiences. Since our understanding develops over the course of research, Becker (1971) tagged the process as one of 'sequential analysis', in which we continually check data against interpretation until satisfied we have the grasped the meaning. Thus, analysis begins while still collecting data and further data gathering is informed by things to which we have become sensitised by provisional analysis.

The analytic process is therefore one of gradual refinement. While this has advantages over methods where, once instruments are designed, analytic interests cannot affect the data collected, it also presents several challenges: knowing when the data are sufficient to form a secure basis for analysis; taking account of the gradual emergence of insight when interpreting data collected at different stages; and finding analytic procedures that accommodate the unpredictability of field data. We also have to cope with the more straightforward problem that qualitative research usually produces voluminous data and requires a clear-headed data management strategy.

While there are many approaches to qualitative data analysis, the procedures most researchers use to manage and prepare data for analysis are quite straightforward. These involve: compiling the corpus of data (fieldnotes, transcripts); searching for categories and patterns in the data; marking the data with category (or 'code') labels; and constructing thematic outlines using the codes to lay out the sequence in which topics will be considered. These procedures formerly involved the physical manipulation of data (literally cutting up data and sorting them into sets of associated extracts) but nowadays the process can be conducted online (although some still prefer 'manual' methods, especially for small-scale studies).

It is not perhaps obvious from this bare statement of procedure that the business of data analysis involves stringent data reduction. As noted, qualitative data are voluminous; Miles and Huberman's (1994) evaluation of innovation in a school system produced over 3,000 pages of fieldnotes. The understanding researchers gain during fieldwork enables them to select the most significant data, guided also by the precepts of the analytic approach they have adopted. Whatever the data management procedure, the essence is that the researcher works up from the data, rather than dipping into it for fragments that support an analysis to which one is already committed.

Grounded theory

The analytic approach most closely reflecting the emphasis on working 'up from the data' is Glaser and Strauss's (1967) *grounded theory*, which also popularised code-based analysis. The *constant comparative method* at its core begins by examining 'incidents' recorded in fieldwork, incidents being discrete acts or the expression of an attitude by research subjects (Becker and Geer, 1960). Each is coded into as many theoretical categories as possible (a process later tagged 'open coding'), with categories being derived from existing analytic constructs (found, for example, in the literature) or terms used by research subjects characterising, for example, aspects of their work. Before assigning a code to a datum, the method requires that we re-examine all incidents previously coded using the same category. This recursive approach ensures that theoretical properties of categories are fleshed out as analysis proceeds. It helps identify different categories and the relationship between categories. Thus, conceptualisation emerges during coding, which is why the second rule of constant comparison is that we should break off coding periodically to prepare 'analytic memos' on the category's meaning.

Glaser and Strauss are in accord with Becker's 'sequential analysis' in maintaining that collecting, coding and analysing data should co-occur, so data collection is guided by *theoretical sampling* (see **Box 5b**) and responsive to the emerging analysis. Having generated a group of categories, the analyst moves to the second stage of constant comparison, 'integrating categories and their properties'. Further incidents are compared against the initial categories, clarifying the categories, their properties and the relationship between the two.

While these first two stages are expansive, in the next the emergent theory is 'delimited'. Major changes are less frequent; the researcher concentrates on clarification, simplification and 'reduction' of the theory. Categories become expressed in more abstract, general terms. This may support a move from substantive to formal theory. To use Glaser and Strauss's classic example, one might now move from a (substantive) theory of how nurses maintain composure in the face of the death of patients to a (formal) theory of how professionals allocate their services in relation to the implicit social worth of their clients. Glaser and Strauss maintain that such an approach facilitates theory that is both parsimonious (offering maximum explanatory power but based on a small number of factors) and has wide scope (applying across a range of situations), while also being well grounded (having a close and demonstrable link to supporting data).

These latter moves reduce the range of categories germane to the emerging theory. Ongoing analysis can now focus just on those categories. The categories become 'theoretically saturated'. It becomes immediately apparent whether a subsequent incident requires modification of the concept. Where it does, the concept is coded and compared to existing categories, if not, the incident need not be coded.

Refinement of grounded theory has seen elaborations of coding procedure. For example, Glaser (1978) and Strauss (1987) stipulated that open coding involves constant questioning of the data (for example, initial data may describe a problem in the setting so one might ask how members deal with it) and treating the data microscopically (sometimes even coding word-by-word). Its formulations are tentative, not conclusive. Strauss and Corbin (1990) offer further open coding strategies.

Open coding is augmented by 'axial coding' (Strauss, 1987), in which a texture of conceptual relationships is built around the 'axis' of the category, 'dimensionalising' the properties of the phenomenon with which the category is concerned. The properties and dimensions are progressively linked to each other by specifying the conditions which generate the phenomenon, the context and intervening conditions bearing on it, the interactional strategies and tactics of those involved, and the consequences that result, a set of considerations constituting 'the coding paradigm'. Moves towards the final theoretical formulation proceed through 'selective coding' – based on a high-level summary of the analysis – and the identification of a 'core category' that integrates the other categories. Work here involves further application of the coding paradigm.

This account of grounded theory, particularly the stages subsequent to open coding, reflects the approach in Strauss and Corbin (1990). Some find their approach appealing for its manual like accessibility and systematic character but others find it untrue to Glaser and Strauss's original inspiration, not least Glaser (1992) himself, who argues that it 'forces' meaning from the data into predetermined templates rather than letting it emerge. Such differences may account for the fact that, while the majority of qualitative researchers claim adherence to grounded theory, inquiry into their working practices reveals substantial variation and deviation from the steps laid down in the canonical texts (Fielding and Lee, 1998).

Analytic induction

Longer-established than grounded theory is Znaniecki's (1934) 'analytic induction', which aims to produce universal statements about social phenomena by identifying conditions always associated with their occurrence. Analytic induction is case-based rather than code-based, examining social phenomena using case studies and focusing on outcomes of social processes. Negative cases indicate the need to modify the universal statement to accommodate them. From Cressey's (1953) application of analytic induction to the case of financial fraudsters we can derive its stages. Step 1 is to identify the phenomenon to be explained. Step 2 involves formulating a working definition of the phenomenon. Step 3 involves formulating a working hypothesis to explain the phenomenon. In Step 4 the researcher studies one case. At Step 5 one considers whether the facts of this case fit the initial hypothesis. If they do, Step 6 is to study the next case. If they don't, Step 6 is *either* to redefine the phenomenon to exclude that case *or* to reformulate the working hypothesis. Step 7 involves continuing Step 6 until there is practical certainty that the emerging theory has accounted for all cases – a 'universal solution'. Any negative case requires either redefinition or reformulation.

Analytic induction encourages researchers to generate and test hypotheses, and was originally commended for systematising causal theory-generation.

However, there is a critical flaw in its logic (Robinson, 1951). The analyst examines instances where the phenomenon is present on the basis that it only occurs when particular conditions apply, not in their absence. This implies the need to look at cases where the phenomenon is *not* present. Only then can we be sure there are no cases where the supposedly universal conditions causing the phenomenon occur in the absence of the phenomenon. As Robinson observed, examining such cases is actually what researchers do in practice; for instance, Cressey (1953) checked the case histories of his fraudsters to see if the conditions under which they violated financial trust had applied earlier in their careers without their committing fraud. But, compromised by its logical flaws (Hicks, 1994), analytic induction suffered from the move away from case-based analysis to the more micro-oriented, code-based analytic approaches. There has, however, been a revival of interest prompted by Ragin's (1987) 'qualitative comparative analysis'.

Computer-assisted qualitative data analysis

The mainstream approaches to qualitative analysis have latterly been supported by computer-assisted qualitative data analysis (CAQDAS). Qualitative software must be able to store data in different formats, and enable researchers to annotate it and 'navigate' the database. Code application and code revision, either globally or in application to particular segments, must be straightforward. When data are coded we need to retrieve them selectively and be able to write analytic memos. Addressing these requirements are three broad types of CAQDAS: *text retrievers*, *code-and-retrieve packages*, and *theory-building software* (Weitzman and Miles, 1995).

Text retrievers, such as Metamorph and askSam, let users recover data pertaining to categories using keywords. Thus, when you search on 'policy', wherever the word appears the software will extract it. If the keyword was not used it must be added to the data. Words and other character strings, in one or many files, can be retrieved, along with things that sound alike or have patterns like the sequences of letters and numbers in social security records. Retrieved text can be sorted into new files, and analytic memos linked to the data.

Code-and-retrieve packages, including WinMAX and The Ethnograph, support attaching codes to data segments and retrieving segments by code. A 'single sort' retrieves all data pertaining to one code. 'Multiple sort' retrievals handle cases where one category is considered in relation to another, for example, where data coded 'age' coincides with data coded 'income'. Searches are also supported which recover data where two characteristics apply but not a third ('Boolean retrievals'); for instance, data from MALE claimants living in URBAN areas who are NOT graduates. Most of these packages support analytic memoing and some alert users that memos pertain whenever relevant segments are inspected. 'Hypertext' features help users to quickly 'navigate' the database.

Such software focuses analytic attention on relationships between categories and data. *Theory-building software*, such as Atlas/ti and N-vivo, emphasise relationships between the categories. It helps users develop higher-order classifications and categories than those derived directly from data, formulate propositions that fit the data and test their applicability, or visualise connections between categories. Full Boolean searching and the ability to 'test' hypotheses may be offered. Some can show code names (or other objects, like memos) as nodes in a graphic display and users can link them to other nodes by specified relationships like 'is a kind of'.

As noted in discussing analytic induction, case-based analysis imposes different requirements to work with codes. Ragin's (1987) 'qualitative comparative analysis' compares outcomes across multiple cases. It uses mathematics to systematically identify 'universal conditions' which are always present in particular combinations when the phenomenon occurs. The 'QCA' package analyses conjunctures of particular elements of cases that bear on the outcome.

Like many innovations, CAQDAS is more readily-adopted by new social researchers, but the field is gradually becoming more familiar with its advantages and limits, and the range of analytic approaches it supports now covers most of those in regular use. **Box 5g** presents an illustration of the use of CAQDAS in social policy research.

Question for discussion

- What is the distinction between case-based and code-based analytic strategies and specify the analytic purposes for which each is best suited?

References

Becker, H. (1971) *Sociological work*, London: Allen Lane.

Becker, H. and Geer, B. (1960) 'Participant observation: the analysis of qualitative field data', in R.N. Adams and J. Preiss (eds) *Human organisation research*, Homewood, IL: Dorsey Press.

Cressey, D. (1953) *Other people's money*, New York, NY: Free Press.

Fielding, N. and Lee, R.M. (1998) *Computer analysis and qualitative research*, London: Sage Publications.

Glaser, B. (1978) *Theoretical sensitivity*, Mill Valley, CA: Sociology Press.

Glaser, B. (1992) *Emergence vs. forcing: Basics of grounded theory analysis*, Mill Valley, CA: Sociology Press.

Glaser, B. and Strauss, A. (1967) *The discovery of grounded theory*, Chicago, IL: Aldine.

Hicks, A. (1994) 'Qualitative comparative analysis and analytic induction: the case for the emergence of the social security state', *Sociological Methods and Research*, vol 23, pp 86-113.

Miles, M. and Huberman, A. (1994) *Qualitative data analysis: An expanded sourcebook*, Beverly Hills, CA: Sage Publications.

Ragin, C. (1987) *The comparative method: Moving beyond qualitative and quantitative strategies*, Berkeley, CA: University of California Press.

Robinson, W. (1951) 'The logical structure of analytical induction', *American Sociological Review*, vol 16, pp 812-18.

Strauss, A. (1987) *Qualitative analysis for social scientists*, Cambridge: Cambridge University Press.

Strauss, A. and Corbin, J. (1990) *Basics of qualitative research: Grounded theory procedures and techniques*, Newbury Park, CA: Sage Publications.

Weitzman, E. and Miles, M. (1995) *Computer programs for qualitative data analysis*, Beverly Hills, CA: Sage Publications.

Znaniecki, F. (1934) *The method of sociology*, New York, NY: Farrar and Rinehart.

Further reading

On qualitative software and its relationship to qualitative analysis:

Fielding, N. and Lee, R.M. (1998) *Computer analysis and qualitative research*, London: Sage Publications.

On the procedures of qualitative data analysis, useful comparisons of different analyses of the same data:

Coffey, A. and Atkinson, P. (1996) *Making sense of qualitative data*, Farnborough: Avebury.

Creswell, J. (1998) *Qualitative inquiry and research design*, London: Sage Publications.

Website resources

For those interested in qualitative software: http://caqdas.soc.surrey.ac.uk

For those interested in social research methods: www.ssmr2003.plus.com/index.htm

Box 5g: An example of the use of hypothesis testing software

Nigel Fielding, *Professor of Sociology, University of Surrey*

Changes in social policy are one means by which society responds to women's changing labour market position. To form policies that will be appropriate for some time, information is needed about the aspirations of women who are currently progressing through education and into the labour market. In our example female students were interviewed about how their careers and family lives might turn out in 20 years. The so-called 'Cinderella complex' would be present where they predicted having a successful, non-traditional career combined with a thriving family life, achieved and sustained unproblematically. The interview data were entered into HyperRESEARCH software, which offers a 'hypothesis test feature'. Users hypothesise a relationship between the occurrence of a particular statement in the data and the occurrence of another (*if* 'this' *then* 'that'). When the two occurrences are found together, this can be made part of another hypothetical relationship. To construct a testable hypothesis, users may need several 'if' and 'then' rules, each using codewords assigned to the data. The hypothesis test searches for cases where the particular codewords occur in the particular combinations the proposition requires. If these are present, that case supports the proposition.

To test for the Cinderella complex, the researchers began by building an expression whose elements (or 'rules') stated the 'if' part of the proposition to be tested and the 'then' part of the proposition. In this case, the first 'if' rule was, 'I am making a high salary and have a fabulous non-traditional job', and the 'then' rule, representing the hypothetical consequence of the 'if' rule, was set as 'high work commitment'. Recall that the proposition may take several 'if' and 'then' rules to build a testable hypothesis and that each rule uses codewords that have been applied to the data. Further rules were added to test for 'high family commitment' and 'high potential for work–family conflict'. The hypothesis test looks for the occurrence of the particular codewords in the particular combinations the proposition requires. If these are present in a case (here, an interview) the proposition is supported for that case. In this case the complete rule-set for the presence of the Cinderella complex was found in only one of eight interviews. The hypothesis was not proven. The conclusion was that, far from harbouring over-optimistic expectations about their work and home life, most students were realistic about their likely future.

It may seem that all this takes us some way from the grounded theory approach. That is so. Theory-building software enables more formal approaches to qualitative data analysis, and some see techniques such as hypothesis-testing as more akin to a positivist orientation than traditional qualitative research. It is necessary for researchers to assume that the data supporting these hypothetical relationships are comparable, because the analytic effort moves away from working with the data itself to working with relationships between the different codes that have been applied to the data.

Box 5h: The 'framework' approach to qualitative data analysis

At the National Centre for Social Research (formerly Social and Community Planning Research) an approach to the analysis of qualitative data has been developed in large part in relation to applied social research of the kind conducted by social policy researchers. The approach is called 'framework', a term that owes its origin to the 'thematic framework' that lies at the heart of the approach. This is used "to classify and organise data according to key themes, concepts and emergent categories" (Ritchie et al, 2003, p 220). The themes derive from an interrogation of the data and the coding (the users of the approach prefer to refer to it as 'indexing') of the data into distinct topics. Once the framework is believed to be inclusive, "each main theme is displayed or 'charted' in its own matrix, where every respondent is allocated a row and each column denotes a separate subtopic" (Ritchie et al, 2003, p 220). The analyst then begins to relate the different themes to each other, draw out abstract categories, and develop explanations out of the matrix. For example, the fact that certain topics surface in more than one thematic column for several research participants can be taken to signal that there are interconnections among the themes concerned. The authors offer the following advice when devising the thematic framework:

1. Make a note of where exactly in a transcript or in fieldnotes the snippet of data has come from.
2. Try as far as possible to keep the language of the research participant.
3. Avoid the temptation to insert in each cell a large amount of quoted material; instead, try to indicate where in the transcript relevant quotations might be found and mark these in the transcript itself.
4. Use abbreviations in the cells so that they do not become clogged up and, if working as part of a team, make sure the abbreviations are agreed.

The matrix is not unlike the kind of spreadsheet that is used in statistical software programs such as SPSS, which has cases going across (as rows) and variables going down (as columns). In a sense, the main contribution of framework is not so much as a set of techniques for doing qualitative data analysis, since it relies very much on well-known approaches like creating an index of codes and developing concepts out of codes. Instead, it provides a useful template for doing qualitative data analysis and in particular, its idea of a data matrix is extremely useful as a tool of qualitative data management.

References

Ritchie, J., Spencer, L. and O'Connor, W. (2003) 'Carrying out qualitative analysis', in J. Ritchie and J. Lewis (eds) *Qualitative research practice: A guide of social science students and researchers*, London: Sage, pp 219-62.

5.15 Discourse analysis

Jonathan Potter, *Professor of Discourse Analysis,*
Loughborough University

Discourse analysis refers to a cluster of methods and approaches (including continental discourse analysis, critical discourse analysis, discursive psychology and conversation analysis) that focus on the role of *talk and texts* in social life. Different forms of discourse analysis place different emphasis on specific practices of interaction and the broader discursive resources that underpin that interaction. On the one hand, for example, Anssi Peräkylä (1995) considered the various practices that make up AIDS counselling (the way questions are asked, 'dreaded' matters broached, advice delivered, and so on). This is characteristic of conversation analysis and the work of Harvey Sacks and Emanuel Schegloff. On the other, for example, Margaret Wetherell and Jonathan Potter (1992) studied the various symbolic resources (or 'interpretative repertoires') that white majority group members draw on to justify ethnic inequalities and to undermine moves towards social change. This is characteristic of critical discourse analysis, and is influenced by the ideas of Michel Foucault.

Discourse research varies in its methodological procedures and assumptions. The following stages are common in many discourse studies:

* *Question formulation:* discourse research typically asks questions of the form 'what is an X?' or 'how is X done?'. What is a complaint, say, and how do complaints get done, get resisted or break down? These kinds of questions contrast to common social science questions such as 'what is the effect of X on Y?'.
* *Data collection:* discourse researchers have used open-ended interviews, focus groups, records of interaction in everyday or institutional settings and formal texts. Interviews have been the method of choice until recently because they enable focus on a topic, standardisation of questions and control over sampling. However, researchers have started to focus more on records of natural interaction because of problems with interviews being flooded with the researcher's expectations and categories. Such records generally have the advantage of directly capturing the initial phenomenon of interest (see **Box 5i**).
* *Data management:* interviews or naturalistic records (audio or video) are most simply worked with in digital form on a PC. This allows instant access, easy searching, filing and categorising, as well as providing a flexible environment for transcription. Unlike grounded theorists or ethnographers, discourse researchers have rarely used qualitative analysis software such as NVivo (see also Section 5.14). Rather, the first move is often transcription. If there is a

small amount of data these will be transcribed directly using a system developed by the conversation analyst Gail Jefferson (see Hutchby and Wooffitt, 1998; see also **Box 5j**). For larger datasets these may be first transcribed in a more coarse manner to allow preliminary searching, filing and categorising.

* *Developing a corpus:* discourse research is intensive. It requires the researcher to engage with the specifics of a set of materials. Depending on the question, this will typically involve the development of a specific corpus of examples. If the materials have been transcribed in only a preliminary manner, it will be at this point that they will be transcribed to full Jeffersonian level. The associated audio or video passage can be selected out so the researcher can work with both recording and transcript in parallel.

* *Analysis:* the precise nature of the analysis will depend to some extent on the question being addressed. It will typically involve working with the corpus to identify some phenomenon or social practice, and to describe its form and regularity. This is an iterative procedure with examples being dropped from the corpus and added to the corpus as the research ideas are refined.

* *Validation:* the process of validation in discursive work is not clearly separate from the process of analysis. Four considerations are central to the justification of analytic findings. First, the analysis should work with, and be sensitive to, the orientations of the participants themselves, which are most powerfully shown in the turn-by-turn unfolding of interaction (this is another reason for preferring naturalistic materials over interviews). Second, the analysis should be able to deal with deviant cases. Departures from standard patterns are highly informative, either showing that a generalisation is suspect, or highlighting its robustness. Third, analysis will build on and mesh with earlier research; if it clashes with earlier work it will need to account for that clash. Fourth, discourse work is validated by readers being able to compare claims and interpretations with materials reproduced in the research report – it is a public and transparent process.

Question for discussion

* What considerations are relevant in the validating of discourse analytic studies?

References

Hutchby, I. and Wooffitt, R. (1998) *Conversation analysis: Principles, practices and applications*, Cambridge: Polity.

Peräkylä, A. (1995) *AIDS counselling: Institutional interaction and clinical practice*, Cambridge: Cambridge University Press.

Wetherell, M. and Potter, J. (1992) *Mapping the language of racism: Discourse and the legitimation of exploitation*, Brighton/New York, NY: Harvester Wheatsheaf/Columbia University Press.

Further reading

Potter, J. (2004) 'Discourse analysis', in M. Hardy and A. Bryman (eds)
  Handbook of data analysis, London: Sage Publications, pp 607-24.
Wetherell, M., Taylor, S. and Yates, S.J. (eds) (2001) *Discourse as data: A guide for analysis*, London: Sage Publications.
Wood, L.A. and Kroger, R.O. (2000) *Doing discourse analysis: Methods for studying action in talk and text*, London: Sage Publications.

Website resources

DA Online – an electronic journal: www.shu.ac.uk/daol/
Ethno/CA news: www.pscw.uva.nl/emca/
Loughborough Discourse and Rhetoric Group: www.lboro.ac.uk/departments/ss/
  centres/dargindex.htm

Box 5i: An analysis of NSPCC call openings

Jonathan Potter, *Professor of Discourse Analysis, and* Alexa Hepburn, *Lecturer in Social Psychology, both at Loughborough University*

One of the aims of discursive research is to explicate the nature of interaction in institutional settings. We have been working on a series of studies with the National Society for the Prevention of Cruelty to Children, focused on calls to their child protection helpline. This involves questions such as: 'How does abuse reporting get done?', 'How do child protection officers deliver appropriate advice?', 'How are frightened or upset callers kept on the line long enough to give their evidence?'. The openings of calls are particularly important, as a number of delicate issues are managed very quickly – the nature of the call, its appropriateness to the helpline, the stance of the caller and so on. The study discussed here is particularly focused on the business managed by callers in the openings by constructions such as "I'm concerned about X" (Potter and Hepburn, 2003; Hepburn and Potter, 2004).

The database for the study was a corpus of 50 openings reporting third party abuse. About 60% of these openings used concerned constructions, about two thirds of which were initiated by the caller and a third initiated by the child protection officer (CPO). The following is typical of caller initiated concern openings:

```
              ((phone rings))
CPO:     Hello NSPCC Helpline can I help you:?
Caller:  Good after[noon      >I     won]der if y'
CPO:               [((clears throat))]
         could.<  .hhh
CPO:     [Ye:s  certainly:,    ]
→ Caller: [I'm concerned about–]
         (0.2)
CPO:     Yeh,
         .h
Caller:  about a child that lives next
         door to me.
CPO:     Tk.h ri :: ght, could- before you go on can I
         ((ethics exchange)
```

Analysis of these openings, working with both canonical and deviant cases, was able to identify a number of ideas about the role of these seemingly very simple openings. First, they are action oriented – they prepare for the caller unpacking their concerns into specific details. Second, they orient to asymmetry – they treat the actionable status of what is being reported as something to be established in collaboration with the CPO (the 'expert' in these matters). Third, these constructions manage the stance of the caller to the abuse – they are treating it as serious (but not so serious the police should be called directly), critical, and reportable; that is, they are 'concerned' about it. Fourth, concern constructions orient to the institutional business of the helpline. They allow the CPO to treat the abuse claim as serious without having to prejudge their truth, accuracy or actionable nature. The concern opening can evolve into a discussion of specifics about abuse – wounds, dates and family relationships – or into a discussion of the caller – their misperceptions, confusions or anxieties.

These analytic points were supported by a close analysis of both the concern openings and the various 'deviant cases'. Particularly strong support comes from the special features of the non-concern openings (they came from callers with institutional identities, such as health visitors; they asked for advice rather than making a direct report; or they showed various kinds of trouble).

This research is intended to identify some of the reasons that callers get into trouble in making calls, and how CPOs may alleviate that trouble. It also provides the material for evidence-based resources for both the training of new CPOs and to help skilled CPOs refine their practice.

Question for discussion
• Why might a caller to an abuse helpline open with a report of their 'concerns'?

References

Potter, J. and Hepburn, A. (2003) 'I'm a bit concerned – early actions and psychological constructions in a child protection helpline', *Research on language and social interaction*, vol 36, pp 197-240.

Hepburn, A. and Potter, J. (2004) 'Discourse analytic practice', in C. Seale, D. Silverman, J. Gubrium and G. Gobo (eds) *Qualitative research practice*, London: Sage Publications.

Further reading

Drew, P. and Heritage, J.C. (eds) (1992) *Talk at work: Interaction in institutional settings*, Cambridge: Cambridge University Press.

Potter, J. (2003) 'Discourse analysis and discursive psychology', in P.M. Camic, J.E. Rhodes and L.Yardley (eds) *Qualitative research in psychology: Expanding perspectives in methodology and design*, Washington, DC: American Psychological Association, pp 73-94.

Silverman, D. (1997) *Discourses of counselling: HIV counselling as social interaction*, London: Sage Publications.

Website resource

The NSPCC: www.nspcc.org.uk/html/homepage/home.htm

5.16 Conversation analysis

Charles Antaki, *Reader in Language and Social Psychology, Loughborough University*

At first sight conversation analysis looks unpromising to the researcher in social policy. Its insistence on working with the fine detail of talk, its curious notational symbols, and its resistance to talking about people's motivations and private feelings all seem to confine it to the linguist's laboratory. But conversation analysis started out as a way of understanding something as applied and urgent as telephone calls to an emergency psychiatric helpline, and has a long tradition of working on routine social trouble including sites of social policy interest like the doctor's surgery, the police interrogation, the interview between claimant and personal adviser, the social worker's assessment of a disabled person or family carer, to name but a few.

The basic idea is that in any of these situations – like life anywhere – the business is transacted through talk. The six minutes' interaction between A and B comes out as a 'doctor's consultation' only because one of them is offering symptoms and complaints, and the other one asks questions, offers a diagnosis and prescribes some course of action. Props may well be used, and posture, gaze and movement all make their contributions, but if we start out with looking at the talk, we shall have got the essence of the interaction in our sights. Once we do, we can ask important questions which cannot be asked on any other basis. We cannot satisfactorily ask doctors or patients how they do what they do on the basis of their recollections, since we know that recollections are partial, faulty and, in any case, likely to be moulded by the question being asked. With a video or audio record, however, we have some reasonably faithful capture of what happened, and we can start very carefully and soberly seeing what was done, and how it was done.

The 'pure' conversation analyst will be satisfied with that, as giving them another chapter in their understanding of the social world; but the 'applied' conversation analyst can go a step further. Remembering that official events like police interrogations and social work assessments have an official set of prescriptions, they can ask: how does what actually happened compare with the official account of what should happen? They can also ask: how does what actually happened, as analysed with the benefit of the video and audio tape, compare with the version that appears on the official record as written in the official file? **Box 5j** provides an illustration of this.

To set about answering such questions, the analyst has to start a long way back. It is no good approaching such complicated data as talk-in-interaction without a set of tools up to the job. Ordinary common sense is tempting, but will leave the analyst utterly unprepared for the sheer complexity of organisation of talk. Fortunately, conversation analysis has now built up – after about 40 years of effort since the pioneering work of the sociologist Harvey Sacks (his fascinating lectures have been reproduced as Sacks, 1992) – a collection of structures that we can identify in talk. The most basic, and the most revealing for the whole principle of conversation analysis' illumination of talk – is what is called the *adjacency pair*. The notion is that a speaker will, by launching something that very strongly projects a certain class of response (a question projects an answer, a request an acceptance), show the next speaker what they are both doing at the moment, and directing (or limiting) what the next speaker can do next. The next speaker is at liberty to respond appropriately or not; but if they do not (and that will be marked by hesitation, a pause and perhaps something like "well ...") then they will suffer – or exploit – the implications of doing so. Hence answering the question "Can you lend me that book?" with a brief pause and a "well ..." will mark the answer as not the expected one, and so economically signal that the answer is no.

Box 5j: The management of delicate questions

Charles Antaki, *Reader in Language and Social Psychology, Loughborough University*

One of the most powerful illustrations of conversational analysis' contribution to the field of social policy is its cool appraisal of what can actually happen in such professional–client encounters as assessments and interviews. The official record of these interactions is based on a complex exchange of questions, answers, observations and commentary, out of which the professional (psychologist, doctor, social worker) distils what he or she feels to be the essentials of the client's situation, state of mind or material circumstances. This goes on the record, and becomes an institutional fact.

Conversation analysis can look very closely at the record of what actually took place. Its findings may confirm that the interviewer's record was soundly based, or it may, as in the case below, throw up something that would make one pause. Consider this question and answer exchange, for example, which comes in a routine assessment of the 'quality of life' of a client with a learning difficulty.

The assessor has established that among J.O's 'recreational activities' are 'parties'. Now the assessment requires her to record how actively he participates in those events. This is the official question as printed on the assessment sheet:

Do you participate actively in those recreational activities? Usually, most of the time; Frequently, about half the time; Seldom or never.

This is how the interviewer (I) actually delivers it:

I   >so (when) you're at- when you're< at your↑ parties? (.4)
     what d'you↑do (.) (>'ve a b't of a<) (.4)have a >bit of a<↑drink do
     you?
JO   yeaéhh::
I   ëeh hehh hehh hehhhehh do you like↑your drink (.) John?=
JO   =yeah
I   heheh (.) what d'you↑drink?
JO   lager
I   heheheheh

Note that the question has been reduced to whether or not he has a drink, and has been cast in such a way as to expect (and get) a positive answer. Nevertheless, the score the interviewer records is that J.O. participates 'Frequently, about half the time'. This may or may not be an accurate guess at what he does at his parties, but it is based on a simplified question, put in a leading way.

We can collect more evidence to see if this is a general pattern, and speculate on why it happens. It seems to be a way of negotiating the routine problem any interviewer has: the dilemma of being literal (and true to the ideals of standardisation and reliability) or being flexible (and adjusting the question to suit the respondent's circumstances) (see Antaki, 2001). Interviewers can manage the dilemma by changing the question, and the way it is meant to be asked, so satisfying the interactional demand – but, at the same time, recording the answer as if it was to the official standard question, so satisfying the institutional one. Conversation analysis identifies the practice, and turns it over to the applied community for any action that it might see as appropriate.

To do this kind of thing one has to collect as good a record of what happened as possible, and then go through it, line by line, making as full a transcription as possible, and analysing it bearing in mind one's knowledge of conversational sequences and structures. Then one will see what the speakers are up to, and – as in this case – how the professional's institutional demands (to make an official record) interact with their conversational imperatives (to conduct the interaction sensibly). Whatever one will find will be based on the strong evidence of first-hand data, analysed by a set of well-developed theoretical tools.

A note on notation

Why all the squiggles? Simply to try and reproduce at least some of the music of ordinary speech. The printed sentence is an artificial, cleaned-up fiction that leaves out a great deal of what makes spoken language work. A pause, for example, between two words can be ... well, significant. And different pauses have different significances, hence the convention of measuring pauses in tenths of a second, as in (.4) or, when it is the briefest of hearable pauses, a simple (.). And to go through some other features of talk that probably carry some weight of meaning: speed (words between > and < are rapidly spoken); intonation (an up or down ↑ arrow signals that the next sound is higher or lower than the surrounding talk); emphasis (an underlined sound is louder than what surrounds it). The last feature that appears in the extract is the overlap between two speakers' words: that is signalled by the square brackets and the matching indentation of the lines. The point always is to try to approximate the actual sounds, because the sounds carry meaning. True, we can never capture sounds perfectly, but even an approximation can help.

Reference

Antaki, C. (2001) '"D'you like a drink?": dissembling language and the construction of an impoverished life', *Journal of Language and Social Psychology*, no 20, pp 196-213.

Basic as that is, it shows up conversation analysis' principle of looking very closely at talk – even down to the pauses and the hesitations. People do not use language carelessly, since it is the best way we have to make our business known to others, and we know that others will take what we say (and how we say it) as significant. That simple fact opens up a rich seam of social research. The business of social life is done in talk, and recording it and analysing it in detail will reveal the detail of how that business is conducted.

Questions for discussion

- Give an example of the kind of systematic regularity that conversation analysis has identified in talk. What would happen if someone flouted this regularity in an actual interaction?
- Pick any line of the extract and imagine it had been transcribed without any notation at all. What difference might it make to its interpretation, if any?

Reference

Sacks, H. (1992) *Lectures on conversation*, vols I and II, edited by G. Jefferson, Oxford: Basil Blackwell.

Further reading

Clayman, S. and Gill, V.T. (2004) 'Conversation analysis', in M. Hardy and A. Bryman (eds) *Handbook of data analysis*, London: Sage Publications, pp 589-606.

Hutchby, I. and Wooffitt, R. (1998) *Conversation analysis*, Cambridge: Polity Press.

Psathas, G. (1995) *Conversation analysis: The study of talk-in-interaction*, Thousand Oaks, CA: Sage Publications.

5.17 Narrative analysis

Brian Roberts, *Principal Lecturer in Sociology, University of Huddersfield*

Narrative analysis has increasingly been used in research in a broad range of social policy areas, including health and education (for example, Hatch and Wisniewski, 1995; Berger, 1997; Barnard et al, 2000; Crossley, 2000; Muller, 2001; Sparkes, 2002). It can also be considered to be part of a wider body of 'biographical work' (see Chamberlayne et al, 2000; Roberts, 2002). The study of narrative grew from literary and folklore studies, with connections to linguistics and psychology, and spread to other social studies around the late 1970s and early 1980s. The notion of *narrative* from its early usage has continued to be subject to differing definitions (Mitchell, 1981, p viv). This difficulty has persisted, as in the study of life accounts, with at one extreme some researchers applying a structural form where a narrative must have a number of key elements, while others have employed a looser notion, as a description of research procedure or merely as a general idea of people talking about their lives (Riessman, 1993, p 17).

There has also been much difficulty in separating narrative, narrative analysis, story and plot (see, Toolan, 1988; McQuillan, 2000; Abbott, 2002). Nevertheless, in the study of lives usually "scholars treat narratives as discrete units, with clear beginnings and endings, as detachable from surrounding discourses rather than as situated events" (Riessman, 1993, p 17). For Abbott, "Simply put, narrative is *the representation of an event or a series of events*", while, just as concisely, Denzin says narrative is "A story, having a plot and existence separate from life of teller" (Abbott, 2002, p 12; Denzin, 1989, p 48; see also McAdams, 1993; Sarbin, 1986). An influential distinction is provided by Polkinghorne who says stories "are concerned with human attempts to progress to a solution, clarification, or unraveling of an incomplete situation" whereas plots "function to select from the myriad of happenings those which are direct contributors to the terminal situation of the story" (Polkinghorne, 1995, pp 6-8; see also Bruner, 1986, 1990; Polkinghorne, 1988). Narrative analysis also draws attention to the 'timing' of experience in accounts. Ricoeur, in particular, has emphasised "the temporal implications of narrativity" and plot as "the intelligible whole that governs a succession of events in any story" (Ricoeur, 1981, p 167; see Polkinghorne, 1995, p 7; Roberts, 2002, pp 123-4). Riessman says we expect certain features (for example, a cast and concluding events) but narratives may be repetitive without a firm conclusion, or focus on certain types of past episodes and events which may have not taken place at all; but, there are various narrative forms (for example, the genres of romance, tragedy and so on) which, as readers, we recognise (Riessman, 1993, p 18). Narratives are relational (told and listened to) and reflect both how individuals see past events and what they intend to do (Muller, 2001, p 224).

There is no single method of narrative analysis of how individuals understand their lives; however, distinctions in narrative analysis can be made. For example, Polkinghorne (1995) makes an interesting contrast between 'analysis of narratives' (identifying themes across narratives) and 'narrative analysis' (with a focus on story or plot, for example, in case study), while a schema of types of narrative analysis has been offered by Lieblich et al, 1998. Narrative research, apart from ideas on 'narrative' from literary and cultural theory (see Toolan, 1988; Berger, 1997; McQuillan, 2000; Abbott, 2002), has also been associated with a broad range of theorisation – including, for example, interactionism, hermeneutics and psychosocial approaches (see Josselson and Lieblich, 1993; Andrews et al, 2000; Chamberlayne et al, 2000; Roberts, 2002).

A number of important methodological and conceptual issues surround narrative analysis and related forms of biographical work (see Roberts, 2002):

- *One case or many?:* while analysis of one life is interesting, should research concentrate on a number of cases as the basis for interpreting and generalising group experience (for example, of patients, family processes)?
- *Realism versus constructionism:* this complex question includes problems of truth and fact in accounts and whether the purpose of the narrative analysis is to gain the current perspective of the interviewed rather than an accurate record of past experience or events.
- *Alternative assessment criteria:* the preceding issues also relate to general questions of qualitative research: whether alternative criteria to the traditional 'scientific' ones of representativeness, validity and reliability, such as authenticity or plausibility should be used.
- *Fragmentation of data:* involves the question of breaking up a narrative/story by the researcher for analysis, including via computer programs, often for comparison with others. Does this not violate the uniqueness, wholeness and interrelatedness of the account?
- *Researcher's role:* many narrativists do not simply argue that interpretation and representation are inevitable in narrative accounts – but that the researchers should be explicit and reflective (as possible) on their own part in constructing and interpreting narratives.
- *The application of the narrative model:* relates to the comprehensiveness and interpretive use of the conceptions of narrative, story and plot: for example, do narrative schemas cover all utterances? How important are stories and story-telling in self-construction? How do stories change according to time and place?
- *Narrative materials:* these are usually transcribed texts of interviews (often on video) but can include a written account (and other material). Therefore, narrative materials may be very different forms of construction, be produced for other purposes and have very dissimilar types of 'subject–researcher– audience' relationship. In the case of the narrative interview itself it is held that the "inherently invasive nature of interviewing means that the narrative approach must place special emphasis upon the interaction between interviewee and interviewer" (Miller, 2000, p 129). In fact, interview procedures differ markedly among narrative researchers with some more 'programmatic' than others (in terms of 'openness', length/number of interviews or stages of interpretation) (see Atkinson, 1998; Jovchelovitch and Bauer, 2000; Wengraf 2001).
- *Individual narratives and social accounts:* this issue concerns the complex interplay between individual and group stories, metaphors, myths and so on and, also,

more general, 'popular' or ideological examples. One source of confusion here can be interchangeable use of the terms 'narrative' and 'discourse' to refer to both individual and broader group or societal accounts.

• Finally, there has been much discussion of *the importance of 'narrative' for social scientists:* whether it represents an important shift in epistemology and methodology at least as significant as other 'turns' (for example, linguistic, cultural, postmodern; see Stanley, 1994; Hinchman and Hinchman, 1997; Andrews et al, 2000; Chamberlayne et al, 2000; Denzin and Lincoln, 2000; Plummer, 2001; Riessman, 2002).

The prime objective of narrative research is to lay bare individual and/or group experience of social context and relationships according to notions of story, plot and time – and, additionally, often some generic or formic ideas such as tragedy, comedy, myth, or similar devices such as metaphor. While there are different types of narrative analysis, of course, there are general procedures as found in other forms of qualitative work – in interviewing, the stress on the complexity of the interviewed–interviewer–audience relation in the processes of interviewing/collecting, analysing/interpreting, and retelling to the audience (see Miller, 2000, p 130). A starting point for understanding and doing narrative analysis is to contrast it with other approaches. For Miller it differs from 'realist' and 'neo-positivist' approaches to biography – while these differ on theorisation (inductive, deductive) the narrative approach takes 'reality' as 'malleable and multiple' and has a concern for the social nature of the interviewed–interviewer interaction but, he adds, this does not mean that it "sees social reality as completely fluid" (Miller, 2000, p 130; see also Denzin and Lincoln, 2000).

Miller demonstrates these differences in assumptions and procedure with reference to a single case. A number of 'practical models' of narrative study, in relation to health and divorce, are considered by Riessman. So, for example, Riessman refers to: a study by Ginsburg of right-to-life and pro-choice abortion activists to compare plot lines and turning points; research by Bell of DES (diethylstilbestrol)-affected daughters using a structural approach to elements of narrative to understand politicisation (how knowledge was transformed to action in linked stories in the same interview by examining the core features of the stories, language or phrases: a textual approach); and Riessman's own study of divorce narratives using a 'poetic structural approach' (Riessman, 1993; see Riessman, 1990). Riessman says, "The first example explores the broad contours of a life story, the second the linked stories in a single interview, and the third the poetic features embedded in a personal narrative" (Riessman, 1993, p 25). Of course, some combination of these approaches could be made.

Various kinds of study (for example, on communal change and illness) have attempted to understand forms of narrative as both changing and interlinked in complex ways with broader, shifting cultural narratives (see Finnegan, 1998; Squire, 2000). Thus, individual narratives are not taken as simply set aside from cultural context. 'Psychosocial approaches', or other research which places narrative study in relation to wider systems of 'discourse' or institutional settings, have attempted such interconnections (Mumby, 1993; Andrews et al, 2000). However, a possible danger is that in analysis of individual narratives their content may become seen as mere expressions of the wider cultural ideologies, representations and so on. Often approaches may make clear that there can be 'non-verbalised' or 'unrecorded' aspects to narrative, and some writers concentrate more on the relation between conscious and unconscious aspects of accounts (Roberts, 2002, p 122; see Hollway and Jefferson, 2000).

The importance of the narrative analysis of lives for social policy research lies in a focus on individual and shared accounts of daily experiences (of clients or practitioners) and responses to significant life changes (for instance, in health or education) and provision of informal and formal services (see Muller, 2001). **Box 5k** gives an example of the use of narrative analysis in this kind of context.

Question for discussion

* How important are 'stories' or 'the telling of stories' to each other for making sense of daily life experience in the family, work or other contexts?

References

Abbott, H.P. (2002) *The Cambridge introduction to narrative*, Cambridge: Cambridge University Press.

Andrews, M., Day Sclater, S., Squire, C. and Treacher, A. (eds) (2000) *Lines of narrative: Psychosocial perspectives*, London: Routledge.

Atkinson, R. (1998) *The life story interview*, London: Sage Publications.

Barnard, D., Towers, A., Boston, P. and Lambrinidou, Y. (2000) *Crossing over: Narratives of palliative care*, Oxford: Oxford University Press.

Berger, A.A. (1997) *Narratives in popular culture, media and everyday life*, London: Sage Publications.

Bruner, J. (1986) *Actual minds, possible worlds*, Cambridge, MA: Harvard University Press.

Bruner, J. (1990) *Acts of meaning*, Cambridge, MA: Harvard University Press.

Chamberlayne, P., Bornat, J. and Wengraf, T. (eds) (2000) *The turn to biographical methods in social science*, London: Routledge.

Crossley, M. (2000) *Introducing narrative psychology: Self, trauma and the construction of meaning*, Buckingham: Open University Press.

Denzin, N.K. (1989) *Interpretive biography*, London: Sage Publications.

Denzin, N.K. and Lincoln, Y.S. (eds) (2000) *Handbook of qualitative research* (2nd edn), London: Sage Publications.

Finnegan, R. (1998) *Tales of the city: A study of narrative and urban life*, Cambridge: Cambridge University Press.

Hatch, J.A. and Wisniewski, R. (eds) (1995) *Life history and narrative*, London: Falmer.

Hinchman, L.P. and Hinchman, S.K. (eds) (1997) *Memory, identity, community: The idea of narrative in the human sciences*, Albany, NY: State University of New York Press.

Hollway, W. and Jefferson, T. (2000) *Doing qualitative research differently*, London: Sage Publications.

Josselson, R. and Lieblich, A. (eds) (1993) *The narrative study of lives 1*, London: Sage Publications.

Jovchelovitch, S. and Bauer, M.W. (2000) 'Narrative interviewing', in M.W. Bauer and G. Gaskell (eds) *Qualitative research with text, image and sound*, London: Sage Publications, pp 57-74.

Lieblich, A., Tuval-Mashiach, R. and Zilber, T. (1998) *Narrative research*, London: Sage Publications.

McAdams, D.P. (1993) *The stories we live by: Personal myths and the making of the self*, New York, NY: Guilford Press.

McQuillan, M. (2000) 'Introduction: aporias of writing: narrative and subjectivity', in M. McQuillan (ed) *The narrative reader*, London: Routledge, pp 1-33.

Miller, R.L. (2000) *Researching life stories and family histories*, London: Sage Publications.

Mitchell, W.J.T. (ed) (1981) *On narrative*, Chicago, IL: University of Chicago Press.

Muller, J.H. (2001) 'Narrative approaches to qualitative research in primary care', in B.F. Crabtree and W.L. Miller (eds) *Doing qualitative research* (2nd edn), London: Sage Publications, pp 221-38.

Mumby, D.K. (ed) (1993) *Narrative and social control*, London: Sage Publications.

Plummer, K. (2001) *Documents of life 2*, London: Sage Publications.

Polkinghorne, D.E. (1988) *Narrative knowing and the human sciences*, Albany, NY: State University of New York.

Polkinghorne, D.E. (1995) 'Narrative configuration in qualitative analysis', in J.A. Hatch and R. Wisniewski (eds) (1995) *Life history and narrative*, London: Falmer, pp 5-23.

Riessman, C.K. (1990) *Divorce talk*, New Brunswick, NJ: Rutgers University Press.

Riessman, C.K. (1993) *Narrative analysis*, London: Sage Publications.

Riessman, C.K. (2002) 'Analysis of personal narratives', in J.F. Gubrium and J.A. Holstein (eds) *Handbook of interview research*, London: Sage Publications, pp 695-710.

Ricoeur, P. (1981) 'Narrative time', in W.J.T. Mitchell (ed) *On narrative*, Chicago, IL: University of Chicago Press, pp 165-86.

Roberts, B. (2002) *Biographical research*, Buckingham: Open University Press.

Sarbin, T. (ed) (1986) *Narrative psychology: The storied nature of human conduct*, New York, NY: Praeger.

Smith, B. and Sparkes, A.C. (2002) 'Men, sport, spinal cord injury and the construction of coherence: narrative practice in action', *Qualitative Research*, vol 2, no 2, pp 143-71.

Sparkes, A.C. (1999) 'Exploring body narratives', *Sport, Education and Society*, vol 4, no 1, pp 17-30.

Sparkes, A.C. (2002) *Telling tales in sport and physical activity: A qualitative journey*, Campaign, IL: Human Kinetics.

Sparkes, A.C. and Smith, B. (2002) 'Sport, spinal cord injury, embodied masculinities, and the dilemmas of narrative identity', *Men and Masculinities*, vol 4, no 3, pp 258-85.

Squire, C. (2000) 'Situated selves, the coming-out of genre and equivalent citizenship in narratives of HIV', in P. Chamberlayne, J. Bornat and T. Wengraf (eds) *The turn to biographical methods in social science*, London: Routledge, pp 196-213.

Stanley, L. (1994) 'Introduction: lives and works and auto/biographical occasions', *Auto/Biography*, vol 3, no 1/2, pp i-ii.

Toolan, M.J. (1988) *Narrative: A critical linguistic introduction*, London: Routledge.

Wengraf, T. (2001) *Qualitative research interviewing: Biographic narrative and semi-structured methods*, London: Sage Publications.

Further reading

Cortazzi, M. (1993) *Narrative analysis*, London: Falmer Press.

Mishler, E.G. (1986) *Research interviewing: Context and narrative*, Cambridge, MA: Harvard University Press.

Riessman, C.K. (1993) *Narrative analysis*, London: Sage Publications.

Box 5k: Narrative analysis in action

Brian Roberts, *Principal Lecturer in Sociology, University of Huddersfield*

Smith and Sparkes (2002) examined the life history interviews of two men – 'Paul' and 'David' – who have suffered spinal cord injury (SCI) through playing sport (Rugby Union). Smith and Sparkes are interested in how 'coherence is constructed' through 'narrative practices' and shaped by 'conventions' in the story telling – with reference to body–self relations and sporting and other pursuits. It is argued that, coherence is not simply a given feature of narrative but is 'artfully crafted' in the telling and utilised from the meanings, linkages and structures shaping stories. The report is part of a wider study of 40 life stories of men who had SCI and defined themselves as disabled. The men's injury was a destabilising and severe event and a significant biographical moment.

Smith and Sparkes began to consider how the men were re-establishing coherence while telling their differing stories; the authors argue that the construction of a coherent life story is understandable only following the narration of the body–self's 'fragmentation' and 'multiplicity' (p 167). They decided to use a variety of forms of analyses to reflect the complexity of experience in the told stories. They found:

> ... with regard to the construction of certain kinds of masculinities through their involvement in aggressive, contact sports like rugby football union ... the experiences of many men faced with major disruptive life events are framed by their relationships towards, and investments in, a disciplined and dominating body.... (p 151)

This body type – formerly held by their respondents – remained even though they were disabled: it had an 'elective affinity' to a 'restitution narrative' (recovery). The finding reflects notions in western societies, especially within sporting activities, regarding health. A capable body is a desired, 'normal' condition – and keen efforts are made to repair it following injury. However, some men had moved from the restitution narrative to a 'quest narrative' where suffering was to be recognised and challenged and disability used (pp 151-2).

Paul was asked what meanings his body had for him. His reply, in a long interview extract, showed various 'narrative shifts' or differing identities, voices and perspectives. Paul also makes 'narrative linkages' that enable him to shape and deliver a story through the connection and contrast of events and objects to produce meaning (p 155). He shifted between 'modalities of body dys-appearance':

> The body as *self*-observed: "I focus on parts of the body and see how useless they are, like my hands".

> The body of *self* as experienced in the modality of appreciation: "All I have to do is look at the lads and its sets off again".

> The body of *self* as observed by the glance of the *other*: "But what does piss me off and which gets me down are the people, stares...."

Paul employed these modalities of body experience to connect his 'ontological narrative' – his personal story – to a 'restitution narrative'. He says that his disability is "something that will be fixed" (p 155). Smith and Sparkes conclude that by the use of linkages, shifts, editing and control in narrative formation, Paul is able to "story" "a dynamic and contradictory process of loss, sustainment, continuity and development in relation to disabled and non-disabled aspects of self" and "masculine hierarchies" (p 159).

Reference

Smith, B. and Sparkes, A.C. (2002) 'Men, sport, spinal cord injury and the construction of coherence: narrative practice in action', *Qualitative research*, vol 2, no 2, pp 143-71.

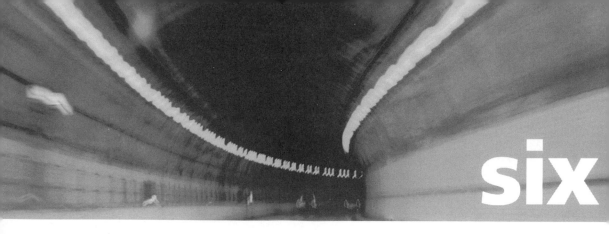

six

Managing social policy research

Detailed contents

6.1 Introduction

To make a judgement as to whether any piece of social policy research has been conducted rigorously requires us to know about how that research was designed and carried out, how data were collected and analysed, and how the conclusions were reached. In this chapter we want to add another indicator of *good* policy research – *the quality and effectiveness of the research management process*. How the research cycle is managed, how it safeguards the safety and integrity of both researchers and respondents, and how it is conducted to high ethical standards, are important indicators of good quality and effectively managed policy research.

There are many aspects of the *research cycle* outlined in Chapter One, Section 1.6 and Figure 11 that require *effective management*. These include the need to manage:

- the ethical context for research (which includes *codes of ethics* which define the moral context of doing research and *research governance* which relates to the specified regulations and standards that should be adhered to);
- the methods used and stages of research, including data collection and analysis;
- the research staff;
- the safety of researchers and respondents;
- confidentiality issues;
- the protection of respondents and the data collected about them;
- the budget and resources for the study and the time available to conduct it;
- the requirements and constraints imposed by the funders of the research.

In this chapter we focus on each of these areas in turn. We discuss why it is important to manage these aspects of the research process, and we offer some guidance as to how to go about making effective management of research a reality.

6.2 The effective management of policy research

Issues of research *management* are rarely discussed in research methods texts. Books generally refer to issues of methodology, research design, research methods, and so on, but few discuss explicitly matters concerned with the *management of the research process* or the implications for the research (and the trustworthiness of the findings and conclusions reached) where management has been poor or ineffective. A distinction can be made between the day-today running of a research project and the activity that research funders undertake as part of the monitoring of a project. Our primary concern here is with the former rather than the latter.

Whether a piece of policy research has been managed effectively is an important indicator of the overall *quality* of that research. Just as research-based texts need to have a discussion of methodological and design issues, and of data collection and analysis techniques, they also need to refer explicitly to specific issues around the management of the research process, including providing details of the ways in which the research has been conducted to ethical standards, how researchers (and respondents) have been kept safe from harm, how data are protected, how the study has been conducted within a budget and to a planned timetable, and how research has met the requirements (and constraints) of funders – be they charitable foundations, large- or small-scale organisations or government departments. These are the concerns of this chapter.

Being systematic

In Chapter One we saw that to count as research an enquiry must be carried out in a systematic and rigorous way and conducted to the highest ethical and procedural standards within the limitations imposed through time, money and opportunity (Figures 1b and 1c, Chapter One). Arber (1993, p 33) reminds us that "You need to adopt a systematic and logical approach to research, the key to which is the planning and management of your time". Planning and managing time and resources, and anticipating the next stages of the research process (and potential difficulties), are key to managing the 'doing' stage of policy research (see Figure 1l). It is critical to plan ahead, to establish the procedures and working practices necessary to ensure that the research progresses smoothly and systematically, both to plan and to budget, and within an ethical framework that respects the integrity of both respondents and researchers, that keeps them safe, and that keeps the information collected secure and confidential.

All stages of the research process modelled in Figure 1l need systematic and effective management, from the *cognitive phase* through to *dissemination* and *change*. Careful planning, ongoing monitoring of progress against a research plan and budget, and always anticipating and preparing in advance for the next phase of the research cycle, are central to effective management. This management function can be overseen by a director of research who may take an instrumental lead, but it is also a function which needs to be undertaken by *all* those working on a research project – including researchers and those involved in administrative and technical support (for example, secretarial staff, data coders, transcribers, computer staff, and so on). This requires each person involved in an investigation not only to plan and monitor their own work, but also to work together to ensure that all aspects of the project 'fit' together, and that each phase of the study progresses according to intention or to plan. Additionally, staff must be kept safe, motivated and supervised adequately; researchers must ensure that data are collected, analysed and stored in ways which are safe, secure and confidential; all staff must be mindful of the budget and timetable. The whole project must be conducted to ethical codes designed to protect and safeguard the integrity of all parties – respondents, researchers, research organisations, funders and users of research, including policy makers and professionals.

Until research management is given a higher priority in published research methods texts, it is unlikely that the research reported in books and journals will include a full discussion of *which* aspects of the research process were managed, and *how*. An absence of this discussion in published research raises an important issue concerning the *reading* of these texts, and the *interpretation* of whether a particular study has been conducted to high ethical, methodological and procedural standards. Put simply, how can we know that a study has been conducted to these high standards if we are not given the necessary information on which to make that judgement? Moreover, can we say that a study is robust and sound when there is little, if any, evidence that it was managed effectively to high ethical and procedural standards (for example, where there appears to be no informed consent by respondents to take part in the study, or where the safety of researchers and respondents was severely compromised, or where data were poorly protected)? Should we value the *findings* of research above all else – regardless of the *process* by which that research was conducted and managed?

In the sections that follow we focus on a number of aspects of the research process that require effective management. These are meant to be illustrative rather than exhaustive – there are many other aspects of the research process, outlined in the preceding chapters, which will require careful management. In focusing on the specific issues covered here, we hope to alert the reader to the need to manage the research process effectively in order for that research to be robust and trustworthy, and especially where the research may be used as *evidence* to inform, and to influence, both policy and practice.

Questions for discussion

- Why is it important that the research process should be managed effectively?
- How should a poorly managed project, which took little account of safety and confidentiality issues, but which nonetheless delivered research findings on time, be judged?

References

Arber, S. (1993) 'The research process', in N. Gilbert (ed) *Researching social life*, London: Sage Publications, pp 32-50.

6.3 Codes of ethics

Many professional and occupational groups in society have *codes of ethics* that are meant to influence the behaviour of their members in a way that is consistent with ethically acceptable practices. As such, these codes would not seem to be contentious but in fact they may be so: some members of a profession may feel that having been trained in the ethos of their profession it should be taken as a matter of trust that they will behave ethically – they have absorbed and accepted their professional obligations and do not need to be dictated to. In an academic context, ethical codes could be construed as being inconsistent with the principle of academic autonomy. On the other hand, ethical codes may be deemed to be helpful to practitioners and the professions themselves. For the former, ethical codes may provide a source for helping to resolve ethical dilemmas and uncertainties and therefore as a means of rationalising how they are resolved; for the profession, a code can represent a way of demonstrating to society at large its credibility and good intentions. The Department of Health's (2001) *Research governance framework for health and social care* identifies key principles and defines the responsibilities of the various parties involved in health and social care research (see **Box 6a**). Research governance is concerned with the regulations and standards that need to be observed when research is carried out. Codes of ethics provide the ethical and moral context for that research.

Box 6a: Research governance framework for health and social care

Jan Pahl, *Professor of Social Policy, University of Kent*

The term *research governance* means the regulations and standards that surround the research process. More specifically, it refers to the *Research governance framework for health and social care*, which was published by the Department of Health in 2001. Because the Department of Health has responsibility for research across a wide span of interest, drawing on the expertise of researchers in both the social sciences and the natural sciences, the *Research governance framework* is likely to have considerable influence on policy and practice in social policy research.

The *Research governance framework* spells out a set of principles and defines the responsibilities of different parties. It aims to promote improvements in the standards of research, to reduce bad practice and to increase public confidence in research. These aims were to be secured by the achievement of key standards, organised into the following domains:

- *Ethics:* ensuring the dignity, rights, safety and wellbeing of research participants, and, where relevant, their involvement in the research process.
- *Science:* ensuring that the design and conduct of the research, and the nature of its findings, are subject to independent review by relevant experts.
- *Information:* providing full and free public access to information on the research and its findings, but protecting intellectual property rights and the confidentiality of data about individuals.
- *Health and safety:* ensuring at all times the safety of participants, research workers and other staff involved in the research.
- *Finance:* ensuring financial probity and compliance with the law and compensation for those suffering harm.

The *Research governance framework* is underpinned by a set of useful principles. These include:

- *Transparency:* that there exist visible and transparent decision-making processes, operating independently of the interests of key stakeholders.
- *Indivisibility:* that there is a single identified agent able to answer for the discharge of a particular duty or responsibility.
- *Checks and balances:* that the different areas of responsibility are discharged with agents with different areas of interest.
- *Enactability:* that those charged with particular responsibilities have the expertise, experience, time and resources to discharge them effectively.
- *Accountability:* that there is a system for monitoring the performance of those given key responsibilities and for calling them to account should they not discharge them.

The *Research governance framework* identifies the key actors in the research process and delineates their different responsibilities. These include:

- *Funders who support research*, ranging from large national bodies to smaller and more local organisations.
- *Reviewers of research proposals*, who may be concerned with the aims and methods of the proposal, or with the ethics of what is proposed.
- *Research employers*, or the organisations that employ those responsible for carrying out research.

- *Researchers*, including grant holders or principal investigators, researchers and support staff.

Good research governance aims to promote a research culture that is characterised by the promotion of excellence, by high standards of personal and scientific integrity, and by respect for diversity and for those who take part in research.

Reference

DoH (Department of Health) (2001) *Research governance framework for health and social care*, London: DoH.

Website resource

Department of Health and the Research Governance Framework: http://www.doh.gov.uk/research/rd1/researchgovernance/researchgovindex.htm

Many of the main disciplines in the social sciences have ethical codes that are meant to influence how research is conducted. The first code of ethics for social scientists was that of the American Psychological Association in 1953 (Sieber, 2004). The Social Policy Association (SPA), the professional group that is closest to the field covered in this volume, has no such code. It is not alone in this respect since other academic groups, such as the British Academy of Management, do not have one either.

Ethical codes are meant to provide guidelines concerning proper ethical practice. They tend to be fairly general so that they can be relevant to a diversity of situations. They also tend to be reviewed fairly regularly, since changes in social values or the arrival of new technologies may require a revision of the recommendations. Ethical codes help to protect both the researcher and the researched. Researchers are protected, for example, because they can fall back on a code of ethics if they are asked to do research they judge to be ethically unjustifiable. Research respondents are protected because codes invariably make reference to some of the principles outlined in Section 6.7, such as protecting privacy, ensuring research participants are given informed consent (see also **Box 3j**, Chapter Three), and making sure that no harm comes to them. Issues such as these are covered by codes such as the British Sociological Association (BSA) *Statement of ethical practice*, which bring out some of the ethical problems that sociologists are likely to face and some precepts that should influence their thinking, most of which are equally applicable to social policy researchers. Like most ethical codes, the BSA *Statement* is very negative about *covert* methods of research, such as covert observation, since they cannot involve informed consent and are likely to be invasions of privacy. On the other hand, as Bryman (2004, p 512) observes, it does not entirely close the door on covert research in sociology and social policy, because there is a recognition that such research may solve problems of highly restricted access to certain groups or organisations. However, in social care and healthcare research it is highly unlikely that covert research would be acceptable given the requirement for research proposals to go before ethical review committees, and the governance framework outlined in **Box 6a**.

Ethical codes, therefore, are not entirely unambiguous in their advice; nor do they have the force of law, although it is conceivable that severe transgressions might result in censure, such as expulsion from a learned society or even difficulty in obtaining a job. However, these forms of censure could feasibly ensue without a code of ethics, although the rationale for expulsion might be difficult to justify without such a code. It is also important to realise that if someone is doing social policy research under the auspices of an institution, such as a university, it too may well have its own code of ethics. These are usually strongly influenced by professional associations' codes. Indeed, in many cases, researchers may not be able to do research on humans (or perhaps certain kinds of research) without approval by a committee or review board to which a proposal for research must be sent for ethical clearance. Flagrantly ignoring codes of ethics at this institutional level could plausibly result in concrete forms of censure, such as termination of employment or a studentship. Consequently, social policy researchers need to be attuned to the ethics codes at the institutional level and those of neighbouring disciplines like sociology, even though the SPA does not have a code of its own.

Questions for discussion

- What part should codes of ethics play in influencing the conduct of social policy research?
- Look at the codes of ethics of a number of organisations, including the Social Research Association and British Sociological Association. What do they have in common? How do they differ? (The websites for these organisations can be found in the Electronic sources section below.)

References

Bryman, A. (2004) *Social research methods* (2nd edn), Oxford: Oxford University Press.

DoH (Department of Health) (2001) *Research governance framework for health and social care*, London: DoH.

Sieber, J. (2004) 'Ethical codes', in M. Lewis-Beck, A. Bryman and T. Futing Liao (eds) *The SAGE encyclopaedia of social science research methods*, Thousand Oaks, CA: Sage Publications, pp 321-2.

Further reading

BPS (British Psychological Society) (2000) *Code of conduct, ethical principles and guidelines*, Leicester: BPS.

Brown, L. (1997) 'Ethics in psychology: cui bono?', in D. Fox and I. Prilleltensky (eds) *Critical psychology: An introduction*, London: Sage Publications, pp 51-67.

Bryman, A. (2001) *Social research methods*, Oxford: Oxford University Press, Chapter 24.

BSA (British Sociological Association) (2000) *Statement of ethical practice*, Durham: BSA.

Butler, I. (2002) 'Critical commentary: a code of ethics for social work and social care research', *British Journal of Social Work*, vol 32, no 2, pp 239-48.

Davis, M. (1991) 'Thinking like an engineer: the place of a code of ethics in the practice of a profession', *Philosophy and Public Affairs*, vol 20, pp 150-67 (also available at: www.iit.edu/departments/csep/publication/md.html).

Glendinning, C. and McKie, L. (2003) 'BSA working in partnership with SPA: ethics in social research', *Network: Newsletter of the British Sociological Association*, no 85, pp 15-16.

Lewis, J. (2002) 'Research and development in social care: governance and good practice', *Research Policy and Planning*, vol 20, no 1, pp 3-10.

SRS (Social Research Association) (2002) *Professional and ethical codes for research*, London: SRA.

Website resources

The British Sociological Association *Statement of ethical practice* can be found at: www.britsoc.org.uk/about/ethic.htm

Another relevant code of ethics for social policy researchers is that of the Social Research Association: www.the-sra.org.uk/Ethicals.htm

The following website contains, and has links with, many useful discussions of codes of ethics, as well as including many professional statements: www.iit.edu/departments/csep/PublicWWW/codes/codes.html

The Department of Health's *Research governance framework*: http://www.doh.gov.uk/research/documents/rd3/rgf2ndeditionv22300403.doc

6.4 Managing particular research methods

In addition to general issues to do with the management of social policy research that are covered in this chapter, each research *method* brings with it a distinctive cluster of issues to do with their management that need to be borne in mind. It is not possible to cover every possible kind of contingency that relates to every research method but in this section we try to bring out some relevant points.

With *survey* research based on structured interviews (face-to-face or telephone), or postal or Internet questionnaires, an important consideration once the final sample has been designed is keeping track of who replies and who does not. All surveys of this kind result in non-response. This is a problem for researchers because it means that even if they have sampled randomly, they are likely to end up with a sample that is less representative than it might otherwise have been because those who decline may differ from those that do not. If the level of non-response can be kept low, there is a greater chance that the sample's representativeness will be less adversely affected. In the case of postal and Internet questionnaire surveys, response rates are often very low so it is especially important to boost responses as far as possible. One way of doing this is to follow up respondents who have not replied. To do this the researcher will need to have some kind of identifying code on the questionnaire that will allow them to identify who has replied (and by implication, who has not). Many survey researchers follow up non-respondents after two to three weeks and again two to three weeks after that. This all means that the researcher needs to keep good records of returns.

A further issue with *quantitative* research is to think about issues of data analysis early on. It is tempting to leave this phase until all the data are in but researchers need to think about what kinds of data they are likely to end up with as a consequence of asking questions in a certain way and what kinds of analysis can be performed on them. Also, researchers need to be familiar with the kinds of statistical tools they can use so that they are not having to learn them at the last minute – when deadlines are possibly tight. An issue related to this is that researchers need to be familiar with the statistical software that they are going to use before the data begin to come in. This point applies as well to qualitative researchers who intend to use a computer-assisted qualitative data analysis package. It is not a good idea to have to learn new software at the last minute when the researcher may be in a rush.

With *qualitative* research methods such as semi-structured and unstructured interviewing and focus groups, the standard advice is to record interviews and transcribe them. Two points stand out here. First, an interviewer needs to make sure that the recording hardware is up to the task in terms of the quality of the microphone and the recording quality of the machine, the batteries, and the possible intrusion of external noise. In this respect, it is always a good idea to test out the equipment first. Also, the researcher needs to be prepared for the possibility that one or two interviewees will decline to be recorded, so that it is necessary to go prepared with a notepad to take notes. Second, researchers should not underestimate how long transcription takes and the volume of paper it generates. A rule of thumb is to allow six hours of transcription for one hour of interview. Ten one-hour interviews mean sixty hours of transcription. However, if an interview is of limited value, it may be wise to transcribe just portions of the interview. Because a large volume of paper is quickly built up by a lot of transcription, it is probably best to begin analysis (coding) of the data as soon as possible to offset the feeling of being overwhelmed by the data and so that if the analysis suggests new leads, these can be followed up while the fieldwork is ongoing.

In the case of *ethnography*, it is crucial to keep a record, often referred to as *fieldnotes*, concerning observations and conversations. These need to be written up as soon as possible, so that key points and reflections are not forgotten, but preferably not in a way that will draw attention to the researcher so that people begin to feel self-conscious about being observed or drawn into conversations. Fieldnotes should be as comprehensive as possible since they are likely to be the ethnographer's main source of data and can even be submitted to analysis through a computer software program.

Surveys employing a *longitudinal design* pose particular management issues to do with keeping respondent attrition to a minimum. With panel designs people may become tired of being regularly interviewed and need to be persuaded to continue their participation (birthday and seasons greetings cards can help in this regard), but also keeping track of new members (children and new partners) and departing members (due to death or marriage break-up) of households needs to be borne in mind. With cohort studies, where there may be several years between interviews, keeping track becomes especially crucial so that members of the cohort are not lost forever to the study when they move home or where other changes take place.

Question for discussion

- Identify some of the main elements that require effective management when conducting: (a) a large postal questionnaire survey; (b) a panel study; and (c) research using semi-structured interviews.

6.5 Managing policy researchers

Bruce Stafford *and* Sue Middleton, *Directors, Centre for Research in Social Policy, Loughborough University*

Research managers seeking to manage staff effectively and efficiently need to follow 'best practice' in human resource management. Having explicit policies on recruitment and selection, staff development, disciplinary procedures, and so on is essential to assure sponsors of the delivery of high quality research outputs, and staff of the fairness and transparency of working practices. It is recognised that such issues are unlikely to impinge on readers of this book who are students. However, an appreciation of such issues is important nonetheless since students need to understand how research is actually conducted and researchers may want some guidance on what is *good practice* in this area.

As in any other business, recruitment and selection procedures should comply with relevant legislation and guidance on equal opportunities. Each post should have a written job description and person specification. Newly recruited staff should receive an induction package that includes guidance on how the organisation works (the office handbook), a mentor and a probation adviser. The mentor aids the integration of the recruit into the community of the research centre, and, most importantly, provides advice and 'on-the-job' training as and when required, and acts as representative for the person if work-related problems arise. The probation adviser will agree work tasks and targets with the individual, and will ultimately recommend to senior managers whether the person's performance warrants confirmation of his or her appointment. Accordingly, the adviser and the probationer should have regular meetings that are minuted and evidence of the latter's performance should be systematically recorded. Sometimes it may be necessary to extend a probationary period for, say, six months in order to collate sufficient evidence of a person's overall performance.

Existing staff will need to renew their intellectual capital and acquire new skills and knowledge in order to effectively and efficiently perform their duties. This cannot be left to chance or done in an ad hoc way. Various staff development schemes and procedures are available and managers must adopt and tailor those that are most suited to the ethos of their organisation. Managers must decide on the extent to which they wish to separate or conflate staff and career development with the appraisal of staff performance. Typically, staff development systems will involve a competency-based assessment of training needs and regular reviews and appraisals. Staff development procedures must also apply to managers.

Social research centres can adopt a team approach to doing research. Managers must select project leaders and team members on the basis of staff:

- competencies and confidence levels;
- past experience in this specific research area and for a particular sponsor; and
- seniority.

Managers must provide intellectual and project leadership and motivate staff once a team is established. This involves maintaining people's intellectual curiosity; setting a timetable with milestones and monitoring work performance; sharing knowledge; providing on-the-job training, personal support and encouragement; and ensuring health and safety, and confidentiality, requirements are met (for a full discussion of the need to ensure the safety of researchers and the confidentiality of data, see Sections 6.6 and 6.7). Motivating staff can entail highlighting the intellectual issues underpinning a project, the principal challenges of the research design, the significance of the study in terms of its potential impact on policy and practice and/or disciplinary knowledge. Different staff will be motivated by different factors.

Managers will want to retain committed and productive researchers. Fixed-term contracts (whereby a person's employment is tied to a specific research project for a limited period of time) mean that staff, concerned about their job prospects, may leave a study before it is completed, often to the detriment of the investigation. Yet the anarchic fixed-term contract pervades the social research community, notably in universities. In addition, job retention can be fostered by adopting progressive family-friendly policies and, when appropriate, managers being proactive in encouraging staff to seek promotion, accelerated increments and lump-sum payments.

However, there are occasions when disciplinary procedures have to be involved. If performance-related they could escalate through informal meetings to formal oral, then written warnings and, even, dismissal. A serious breach of conduct might justify jumping some stages. Managers should involve, if available, personnel services at an early stage and a written record of all actions and documents must be kept.

The above discussion focuses on research staff, but in a research centre, complementary policies and practices are required for secretarial and administrative staff. Similarly, the discussion assumes that the researchers are in the managers' own organisation. However, sometimes research is conducted by consortia, which involve subcontracts. Having clear lines of accountability for the management of staff both within and across organisations is vital if timely, high quality, research is to be achieved.

The management of research and support staff is not an optional extra. Sponsors of social research should be more proactive and require research centres to demonstrate that the researchers are managed to the highest standards. Moreover, as we shall see in the next sections, it is also vital that research staff are kept safe in their work, and that research respects the confidentiality of respondents. Again, managers, and research sponsors, need to be fully aware of their responsibilities in these respects.

Question for discussion

• What steps would you take to deal with a researcher on probation whose work was unsatisfactory? What would you say to him/her?

Website resources

Higher Education Staff Development Agency: www.hesda.org.uk/
Investors in People in Higher Education: www.lboro.ac.uk/service/sd/iipinhe/
 iipinhe.htm
www.iipuk.co.uk/
Research careers initiative/contract research staff concordat and other materials
 from Universities UK: www.universitiesuk.ac.uk/activities/RCIdownloads/
 rci_final.pdf
Mentoring guidelines: http://wendwell.co.uk/Resources/Mentor%20Guides.htm
www.sussex.ac.uk/Units/staffing/staffdev/policies/mentor.html

6.6 Managing safety in policy research

Gary Craig, *Professor of Social Justice, University of Hull*

Safety is an issue of growing importance for many people, both individually and professionally, as the disappearance of the estate agent Suzie Lamplugh (Suzie Lamplugh Trust, 1999) and the racist murder of Stephen Lawrence demonstrate. Issues of community safety (Alcock et al, 1999) have achieved recent prominence and *Community Care* magazine ran a special campaign throughout 1999 that focused on the issue of violence to social work staff. Professions which require individuals to be alone in the normal course of their duties, such as social security officials, have developed guidance and protective measures to help staff avoid dangerous or compromising situations. In the case of social work and education, guidance has addressed members' fears of having allegations of abuse made against them.

 Social policy research often also requires researchers to work on their own, and qualitative social research with individual respondents in particular characteristically involves one-to-one relationships, typically conducted in situations of privacy. Until fairly recently, however, despite small-scale initiatives, and a limited literature on the subject (Arksey and Knight, 1999; Paterson et al, 1999), there has been no consolidated guidance for the safety of social researchers.

Safety is now, however, a pressing issue for research units, research managers and for the researchers themselves, who are frequently sent alone into potentially dangerous situations. An exploration of the issue in 2000 identified quite unpredictable events – such as the case of a lone researcher visiting a bedridden respondent who drew a revolver on him – and suggested that the issue of safety was shared by cognate professional groupings such as GPs and other health professionals (Sandell, 1998), and others whose members work alone, such as political party canvassers. It also demonstrated that the scope of safety issues was very wide, going way beyond ensuring the personal safety of individual researchers conducting fieldwork. It indicated that the boundary between safety and ethics is, at times, a blurred one and that the boundaries of 'safety' itself need to be thought of flexibly. One researcher, for example, conducted a study with respondents about subjects potentially distressing for both respondents and researchers. This study provided counselling support for researchers, the mental health of the researcher being regarded as a legitimate aspect of their general safety.

The interest generated by this exploration led to a small group devising a code of safety for social researchers for the Social Research Association (SRA)[1]. The following section briefly raises the key issues elaborated within this code.

The main focus of safety in relation to a social researcher might be thought to be with the researcher's own needs. However, there are other parties for whom researcher safety is important. Researchers are, generally, employees; and employers (usually universities or research institutes), under both UK and European legislation, have a general 'duty of care' to employees. There are, nevertheless, situations arising in the context of social research, where this responsibility might be contested. How far does this duty of care extend to a researcher conducting interviews on the street at night in a 'foreign' town, on his/her own? What might be regarded as reasonable precautions? Who should be responsible for taking them?

Although a university personnel office might legally stand as the employer, this duty of care would normally revert to the research manager – the head of a unit or a particular budget holder (see Section 6.5). However, despite the existence of a code of safety, brought to the attention of a researcher as part of

---

[1] The team devising the Code of Safety comprised Gary Craig (University of Hull), Anne Corden and Trish Thornton (both University of York); the code can be accessed at www.the-sra.org.uk

the contractual framework within which they work, how much control can a manager reasonably exercise over a researcher during fieldwork? Where do contractual liabilities cease? For example, a fieldworker may have to stay overnight in a hotel – who chooses these hotels and on what basis? Managers can put safety provisos in place – for example clear procedures for ongoing reporting back, monitoring incidents, written guidelines and the provision of safety aids – but they cannot be on the 'fieldwork spot' all the time. And when does fieldwork start and finish? Many universities appear not to have insurance policies which cover the use of private cars travelling to and from work; yet the use of a private car may be the only transport option – or the only safe one – open to researchers in remote or potentially dangerous contexts. Who, then, is responsible for meeting the costs of damage in the event of an accident or of violence done to the vehicle? And, are researchers insured for personal injury in all situations related to the conduct of fieldwork?

These issues become more critical where researchers are studying phenomena on or beyond the boundaries of criminality, working with higher risk groups such as ex-offenders or those with a history of psychological disturbance, or exploring issues where the threat of violence is greater – for example, working across sectarian divides, or studying homophobic violence. The effects of actual or threatened violence on a researcher may be traumatic. Is it the responsibility of employers to ensure that suitable debriefing or therapeutic help should be available after such incidents? How many research units have access to such professional help?

It is equally necessary to consider safety from the perspective of research respondents. Ethical guidelines developed by professional bodies (see Chapter Three, Section 3.14, and Chapter Six, Section 6.3) remind researchers of the need to protect respondents' interests through respecting their privacy, the confidentiality of data collection, ensuring informed consent and by being alert to the possibilities of harm or discomfort (see also Section 6.7, **Boxes 6b** and **6c** and **Box 3j**, Chapter Three). Ethical considerations, however, often emerge in complicated ways. One study with children of lone parents might have prompted revelations about undisclosed child abuse. Researchers here needed, through an appropriate protocol, both to protect their own situation and also to make it clear to children that they would act if 'they thought anyone was in danger'. Section 6.7 expands on these issues of confidentiality. There are, however, no firm safeguards preventing respondents from exploitation by researchers.

Issues of race, culture and gender may impact significantly on the safety of researchers, particularly in violently divided societies. Lone female researchers are generally more vulnerable than lone male researchers. Even where the threat of physical violence is not pressing, some cultures may react with hostility to the presence of female researchers. Certain racialised contexts may make the conduct of non-ethnically-matched interviewing fraught. Male researchers are increasingly anxious about the risks to themselves in interviewing children alone.

There are more subtle issues, including the use of body language, the way researchers dress and the acceptability or not of physical contact, where researchers may inadvertently increase risks to themselves. Sitting on a bed is an obvious example; even going into a bed-sitting room may be another. GPs constitute one professional group which has been given advice as to what constitutes 'unsafe' territory, but there are many nuanced situations where researchers are left to rely on their own intuition as to when an interview should be terminated. Should a door always be left open (even if this compromises confidentiality)? Should interviews only be conducted in rooms where there is a clear exit route if researchers need to leave in a hurry? The quality of social research frequently depends on establishing the appropriate distance – neither over familiar nor too detached – between researcher and interviewee, but that distance will vary. Too much intimacy or too little rapport may send out the wrong signals.

Some research funders now acknowledge that they have to address the resource implications of research which is both ethically robust and carried out in safety, recognising that its quality suffers if researchers feel vulnerable and frightened. Proposals are beginning to include a budget line covering the use of mobile phones, the carrying of personal alarms and phonecards, the use of hire cars or taxis, and appropriately priced and located overnight accommodation (see also Section 6.8 on budgets). There are, however, more significant safety costs, particularly where it is inappropriate for researchers to visit respondents alone. More costly strategies open to research managers include having researchers work in pairs, with non-researcher friends who are paid simply to wait while interviews are conducted, or to conduct interviews only in public places (for example, community centres). What is now clear is that an effective safety strategy for social policy research requires employers, researchers and funders to work collaboratively.

Question for discussion

- What are the key aspects of safety that a researcher working alone needs to think about? Do these aspects have gender and 'race' dimensions?

References

Alcock, P., Barnes, C., Craig, G., Harvey, A. and Pearson, S. (1999) *What counts? What works? The evaluation and monitoring of local government anti-poverty work*, London: Improvement and Development Agency.
Arksey, H. and Knight, P. (1999) *Interviewing for social scientists*, London: Sage Publications.

Paterson, B., Gregory, D. and Thorne, S. (1999) 'A protocol for researcher safety', *Qualitative Health Research*, vol 9, no 2, pp 259-69.

Sandell, A. (1998) *Oxford handbook of patients' welfare: A doctor's guide to benefits and services*, Oxford: Oxford University Press.

Suzie Lamplugh Trust (1999) *Personal safety at work: Guidance for all employees*, London: Suzie Lamplugh Trust.

Further reading

Arksey, H. and Knight, P. (1999) *Interviewing for social scientists*, London: Sage Publications.

Paterson, B., Gregory, D. and Thorne, S. (1999) 'A protocol for researcher safety', *Qualitative Health Research*, vol 9, no 2, pp 259-69.

Website resource

The code of safety and code of ethics for social researchers published by the Social Research Association is available at www.the-sra.org.uk

6.7 Managing confidentiality in policy research

Harriet Ward, *Senior Research Fellow, and Director of the Centre for Child and Family Research, Loughborough University*

Social policy research often involves the collection and analysis of empirical data which, when gathered or explored at the individual level, can be extremely sensitive. Nobody wants it to be publicly known that information about them was used in a study of the treatment of offenders or of the victims of child abuse. Yet, without access to empirical data from individuals, either held on records or given at interview, it is virtually impossible to generate the findings that allow for the construction of evidence–based social policy and practice (see also Chapter One, Sections 1.4, 1.5, and Chapter Seven, Sections 7.4 and 7.5). *Confidentiality* is therefore a major issue in policy research, and needs to be addressed at all stages of the process, including access to potential subjects and to records held by professional agencies, collection and storage of data and the analysis and reporting of findings. Researchers need to be aware of the provisions of the 1998 Data Protection Act and the 1998 Human Rights Act (see Figure 6a for details), as well as of protocols set by some funding bodies, such as the Department of Health's *Research Governance Framework* (2001; see also **Box 6a**). Healthcare researchers will also need to be mindful of Section 60 of the 2001 Health and Social Care Act.

Figure 6a: **The 1998 Data Protection Act and 1998 Human Rights Act**

The 1998 Data Protection Act sets out eight principles for the protection of personal data. Some relate to the collection and processing of data: it must be processed fairly and lawfully and only with the consent of the data subject; it must be adequate, relevant and not excessive; it must be accurate and kept up to date; it must be processed according to the rights of data subjects. Others relate to the storage of data: it shall not be kept for longer than is necessary; appropriate technical and organisational measures shall be taken against unauthorised or unlawful processing, and against accidental loss, destruction or damage; it shall not be transferred outside the European Economic Area unless there is an adequate level of protection. Finally, the Act lays down principles for its use: personal data cannot be processed in any manner that is incompatible with the purposes for which it was obtained (see Data Protection Act, Schedule 1 [Part 1]; Schedule 2 [1] and Schedule 3 [2]).

Under Section 33 of the Data Protection Act, the storage and handling of data for research purposes is exempt from some of these principles, provided that it is not used to support measures or decisions concerning particular individuals, and as long as it is not processed in such a way that substantial damage or distress is, or is likely to be, caused to any data subject (see Data Protection Act Part IV, Section 33). This section of the Act is interpreted differently by the various organisations which hold personal data about vulnerable people. In one recent study, for instance, three local authorities agreed to researchers examining files of children who had been in care 20 years ago to see whether it might be possible to trace them, while a fourth refused on the grounds that it would be contrary to the provisions of the Act to do this without first obtaining their consent.

The 1998 Human Rights Act incorporates the European Convention on Human Rights into United Kingdom law. Article eight of the Convention states that "everyone has the right to respect for his private and family life, his home and his correspondence". This right can be deemed to have been violated if, for instance, personal data are not kept private (see Wadham and Mountfield, 1999).

It is difficult to invite users of public services directly to participate in research which relates closely to their experiences: advertisements are likely to produce a biased sample group, particularly if the service received can be interpreted as stigmatising, such as apprehension by the police, or support from social services or a benefits-related agency. Service users are therefore more usually approached indirectly, through negotiation with those agencies to which they are already known, and whose interpretation and implementation of policy is being evaluated. The need to adopt this indirect approach is one of the major reasons why issues of confidentiality and consent can become thorny problems if not adequately addressed.

Agencies have a duty to protect the identities of service users, to safeguard information that is given to them in confidence and to ensure that it is not inappropriately used. However, despite the legislation, agencies hold varying views as to what information can be made available to researchers when the consent of service users cannot be obtained and as to what may constitute a consent to pass on information that makes it possible to arrange interviews (see **Box 6b**). At times, their duty of confidentiality can appear to conflict with the researcher's responsibility to gather information and to meet research deadlines. These and other pressures may tempt researchers to cut corners, but to do so is counterproductive. Research of this nature can only be successfully conducted if all parties are confident that the work will be undertaken within a strict ethical framework.

Box 6b: Confidentiality in practice

As part of a number of government-funded studies to evaluate the outcomes of placing children away from home, a research team were contracted to interview cohorts of children who are looked after by the local authority. The researchers could not be given access to the names and addresses of children without the consent of both themselves and their parents, and so the social services departments had to send out the initial letters of invitation to participate in the research. No social services staff had dedicated time available for this task, and it took several weeks for invitations to be sent.

Four authorities adopted an opt-out arrangement whereby the letter explicitly stated that consent for information to be passed to the research team would be deemed to have been given if the subject had not responded within a certain period – children and parents made no objection to this arrangement and 59% agreed to be interviewed. In two authorities consent was only regarded as given if the child and parent had formally replied to the letter (opt in) – the numbers who came forward for interview were reduced to 13% although there was no evidence that more families were unwilling to participate. Ensuring that the issue of confidentiality was properly observed was a necessary part of the research process, but it led to a reduced and unbalanced interview sample, and added substantially to the research timetable and therefore costs. The research teams made considerable efforts to ensure that all data were anonymised and stored in locked cabinets and that identifying codes were kept separately. In principle, identifying information was never held on computer. However, although this was adhered to with the datasets, a research assistant was in the process of writing letters to the authorities when she was mugged and her laptop computer was stolen (in this respect, it is worth considering issues concerned with keeping researchers safe, as outlined in Section 6.6). Children's names had, by then, been given to the research team and were included as a necessary part of the letter. Addresses had not been held on the laptop and so the chances of the information being useful to third parties were minimal. However, the computer had not been password protected and the letters were not encrypted. The research team immediately informed the authorities, some of which were extremely concerned about the incident. Their worries were openly discussed and security increased.

During the course of one of the research interviews, a teenager disclosed that he had previously lived with foster carers who regularly drove him in the car when they had been drinking. They had also refused to allow him a key so that he was frequently locked out of the house after school until they returned from work. He was advised that the information might need to be passed on to the local authority, particularly as these carers were now fostering other children.

Researchers therefore have to go through what are often lengthy and time consuming procedures in order to obtain access to confidential information, not only because they are required to do so by the Data Protection Act, but also because they need to demonstrate to the agencies with which they work that they will respect the rights of service users. The time taken to obtain access should not be underestimated and should be built into every research timetable.

While researchers may make every effort to preserve confidentiality, errors quite frequently arise. These need to be dealt with openly and not concealed, for unless agencies and service users have full confidence in the research team, the type of problem shown in **Box 6b** can irrevocably damage the relationship and lead to withdrawal from the project. It is helpful for research teams to draw up contracts with participating agencies, stating explicitly how confidential data will be accessed, stored and used. Some agencies, particularly social services departments, now require research teams to be police-checked before allowing access. Issues concerning confidentiality should also be spelled out at the start of each interview with service users; the way in which the information will be used should be explained and consent formally obtained (see Chapter Three, **Box 3j**, for further discussion on informed consent).

Researchers also need to ensure that information of a sensitive and personal nature is collected and stored in such a way that confidentiality is preserved. It is a relatively simple task to anonymise all data by replacing names and addresses with research codes and by keeping any identifying information separate from the main dataset; it is also relatively easy to password protect and/or to encrypt data held on a computer. However, anonymising data can itself lead to difficulties – and not only when the computer password or the keys to the filing cabinet are mislaid. If too little identifying data are held, or too little thought has gone into the way in which it is coded, valuable information can be lost. For instance, in one study the aim was to record the frequent changes of household that were experienced by very young children in need. Identifying data were only recorded where absolutely necessary and held separately; names and addresses of successive foster carers who were identified numerically on the dataset were not regarded as essential and therefore not recorded. However, carers were coded in such a way that it later proved impossible to identify those who had looked after more than one child in the sample, and an important issue could not be explored. **Box 6c** provides some practical guidance on how to ensure confidentiality and data protection.

Box 6c: Guidance for ensuring confidentiality and the protection of data
Lisa Holmes, *Research Associate, Centre for Child and Family Research, Loughborough University*

Data stored on hard drives
- Research participants' names and addresses should not be stored on the hard drive of either laptop or desktop computers.
- All participants are identified on data files saved to the hard drive by research and authority identifier codes.
- These data files (including Access databases, Excel spreadsheets and SPSS files) are all encrypted using AEP pro 2002 or an equivalent package.
- A corresponding paper list containing names along with identifier codes is stored separately in a locked filing cabinet; alternatively, an electronic version of the document is saved onto a floppy disc that is also stored separately in a locked filing cabinet.

Correspondence by e-mail with local authorities and other agencies

- There is an agreement with authorities that research participants, especially children, will not be referred to by name in e-mails.
- Participants should only be identifiable by either their research ID or local authority ID.

Correspondence by letter

- Copies of letters sent to research participants are not saved to the hard drive of laptop or desktop computers.
- A copy of the letter containing the participant's name and address is either saved onto a floppy disc or a copy of the letter is printed.
- Both the floppy disc and copies of letters are stored in locked filing cabinets.
- All letters to research participants are sent by special delivery.

Data collection

- When gathering data in a local authority or other agency office, information is transferred from the case files to an Access (or other) database on the researcher's laptop. All these databases are encrypted.
- Participants' names are not recorded on the database, they are identified only by research or authority IDs.
- An encrypted version of the database is saved onto a zip disc at the end of every day. The zip disc is then stored and transported in a separate bag to the laptop.
- To assist with locating the relevant case files, the researcher uses a paper list containing both names and the corresponding research/authority identifier codes.
- If possible, this list is stored securely at the authority office at the end of the day. If the researcher keeps the list it should be stored and transported separately from the laptop.

Interviews

- All information gathered during interviews is recorded by research ID only; participants, especially children and young people's names, are not recorded on the interview schedules.
- The exceptions to this are the consent form and, where appropriate, the gift voucher receipt (a voucher may be given in some cases by way of a 'thank you' for participation) that the parent, young person or other participant has to sign.
- These forms are stored in a separate locked filing cabinet.
- All tapes of the interviews are stored in a locked filing cabinet.

Transcription

- All transcribers should be asked to sign a letter stating that they will abide by the 1998 Data Protection Act, including an agreement that all transcriptions of interviews are not stored on the hard drive of their computer.
- The transcripts should not contain participants' or children's names; all names mentioned in the interview are translated into initials only.
- All tapes sent to transcribers are sent by special delivery, likewise, all transcribed interviews are returned by special delivery.

Paper copies of interview schedules and transcriptions

- All copies of interview schedules and transcriptions for current research projects are stored in locked filing cabinets.
- These documents are stored separately to any records of names and addresses.

Travelling

- Travelling to and from an authority or organisation can present a risk to the security of information. As much care as possible must be taken to ensure that breaches of security do not occur. For example, if travelling by train confidential information should not be left unattended.

Risk

- It is not feasible to take computers and briefcases everywhere and at times they do have to be left. However, as much care as possible should be taken to ensure that researchers stay in reputable hotels in lower risk areas of towns and cities.
- If computers do have to be left unattended, rooms should always be locked and research materials should always be packed away rather than left spread out.

Confidentiality also needs to be taken into account in writing reports. In addition to the obvious requirement to hide the identities of both organisations and individuals, quotations need to be disguised in such a way that they cannot be attributed to a particular participant. Again, there is a tension between the researcher's need to provide detailed information and the subject's need not to be identified. There is, therefore, some controversy concerning the extent to which material in case studies or quotations should be altered to disguise its provenance, with some researchers holding the view that it should be totally unidentifiable and others that it should only be recognisable to the subjects concerned.

While researchers need to devote considerable effort to preserving confidentiality, there are also occasions when other considerations can override this requirement. It is not uncommon, for instance, for vulnerable children to disclose abuse within the relatively safe parameters of a research interview, and procedures need to be already in place for dealing with such issues (see also the discussion on safety in Section 6.6). Research interviews do not have the sanctity of the confessional and the researcher's duty as a citizen to ensure that vulnerable members of the public are protected from harm is usually thought to override his or her duty to preserve confidentiality. However, *before the interview begins*, subjects need to be forewarned of any circumstances in which it may be thought necessary to pass confidential information on to others, and if disclosures are then made, they need to be advised as to how the information will be dealt with. Once again, confidentiality and trust turn out to be closely interrelated.

Question for discussion

• Under what circumstances can the need to preserve the confidentiality of research subjects and participating organisations conflict with the researcher's need to gather data, analyse findings and produce a report within a fixed timescale? How can such conflicting demands be reconciled?

References

DoH (Department of Health) (2001) *Research governance framework for health and social care*, London: DoH.

Further reading

DoH (Department of Health) (2001) *Research governance framework for health and social care*, London: DoH.
Wadham, J. and Mountfield, H. (1999) *Blackstone's guide to the Human Rights Act 1998*, London: Blackstone Press.
Ward, H., Soper, J., Elson, L. and Olsen, R. (2004) *The costs and consequences of different types of child care provision: Report to the department of health*, Loughborough: Centre for Child and Family Research, Loughborough University.

Website resources

Data Protection Act: www.legislation.hmso.gov.uk/acts/acts/1998/ 19980029.htm
Human Rights Act: www.legislation.hmso.gov.uk/acts/acts/1998/19980042.htm
2001 Health and Social Care Act, Section 60: www.hmso.gov.uk/acts/acts2001/ 10015—g.htm#60

6.8 Managing budgets and budgetary constraints

Nigel Bilsbrough, *Finance and Resources Manager, Centre for Research in Social Policy, Loughborough University*

In this section we are concerned with managing budgets in a social policy research context. Keeping within predetermined cost is affected by a number of factors, not least the need to deliver results to a deadline and to the requisite standard. It is recognised that these issues may not be of immediate interest to readers of this book who are students. However, an appreciation of budgetary issues is important nonetheless since students need to understand that research is always conducted within a budget and within other resource constraints, and established researchers may appreciate some guidance in this area, particularly if they are involved in costing out a new research proposal.

However, before looking at managing budgets and budgetary constraints in more detail we need to consider what is meant by a *budget* and what constraints may be imposed. A *budget* is defined as *a plan of expenditure*, but in the area of policy research this has come to mean *an allocation of financial resources within which a particular research project is to be undertaken.* In some cases (for example, where a lone researcher or student is working on a study which has no funding source), there may not be an explicit or planned budget per se, although even here the researcher will still be conscious of the real costs of time and, especially, money.

However, in many other cases, policy research will be funded in some way. When devising a budget for a research project, the researcher or research organisation will need to take various factors into account, not least of which are the often stringent requirements of the particular sponsor concerned. Any expenditure included in the budget must be *eligible* (see, for example, the Economic and Social Research Council website at www.esrc.ac.uk/, also see 'research costs' in the **Glossary**).

It is also important to determine whether the project is to be undertaken for a fixed price, as is often the case with government funded projects (and where the sponsor will pay a set sum of money in return for a specified outcome). In this case the researcher will be required to submit claims to the sponsor justifying the expenditure incurred. If the budget is underspent then the money will effectively be lost.

Many other points will need to be considered when preparing a project budget, and some of the key ones are outlined in Figure 6b.

Figure 6b: **Issues to consider when preparing a research project budget**

- The *level* of staff employed. For example, research councils will specify the maximum grade of staff they would normally consider funding.
- Can nationally agreed *pay awards* be included or will the budget be inflation-linked?
- Can the costs of *recruiting* staff be included?
- Can the costs of *support staff* be included or are these to be treated as part of the overheads contribution?
- What level of *overheads* (see **Glossary**, 'research costs'), if any, can be included and on what can they be charged? For example, research councils allow for 46% overheads to be paid on *all research staff salaries* claimed; European Union funded projects allow for 20% overheads but on *all eligible costs*; government sponsors typically allow 40% to 50% overheads on *staff costs*; charitable foundations will not pay any overheads at all.
- Is any specialist *equipment* required to undertake the project? In policy research the costs of equipment are often neglected but there may be a need for a high quality recording machine to undertake interviews or a transcribing machine.
- Can *office costs* and *consumables* be included or are these considered to be part of the overhead costs?
- Other *direct costs* (see **Glossary**, 'research costs') will need to be considered, such as:
  - travel and subsistence (which should not be underestimated);
  - recruitment of respondents;
  - payment of expenses to respondents;
  - transcription of interviews;
  - preparation and printing of questionnaires;
  - telephone and postal costs and costs of follow-ups.

Figure 6b is by no means an exhaustive list, but it is hoped that this will provide some guidance. Above all, it needs to be remembered that very few research proposals will fail on the grounds of cost alone. Most sponsors will be prepared to negotiate the costs, invariably downwards, if they are otherwise happy with the proposal, but it is almost impossible to increase costs at a later stage.

Once a budget for a research proposal is finalised and agreed, it is important that it is adhered to. It may seem an obvious point to make but many researchers will continue to try and produce for the sponsor everything that was included in the original proposal, and often more as enthusiasm for the work takes hold, ignoring the fact that the funding may have been cut. It is therefore imperative that a project plan is devised for the project and that fully costed resources are allocated to it.

In addition, the project plan must be monitored on a regular basis to ensure that the appropriate resources are being utilised and that agreed milestones are being met. The project plan may require periodic adjustment. The very nature of research means that the outcomes are not necessarily predictable. Problems and attendant delays may be encountered along the way. But at least if regular reviews of the work in progress are undertaken potential pitfalls can be identified at an early stage and remedial action can be taken. This is preferable to the sickening realisation that a project is rapidly coming to a close, that all available resources have been consumed, but yet the final output (in whatever form it may take) is still nowhere near completion.

Question for discussion

- Why is it important to have a fully costed and adequate budget for any piece of policy research?

6.9 Managing funders' constraints

Janet Lewis, *formerly Research Director, Joseph Rowntree Foundation*

The big constraint set by research funders is the *application process*. Every funder has a different set of requirements and interests which those applying for money have to follow if they are to be successful. The process of making an application varies along a number of dimensions:

- *Mode of application:* a standard application form; a proposal in a standard format; or a response to a tender document. Submission might be electronically or on paper.
- *Subject and focus:* the Economic and Social Research Council's (ESRC) Research Grants programme operates in a 'responsive mode', so this is one of very few avenues, apart from postgraduate work or postdoctoral fellowships, for researchers to propose social policy investigations, pursuing any topic and theoretical or applied approach. More limited parameters, in terms of programmes of research on specific topics, are set by the various ESRC initiatives and by many of the charitable trusts. Those who directly commission research will be focusing on a particular issue and often a specific way of approaching it.

- *Approach:* the majority of funders of research, outside the funding councils, are seeking work that is going to be 'useful' or which can be applied in some way. The Leverhulme Trust is one of a few organisations that funds the pursuit of knowledge 'for its own sake'. Many funders expect that those putting in proposals will have involved 'users and beneficiaries' in the process of developing the proposal, sometimes as key people in setting the research agenda (see Chapter Three, Section 3.6, on user participatory research).
- *Timescales and restrictions:* all funders follow similar kinds of procedures for assessing proposals but the details vary. The timetables for submission and decision differ and the detail required on budgets, timetables and staffing are specific to each funder, as well as what can be included in the budget. For example, as Section 6.8 has already made clear, the charitable trusts will only meet the *direct costs* of the research so they do not pay *overheads*. However, the definition of what constitutes a direct cost is often quite broad.

It clearly pays to be aware of the way the body from which you would like funding actually works and what its requirements are. Most funders publish their details. But the fact that they have requirements does not mean the researcher is not expected to contribute knowledge and creativity. *The best proposals are those where the researcher has managed to combine their own interests with those of the funder.*

The constraints imposed by funders once the funding has been agreed depend on the way in which they choose to operate. Where the funds are essentially a grant, the researcher(s) are expected to get on with the work. The requirements are usually straightforward, in that there is an expectation that the work will be done, the financial and staff management will be sound, and a final report or publication produced at the end.

There are other models that provide more involvement and support from people outside the team. ESRC programmes usually have programme directors and advisory/steering groups who become engaged with the work of the projects in the programme. The aim is to 'add value' to the work of the individual projects through synthesising and disseminating the work of the programme as a whole. Some of the charitable trusts, such as the Joseph Rowntree Foundation, see their role as one of working in partnership with the projects that they support. Many projects funded by the Joseph Rowntree Foundation have advisory groups whose members take an active role, along with the staff, in supporting the research team. The role of all steering/advisory groups can include discussion of research methods and the details of how the work is done, for example, helping to resolve a problem of access to samples or delays in the timetable – problems that often arise in research projects. The groups also give advice and guidance about dissemination at the end of the project. The aim of these arrangements is not to constrain the researchers but to help them make the most of the work they are doing.

What happens at the end of a project is another area where funders have different expectations. The Joseph Rowntree Foundation takes responsibility for ensuring that particular kinds of dissemination happen. The emphasis is on summaries of findings and short reports (20,000 words) written in language that is accessible to non–academics. This requirement clearly constrains those researchers who only wish to publish in academic journals, although the Foundation is happy to see this happen once the accessible material has been completed. The Foundation requirement provides opportunities for researchers to address policy and practice issues and audiences that may not be available in other ways. Issues of dissemination are examined in more detail in Chapter Seven of this volume.

Questions for discussion

* What kinds of factors do you have to consider when developing a research proposal for a funding body such as the Joseph Rowntree Foundation?
* What is the purpose of an advisory board for a research project?

Further reading

Fitzherbert, L. and Richards, G. (2001) *A guide to the major trusts 2001/2002, Volume 1 Top 300 trusts*, London: Directory of Social Change.
Lewis, J. (2000) 'Funding social science research in academia', *Social Policy and Administration*, vol 34, no 4, pp 361-376 (special issue on 'The business of research: issues of politics and practice').

Website resources

Most of the major funders have information for applicants in both written and electronic forms. For example, the Joseph Rowntree Foundation has a section on its website, on 'How to apply for funding', which includes details about the information it seeks in research proposals and the way in which the Foundation works.

ESRC: www.esrc.ac.uk
JRF: www.jrf.org.uk
Nuffield: www.nuffieldfoundation.org
Social Research Association: www.the-sra.org.uk

seven

Disseminating social policy research

Detailed contents

7.1 Introduction

Dissemination is concerned with the communication to relevant audiences of information and knowledge gained from research. This is an integral part of the policy research process. Whether research then goes on to inform or to influence social policy or practice requires us to examine the process by which research is adopted and used by policy makers and professionals. These are some of the main concerns of this chapter.

In this chapter we examine and discuss:

- what is meant by *dissemination* and how this phase of research 'fits' with the other stages of the research cycle;
- the main vehicle for dissemination – the *written report* – and we offer practical guidance on how to make reports accessible and well structured, and how to relate research findings to an established body of knowledge;
- the *postmodernist critique* of written outputs;
- ten key issues that need to be addressed when considering a *dissemination strategy* for any piece of policy research;
- the role that the *media* can play; and
- how research can *inform change* in policy and practice.

7.2 Dissemination as part of the research process

Defining dissemination

The dictionary defines *dissemination* as: "To spread (information, ideas, etc.) widely" (Collins, 2001, p 227). Other terms closely associated with dissemination include "broadcast, circulate, diffuse, disperse, distribute, propagate, publish, scatter, sow, spread" (Collins, 1996, p 174). In the context of policy research, dissemination is thus concerned with *communicating information and knowledge gained from research to relevant audiences*. This dissemination can include the communication of information about research findings, about messages from research, implications for policy and practice, about methodologies employed, and so on.

For any piece of policy research it will be important for the researchers, in discussion with their funders and other involved parties, to identify the appropriate and relevant audiences for dissemination. These audiences can include policy makers, politicians, practitioners, users of services, research funders, other researchers and academics, and, potentially, the public as a whole. Dissemination will also include letting research respondents know about the findings, and in some cases this can act as an important test of validity for the study as a whole. Different audiences will need to know about different aspects, for example, some may need to know specifically about the findings, others may be more interested in knowing about the application of methods or research designs. We return to these issues in Section 7.4.

Locating dissemination in the research cycle

Figure 11 in Chapter One shows that dissemination is a distinct phase of a dynamic research cycle. The dissemination of research findings to relevant audiences, and the promotion of the findings as research evidence, follows a *cognitive phase* and the *doing research phase*, all of which need to be managed effectively if the research process is to be rigorous and the findings are to be trustworthy. As we have said, the *dissemination phase* is concerned with *communicating* information and knowledge gained from the other stages of the research cycle, particularly the findings, to relevant audiences. In the context of *evidence-based policy making*, and *evidence-based practice* (see Chapter One, Sections 1.4 and 1.5), dissemination becomes especially critical. Put simply, unless policy makers and practitioners have the information and knowledge gained from research, there is little chance that research will either inform, or influence, policy or practice. However, it is important to be aware that for some commentators, the *publications* that report research findings are not neutral devices for conveying information. The *postmodernist* position problematises research reports and regards them as just one possible mirror on social policy (see **Box 7a**).

Box 7a: The postmodernist critique of published outputs

Until relatively recently, the published outputs of social researchers, such as those described in Section 7.3, were treated as essentially unproblematic in their nature. However, the growing influence of postmodernist thinking since the mid-to-late 1980s has changed the way that in particular publications based on research are perceived. Traditionally, we have tended to think of an academic article or a book that reports the results of research simply as giving us an insight into an aspect of social reality. There may be technical problems with the way the research was done or we might disagree with some of its inferences or its theoretical basis, but other than that a publication of this kind was thought of as unremarkable.

Postmodernists are sceptical about the notion that social policy researchers can capture reality definitively. Instead, they argue that all we can do as researchers is to recognise that we are presenting one of many different versions. The crucial point from this perspective is to realise that researchers are engaged in a kind of game in which they must persuade readers of the trustworthiness of their conclusions and inferences. As noted in Chapter Three, Section 3.10, according to this viewpoint adopting such procedures as triangulation or member checks is significant only insofar as such techniques make the results look more convincing. Because it adopts an essentially anti-realist position, postmodernism denies that the techniques and concepts of the social scientist provide a privileged access to reality. Van Maanen (1988), for example, has argued that ethnographers have adopted a variety of tactics to give a sense that they are providing an authoritative account of the society and culture with which they came into contact. Reference to their prolonged immersion in the field and their language skills are meant to act as indicators of the authenticity of their accounts. However, when it comes to presenting the findings and conclusions, the author disappears from sight, giving the impression that he or she is simply a vessel for projecting the findings and conclusions that anyone similarly placed and with the same skills would have found.

The postmodernist position is deeply unsettling about the publications that we read and the research on which they are based. It tells us that there are many truths and that what we end up with is publications that are little more than acts of persuasion that one truth is more viable than another. This line of thinking has ushered in a period in which reflexivity has come to be viewed as an important component of writing up research findings in some quarters. With reflexivity the author presents reflections about the circumstances of the research process and the way in which his or her personal characteristics may have impinged on the findings. The author is no longer regarded by postmodernists as a neutral device for conveying information but a component of the research setting and the findings. In a postmodernist environment, the author can no longer hide and pretend to have cracked social reality. Since readers of a postmodernist persuasion will always be sensitive to the provisional nature of findings, authors who are influenced by postmodernism adopt a reflexive posture since they are insightful about the partial nature of the truths they are conveying. While traditional writing based on realist assumptions still exists and almost certainly remains the dominant discourse for couching publications, there is a significant body of work that is self-consciously anti-realist in its accommodation to the belief in multiple versions of truth and in the need for reflexively inspired writing.

Question for discussion
- To what extent does the postmodernist position undermine our sense that there are verifiable truths?

Reference
Van Maanen, J. (1988) *Tales from the field: On writing ethnography*, Chicago, IL: University of Chicago Press.

Further reading
Alvesson, M. (2002) *Postmodernism and social research*, Buckingham: Open University Press.
Atkinson, P. and Coffey, A. (1995) 'Realism and its discontents: on the crisis of cultural representation in ethnographic texts', in B. Adam and S. Allan (eds) *Theorizing culture: An interdisciplinary critique after postmodernism*, London: UCL Press, pp 41-57.

Given the concern in social policy research both to understand and to improve policy making and implementation (see Chapter One, Section 1.3), it is possible to identify five underlying principles which should govern any approach to dissemination in policy research. These are shown in Figure 7a.

Figure 7a: **Five principles for policy research dissemination**

1 Dissemination needs to be seen as an integral part of the policy research process – not as an optional extra or 'luxury'.
2 The essence of dissemination is *communication*. This requires clarity of expression and the use of appropriate vehicles of communication that are relevant to particular audiences. Thus, dissemination is about making research and research findings accessible, understandable, useful and relevant to a range of specialist, lay and user audiences.
3 Dissemination of research is about generating, transferring and circulating information and evidence, for knowledge, for power and, where appropriate, for change.
4 Dissemination is essential if research is to inform or to influence policy, policy making and implementation.
5 Dissemination is an integral aspect of the researcher's task. It helps to get their work better known and develops their own profile; it contributes to their publication list and academic credibility (the number and quality of publications are ways in which researchers are judged by the academic community); and it can give them a sense of value and satisfaction that their work is known and may be influential for policy and practice.

Question for discussion

- What is dissemination and why is it important?

References

Collins (2001) *Collins paperback English dictionary*, Glasgow: HarperCollins Publishers.

Collins (1996) *Collins paperback dictionary and thesaurus*, Glasgow: HarperCollins Publishers.

7.3 How to write up policy research

Stephen Potter, *Senior Research Fellow, The Open University*

Before any piece of research can be disseminated, there needs to be an 'output' – *a vehicle for communicating the research to relevant audiences*. In most cases, this will be a *written report* which contains, not least, the findings as well as broader discussions of methodology, conclusions, and so on. In this section we focus on the written report and in particular the *process of writing up research*. We offer *practical suggestions and guidance* on how to write up research so that it can be accessible and relevant for different audiences. However, we must also introduce a note of caution. As **Box 7a** shows, there has developed over recent years a *postmodernist critique of published outputs* that challenges the very nature of the written report as a vehicle for communicating research both as *evidence* and as *truth*.

Guidance for writing up research

There are dangers in the term *writing up research*. First, it implies that writing is something you do at the *end* of a research project – little more than an add-on to the 'real' work of doing the research itself. But until your research is written up, nobody will know of it. A second danger is that the idea that writing is only done at the end of a project can undermine the need to write *throughout* the project. Getting feedback on a proposed investigation calls out for a paper, conference or workshop presentation at the *start* of a project. There are also pilot studies or work-in-progress reports that provide that all so necessary feedback as a project progresses. Take these as real opportunities to develop and hone your writing skills and style.

Organising research writing

Reporting research can take many forms, from conference papers, reports through to a dissertation or thesis. Particularly for a large work, such as a report or dissertation, it is useful to start by putting together an outline. List the section headings and say what each of these will contain and how they will develop the work's 'storyline' (in other words, where things will be at the beginning of the section and where they will be at the end).

For a *thesis*, *research report* or *major article*, the structure could involve:

- *Analysing the research question you are addressing:* explain the questions or issues involved. Defining the research question or questions you are answering is vital to understanding your research, yet this is often skimped leading to considerable problems.
- *Reviewing what others have done:* in any type of research paper you have to show that you know where your research fits with what others have done on your subject (see also Chapter Two, Section 2.3 and **Box 7b**). Structure this review of existing knowledge into arguments and themes. Do the ideas of others make sense to you? Are there conflicts or contradictions – or do you detect undue bias? If so, is there a reason (for example, do writers approach the subject from the viewpoint of different stakeholders)? Do these ideas relate to the 'real world' of social practice that you know? Work towards an end point that shows your research is about something that needs investigating.
- *Your research project and method:* explain your project and the methods used to gather and analyse data. Do not forget to report the logic behind the research method used. Particularly in social policy, it is crucial to explain how you researched an issue as well as presenting your results.
- *Reporting your research results:* a 'classic' approach in writing up research is first to report results and then to have a separate section on discussion and conclusions. This can work well, but particularly in a subject such as social policy, researchers develop a 'storyline' that takes their reader into an exploration of what they have discovered. For example, if there is a key argument that someone else has put forward, the new findings are structured around this, showing if the new information supports or contradicts viewpoints within this debate.
- *Analysis, discussion, conclusions and recommendations:* this is the most important part of your writing. Whatever you do, do not just say 'the facts speak for themselves' and leave it at that. The whole thing about research writing is demonstrating your ability to analyse, discuss and contribute to social policy's community of knowledge (see **Box 7b**). If you have integrated discussion and evaluation as you reported your results, the boundary between reporting and this section could seem arbitrary. However, it is here that you might

pull together observations and basic analysis that took place while reporting results and draw a bigger picture. You might also want to discuss the weaknesses and limitations of your research.

Box 7b: Relating findings to the established body of knowledge

Stephen Potter, *Senior Research Fellow, The Open University*

Section 7.3 considers 'structure' when writing up research and provides some outline guidance on relating your findings to existing knowledge. This is a crucial part of your research; through it you will show the relationship of your findings to that of your colleagues in the field. The foundations of this relationship should have been set when you reviewed and evaluated your topic area (which was covered in Chapter Two). Indeed, before you even start reporting your findings, you should return to your topic or literature review and particularly to your evaluation of issues, debates and choice of methodology that informed the design of your own research project.

Once you have your results, it is useful to think through the strategic ways your own research relates to existing knowledge. Is your research:

1 *An extension of the existing way of understanding and researching this topic?* For example, a study of health inequality that has applied an established theory and research approach to a new group of people or a new situation.
2 *Comparing or challenging the results of other studies?* For example, you may have found that important factors were missing in other studies and you have sought to fill that data gap.
3 *Comparing or challenging the method of measurement or evaluation indicators used?* This is not just about adding new information, but questioning the form of the information. For example, you may say that, as a measure of 'success', your research has shown that a particular indicator is misleading.
4 *Challenging the research methodology used?* This is further on from challenging a measure used, saying that a different methodology is needed. For example, using a qualitative approach assessing residents' perceptions of road safety rather than a quantitative approach.
5 *Challenging a theoretical approach to the subject?* Your research may throw doubts on a particular theoretical approach, or provide evidence to support one theory of social policy rather than another.
6 *Challenging a policy response?* The above points will inevitably have policy and practice implications, but research can focus on policy formulation and implementation itself. However, it is important to explain the research

justifications (such as data, method and theory) behind a policy response recommendation.

You may find it useful to make a list of the ways in which your research relates to existing knowledge. The list above is not exhaustive, so use it as a starting point. However, it is important to establish a sequence or structure in relating your results to existing knowledge. You may start by comparing your research at the level of the data and information it contains, and then move on to how that relates to measurement and meaning, which could go on to a discussion of methodology and possibly theory. So, having made a list of the strategic ways your research relates to existing knowledge, see if you can then structure this into a sequence that allows you to make comparisons to existing knowledge at different levels – from data, to indicators, to techniques, to method, to theory (or any other level that you identify yourself). Policy implications may be picked up at any of these levels.

Of course, in structuring your discussion, you are not starting from scratch. Your topic or literature review should have started to set up the broad approach of your research and this will have informed your research project design. You could return to that and pick up the discussion and debate where you left off. Equally, in reporting your results, you may have started to make some initial comparisons to existing knowledge. This is most likely at the level of comparing data, such as to existing studies, and you may have already pointed out some areas where there are similarities and differences. You might also have provided some comments on some implications of the results.

Seek to build up a picture that relates your findings to what others have done in your subject area. Think through a 'storyline' that will guide your reader. You could start by summarising what were the crucial issues that had resulted in you undertaking the research in the first place. In undertaking the research you may have changed your understanding and modified the information that you sought to gather. Explain this, and why. You can then pick up key results (particularly if you had highlighted them already when reporting your results) and work your way towards what you see as your most strategic findings. Invite your reader to join you in your research journey and share with them how you have built up a picture of your discoveries.

Question for discussion
- Starting with the six numbered categories above, make a list of the ways in which *your* research relates to existing knowledge.

Further reading
Potter, S. (ed) (2003) *Doing postgraduate research*, London: Sage
  Publications.

Flow and comprehension

Structuring a piece of research work, particularly a large work, is not an easy job. You should allow time for development and revision. Guiding your reader through your work is very important; sometimes you make connections in your mind rather than stating clearly how your points link up. You could include 'signposts' to help, for example:

- At the start of each section or chapter of a report, say *what the section contains* and its *purpose*. That will prepare the reader for the contents and the sequence in which they are tackled.
- In larger works, it is useful to have a *summary* at the end of the sections, pulling together the key issues in that section and indicating how these will be followed up in the next.
- *'Pulling together' summary points* should feature where your writing takes any new direction. You might say "this is what I have discovered, the implications are these, and so we need to explore the following to develop our understanding further".

Also, you should make sure that your work answers the question you posed at the start. You should not drift off the subject, although it may be that the question you started with was the wrong one or was more complex than you first thought.

Writing style

As well as the structure of your writing, there is the detailed question of style. Look at some social policy research articles or reports. First, there is *academic style*. You should try to find a style of writing that you find comfortable but equally works academically. Seek to find your 'own voice' within the style of your discipline.

At a more detailed level there are issues of style and grammar that can make all the difference in how your writing is received – quite aside from the research and arguments it contains. Devise a list of things that make it difficult for you to understand social policy articles or reports (see Figure 7b).

Figure 7b: Things that can make social policy publications difficult to understand

- Over-complex and long sentences.
- Undefined jargon and technical terms.
- Very 'dense' writing: saying a lot in a very few words that need to be read several times to get the meaning.
- Simply presenting a list of 'facts' that may, or may not, have some links.
- Shifting from one subject of discussion to another with no explanation as to why one follows on from another.
- Conclusions that are not backed up by evidence.

Go back and check that you have not included in your writing any of the stylistic traits that annoy you! And finally, it is very useful to get someone else to read your draft for style, flow and comprehension. Often you cannot spot where you have lost your reader.

Questions for discussion

Take an article or piece of written work that you have had to read for your studies:

- What sections did you find most difficult to understand and why? Did anything annoy you?
- Does the written piece have a 'story' or argument that develops through it? What 'signposts' are used?
- Are the conclusions or recommendations clear?
- Were there any bits you simply did not understand at all? (Could you rewrite this to make it understandable?)
- What part did you find most enjoyable to read? Why was this?
- Would you have inserted a summary at any point?
- Would you have reordered the material?

Pulling apart someone else's written work should help you to think through these issues for your own writing. Go now and follow your own advice!

Further reading

Dunleavy, P. (2003) *Authoring a PhD: How to plan, draft, write and finish a doctoral thesis or dissertation*, Basingstoke: Palgrave Macmillan.

Ward, A. (2003) 'The writing process', in S. Potter (ed) *Doing postgraduate research*, London: Sage Publications, pp 71-109.

The Research Methods Knowledge Base: http://trochim.human.cornell.edu/kb/

7.4 Ten questions to inform dissemination

As researchers embark on the dissemination phase of the research cycle (see Section 7.2), they need to consider a range of strategic and practical issues. In this section we identify ten key questions that will need to be addressed both *before* and *during* the dissemination of any piece of policy research:

1 Who 'owns' the research and who is responsible for dissemination and promotion? For example, is it the researchers, the funding agency, the university or research unit – or others? This issue needs to be transparent and resolved *before* the research commences, as it may mean that in some cases researchers may have little ownership of the data and little control over whether or not the results can ever be made public. Matters of ownership and responsibility for dissemination can be resolved by agreeing these issues in advance and by demarcating these responsibilities as distinct clauses in any research *contract* or *agreement*.

2 What type of 'product' or 'output' do the researchers, funders or other stakeholders want and expect? Is there a need for:

- a report (brief or detailed?);
- an executive summary;
- a short article (in a professional or academic journal?);
- a video or audio tape;
- a presentation (seminar, conference paper, presentation to respondents, to professionals?);
- a book;
- or a combination of outputs?

It is important to have a clear view of the output(s) required from the earliest opportunity – at the research design stage if possible. Section 7.3 focused on *published outputs*, particularly on how to write up research.

3 What 'style' of dissemination needs to be pursued? Should there be active dissemination – whereby those responsible for dissemination actively pursue the promotion of the research output, perhaps using multimedia – or more passive dissemination? Is 'low-key' dissemination or a high profile launch or campaign required? Much policy research is published in report or monograph form and is rarely disseminated widely. Some large research studies never see the light of day. Some research (often small-scale) manages to get high profile reporting. Sometimes this is by accident, most often it is a careful strategy of active promotion with careful use of 'launches' and the media (see **Box 7c**). What style of promotion is required, and why? What does the research funder want?

4 What are the (perceived) costs and benefits of each dissemination strategy? An active dissemination strategy requires considerable time, resources and effort. Are there the resources to handle specialist or media enquiries? Do you want the attention? How will the commitment required for dissemination affect your other work and responsibilities?

5 Who should receive the research output(s), and why? What do you want them to do with it? (It's always worth letting them know in a covering letter.) Different target audiences will require different types of output because their own needs to know, and what you want from them, are likely to be different. For example, in typical hierarchical organisations (such as social services and health departments) different layers of the organisational structure have different needs for information. This is because people have different responsibilities, duties and information requirements:

- top managers will most often require *strategic* information to allow them to plan and evaluate service direction and effectiveness from year-to-year;
- middle managers will require more *tactical* information, on similar issues, but to enable operation from month-to-month;
- first line managers will require *operational* information – often for day-to-day management;
- front-line workers most often require the *facts* – raw data – on which they can make immediate informed decisions.

This is not to say that front-line workers (or *street-level bureaucrats* – see Chapter One, Section 1.4) should not have access to other strategic information, or that top or middle managers should not have access to the facts, but that their immediate information needs are for useful, understandable and relevant information – requiring those responsible for dissemination to target and refine the output *according to who is to receive it* – and *why* they need to know.

Linked to this are the different emphasis and focus needs of diverse audiences.

Some will only be concerned with a particular part of the research or research findings because their concerns are more specialist or narrow. This may require researchers to use different language for different audiences, as well as a different form of presentation (for example, audio-visual or PowerPoint rather than written).

In some instances those responsible for dissemination may need to reframe the findings into a style and manner relevant to a specific audience. In some cases it will be necessary to present only the main findings and 'messages' from research (messages for *that* particular audience); others might need 'recommendations' and an executive summary of just a few pages. In other instances it may be necessary to present the information in more diagrammatic form, using key charts or tables, or even as a 'clinical guideline' (see **Box 1f**, Chapter One).

It is usually helpful to seize, or create, opportunities to frame the findings in a popular discussion or concern that is topical. For example, if the research includes some information on a theme that is of popular interest – then it may be particularly attractive to the wider media (see **Box 7c**). Sometimes, researchers will be concerned to reach a specialist audience part of a particular community of interest. Again, these targets can be identified and use made of *their* appropriate vehicles of communication (such as specialist journals, newsletters, magazines, radio shows and so on).

It is also important to ensure that the research is communicated to *all* relevant groups. Researchers should make use of 'minority' publications and outlets where appropriate. Material should be tailored for particular readerships and needs. For example, sometimes this will require research findings to be translated into other languages or to be put on audiotape where, for instance, an audience has a visual impairment.

6 When should information or findings be disseminated? Here we need to consider *when* we want to disseminate material, not just *how*. Is dissemination something that happens at the end of a project, or at other stages (as well)? This will depend to a large extent on *why* those responsible for dissemination actually *want* to disseminate research findings and what kind of research it is. For example, the findings of theoretical research can only be disseminated when there is sufficient evidence to enable theoretical development – this will generally follow a lengthy period of research, reflection and peer review, and attempts at verification and falsification (see Chapter One, Section 1.5). Researchers concerned more with action policy research are more likely to disseminate material as they go along. Some of this will be in the form of tentative findings and interpretations, 'in progress' research reports or as working papers. If those responsible for dissemination want to influence policy, or are concerned with wider social change, they must weigh up whether ongoing dissemination will be more effective for these purposes than 'end of project' dissemination and promotion (see also point 10, below).

The timing will also depend on what and who researchers want to influence. To achieve 'maximum' impact researchers need to ensure that their outputs are, for example, released when the local authority or health authority are planning/reviewing the policy or practice, or when Parliament is sitting and not in recess.

7 Who else is working on this or a similar issue? Can the dissemination of the research coincide with the publication or dissemination of their work? Is it possible to work together, or make use of any other topical issue, to promote the research? Having 'allies' in the dissemination process can be very useful in helping to get research 'noticed' by policy makers.

8 Can, or should, the media be used to disseminate and promote the research? Media work requires its own knowledge and skills. Those responsible for dissemination need to be prepared to seek advice about how best to use the popular and professional media, including press releases, radio and television interviews, and so on. They need to make the media work for them, rather than ending up working for the media. **Box 7c** provides a discussion on the use of the media for disseminating social policy research.

Box 7c: Using the media to disseminate policy research
Polly Neate, *Editor*, Community Care *magazine*

There can be no doubt that the media are interested in social care, social work and social policy issues. In one study by Bob Franklin (1998), nine newspapers published 1,958 reports about social issues in a single year, an average of four per newspaper per week.

Neither can there be any doubt that the tone of this coverage is overwhelmingly negative. Franklin writes: "Newspaper reporting of social work and social services is overwhelmingly negative and critical. This is true for effectively all newspapers: tabloid or broadsheet" (1998, p 5). This is the background against which research enters the newsroom. It is axiomatic to many journalists, for example, that social workers do more harm than good. They will view research findings through this prism.

Even responsible reporting simplifies and selects from research findings, and focuses on the most 'newsworthy' elements, not necessarily those which researchers consider most significant. Research which is seen as controversial or alarming will get more prominent coverage than those which seek to affirm the status quo, or calm fears – particularly when journalists have a stake in continuing fears which they excited in the first place. The potentially harmful panic about the MMR vaccine is a case in point (BBCi).

On top of all this, the intellectual status of social sciences is low in the minds of many journalists in comparison with, say, medical research. Highly complex information is hard to obtain from the most vulnerable groups. By definition, those who are socially excluded are hard to find, meaning sample sizes are inevitably smaller. Journalists have only a basic (if any) grasp of what makes good research, so they feel less confident about the significance of much social science material. Unless the extent and limits of its significance are clearly explained, they will probably just bin it. By contrast, as Vikki Entwistle has written (1995), journalists regularly scour the medical press for nuggets from research, which they assume to need no further checking. Journalists are not exempt from the general ignorance about social policy and social care. We all know what teachers, doctors and nurses do, but who has any idea how social workers, for example, spend their days?

Yet despite these pressures, it is no longer fair to say that social science researchers dismiss the mass media as irrelevant, although this was once the case. They couldn't do so anyway, because funders of research increasingly insist on dissemination outside the research community (see also Chapter Six, Section 6.9). The Economic and Social Research Council offers quite detailed advice on its website, citing the sociologist Graham Murdock, who has argued (1994) that television is an essential forum for anyone who wishes to influence the national debate about our society, its problems and their possible solutions.

The Joseph Rowntree Foundation handles media liaison itself, for research it has funded, and is highly successful in terms of volume of coverage. Authors are prepared for the questions they may be asked – questions which are obvious to anyone with a media background, but not necessarily to researchers. When journalists ask "What do these findings mean?", they really mean "What's the story?", and that is a question whose meaning few researchers actually understand.

Even for professional communicators, it is impossible to control the coding process which research undergoes as it passes through the media machine and comes out the other end. Research findings on a particular subject emerge into a context that already exists around that subject. For example, a longitudinal study on the effects on children of parental employment was published by the Joseph Rowntree Foundation (Ermisch and Francesconi, 2001). It received substantial coverage in the press and broadcast media, focusing on a finding that children whose mothers worked full time during their early years gained lower A level results than those whose mothers did not work. A simple message, tying into a high-profile debate, and great fodder for columnists too, who endlessly related their personal experiences, pulling the debate ever further from the research itself, but right into the mainstream media agenda. What about the findings on fathers? What about the benefits of the additional income from working mothers? Forget it. Meanwhile, various tactics were used by those who didn't like the message (although, ironically, they might have had fewer problems with the 'real', as opposed to the media, message), such as criticising the research as out-of-date, despite the accepted importance of longitudinal data.

It is early days to ascertain the real effect of all that publicity. Going further back in time, it is easier to see the positive effects of disseminating research through the mass media, even if the debate at the time is oversimplified. A review of the literature on the effects of divorce and separation on children, for example, was published by the Joseph Rowntree Foundation in the late 1990s (Rodgers and Pryor, 1998; see also **Box 3i**, Chapter Three, for a discussion of this study as an example of a *systematic review*). The messages were complex and subtle. Some media hated the findings because they weren't negative enough about divorce. Others hated it because it did point to some damaging effects. But the debate has become less highly polarised, and the research contributed to that consensus. As David Utting, Associate Director (public affairs) at the Joseph Rowntree Foundation, told me: "It matters to children that neither extreme should be seen to have right on its side, when the evidence is elsewhere". His advice: "You have to understand that there is no capacity to deal with grey areas". Just give out a small amount of information, he adds, and remember that part of the reason for publicising research is so that those who really want to understand will come and find the real answers.

Researchers who want their findings to influence social policy simply must be media-savvy, particularly in this age of government hypersensitivity to the media agenda. But there is a real danger that the simplistic, politicised version presented by some journalists will be what influences government, rather than the findings themselves. The seductive power of becoming a well-known commentator, with ready access to the top of government, can be dangerous for the truth as well. Currently, however, for every researcher with ambitions to be a talking head, there are dozens more who face the opposite pressure: a government which commissions an increasing volume of research, but wants to control when and how findings are disseminated – and even which findings are released at all (see also Chapter One, Section 1.4).

It's a jungle out there. Don't try to survive without the right support and equipment. Decisions on dissemination must ultimately be taken by authors themselves, with respect to those who have been 'researched'. It may even be time to remind ourselves that before assuming mass dissemination is needed, some questions – like the ten identified in Section 7.4 – should be asked.

Question for discussion
- Why is there a need for caution when debating whether to gain mass media coverage of research findings?

References
Franklin, B. (1998) *Hard pressed: National newspaper reporting of social work and social services*, Sutton: Reed Business Information.

BBCi (http://news.bbc.co.uk), *MMR research timeline*.

Entwistle, V. (1995) 'Reporting research in medical journals and newspapers', *British Medical Journal*, 310, pp 920-23.

Murdock, G. (1994) 'Tales of expertise and experience: sociological reasoning and popular representation', in C. Haslam and A. Bryman (eds) *Social scientists meet the media*, London: Routledge, quoted at http://www.esrc.ac.uk/index.asp (ESRC website), under 'Information for award-holders'.

Ermisch, J. and Francesconi, M. (2001) *The effects of parents' employment on children's lives*, York: Joseph Rowntree Foundation.

Rodgers, B. and Pryor, J. (1998) *Divorce and separation: The outcomes for children*, York: Joseph Rowntree Foundation.

Further reading
Philpot, T. and Neate, P. (eds) (1997) *The media and the message: A guide to the media for everyone in social care*, Sutton: Reed Business Information.

Website resources
Advice on media interviews for academics: http://gradschool.about.com/cs/mediainterviews/

Community Care magazine: www.communitycare.co.uk

The Media Trust is a useful site aimed at charities but helpful for anyone dealing with sensitive issues: www.mediatrust.org/advice/

Advice for university academics is available from Southern Connecticut State University: www.southernct.edu/faculty/paffairs/index.php?file=mediatips.html

9 What should research respondents be told about the findings? A 'user-conscious' dissemination strategy will consider the research respondents' dissemination needs at an early stage, and will decide the appropriate form, and timing, of dissemination so that respondents (and other service users) can be kept informed of developments and findings. Many respondents are never given the results of the research in which they participated (the same applies to many professionals as well as service users who take part in research). This is a source of constant criticism and gives policy research a bad name. At the very least, respondents should be given some form of accessible summary of the findings so that they can see how their contribution to the study was used and interpreted; for many respondents this may be a valuable source of information on a topic or issue that interested them enough for them to become research participants in the first place.

For some forms of research, particularly qualitative approaches such as participant observation, providing the findings to respondents (in summary or more elaborate form) can act as an important source of validation for the findings and interpretations, and for the project as a whole, particularly where respondents are able to influence the final output or report.

Finally, communicating findings to a wider population of *service users* (not just the service users who were the respondents for the research study itself) will enable users to make informed judgements and choices based, to some extent, on research evidence. This will sometimes require communication of research in languages other than English, and/or using specialist forms of communication, where, for example, service users may have impaired vision or where there are learning or other disabilities.

10 Is the dissemination strategy aimed at informing or influencing policy and professional practice? If an aim of communicating research to relevant audiences is to have some impact on policy, policy making and the implementation of policy, then it will be important for researchers to address many of the issues outlined in the earlier discussion of evidence-based policy and practice (Chapter One, Sections 1.4 and 1.5). In these sections we discussed in detail the issues, strengths and limitations of using research as evidence to inform policy and practice, and the interested reader should revisit that earlier discussion. Here, we want to add just a few points about the *communication* of research evidence to inform policy and practice. It must be emphasised, however, that dissemination of results on its own will not produce change in policy and practice. For change to occur, findings must be understood, adopted and implemented by policy makers and practitioners – a theme we return to in Section 7.5.

Gomm and Davies (2000) identify a number of reasons why poor communication of research helps to maintain a gap between research evidence and its adoption by professionals (Figure 7c).

Figure 7c: How poor communication of research helps to maintain the research–practice gap

- Research findings tend to be published in 'academic' or obscure' journals which are read by academics rather than by practitioners.
- Many healthcare professionals and the majority of social workers have poor access to specialist libraries and sources of information.
- Where practitioners work in semi-isolation (in the community or primary care) there is less chance of messages from new research being disseminated by person-to-person communication.
- Information overload – the sheer weight of new information being produced.
- When research findings reach and are read by practitioners they are not sufficiently accessible to be understood and valued.

Source: Gomm and Davies (2000, p 135)

Gomm and Davies (2000) suggest that many practitioners express a preference for easy-to-read summaries with clear messages about implications for practice. This is confirmed by research conducted in local authorities examining how research can bring about change (Percy-Smith et al, 2002). The researchers found that the way in which research is *presented* affects the likelihood of it being read, disseminated further within an organisation and to other professionals, and whether the findings will be acted upon. Figure 7d lists the factors that contribute to good presentation of research and which thus increase the likelihood of findings being used to inform policy and practice (see also the guidance in Section 7.3 on how to write up research).

Figure 7d: Factors contributing to effective presentation of research

- A concise summary of research findings.
- Inclusion of recommendations, action points or checklists.
- Clearly presented data, case studies or examples.
- Orientation towards practitioners.
- Limited use of academic references, footnotes and so on.
- Clear identification of the key issues, why the research is important.
- Awareness of the multiple audiences for research, and who should read this particular document.
- Relevance and timeliness.

Source: Percy-Smith et al (2002, p 29)

This approach to dissemination, of *making research accessible, meaningful and relevant for different audiences, so that it can inform policy and practice*, has manifested itself in a range of strategic national initiatives in the last few years, particularly in the health and social care spheres:

- The *National Institute for Clinical Excellence* (NICE), the *NHS Centre for Reviews and Dissemination* (NHSCRD), and the *Social Care Institute for Excellence* (SCIE) aim to make the best research evidence available to policy makers and professionals in medicine and healthcare (NICE, NHSCRD), and in social care (SCIE) (see also **Boxes 1f** and **1h**, Chapter One). The NHS Centre's role includes the dissemination of reviews to practitioners and users, including the production of *Effective Health Care Bulletins*. These *Bulletins* are systematic reviews produced in an accessible format with the implications for healthcare practice clearly identified. The dissemination of best evidence by NICE most often involves the use of systematic reviews and meta-analysis (see also Chapter Three, Section 3.12), and *Clinical guidelines*. SCIE's remit appears broader, *to develop and promote knowledge about what works best in social care*, which includes not only the dissemination of reviews of evidence from research, but also disseminating knowledge from other sources, including users of services, those who deliver services and other stakeholders. In developing a knowledge base for social care, SCIE also intends to publish best practice and other guides for the benefit of policy makers and professionals, and to provide an electronic library, all with an explicit intention of contributing to positive change in both policy and practice. The NHS also has developed an electronic library for clinicians and other professionals that is designed to inform them of the best current know-how and knowledge to support healthcare-related decisions.
- The *Cochrane Collaboration* and the *Campbell Collaboration* are concerned with the preparation, maintenance and dissemination of systematic reviews of studies of interventions in the medical and health spheres (Cochrane), and in the social, behavioural and educational arenas (Campbell) (see also **Boxes 1f** and **1h**, Chapter One, for further details). Both have extensive libraries and databases of relevant studies.
- The *EvidenceNetwork*, as discussed in **Box 1h** (Chapter One), comprises nine ESRC-funded teams all committed to specialist review work in policy areas such as public health, neighbourhood, economic evaluation, ethnicity, social policy and social care, European policy and children's services.
- *Research in Practice* and *Making Research Count* are two national network organisations comprising universities, local and health authorities, voluntary organisations and other agencies, aimed at disseminating the findings of research to relevant audiences to inform policy making and professional practice in health and social care. Both produce research-based reports,

newsletters and other publications, and provide conferences, seminars and other events for members.

* *Research Matters* is a thrice-yearly journal for health and social care policy makers and professionals, published by the weekly magazine *Community Care*, which disseminates research findings on a wide range of topics (for example, adult and child care, carers, families and parenting, learning difficulties, mental health, older people, poverty, residential care, sexual health, to name a few). Research findings are summarised and reviewed, and the implications for practice are clearly identified.
* Some research funders are disseminating research findings directly to relevant audiences with an explicit intention of informing policy and practice. The Joseph Rowntree Foundation, for example, produces 4-page summaries of all its funded research, called *Findings*, as well as more detailed reports and synthesis of research (see also Chapter Six, Section 6.9 and **Box 7c** for more on the Joseph Rowntree Foundation).

Question for discussion

* What are the main issues that need to be taken into account when deciding a dissemination strategy for any piece of policy research?

References

Gomm, R. and Davies, C. (2000) *Using evidence in health and social care*, London: Sage Publications.

Percy-Smith, J. with Burden, T., Darlow, A., Dowson, L., Hawtin, M. and Ladi, S. (2002) *Promoting change through research: The impact of research in local government*, York: Joseph Rowntree Foundation.

Further reading

Gomm, R. and Davies, C. (2000) *Using evidence in health and social care*, London: Sage Publications, Chapter 7.

Relevant organisations

Campbell Collaboration

Dr Dorothy de Maya, Executive Officer Campbell Collaboration Secretariat, University of Pennsylvania, 6417 Wissahickon Avenue, Philadelphia, PA 19119, US
Telephone +1 215 848 5489; www.campbellcollaboration.org

Joseph Rowntree Foundation
The Homestead, 40 Water End, York YO30 6WP
Telephone 01904 629241; www.jrf.org.uk
Making Research Count
School of Social Work and Psychological Studies, Elizabeth Fry Building,
University of East Anglia, Norwich NR4 7TJ
Telephone 01603 593557; www.uea.ac.uk/swk/research/MRC.htm
NHS Centre for Reviews and Dissemination
University of York, Heslington, York YO10 5DD
Telephone 01904 433634; www.york.ac.uk/inst/crd/crdrep.htm
National Institute for Clinical Excellence
11 The Strand, London WC2N 5HR
Telephone 020 7766 9191; www.nice.org.uk
Research in Practice
Warren House, Dartington, Totnes, Devon TQ9 6EG
Telephone 01803 867692; www.rip.org.uk
Research Matters
Community Care, 6th floor, Quadrant House, The Quadrant, Sutton, Surrey
SM2 5AS
www.communitycare.co.uk
Social Care Institute for Excellence
1st floor, Goldings House, 2 Hay's Lane, London SE1 2HB
Telephone 020 7089 6840; www.scie.org.uk
UK Cochrane Centre
Summertown Pavilion, Middle Way, Oxford OX2 7LG
Telephone 01865 516300; www.cochrane.de/cochrane/general.htm

Website resources

ESRC EvidenceNetwork: www.evidencenetwork.org
National Electronic Library for Health: www.nelh.nhs.uk

7.5 Making a difference

Adoption, utilisation and change

In the final phase of the research cycle (Figure 11, Chapter One) we are
concerned specifically with the *adoption of research evidence* and its *use to inform,
influence, and where appropriate, to change policy and practice*. This phase is closely
linked with the *dissemination and promotion phase*. Adoption, and the utilisation
of research, cannot lead to change in policy and practice without adequate

dissemination, and any dissemination strategy requires the ten issues outlined in Section 7.4 to be considered from an early stage in the research itself.

In Figure 1h (Chapter One) we identified the circumstances that are favourable to research having an impact on both policy and practice. So, for example, research is more likely to influence policy and practice where the researcher is trusted and authoritative, and where the methodology is relatively uncontested. These factors will help increase the adoption of research by policy makers and professionals. It is also important to be aware that the 'loudest' research voice will not necessarily lead to the greatest adoption and utilisation of research, or to the largest change in policy and practice. Targeted dissemination and promotion, on a softly-softly basis, can be as effective, if not more so, than, for example, attempts to embarrass a government, an organisation, agency or person.

All researchers will have their own personal goals and values in doing and disseminating research. Some will be concerned to disseminate findings to change the practice (or certainly to inform it) of a specified group of people – perhaps social workers, care managers, benefit advisers or health workers. Others will be concerned to influence organisations – at a micro- or macro-level. Others may wish to inform or change public attitudes through the process of adding to knowledge on a particular issue. Others will be concerned to contribute to a movement for wider social (and political) change. These considerations will affect the style, manner, timing and form of dissemination (see Section 7.4).

Dissemination can also be an empowering force for research *participants*, other users of services and their carers. Research evidence can highlight the circumstances and experiences of particular groups, and may help to enable a transfer of resources to them. Where service users and carers are involved directly in the design, management, implementation and dissemination of research, this process may be particularly effective and empowering (see also Chapter Three, Sections 3.6 and 3.7).

For research to influence and change policy, actions or practices, however, we need to be clear about *what contributes to change* in these spheres of activity. So, for example, do people need information and knowledge to change their policies or practices, or can they be *instructed* to change? Should information and knowledge be provided through training and staff development, or through policy, organisational and cultural change?

If an aim is to change policy and practice, the dissemination process needs to be used (and devised) in such a way as to maximise the potential for change. In some instances this will require a concentration on inappropriate attitudes and to try and highlight 'myths'; in other circumstances it will require close working between researchers and trainers to develop training materials based upon messages from research; in other instances it will require the concentration of findings and messages on crucial *change agents* within an organisation –

those who can go on to change the service or organisation itself. Those responsible for dissemination will need to engage with many other actors, stakeholders and networks of interest if individual or organisational change is to be an outcome of the research process. Figure 7e identifies six issues that need to be considered where it is a goal for dissemination to achieve change in policy or practice.

Figure 7e: **Dissemination for a change: six issues to consider**

1 *What* do you want to change, and *why*? Are you concerned with professional practice, organisational structure, organisational culture, policy or wider social change? Be specific and be precise. Identify and list the key 'targets' for change.
2 *Who* do you want to change? Can you identify specific groups or individuals? Are there six key people who should be targeted with research findings/messages and who could play a strategic role in bringing about these changes?
3 In what *direction* do you want change to occur? What are the *outcomes* that you want from any change? For whose benefit is this change to occur?
4 How can you bring about and secure change? What needs to happen to X before Y will change? What happens to Z as a direct or indirect consequence?
5 What is your timescale? Can you identify and list clear targets for change in the short, medium and long term?
6 How will you know when something has changed? How can you monitor change and evaluate whether it has been successful or not?

With change, one round of the research cycle identified in Figure 11 (Chapter One) becomes complete. The original 'seeing' of a social issue or social problem, has, with some research skill and a little luck, led to changes in policy and/or practice and, hopefully, an improvement in whatever aspect of social life, social welfare or wellbeing that has been the subject of the research focus. However, the research *cycle* does not end here – it is dynamic and ongoing, with the monitoring and evaluation of new policies and practices.

This cycle of research, dissemination and change does not take place in a vacuum. What can be understood through research, what can be achieved by it, and the type of change that can be brought about, are all influenced by the many factors which we have considered throughout this volume, including the political climate at the time, whether research is accepted as an evidence base for policy and practice, the quality and trustworthiness of the research, and so on.

Research has the potential to inform change – but it is a time consuming and a difficult process, with no guarantee that policy or practice will change. Sometimes the best executed research changes nothing, is misrepresented or ignored, as we have already seen in Chapter One. At other times, a small study can have an effect on policy that few would have thought possible. This is *not* a lottery. Developing the expertise in doing and managing policy research, and in disseminating research to relevant audiences, will maximise the potential for research to form a trustworthy evidence base for future social policy and practice. As one *way of knowing* (Figure 1i, Chapter One), research is the *only* foundation for policy and practice that allows self-correction through further research – which can check, verify or refute the knowledge base.

Question for discussion

- Can and should research lead to change? Outline and discuss some of the issues involved.

Further reading

Wilson, D. (1984) *Pressure: The A to Z of campaigning in Britain*, London: Heinemann.

Nutley, S., Percy-Smith, J. and Solesbury, W. (2003) *Models of research impact: A cross-sector review of literature and practice*, London: Learning and Skills Research Centre.

Website resource

Research Unit for Research Utilisation at the University of St Andrews, Scotland. The overall aim of RURU is to facilitate the production and use of practical knowledge that will assist in enhancing the role of evidence in public policy and public services: www.standrews.ac.uk/~ruru/home.htm

Glossary

Note: all glossary items have been compiled by the contributors and editors.

Accessible: Materials or environments designed or adapted to be easily used/ understood by disabled people, people with learning disabilities or others.

Action orientation: The way people's talk or text are designed to perform actions in particular settings.

Action research: An orientation to inquiry rather than a methodology. Action research is a participatory, democratic process concerned with developing practical knowing in the pursuit of worthwhile human purposes and grounded in a participatory worldview. Action research seeks to bring together action and reflection, theory and practice, in participation with others, in the pursuit of practical solutions to issues of pressing concern to people, and more generally the flourishing of individual persons and their communities

Adoption (of research): The use made of research to understand, inform or to change policy and practice.

Advisory groups: These are often set up by funders of research to support a project in various ways. Members of such groups are usually people with particular knowledge of the issues, including policy makers and practitioners, or knowledge of the approach being adopted (for example, qualitative methods). Advisory groups have no executive authority in relation to projects and simply offer advice and support. Some steering groups, particularly those set up by some government departments, can take a more active role in specifying the work to be done or taking part in decisions that can change the project's work.

Aggregate data: Statistics that relate to broad classes, groups or categories, so that it is not possible to distinguish the properties of individuals within those classes, groups or categories. Examples are population statistics on gender or national estimates compiled from regional data sources.

Analytic induction: An account of the process of scientific inquiry that has been appealed to by some qualitative researchers. It assumes that research begins with investigation of instances of the phenomenon to be explained, and leads into the formulation and testing of explanatory hypotheses. Initially, the hypotheses will usually fail to fit the cases studied, and this will lead to their modification or abandonment, and/or to a reformulation of the nature of the phenomenon to be explained. Only when investigation of further cases throws up no exceptions can a hypothetical explanation be accepted as true, and only then provisionally – contradictory evidence may arise in the future, stimulating a resumption of the inquiry process. Those who developed analytic induction contrasted it with statistical method, in which hypotheses are accepted so long as the bulk of cases investigated do not contradict them.

Analytic memo: See **Memo**.

Anti-realism: This is an approach to knowledge that attacks realism by disputing its central tenets. It therefore denies that there is an externally knowable world that can be accurately and objectively represented and studied.

Asymmetry: Differences between different parties to an interaction in terms of their power, knowledge, institutional identities and so on.

Asynchronous/Non-real time: Communication that takes place at different times, for example, e-mail communication which is not simultaneous and does not require users to be online at the same time.

Bar chart: A graphical display of categorical data in which each category is represented by a bar or rectangle and where the height of the bar indicates the number of cases.

Bias: A measure of the difference between the average estimate (from the sampling distribution of means) and the true population parameter. It arises when some population members have unequal selection probabilities.

Biography: An account of a person's life written by another individual; the practice of writing about another person.

Boolean retrieval: Text recovered in qualitative software using a search rule based on the AND, OR, NOT relations of Boolean algebra.

Booster sample: Sampling for surveys usually involves taking a representative or random sample of the whole population or obtaining a stratified sample to make sure that all target groups are proportionately represented within the final sample population. However, in some cases, for example where the overall population of minorities may be very low compared with the population as a whole, it may be necessary to boost – that is, deliberately increase – the sample of minorities to ensure that the sample is large enough to provide adequate good quality data. This is called booster sampling. The more formal term for this is 'disproportionate stratification'.

Budget: (a) A plan of expenditure; (b) an allocation of financial resources within which a particular research project is to be undertaken.

Campbell Collaboration: Analogous to the **Cochrane Collaboration** (see later), but is concerned with the preparation, maintenance and dissemination of systematic reviews of studies of interventions in the social, behavioural and educational arenas.

Canonical cases: Standard or expected cases which are characteristic of a practice; for example, 'fine thanks' in response to a 'howareyou' greeting.

Case study: A case can be defined as any phenomenon located in space and time about which data are collected and analysed, and can comprise single individuals or a group, particular events or situations, a specific organisation, a social institution, neighbourhood, national society or global process. Case studies can address the micro situation of a single person in everyday life or the macro-situation of a nation state in the global world.

Clinical guideline: A statement of how clinical professionals should act in respect of treatment or diagnosis in specified circumstances. Such guidelines may be more or less specific and may or may not be in some sense 'evidence-based'.

Closed questions: These are questions that supply the answers from which respondents are asked to select and are commonly used in survey research with questionnaires. Sometimes they include an open-ended option (for example, 'other') at the end.

Cluster sampling: A sampling technique that aggregates population members into groups (clusters) and it is these groups that are initially randomly selected.

Cochrane Collaboration: A well-established international network of specialists developing the evidence base for medical practice on an open and responsive basis with regular updating of systematic reviews posted on the Collaboration's website.

Code of ethics: A formal set of guidelines intended to influence the behaviour of researchers in a way that is consistent with ethically acceptable practices.

Cohort design: A continuing research study that collects data over time about a group of individuals born in the same time period, and which may be conducted prospectively or retrospectively. A **prospective cohort study** involves a systematic follow-up for a defined period of time or until the occurrence of a specified event (for example, onset of illness, retirement, or death). For a **retrospective cohort study**, data on the group's background, experience or life history are already available.

Comparative method: A very general term referring to the fundamental approach of most scientific inquiry, in which cases are compared in order to try to identify the causes which bring about some type of phenomenon. Experiments, survey analysis, grounded theorising and analytic induction all employ the comparative method.

Comparative research: Research which aims to identify and explain similarities and differences between social phenomena – events, processes, actors, social groups – in two or more contexts. It can involve comparisons of phenomena within one country, but more usually it refers to comparisons of socio-economic and political phenomena in two or more countries, which is also known as 'cross-national research'.

Computer-assisted interviewing (CAI): The use of computers to assist in conducting interviews. The most common form of CAI is to use pre-programmed questionnaires and administering the questionnaire either personally (CAPI), over the telephone (CATI) or allowing the respondent to self-administer the questionnaire (CASI). Self-administration may be conducted in a variety of ways including via e-mail or the Internet. These computer-assisted forms of data collection contrast with surveys that use paper questionnaires (commonly known as **PAPI**, **Pen/Pencil Assisted Personal Interviewing**).

Confidence intervals: The upper and lower bounds of an estimate that describe the range within which the population parameter will fall, with a given degree of probability, set by the researcher.

Conjecture: The first stage in the development of a scientific hypothesis that will give focus to the research and direction in the collection of relevant data.

Constructionism: This is a theoretical approach within the social sciences that emphasises that social phenomena are constructed by people in and through their actions, rather than existing independently of those actions. In this respect, it contrasts with those approaches that emphasise the way in which people and their actions are shaped by external social structures and institutions.

Constructionism takes its most radical forms when it is applied to people's understandings of the world, and even to social scientists' own research reports. Here it involves a rejection of the idea that accounts, even scientific accounts, represent the world. Rather, emphasis is given to the functions which accounts are designed to serve and their role in constructing the reality they purport merely to represent.

Content analysis: A term mainly used to describe the statistical analysis of content. Quantitative content analysis mainly focuses on the manifest features of texts, and requires the development of a coding frame that identifies which aspects should be counted, and in what way.

Contingency table: A table showing the frequencies of cases in the categories of two or more variables.

Convenience sampling: A type of sampling where the researcher uses cases that are most convenient or available. The sample is made up of whoever is willing and available to participate. This is a non-probability method of sampling.

Conversation analysis: A way of understanding the joint production of everyday life through a labour-intensive (qualitative) analysis of conversation. It promises an empirically grounded basis for understanding how issues in social policy are actually realised in interaction.

Correlation, Pearson's (r): An index of the strength and direction of the linear relationship between two quantitative variables.

Credibility: The question of whether a set of findings are believable.

Cross-sectional survey designs: Research design in which data are collected for all cases and all variables that apply to a single period in time.

Data: Social science data are the raw material out of which social and economic statistics and other research outputs are produced. Social science data originate from social research methodologies or administrative records, while statistics can be produced from data. Data are the information collected and stored at the level at which the unit of analysis was observed, such as an individual or household. Data are processed to enable them to be analysed, such as with statistical or qualitative data software, which read the raw data from computer files, or data can be analysed using one or more other techniques, such as grounded theory, discourse analysis, and so on.

Data archives: resource centres that acquire, store and disseminate digital data for secondary analysis in research and teaching.

Data archiving: A method of conserving expensive data resources and ensuring that their research potential is fully exploited by researchers and others.

Data editing: Process of checking the quality of data and, where possible, correcting any errors.

Data management strategy: A systematic approach to organising the data from a research project ready for analysis; may be a paper-based filing system or use data management software, or both.

Dataset: A collection of data records, such as numerical responses to a survey or texts transcribed from qualitative interviews, associated with a particular study. A dataset can be a file or group of files associated with one part of a study.

Deductive approach: The research process is conducted with reference to pre-existing theoretical ideas and concepts. Deductivists start by formulating a theory and then proceed from this general proposition to a consideration of particular cases in order to test their theory. This approach contrasts with inductivists who start by drawing inferences from particular cases from which they proceed towards the formulation of general theoretical conclusions.

Degrees of freedom (*df*): The number of values in a statistic that are free to vary.

Dependability: The question of how far we can rely on a set of findings.

Deviant case: Sometimes also known as 'negative instance', this is a term from qualitative data analysis to describe an instance in which data do not fit, or initially appear to contradict, an emerging generalisation or theoretical proposition. Frequently such instances can extend or deepen a theory by requiring its reformulation to take account of the anomaly.

Deviant case analysis: Exploration of exceptional examples as part of the validation of analytic claims.

Dichotomous variable: A variable that only has two categories or values.

Discourse: Texts and talk in social practices.

Discourse analysis: A cluster of methods and approaches (including continental discourse analysis, critical discourse analysis, discursive psychology and conversation analysis) that focus on the role of talk and texts in social life. Different forms of discourse analysis place different emphasis on specific practices of interaction and the broader discursive resources that underpin that interaction.

Dissemination: The communication to relevant audiences of information and knowledge gained from research.

Epistemological: Refers to a concern with what should be regarded and accepted as legitimate knowledge.

Epistemology: A set of assumptions about what should be regarded as acceptable knowledge.

Epsem (equal probability of selection method): A technique that ensures that each subset of size *n* population members has an equal chance of selection into the study.

Equivalence scale: A scale used to adjust household income so that it takes into account the number of people who have to live on that income and economies of scale.

Ethnography: A style of research rather than a single method. The study of people in naturally occurring settings or 'fields' by means of methods which capture their social meanings and ordinary activities, involving the researcher participating directly in the setting, if not also the activities, in order to collect data in a systematic manner but without meaning being imposed on them externally.

Evaluation research: Research that seeks to assess the worth or value of an innovation, intervention, programme, policy or service.

Evidence: (a) Means of proving an unknown or disputed fact; (b) support for a belief; (c) an indication; (d) information in a law case; (e) testimony; (f) witness or witnesses collectively; (g) the results or findings of systematic, robust and trustworthy empirical enquiry.

Evidence-based medicine (EBM): The integration of best research evidence with clinical expertise and patient values.

Evidence-based policy and practice: The formulation and implementation of policy and practice based on the best evidence available, including research evidence and evidence from other sources such as 'service users', professionals and other stakeholders.

Experiment: Often seen as the most fundamental modern scientific method. It can be contrasted most sharply with observation of naturally occurring events. It involves active intervention on the part of the researcher to set up a situation in which what is taken to be a key causal factor is varied and the effects of other relevant causal factors are minimised or maintained at the same level. The aim is to identify the independent effect of the key variable: to discover whether it has the effects hypothesised, or whether these are a product of other factors.

Feminism: A position with the political aim of challenging discrimination against women and/or promoting greater equality between the sexes. It involves some sense of women having common interests as a result of unjust gender relations. There are, however, a great variety of different feminist theories and corresponding political strategies for change.

Feminist research: Challenges the 'myth' of objective, value-free research and acknowledges the centrality of the researchers' values and interpretations. It values the experiences and opinions of women, is politically *for* women and seeks to improve women's lives in some way.

Fieldnotes: A record of field observation. Usually divided into three types: mental 'notes', jotted notes (prepared in the field) and full fieldnotes (a detailed description of the round of observation).

Files: A discrete set of data held in computer software, for example, the complete transcript of a single interview.

Finding aids: Inventories, registers, indexes or guides to collections held by archives and manuscript repositories, libraries and museums. Finding aids provide detailed descriptions of collections, their intellectual organisation and sometimes of individual items in the collections.

Finite Population Correction (*fpc*): An adjustment made in simple random sampling to reflect the fact that samples are drawn from a finite population, compared to the infinite populations that are used in theoretical procedures.

Focus groups: Group discussions that are organised to explore a specific set of issues and involve some kind of collective activity. What is important in the focus group is the emphasis on interaction within the group based on topics that are of interest to the researcher.

Frequency distribution: A table that shows the number of cases in each category of a variable.

Funnelling: A technique used in questionnaire design to introduce sensitive questions. Questions begin broadly and increasingly narrow down to the point where the revelation of sensitive, personal or intimate information appears less sudden or surprising.

Generalisability: This means the applicability of the data to other like cases (also sometimes called 'external validity').

Governance: The study of governance focuses on the exercise of political power and the patterns of power in the relationships between different actors – state, civil society, public and private sectors, citizens and communities.

Governmentality: The study of governmentality is concerned with the sorts of knowledges, ideas and beliefs about aspects of society that contribute to the ways in which issues are problematised, and the strategies and tactics that governments use to deal with these.

Grounded theory: A collection of (largely qualitative) data gathering and data analysis procedures in which the objective is to generate theories from data. Grounded theories can be of two types: 'substantive' (applicable to the setting studied) or 'formal' (applicable to a range of similar settings).

Haphazard sampling: A method of selecting sample members without conscious choice, but one that is still subject to unconscious effects and is still therefore subjective and likely to be biased.

Harmonised data: Data that have been collected for particular purposes, and which are afterwards adjusted so that as far as possible the variables in different datasets measure the same thing – such as the number of hours that constitutes part-time employment in different countries.

Hypotheses: A kind of research question, namely, one that postulates a possible relationship between two or more variables. Scientific hypotheses must be set out in ways that allow them to be tested and falsified by methods of observation and experiment. See also **Conjecture**.

Indicator: A measure that is used to represent a concept, such as 'occupation' as an indicator of social class.

Inductive orientation: A contrast is sometimes drawn between two views of scientific method: inductive and deductive. The inductive view argues that science ought to start with the collection and analysis of data, from which theoretical ideas will then emerge. These may then be tested against further data.

Informal carers: People who provide unpaid care to other family members or friends who need personal help, practical assistance or watching over because of frailty, physical impairment, learning disability or ill-health, including mental illness. Some informal carers can be children and young people ('young carers').

Informant: A term referring to an interviewee, especially where what the interviewee provides is information not accessible to the researcher by means of direct observation, for example because the events described occurred in the past or took place in settings to which the researcher does not have access. The role of informants is particularly important in ethnographic research, especially in anthropology. The interviewee as informant is sometimes contrasted with the interviewee as respondent (see **Respondent**).

Informed consent: A knowing agreement to take part in research.

Institutional interaction: The talk in institutional settings that performs and constitutes the nature of that institution.

Internet server: Individuals connect to the Internet by attaching to a server (computer) that has links to numerous other servers that form the Internet. As well as providing access to the Internet, servers store web pages and associated files. Files such as electronic questionnaires can be stored on a server and made available to all users of the Internet or may be configured to allow restricted access based on passwords or some other identifier.

Interpretative repertoires: An organised cluster of terms; metaphors that are a resource for constructing versions of actions and events.

Interpretivism: A term sometimes used to refer to an approach in social research that emphasises the role of interpretation on the part of both those studied and the researcher. Interpretivists reject those views of human behaviour which portray it as a mechanical product of causes, whether biological, psychological, social structural or cultural. Instead, human action is treated as following a contingent course as a result of a process of interpretation by which actors make sense of the situations they face, and of their own concerns and goals in light of that situation. Moreover, it is taken to follow from this that any attempt on the part of researchers to understand the social world must rely on their ability to interpret the behaviour of those they are studying: scientific understanding of social life cannot take the form simply of following some abstract scientific method, it relies on a cultural capacity to make sense of other people's behaviour in the same way that they do themselves.

Interview mode: The manner in which an interview is carried out. The most common modes are face-to-face or telephone.

Learning difficulty/disability (also **intellectual impairment**): People with an intellectual disability, formerly described as a 'mental handicap' (now regarded as a derogatory label).

Life history: Life history interviewing is one of the methods used by social scientists. It involves in-depth questioning of a person, or a small number of people, about their lives, often over several interview sessions. The usual rationale for this method is the argument that we can only understand a person's actions properly if we can see what they do in the context of their life as a whole. However, life history work is also sometimes motivated by an interest in how people's lives develop, or in the experiences of a particular historical generation.

Likert Scale: Widely used technique for measuring attitudes. Consists of a set of statements that respondents have to rate. Each respondent's replies are then scored and aggregated.

Longitudinal design: A research design in which data are gathered from a selected group of individuals at intervals over a period of time. The two main types are **cohort designs** (see separate Glossary entry) and **panel designs**. Examples of panel studies include the British Household Panel Study (BHPS) and ONS Longitudinal Study (LS) based on the Census and vital event data (births, cancers, deaths) routinely collected for 1% of the population of England and Wales.

Longitudinal qualitative research: Repeat observations of, ideally, the same research subjects over time, using qualitative data collection techniques, and focused on change at an individual rather than group level.

Mean, arithmetic (M): A measure of central tendency whereby the sum of values is divided by the number of values.

Measures of central tendency: Indices that describe the central or typical value of a set of values such as the mean.

Measures of dispersion: Indices that describe the dispersion or spread of values in a set of values such as the standard deviation.

Median: The value of the mid-point of a set of values ordered in size.

Memo: A succinct statement of the meaning of an analytic category or the definition of a code applied to the data.

Mental health service user/survivor: Someone who uses, or has used, mental health services.

Meta-analysis: A method of combining the findings of several research studies so as to reach an overall conclusion. In the context of healthcare, meta-analysis normally employs statistical techniques to pool the results of studies that in some cases may be too small to provide convincing conclusions.

Metadata: Defined as 'data about data', such as the information contained in a library or data archive catalogue. For social science data, metadata include information about the data file, the research study, such as describing the sample from which the data were drawn, the time period covered, and at a finer level, definitions of survey codes in a file, such as their description and values.

Method: Procedure for collecting research data.

Methodology: (a) The broad theoretical and philosophical framework within which methods operate and which give them their intellectual authority and legitimacy; (b) the study of methods.

Microdata: Data collected from surveys or compiled from other sources, at the level of the individual or group, rather than at the aggregate level. An example is a Census or survey that has collected information about behaviour and the surrounding social and economic environment. Typically, certain information is removed to protect the confidentiality of the respondent.

Mode: The most frequently occurring value in a set of values.

Modernity: The social organisation of industrialising and industrialised societies of the West characterised by separations of church and state, art and science, the public sphere of work and politics from the private sphere of home, by the institution of economic, political and social rights attached to citizenship which serve to distinguish between nationalities, men and women, disabled and 'able-bodied' and so on. It involves the rise of new institutions, such as education and welfare, which organise people into categories, and become key sites for the acting out of collective norms and values. Rational and bureaucratic selection and allocation processes, backed up by scientific theories, are seen to provide a break with old forms of patronage and preferential distribution.

Multi-stage sampling: Repeated drawing of subunits from higher order units, for example, at Stage 1 drawing a sample of postcode sectors from all postcode sectors and at Stage 2 drawing a sample of addresses from the postcode sectors selected at Stage 1.

Multi-strategy research: Research that combines quantitative and qualitative research.

Narrative analysis: The collection and interpretation of life accounts in interview or other forms with reference to story (and plot) construction and attention to the teller's temporal ordering of events, use of descriptive or explanatory devices such as metaphor, and experiences.

Naturalism: An approach to the study of the social world that argues that the fundamental source of evidence is observation of how people actually behave in the natural settings in which they normally participate. What is opposed here is both primary reliance by social scientists on experimental method – in which people are studied in specially constructed settings designed to control causal variables – or on interview data – where what people say about the world is treated as data about what happens or what they actually do in other settings.

Naturalistic records: Video or audio recordings of people interacting in everyday or institutional settings (not set up by the researcher).

Navigate: To move around a database held in a software package.

Negative case: A case that does not work as proposed in a hypothetical universal statement.

Neo-positivist: An approach influenced by 'positivism' in social science – the application of the scientific method to social life, including deductive reasoning and hypothesis testing, the collection of 'empirical data' and the use of scientific findings to make social changes.

Normative: Concerned with how society *should* be organised, rather than describing how it *is* organised, or trying to provide an explanation for *why* it is organised as it is.

Objectivity: A term that has a variety of meanings, and can therefore generate confusion and spurious disagreement. The most prominent meaning of 'objectivity' refers to a process of inquiry. Inquiry is objective if it follows the most rational course in seeking to produce knowledge; in other words, if it is not deflected from that course by prior assumptions, personal preferences, and so on. Here, the opposite of objectivity is bias: systematic error caused by features of the researcher.

Operationalisation: The process of generating one or more indicators of a concept.

Opt-in: To agree to participate in a research project by formally responding to a letter of invitation.

Opt-out: To be deemed to have given consent to be approached by a research team by not having formally refused or declined within a given timescale.

Output: A vehicle for communicating research to relevant audiences, such as a report, presentation and so on.

Panel attrition: Refers to the cumulative loss of respondents in successive waves of data collection through refusal, non-contact, moving overseas, being out-of-scope or death.

Panel designs: Collect comparable data about the same individuals on two or more occasions. The British Household Panel Survey is a prospective panel design, following up the same individuals over time.

Paradigm: A cluster of beliefs and practices associated with a particular worldview about how scientific practice should take place.

Parameter: A population value of a distribution (such as the mean or variance).

Participant observation: A method in which observers participate in the daily life of a people under study.

Phenomenology: A philosophical position concerned with how we comprehend the world around us and with the ways in which that process of comprehension might be studied. The position places an emphasis on the bracketing of the analyst's experience.

Photo-elicitation: The use of photographs to elicit information in interviews.

Plot: A term used in narrative analysis. A length of time – the time limits of start and end – within which selected events are given meaning and connected as part of a specific storied outcome.

Policy implementation: The business of translating decisions into events, of 'getting things done'. Implementation relates to 'specified objectives', the translation into practice of the policies that emerge from the process of decision making.

Policy research: Research designed to *inform* or to *understand* one or more aspects of the public and social policy process, including decision making and policy formulation, implementation and evaluation. Policy research also aims to provide answers and evidence that can contribute to the improvement of 'policy' and policy making, can lead to better practice and interventions, the reduction of social problems and social distress, and the promotion of welfare and wellbeing. Policy research draws from the full range of research designs, methods and approaches outlined in this volume.

Population: The term given to all units that are defined by particular characteristics.

Positivism: A philosophical position that stipulates that both the natural and the social worlds can and should be studied using the same procedures and criteria of truth. Positivists emphasise the importance of the scientist's ability to observe the natural or social phenomena that are the objects of their study.

Postmodernism: This is a set of theories that in relation to knowledge argue that objective truth is unattainable. The search for objective truth is deconstructed and shown to dissolve into various language games about 'truth'. Knowledge is therefore relative, and people should thus be sceptical about truth claims. Postmodernism thus encourages us to examine the contingent social processes that affect research and which undermine the objectivity and truthfulness of the knowledge.

Postmodernity: This term is more problematic than both post-structuralism and postmodernism, for it presupposes that society has broken from modernity and now exists within a new epoch. Most social theorists do not go that far, recognising that some aspects of modernity still coexist with some significant changes. Thus, Giddens talks of 'reflexive modernisation' as the period we are now in, marked by globalisation, a post-traditional social order (where class, gender, sexuality, age and ethnicity are far more fluid and less fixed) and reflexivity, where people do not follow fixed biographies, but are engaged in continual negotiation of the courses of their lives.

Post-structuralism: The body of theory to emerge in the 1960s from French philosophers, Foucault, Derrida and Lacan, as a critique of Enlightenment thinking. It thus involves the rejection of the 'grand narrative', of the human subject as powerful, unitary and self-consciously political, of the necessity of progress, the belief in universal truths and unquestionable or scientific facts. Post-structuralists resist the construction of the world into oppositional categories: man/woman; ruling class/working class; civilised/uncivilised; culture/nature; tradition/reason. Instead, they focus on fragmented and changing subjectivities, on the way 'truths' about phenomena are constituted through the way people speak about them. Power and knowledge are thus interconnected, for discourses (sets of linked utterances or texts) are the vehicles that hold domination in place (for example, the power of medical discourses to define a person as 'disabled' or 'mad'), but also provide opportunities for contestation.

PPS (probability proportionate to size): Adjusts the probability of a higher order unit (cluster) being selected to be in proportion to the number of units in that cluster.

Precision: The extent to which an estimate lies close to the population parameter.

Protocol: A plan of action, giving details of all the steps that will be followed in an investigation, and adopted as the key procedure for systematic reviews in medical and social science.

Qualitative data: Qualitative data are collected using qualitative research methodology and techniques across the range of social science disciplines. Strategies often encompass a diversity of methods and tools rather than a single one and the types of data collected depend on the aims of the study, the nature of the sample and the discipline. As a result, data types extend to: in-depth or unstructured, individual or group discussion interviews, field and observation notes, unstructured diaries, observational recordings, personal documents and photographs.

Qualitative variable: A variable in which the categories have no numerical relationship to one another.

Quantitative data: Quantitative data are collected using quantitative research methodologies and techniques across the range of social science disciplines. Strategies often encompass a diversity of methods and tools rather than a single one and the types of data collected depend on the aims of the study, the nature of the sample and the discipline. As a result, data types extend to: structured interviews, questionnaires, behavioural data from structured observation and data deriving from content analysis.

Quantitative variable: A variable in which the categories have a numerical relationship to one another and can be ordered in terms of size.

Questionnaire: The instrument used to collect information from a respondent. It can either be completed by an interviewer interviewing the respondent or by the respondent him/herself (in which case it is referred to as a self-completion questionnaire).

Quota: A set number of interviews.

Quota control: The specification of particular characteristics of units that are to be selected.

'Race': A term introduced into anthropological discussion of the differences between people of differing ethnic groupings, to denote innate biological-physiological or intellectual and cultural differences between people. The term was part of a wider discourse that justified prejudicial, discriminatory and oppressive practices by those with power against those without. These practices are now generally brought together under the term 'racism' but, in the period of slavery, for example, these allegedly inherent racial differences were used to justify economic, political and physical exploitation of weaker ethnic groups by stronger ones.

Random selection: A method of selecting a sample that is objective, in other words it does not allow any subjective influence over which units are included in the sample.

Randomised controlled trial: A research study in which subjects are randomly allocated between treatment and control or comparison groups. Sometimes regarded as the 'gold standard' in medical and health research.

Range: The difference between the highest and lowest value in a distribution of values.

Realism: This reflects a methodological position which advances two claims: that there is an external world independent of people's perceptions of it (so that there is more to find out about the social world than people's meanings); and that it is possible to obtain direct access to, and 'objective' knowledge about, this world. It permeates positivism to the point where the two terms are used interchangeably. However, the second principle is also a feature of naturalism.

Reflexivity: Involves reflection by researchers on the social processes that impinge upon and influence data. It requires a critical attitude towards data, and recognition of the influence on the research of such factors as the location of the setting, the sensitivity of the topic, and the nature of the social interaction between the researcher and researched. In the absence of reflexivity, the strengths of the data are exaggerated and/or the weaknesses underemphasised.

Reliability: This describes the extent to which measurements are consistent when repeating a study using the same instruments under the same conditions.

Representativeness: The requirement that the structure and characteristics of the sample reflect those of the population.

Research costs: Funds for research are usually broken down into different categories. 'Direct costs' are those that are incurred only if the work goes ahead, for example, the salary of the researcher and the fieldwork costs. 'Indirect costs' are those incurred by the organisation employing the researcher, for example, the accommodation costs or those of central services that have to be paid for, whether or not the particular project goes ahead. If a piece of work is funded there will be a number of indirect costs that are then attributed to the project. 'Overheads' is sometimes the term used instead of 'indirect costs' and is usually calculated as a percentage of the direct costs. There are often disputes on exactly what constitutes a direct or indirect cost, for example, the costs of senior staff who help to support and manage the project. Those funders who pay indirect costs (and not all do) will usually prefer to pay specific amounts for particular things, for example, accommodation, rather than a percentage of the direct costs.

Research design: A structure or framework within which data are collected. A research design is selected for its capacity to answer the research questions that drive an investigation.

Research governance: Regulations and standards that surround the research process.

Research synthesis: a broader term than **systematic review**, more inclusive in scope, and referring to a wider range of techniques for collating and assessing research evidence. Arguably research synthesis is more closely tailored to the pluralism of social policy research.

Respondent: A term used to refer to a person whose responses to questions are collected and analysed, usually with a view to documenting the person's attitudes or opinions, rather than using him or her as a source of direct information about the world.

Response bias: Where the final sample of respondents is unrepresentative of the population because some types of selected sample members fail to respond at a greater rate than other types of selected sample members.

Response rate: The percentage of a sample from which information is successfully obtained. Response rates are calculated differently depending on the method of questionnaire administration.

Responsive mode: Research proposals where the ideas for the piece of work come from the individual researcher, so that the funder is 'responding' to the application submitted, rather than seeking a project on a specific topic.

Sample: A subset of a population.

Sampling: Sampling entails the selection of cases for study from among the basic unit of study where it is impossible to cover all instances of the unit. In probability sampling, each instance of the unit has the same probability of being included in the sample; in non-probability sampling there is no way of estimating this probability or even any certainty that every instance has some chance.

Sampling distribution of the means: A hypothetical distribution that occurs through repeatedly sampling (with replacement) a fixed number of units from the same population, under the same conditions.

Sampling error (variability): The difference between an estimate and parameter that arises randomly through the chance inclusion of the particular set of population members realised in a particular sample.

Sampling fraction: The number of units selected relative to the total number of population units.

Sampling frame: A list of population members that are numbered in such a way that their numbering corresponds to numbers randomly generated for selection from that list.

Sampling interval: The distance between two numbers on a list defined by the sampling fraction (see **systematic sampling**).

Secondary analysis: Method used when a researcher analyses data that they themselves did not collect. Secondary analysis is also the method used when a researcher analyses data that they had collected in the past for a different purpose from the one that they now have. Secondary analysis is most often assumed to involve quantitative data but can also involve qualitative data.

Self-completion methods: Methods which require respondents to work through and complete a questionnaire on their own, for example, a paper or electronic questionnaire.

Semi-structured interviews: A conversation directed by an interview guide organised around key areas of interest to the topic under investigation. The interviewer has flexibility to modify the sequence and wording of questions.

Sensitive research: Research that has potential implications for society or key social groups, and is potentially threatening to the researcher or subjects in bringing economic, social, political or physical costs.

Snowball sampling: Choosing respondents on the basis of previous respondents' recommendations or relationship networks, so that the eventual sample is likely to be a single or several networks of people. This is a non-probability method of sampling.

Social Policy: (a) An academic subject concerned with how and why policies have developed and how they operate in the social world; (b) the practice of social intervention and action aimed at securing social change to promote the welfare and wellbeing of citizens.

Social problems: Those conditions that are perceived as a collective rather than individual source of concern and which can be remedied or ameliorated by social action. There are competing explanations as to why certain social conditions or behaviours come to be regarded as social problems.

SPSS: An abbreviation for a package of computer programs called the Statistical Package for the Social Sciences and the name of the company that is responsible for it.

Standard deviation (SD): A measure of dispersion that is the square root of the variance or mean squared deviations.

Standard error: The standard deviation of the sampling distribution of means. It provides a measure of imprecision in the estimate.

Statistical significance: The probability of a finding being due to chance or sampling error.

Steering groups: See **Advisory groups**.

Story: A term used in narrative analysis. Stories attempt to give coherence to lives by joining elements of experience together by use of a plot and expressed through written, oral and visual means in autobiographies, biographies and related forms.

Stratification: The division of the population elements into groups defined by particular characteristics.

Stratified sampling: The random selection of units within each stratum defined by the stratification procedure, in advance of sampling.

Stratum: Particular groups defined by the process of stratification.

Survey: This is a generic research design used by social scientists in which data are collected from a relatively large number of cases at a single point in time.

Synchronous/Real time: Communication or 'chat' which takes place simultaneously, that is, messages are written and read at the same time by those online in different locations.

Systematic reviews: Reviews that draw together the results from a number of different research studies that are selected according to clear criteria, and which summarise these studies using standard protocols.

Systematic sampling: A process that uses a randomly selected starting point between 1 and k, then chooses every kth member on the list, where k is defined as the overall sampling fraction.

Theory: Refers to our existing knowledge and understanding surrounding an issue – what do we know about the issue. Theories set out explanatory and predictive propositions about the causal relationships between phenomena.

Theoretical sampling: A procedure involved in grounded theorising and requires a researcher to sample in order to extend and broaden the scope of an emerging theory. Cases, settings or people are chosen to study with a view to finding things that might challenge and extend the limitations of the existing theory.

Theoretical saturation: A procedure involved in grounded theorising and is said to be reached when new data generate no further theory development, with categories and their properties therefore appearing fully developed.

Third party payment: In the context of healthcare systems, an arrangement by which individuals make financial contributions to a pool of resources against which they may subsequently claim the provision of healthcare. Such systems may be based on taxation, on social insurance or on private insurance.

Transcription: A system of representing speech delivery using written text.

Transferability: Whether a set of findings is relevant to settings other than the one or ones in which it was conducted.

Triangulation: Traditionally, defined as the use of more than one method or more than one source of data to investigate the same research question. The primary aim of triangulation is to provide a check on the validity and reliability of the research. More recently, the definition of triangulation has expanded to encompass the combination of methods to answer different research questions within the same overarching study.

Unbiased sampling frame: A sampling frame is the list of elements of a population from which a sample will be drawn. This list is unbiased if it is a complete list of population elements or, if incomplete, the omitted elements are randomly rather than systematically missing.

Unobtrusive methods: Data collection techniques that do not involve direct elicitation from respondents so that the information is obtained without the subject's prior knowledge, thus avoiding the 'reactive effect'.

Unstructured data: Data that are not structured in terms of categories relevant to the research at the point of collection.

Unstructured interviews: An informal conversation that is interviewee-oriented and that follows the interviewee's agenda.

User participatory research: Research in which users are active participants in the process of commissioning, designing and/or carrying out individual research projects or programmes.

Utilisation (of research): (a) Instrumental utilisation – when there is evidence of policy makers or practitioners acting on the findings of specific research studies; (b) conceptual utilisation – where research influences how policy makers and practitioners interpret and think about a social issue or problem.

Validity: Extent to which the data accurately reflect the phenomena under study.

Variable: An attribute in relation to which people (or any other units of analysis) differ.

Variance: A statistic that measures dispersion around the mean. It is the sum of squared deviations divided by the number of cases (sample variance) or the degrees of freedom (estimated population variance).

Vignette: A term with a double meaning. In one sense it describes a data collection technique, in which researchers present subjects with a hypothetical situation or scenario and ask them to write down how they or a third person would respond to it. It is particularly useful in dealing with very sensitive material. Its other meaning relates to the presentation of data where some aspect of the data are extracted and given special close analysis or description to act as an exemplar of a broader process.

Visual ethnography: Ethnographic research in which the visual forms a part.

Volunteer sampling: Sampling by asking for volunteers to take part in a study. This is a non-probability method of sampling.

Weighting: The procedure used to adjust samples so that the sample characteristics resemble those of the population. Sample weighting results in some individuals counting as less than one case while others may contribute more than one case.

Index

Page references for the glossary are in **bold**

Murray, T. 264
Murtagh, B. 123, 124-5
Musgrave, S. 150

N

narrative analysis 267, 268, 299, 300,
   317-25, **399**
Nassar-McMillan, S.C. 99
National Child Development Study
   (NCDS) 149, 194
National Co-ordinating Centre for
   Health Technology Assessment 47
National Institute for Clinical Excellence
   (NICE) 44, 47, 54, 380, 382
National Lottery 199
National Pensioners Convention 8
National Readership Survey 139
naturalism 281, **399**
naturalistic records **399**
navigate **399**
Needham, G. 35
negative case 251, **399**
neighbourhood research 52
neo-positivist 320, **399**
New Deal for Disabled People 27
Newby, H. 164
Newman, J. 136
NHS Centre for Reviews and
   Dissemination (NHSCRD) 380, 382
Nicholls, V. 174
Nolan, M. 191
nominal variables 235-8, **402**
non-probability sampling 202-3
non-real time **388**
Norah Fry Research Centre 174, 176
normative **400**
NSPCC (National Society for the
   Prevention of Cruelty to Children)
   172, 311-13
Nuremburg Code 153
Nutley, S. 22, 29, 35, 36, 40-1, 55

O

Oakley, Ann 16, 17, 51, 57-8, 105, 273
objectivist position 181
objectivity 105-6, 255, **400**
O'Brien, M. 135
observation schedule 225
O'Connor, H. 295
Office for National Statistics (ONS) 83,
   151, 229
official statistics 204, 228-35
Olesen, V. 106
Oliver, M. 111

Olsen, R. 24
Omnibus Survey 230
open questions 205, 211
operationalisation 89, **400**
opt-in **400**
opt-out **400**
Organisation for Economic
   Co-operation and Development
   (OECD) 127, 128
organisational change 116
output **400**
Oxley, H. 127

P

Page, R.M. 9
panel attrition 191, 194, 338, **400**
panel designs 190-4, **397**, **400**
PAPI (pen/pencil assisted personal
   interviewing) 206, 215, **390**
paradigms **400**
parameter 197, **400**
parental separation 146-7
Park, A. 207, 208
Parker, G. 24
Parks, M.R. 294
participant observation 97, **400**
participative action research (PAR)
   117-18
participatory research 108-14, **409**
Pascall, G. 104
Patel, N. 174
Paterson, B. 342
Pearlman, V. 191
Pearson's correlation 241-2, **391**
Peel, E. 156
Pelassey, M. 130
Pendergrass, S. 296
Penna, S. 135
pensions 74-5
Peräkylä, Anssi 309
Percy-Smith, J. 36, 37, 379
periodicals 76
Peters, B.G. 129
phenomenology 96, **400-1**
photo-elicitation 272, **401**
Pickard, S. 93-5
Pink, S. 276, 278
Pittman, D. 164
plot 318, 319, **401**
Plummer, K. 320
Polanyi, M. 45
policy
   definitions and attributes 13-14
   and research 19, 36-7
policy implementation 34, **401**